CW01648471

WHAT'S IT WORTH?

Tony Curtis

A Lyle Price Guide

WHAT'S IT WORTH ?

WHSMITH
EXCLUSIVE
· BOOKS ·

While every care has been taken in the compiling of information contained in this volume the publishers cannot accept any liability for loss, financial or otherwise, incurred by reliance placed on the information herein.

The publishers wish to express their sincere thanks to the following
for their involvement and assistance in the production of this volume:–

TEXT BY LIZ TAYLOR AND ANNETTE CURTIS
EDITED BY TONY CURTIS

KAREN DOUGLASS (Art Editor)
JANICE MONCRIEFF (Assistant Editor)
SUSAN CAMERON
TANYA FAIRBAIRN
SALLY DALGLIESH
FRANK BURRELL
ROBERT NISBET
EILEEN BURRELL

This edition produced exclusively for W. H. Smith Ltd.,
Greenbridge Road, Swindon SN3 3RD.

Produced by Lyle Publications

ISBN 0-86248-102-3

Copyright © Lyle Publications MCMLXXXVII
Glenmayne, Galashiels, Scotland.

No part of this book(issue) may be reproduced in any form by print, photoprint, microfilm or any other means without written permission from the publisher unless for review purposes.

Printed by A. Wheaton & Co. Ltd., Exeter, Devon.
Bound by Dorstel Press, Harlow, Essex.

CONTENTS

ACKNOWLEDGEMENTS

Abbots, *The Hill, Wickham Market, Suffolk.*
Abridge Auctions, *(Michael Yewman), Market Place, Abridge, Essex*
Aldridge's, *130-132 Walcot Street, Bath, Avon.*
Alfie's Antique Market, *13-15 Church Street, London.*
Allen & May, *18 Bridge Street, Andover.*
Anderson & Garland, *Anderson House, Market Street, Newcastle.*
Gilbert Baitson, *194 Anlaby Road, Hull, Yorks.*
Richard Baker & Thomson, *9 Hamilton Street, Birkenhead, Merseyside.*
T. Bannister & Co., *7 Calbourne, Haywards Heath, W. Sussex.*
Barber's, *Town Mill, Bagshot Road, Chobham, Surrey.*
Stan Beaumont, *13a Oakfield, Off Oakfield Road, Anfield, Liverpool. (Cigar Bands)*
R.A. Beck, *23 Basing Hill, London NW11 8TE (Butlin's Badges)*
Tessa Bennett, *Bennett Book Auctions, 72 Radcliffe Terrace, Edinburgh. (Cigarette Cards)*
Biddle & Webb, *Ladywood, Middleway, Birmingham.*
Boardman's, *Station Road Corner, Haverhill, Suffolk.*
Bonhams, *Montpelier Galleries, Montpelier Street, London.*
Bonsor Penningtons, *82 Eden Street, Kingston-on-Thames.*
John F. Bradshaw, *33 Shaw Crescent, Sanderstead, Surrey. (Railway Tickets)*
British Antique Exporters, *206 London Road, Burgess Hill, W. Sussex.*
Brogden & Co., *38 & 39 Silver Street, Lincoln.*
Wm. H. Brown, *31 St. Peter's Hill, Grantham, Lincs.*
Bruton, Knowles & Co., *Albion Chambers, 55 Barton Street, Gloucester.*
Buckell & Ballard, *49 Parsons Street, Banbury, Oxfordshire.*
Burrows & Day, *39/41 Bank Street, Ashford, Kent.*
Burtenshaw Walker, *66 High Street, Lewes, Suffolk.*
Butler & Hatch Waterman, *86 High Street, Hythe, Kent.*
Butterfield & Butterfield, *1244 Sutter Street, San Francisco.*
Button, Menhenitt & Mutton, *Belmont Auction Rooms, Wadebridge.*
Alan Cadwallender, *63 Green Street, Middleton, Manchester. (Comics)*
Capes, Dunn & Co., *The Auction Galleries, 38 Charles Street, Manchester.*
Chancellor's, *31 High Street, Ascot, Berks.*
H.C. Chapman & Son, *The Auction Mart, North Street, Scarborough.*
Christie's, *8 King Street, St. James's, London.*
Christie's & Edmiston's, *164-166 Bath Street, Glasgow.*
Christie's S. Kensington, *85 Old Brompton Road, London.*
Clarke Gammon, *45 High Street, Guildford, Surrey.*
Coles, Knapp & Kennedy, *Georgian Rooms, Ross-on-Wye.*
D.G. Cook, *275 Locking Road, Weston-super-Mare, Avon. (Tobacco Tins)*
Cooper Hirst, *Goldway House, Parkway, Chelmsford.*
Crystals Auctions, *Athol Street, Douglas, I.O.M.*
Dacre, Son & Hartley, *1-5 The Grove, Ilkley, Yorks.*
Dee & Atkinson, *The Exchange, Driffield, Yorks.*
Dickinson, Davy & Markham, *10 Wrawby Street, Brigg, S. Humberside.*
D.A. Dolbey Jones, *35a Maclise Road, London W14*
Wm. Doyle Galleries Inc., *175 East 87th Street, New York.*
Dreweatt, Watson & Barton, *Donnington Priory, Newbury, Berks.*
Hy. Duke & Son, *40 South Street, Dorchester, Dorset.*
Edwards, Bigwood & Bewlay, *The Old School, Tiddington, Stratford-on-Avon.*
Elliott & Green, *40 High Street, Lymington, Hants.*
R.H. Ellis & Sons, *44-46 High Street, Worthing, Sussex.*
H. Evans & Sons, *Hull, Yorks.*
Farrant & Wightman, *2/3 Newport Street, Old Town, Swindon.*
John Francis, Thomas Jones & Sons, *King Street, Carmarthen.*
Frank H. Fellows & Sons, *Bedford House, 88 Hagley Road, Birmingham.*
John D. Fleming & Co., *Melton House, High Street, Dulverton.*
Fox & Sons, *5 & 7 Salisbury Street, Fordingbridge, Hants.*
Kathleen Fullerton, *Singleton, Fernhill Heath, Worcester WR3 7UA (Hatpins)*
Garrod Turner, *50 St. Nicholas Street, Ipswich, Suffolk.*
Geering & Colyer, *Highgate, Hawkhurst, Kent.*
Mike Gosling, *Philmont, 78 Skip Lane, Walsall, West Midlands (Scout Badges)*
Goss & Crested China Ltd., *N. J. Pine, 62 Murray Road, Horndean, Hants. PO8 9JL. Tel. No: 0705-597440*
Andrew Grant, *59-60 Foregate Street, Worcester.*
Mrs. Ivy Grant, *Seas-Gu-Daighean, Lynden Lane, Stonegate, Nr. Waldhurst, Sussex TN5 7EF (Miniature Bottles)*
Graves, Son & Pilcher, *38 Holland Road, Hove, Sussex.*
Gray's Antique Market, *58 Davies Street, London.*
Alistair Grey, *67 Braddon Road, Loughborough, Leics. (Bus Tickets)*
Gribble, Booth & Taylor, *West Street, Axminster, Devon.*
Arthur G. Griffiths & Sons, *57 Foregate Street, Worcester.*
Rowland Gorringe, *15 North Street, Lewes, Sussex.*
Hall Wateridge & Owen, *Welsh Bridge, Shrewsbury.*
James Harrison, *35 West End, Hebden Bridge, W. Yorks.*
Heathcote Ball & Co., *47 New Walk, Leicester.*
John Hogbin & Son, *53 High Street, Tenterden, Kent.*
Honiton Galleries, *High Street, Honiton, Devon.*
Edgar Horn, *47 Cornfield Road, Eastbourne, Sussex.*
Hilary Humphries, *15 Dullingham Road, Newmarket, Cambs. (Cigarette Packets)*
Jackson-Stops & Staff, *Fine Art Dept., 14 Curzon Street, London W1.*
Michael Jones, *27 Chinbrook Road, Grove Park, London, SE12 9TQ. (Beer Bottle Labels)*
G.A. Key, *Market Place, Aylesham.*
Lacy Scott & Sons, *3 Hatter Street, Bury St. Edmunds.*
Lalonde Bros. & Parham, *Station Road, Weston-super-Mare.*
Ruth Lambert, *Weston Favell, Northampton. (Gramophone Needle Tins)*
W.H. Lane & Son, *Morrab Road, Penzance, Cornwall.*
Langlois, *10 Waterloo Street, Jersey, C.I.*
Lawrence Fine Art, *South Street, Crewkerne.*
James & Lister Lea, *11 Newhall Street, Birmingham.*
Locke & England, *Walton House, 11 The Parade, Leamington Spa.*
Love's, *St. John's Place, Perth.*
Mallams, *24 St. Michael's Street, Oxford.*
S. Marshall, *23 Lock Laxford, East Kilbride. (Cigarette Cards)*
Brian & Vera Matthews, *8 The Vale, Oakley, Hamps. RG23 7LB (Sewing Machines)*
May, Whetter & Grose, *Cornubia Hall, Par, Cornwall.*
John Milne, *9-11 North Silver Street, Aberdeen.*
Moore, Allen & Innocent, *33 Castle Street, Cirencester.*
Morphets, *4-6 Albert Street, Harrogate, Yorks.*
Morris, Marshall & Poole, *2 Short Bridge Street, Newtown, Powys.*
Alfred Mossop & Co., *Kelsick Road, Ambleside, Cumbria.*
McCartney, Morris & Barker, *Corve Street, Ludlow, Salop.*
Bridget McConnel, *Grays Antique Market, 58 Davies Street, London W1* (Thimble Society of London) *(Thimbles, Tape Measures & Sewing Items)*
Peter McConnell, *37 Oakhurst Road, West Moors, Wimbourne BH22 ODW (Postal Scales)*
Neales, *192 Mansfield Road, Nottingham.*
D.M. Nesbit & Co., *7 Clarendon Road, Southsea, Hants.*
Northampton Auction Galleries, *33-39 Sheep Street, Northampton.*
Nostalgia, *13 Harleslade, Brandy Cove, Bishopston. (Advertising Signs)*
Olivers, *23-24 Market Hill, Sudbury, Suffolk.*
Osmond, Tricks, *Regent Street Auction Rooms, Clifton, Bristol.*
Outhwaite & Litherland, *Kingsway Galleries, Fontenoy Street, Liverpool.*
J.R. Parkinson, Son & Hamer, *14 Bolton Street, Bury, Lancs.*
Parsons, Welch & Cowell, *129 High Street, Sevenoaks, Kent.*
Pattison Partners & Scott, *Ryton.*
Pearsons, *Walcote Chambers, High Street, Winchester.*
Phillips, *7 Blenheim Street, New Bond Street, London.*
Phillips & Brooks, *39 Park End Street, Oxford.*
Phillips & Jolly's, *The Auction Rooms, Old King Street, Bath.*
Geoff Price, *37 Comberford Drive, Tiffany Green, Wednesday, West Midlands (Model Bus & Tram)*
John H. Raby & Son, *St. Mary's Road, Bradford.*
Samuel Rains & Son, *Trinity House, 114 Northenden Road, Sale, Manchester.*
S. Reeve & V. Gladwish, *17 Montague Road, Uxbridge, Middx. (Match Box Labels)*
Renton & Renton, *16 Albert Street, Harrogate, Yorks.*
Riddetts, *Richmond Hill, The Square, Bournemouth.*
Russell, Baldwin & Bright, *Ryelands Road, Leominster.*
Sandoe, Luce Panes, *Chipping Manor Salerooms, Wotton-under-Edge.*
M. Philip H. Scott, *East View, Bedale, Yorks.*
Shouler & Son, *43 Nottingham Street, Melton Mowbray.*
Robert W. Skinner Inc., *Bolton Gallery, Mass.*
Andrea Smith, *Manderley, 27 Sutton Lane, Adlington, Lancs. (Robertson's Golly Badges)*
Smith-Woolley & Perry, *43 Castle Hill Avenue, Folkestone.*
Jonathan H. Sneath, *Eastlyn, Fen Gate, Moulton Chapel, Nr. Spalding, Lincs.*
Spear & Sons, *The Hill, Wickham Market, Suffolk.*
H. Spencer & Sons Ltd., *20 The Square, Retford, Notts.*
"Street Jewellery" & "More Street Jewellery" *by* **New Cavendish Books**
Street Jewellery Society, *48 St. Georges Terrace, Newcastle upon Tyne NE2 2SY*
Stride & Son, *Southdown House, St. John's Street, Chichester.*
T.K. Suttie, *Riverside Cottage, 13 Bridge End, Billington, Nr. Blackburn. (Pictorial China)*
Christopher Sykes, *11 Market Place, Woburn, Milton Keynes.*
David Symonds, *High Street, Crediton, Devon.*
Taylor, Lane & Creber, *Western Auction Rooms, Plymouth.*
Laurence & Martin Taylor, *63 High Street, Honiton, Devon.*
Liz Taylor, *Ancrum, Jedburgh, Roxburghshire.*
Louis Taylor & Sons, *Percy Street, Hanley, Stoke-on-Trent.*
Terry Antiques, *175 Junction Road, London N19.*
Theriault, *P.O. Box 151, Annapolis, Maryland, 21404.*
Turner, Rudge & Turner, *29 High Street, East Grinstead.*
V. & V.'s, *The Memorial Hall, Shiplake-on-Thames.*
Vidler & Co., *Auction Offices, Cinque Ports St., Rye, Sussex.*
Wallis & Wallis, *Regency House, 1 Albion Street, Lewes, Sussex.*
Tom Walsh, *Capricorn Curios, 48 St. Annes Road, Blackpool. (Radios)*
Warren & Wignall, *113 Towngate, Leyland, Lancs.*
Thomas Watson, *27 North Street, Bishops Stortford.*
Way, Riddett & Co., *Town Hall Chambers, Lind Street, Ryde, I.O.W.*
Neil Wayne, *Old Chapel, Bridge Street, Belper, Derby. (Razors)*
J.M. Welsh & Son, *The Old Town Hall, Great Dunmow, Essex.*
Whitehead's, *111-113 Elm Grove, Southsea, Hants.*
Whitton & Laing, *32 Okehampton Street, Exeter.*
Keith Wilkinson, *18 Hinton Street, Fairfield, Liverpool L1 3AR (Enamel Football Club Badges)*
Richard Withington, *Hillsboro, New Hampshire 03244.*
Woolley & Wallis, *The Castle Auction Mart, Salisbury.*
Eldon E. Worrall & Co., *15 Seel Street, Liverpool.*
Wyatt & Son with Whiteheads, *59 East Street, Chichester, Sussex.*
Yesterday's Paper, *40 South View, Holcombe, Rogus, Wellington, Somerset TA21 0PP*

WHAT'S IT WORTH ?

Hold on! Don't throw that away! So it's only perhaps an old railway ticket or a matchbox that you're about to chuck into the wastepaper basket but, unlikely as it sounds, it's worth something. That unregarded piece of rubbish could be the source of a useful sum of money or the beginning of a lifelong passion for you.

A fine Louis XV kingwood floral marquetry bombe commode, stamped by Nicholas Petit, 98cm. wide, 72cm. high. (Phillips) £13,500

A superb George I walnut and beechwood settee covered in petit and gros point floral needlework, 64in. wide. (Christie's) £41,800

An unusual George III satinwood canterbury, the hinged rectangular top with three-quarter gallery above three dividers, on ring-turned tapering legs. (Christie's) £8,250

There is no limit to the sort of things that have unexpected value. True collectors do not only seek out bisque headed dolls, vintage cars, Old Master prints or Chelsea china. Not all of them go to the big London sale rooms and bid in telephone number sums; they also dig in rubbish tips, haunt jumble sales and street markets, turn out their attics and use their eyes to appreciate the attractive quality of hitherto little regarded every day items. There is a profit to be made in such assorted things as railway porters' badges, soup can labels, light bulbs, beer mats, bicycles or pictures of film stars, just as much as in Chinese porcelain or fine French furniture.

There is absolutely no limit to what is worth money. One man's rubbish is certainly another man's treasure and, strangely enough, once something starts to be collected, it acquires a new value. One railway ticket crumpled up on a station platform is worth nothing. Ten railway tickets, neatly arranged in order, form the basis of a collection that could in time be worth hundreds of pounds.

Collectors of railway tickets usually concentrate on a specific category such as misprinted tickets or specialist tickets such as those issued for Anglers, Hop Pickers or from pre-nationalised companies. One of the rarest platform tickets is one for Ludgate Hill, closed in 1929, which sold recently for a record £340.

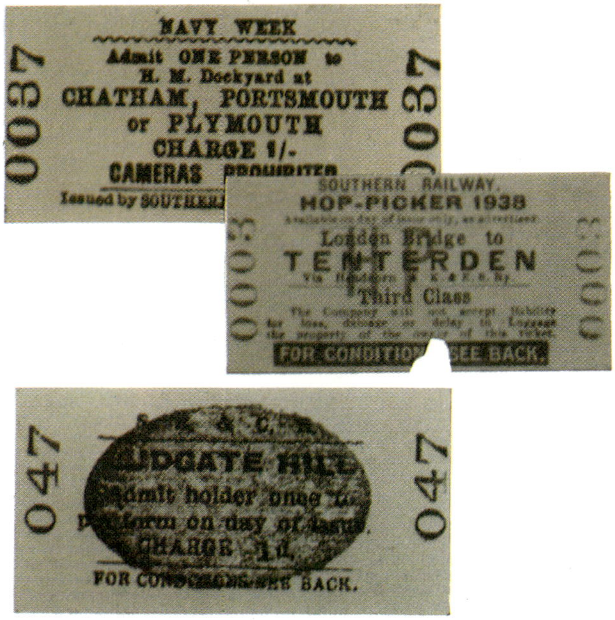

The Navy Week ticket is worth £5 and the Hop Picker ticket £2.50, but the rare 'Ludgate Hill' platform ticket is worth £340.

A set of twenty 'Clowns and Circus Artistes', by Taddy sold for over £4,000 by Phillips.

Another area for collecting are cigarette cards, first introduced into Britain by the firm of W. D. & H. O. Wills of Bristol around 1885 and most of the 5000 or so sets produced are only worth a few pounds. Early examples produced by Taddy & Co. however can be worth hundreds of pounds and if they are a set of 20 Clowns and Circus Artistes you are talking about £4,000 plus, depending on condition.

Beer cans were first introduced in 1935 and early examples feature a cone-shaped top. Over 25,000 different cans have been made and collectors prefer ringpull cans to be intact therefore, empty the contents of the can from the bottom. A 12 oz. example of Pilsner Lager, made in 1955, is worth about £20.

One of the earliest patents for a cast iron mechanical novelty bank was taken out by J. Hall on 21st December 1869 for his Excelsior bank. Many of the hundreds of designs were of American manufacture and sell for between £100 and £500 depending on rarity. Occasionally however, a hitherto unknown example comes onto the market like one featuring a girl skipping which sold for a mammoth £8,250.

One of the more common money banks which swallows the coin when a lever is activated at the back.

Few collectors however start out only with the aim of making money. For many of them, profit comes by accident. They collect because they like the look of something and want to own it; because it reminds them of a time when they were happy or of someone they love. Usually the initial impulse to collect begins in childhood and most of us can remember the thrill of hunting out special coloured marbles; filling up scrap books or cigarette card albums; the enthusiastic swopping with friends; the anxious hunt for that elusive scrap or card that somehow always refused to come our way. It's the hunt that's the pleasure; the search combined with the gradual amassing of knowledge about the chosen subject. Only when someone has been well and truly bitten by the collecting bug, do they come to realise that their treasures represent a nest egg, worth far more than it cost to collect them in the first place.

For example, take the case of the middle aged Englishman who began buying second hand books while he was a student. Twenty years later he found, to his surprise, that he had assets worth well over £50,000 stacked away on his book shelves.

When he worked out how much the books had originally cost him, he discovered that no volume had been bought for more than £2 and most of them were picked up for less than 50p. His treasures had been found on market stalls and at jumble sales simply because his limited income as a student meant that he could not afford new books. By 1987 some of the books were worth at least £500 each and none were valued at less than £70. The book collector, worried that if he sold his collection it would attract tax, wrote to the Letters Page of the *Financial Times* about it and the reply was that windfalls made in this way are free of Capital Gains Tax. His hours spent browsing in second hand bookshops paid off in a big way.

First Edition in three volumes of Dickens' 'Great Expectations' 1861. (Phillips) £12,000

Comics are collected by enthusiasts all over the world, particularly American, reflecting the extensive distribution they have always had. Few collectibles have such a huge range of items available and such a vast range of prices from 10p to £7,500 for the No. 1 *Action* comic from June 1938 which launched Superman for its creators, Joe Schuster and Jerry Seigal.

'The Dandy' and 'The Beano', two of the most popular comics among British collectors.

The most widely collected British comics are the *Dandy, Film Fun, Eagle, Radio Fun, Knockout* and the *Beano* of which the first edition of July 30 1938, complete with free Whoopee mask, is worth about £300.

A very rare Lalique glass amethyst tinted car mascot, 'Victoire', 14.7cm. high. (Christie's) £9,680

It is easier to spot something that is worth money, if you specialise in things that appeal to you. Motor enthusiasts who cannot afford vintage cars can buy car bonnet ornaments, or, like a man in Northern Ireland, jerry cans for petrol. Unlikely as it seems he discovered that his collection of old cans was worth money and he began travelling all over the country picking up more unusual cans. Today he has the finest collection of jerry cans in the country, most of them picked up from old garages, garden sheds or rubbish tips for next to nothing. Another car enthusiast realised that the introduction of modern petrol stations spelt the end for the old glass globes that used to decorate petrol pumps. He bought one or two for the sake of nostalgia and the collection has grown into a motoring museum.

Oiliana is a comparatively new collecting field, the attraction being the functional advertising in the form of oil cans and pourers by firms such as Shell, Castrol and Pratts. Some of the early enamel signs might make over £100 but even humble oil pourers are keenly sought by collectors and can make as much as £20.

With motoring in mind cars on a smaller scale are also keenly sought after, particularly those produced by Dinky. Although most are worth only a few pounds, find one from the 30's and it could be worth over £400.

Pre war aeroplane sets by Dinky, worth well over £1,000 each.

Probably the most sought after model to any Dinky collector, however, is number 992 Avro Vulcan. This model of the most famous of the R.A.F. V bombers was produced between 1955 and 1956 and differed from others in that it was made of aluminium. The bulk of the 500 or so produced were sold in North America for $1.40 cents each but it is estimated that there must be about 25 examples somewhere in the U.K. Find one of these complete with its original box and you can expect to make £1,400 at auction.

Many people find that their acquisitions have a value over and above what other collectors will pay for each item because they are able to turn their hobby into a way of living. There are several museums over the country that were started by an enthusiastic collector who fell in love with something unlikely. In Wales, a redundant miner runs his own museum specialising in old pit lamps and miners' tokens. Because of his regret for the passing of an era, he picked up a few lamps and tokens when the mines were closing. He wanted something of the old way of life in the valleys to be preserved. Today his collection is not only valuable in terms of money – some of the lamps he bought for a couple of pounds are worth £200 each – but it is also a rich source of historical evidence about the life of the past and parties of school children are brought from

A fine Marklin clockwork tinplate Nassau-class battleship, the motor driving three propellors, the hull painted brown and two-tone grey with simulated planked deck, in its original wooden crate bearing Marklin trade label, the model 39in. long. (Christie's) £10,500

all over Wales to see it. Instead of being on the dole, he is a museum owner and his collection, picked up on pithead rubbish tips or bought for pence, is worth many thousands of pounds to any museum should he choose to sell it.

A man in Edinburgh owns a shop selling football memorabilia because as a boy he saved the programmes of every football match he attended and after a few years discovered that he had a large and valuable archive on his hands. Prices for old football programmes now range from 75p to £25 or even more for rare examples, so next time you go to a match, don't throw the programme away. Save it.

Football programmes have been collected for almost as long as the game has been played but it is only since the late '50's that this has been a recognisable hobby. The earliest examples date back to the 1880's and are little more than teamsheets surrounded by advertising, they can however change hands for substantial sums of money. An example of the 1922/23 first Wembley final between West Ham and Bolton is worth about £140.

Another collector in Edinburgh, a retired Colonel, shares his home with over seven hundred teddy bears, which have proved over the last year or so to be a phenominal growth area. Not long after the world record of £5,750 was established at Sothebys for a short plush Steiff bear named Archibald, an even rarer muzzled bear was sold to the same buyer from California for over £8,000.

Margaret Steiff, a crippled dressmaker, is credited with making the first bear about 1900, but it wasn't until Teddy Roosevelt refused to shoot a bear on an organised hunt (it was after all tied to a stake by someone eager to please) that the Teddy Bear really took off in popularity.

The first Wembly Cup Final Programme, April 28th 1923. (Football Crazy) £140

An early straw filled Teddy bear from 1905 which is worth a few hundred pounds, but if it had a Steiff button in its ear it could be worth thousands.

Typical late 19th century dolls so eagerly sought after by collectors, all worth over £200 each.

Dolls too have been hitting the headlines with new world records, for over £67,000 was paid for a rare William and Mary wooden doll which, unfortunately, was devoid of a hand and part of a lower leg.

People buy old pub signs, advertising boards, paper window displays, enamel signs, railway station nameboards just because they like the look of them – and later find that they have picked up a valuable asset. A man whose hobby was fishing became interested in old fishing tackle and is now one of the best known international dealers in the field for the sport of angling has been a rich source for

These colourful enamel signs are worth from £45 for the 'Rowntree's Chocolates and Pastilles', to an amazing £300 for the 'Zebra Grate Polish'.

the collector ever since the days of Isaac Walton. Salmon flies, spoons, floats, gaffs and even weights have their specialist following but the fishing reel is without doubt the most sought after item by collectors. Rare examples such as a Victorian gilt brass reel with ivory handle and spring and cog mechanism recently sold for £2,700.

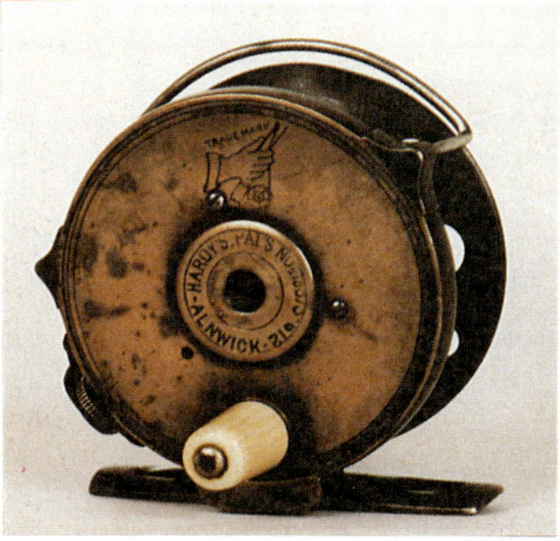

A rare Hardy Bros. 2½in. Perfect brass fly reel of the 1891 pattern. (Phillips) £2,700

A dentist gave up looking after patients' teeth when his collection of old dental instruments took over his life. Today he deals in the instruments and also writes books about them. A couple whose hobby was swimming and badminton began collecting postcards and advertising material about these sports. They've written books on the subject, deal in cards concerned with sporting subjects and travel all over the country giving lectures on their collection.

Because of his job, a lighthouse keeper started collecting old postcards with pictures of lighthouses on them. Today he has one of the best collections in existence and his cards are valuable not only in money terms but also from a historian's point of view because they provide information about lighthouses which are no longer in use or sometimes even in existence. He found his cards through other dealers, in jumble sales and saleroom job lots. Few of them cost more than a couple of pence to buy and some were swopped with other collectors for cards he did not want himself, because as far as postcards are concerned there are collectors interested in every subject under the sun from bridges to bathing beauties; railway stations to rude cartoons; foreign cities to farm yards. Today collectors pay prices ranging from £1.50 for a postcard of Cary Grant to anything up to £8 for one of the erotic French postcards of the 1920's.

Typical saucy French postcards worth between £3 and £7.

A very rare ballooning postcard 'Lifeboat Saturday', sold by Neales of Nottingham for an amazing £1,675.

The first British postcards issued by the G.P.O. in 1870 were designed to take the address only on one side and the message alongside the illustration on the other side. An Act of Parliament in 1902 allowed the message and address to be written on the same side leaving the other side free for a picture which greatly increased their popularity. One of the rarest examples is 'Lifeboat Saturday' which was delivered by Balloon Post from Manchester to Haslingden on 20th September 1902 and sold for the not inconsiderable sum of £1,675.

A policeman in London has shelves in his sitting room full of valuable and attractively coloured Victorian poison bottles because one day, when he was chasing a suspect through rough ground, he tripped over a bottle sticking up out of a rubbish dump. It was a poison bottle and because he liked the look of it, he went back to the dump and dug up several more. Then he began reading up about poison bottles and gradually his collection grew. Today he has bottles which are worth up to £40 each – all dug from dumps where they had been thrown away as worthless.

An Art Nouveau rectangular leaded glass panel by Jacques Gruber, 256cm. high. (Christie's) £9,720

The scope for finding something that is worth money is immense, it covers every

A Clarice Cliff 'Age of Jazz', two sided plaque, 17.5cm. high. (Phillips) £4,000

A Goldscheider painted terracotta group, 57cm. high. (Phillips) £1,500

One of a pair of George III giltwood mirrors, by Thomas Chippendale. (Christie's) £64,800

A calendar for 1900 by E. P. Dutton & Co. with the boat moving under the bridge when the strings are pulled — now worth over £20 to the collector.

Even Christmas cards are now a serious collectible, with this fine Victorian example with its delicate soft colouring worth over £5.

possible aspect of life and every interest, no matter how bizarre. Every week someone finds something new worth collecting and so another speciality is born; another market opens up for items that were disregarded before. Anything connected with golf for instance is very popular. The earliest golf balls were made of leather and filled with a concoction of boiled feathers, enough to fill a top hat. They were then hammered to a round shape and painted white. In time these were followed by the Gutta-Percha balls which were of smooth appearance and patented by Dr Paterson of St. Andrews. Early balls are extremely rare and highly collectible as can be judged by a Gourlay feather ball in mint condition which recently sold for £4,500.

'Historical Gossip about Golf and Golfers', Edinburgh 1863, a very rare book sold by Phillips for £11,200 together with the golf ball which sold for a mammoth £4,500.

Photograph of Sir Winston Churchill, signed, depicting him as a Lieutenant in the 4th Hussars, Cairo, September 1898. (Phillips) *£1,500*

An album of 27 calotypes by D. O. Hill and R. Adamson. (Christie's) *£17,000*

Photography is another fertile area for collectors. One of the rarest cameras to come on the market was the Sutton Panoramic Wet Plate camera made of mahogany and brass which sold for £11,000. Just as surprising was a Kodak No. 1 from 1880 with its 57mm. F9 Periscopic Lens and Guillotine Sector Shutter which although less impressive to look at made £800. Don't get excited, your box Brownie which looks very similar is hardly worth anything.

One of three glass negatives taken by the Rev. Charles Lutwidge Dodgson – Lewis Carroll – in 1879. (Phillips) *£8,000*

If there was any doubt that collecting weathervanes is a subject for serious investment it was dispelled recently in America when an entire auction was devoted to the sale of just one weathervane with historical connections to the patriot Paul Revere. Weathervanes have also been disappearing mysteriously from atop some of the highest churches in New York State as a result of daring helicopter raids at dawn – a sure indication of their worth. A rare late 19th century example of a leaping horse made of copper and zinc recently sold for £24,285 – really.

Treasures can turn up anywhere – antique shops, junk shops, car boot sales or jumble sales are all good sources.

An extremely rare American locomotive and tender copper weathervane, circa 1882, the locomotive reproduced in fine detail is mounted on track with two ball finials at tracks end, and attached ball counterweight, in fine original condition with verdigris surface, 17in. high, 61in. long, 8in. deep. (Robt. W. Skinner Inc.) £115,625

A pictorial framed advertisement for Green's Lawn Mowers, 'Hundreds of Thousands in Use' 18 x 24in. (Onslows) £110

A rare German Cupid Plane, probably 17th century, 6¾in. long, 2in. wide. (David Stanley Auctions) £2,900

Britains extremely rare display set 131, the largest set ever made by Britains, consisting of 281 figures including cavalrymen, infantrymen, bandsmen, sailors and Camel Corps soldiers, circa 1905. (Phillips) £10,000

A pair of 16th century leather nose spectacles, 9cm. wide, discovered in the roof of a house. (Phillips) £1,600

A rectangular conversation piece by Wm. Welling, of a husband and wife taking tea, signed and dated 1874, 280 x 380mm. (Phillips) £3,200

A Liberty & Co. 'Cymric' silver timepiece, the design attributed to Archibald Knox, 17cm. high, hallmarks for 1901. (Phillips) £3,200

A mid 18th century beadwork bag, circa 1760's. (Phillips) £420

A Marinot enamelled glass vase, the clear glass enamelled with a frieze of three nude female figures, 20.2cm. high. (Christie's) £4,540

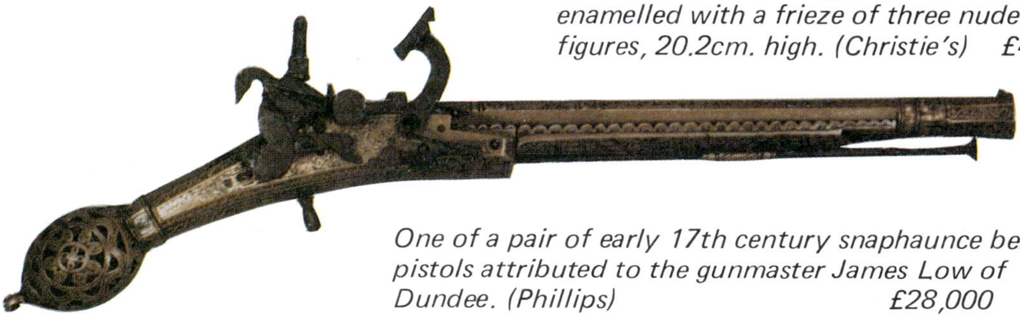

One of a pair of early 17th century snaphaunce belt pistols attributed to the gunmaster James Low of Dundee. (Phillips) £28,000

The Archer, a figure by Ferdinand Preiss, 23½in. high. (Christie's) £11,500

A Gustave Serrurier Bovy three-fold screen of mahogany and stained glass, 376 x 165cm. high. (Christie's) £6,571

A classic Navajo chief's blanket, woven in single strand homespun and ravelled yarn, 82 x 62in. (Robt. W. Skinner Inc.) £20,978

A rare and unusual James Dixon & Sons plated teapot designed by Christopher Dresser, circa 1879, 16.75cm. high. (Phillips) £36,000

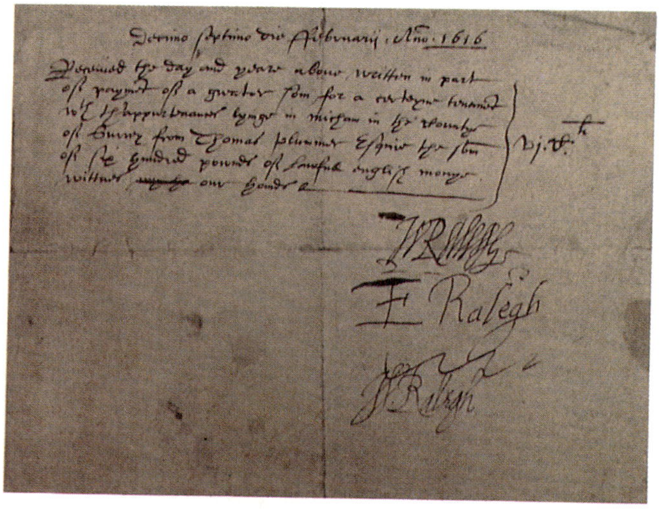

Some early signed documents can have considerable value such as this Receipt for the sale of a property signed by Sir Walter Ralegh, his wife, Elizabeth, and son Walter, which could be worth over £5,000 at auction. (Christie's)

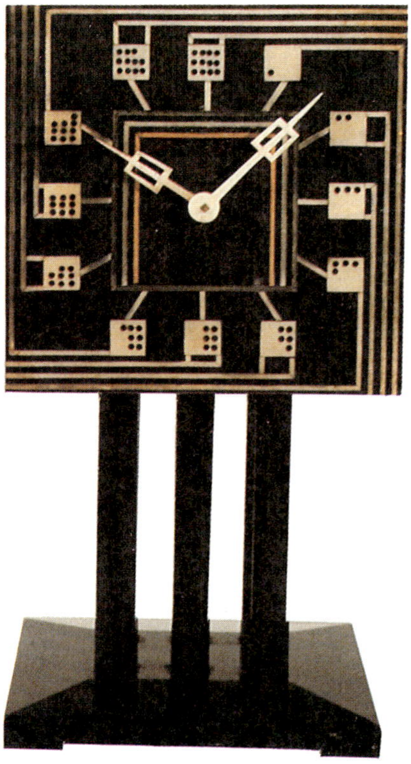

The Sturrock Domino clock, designed by Charles Rennie Mackintosh as a wedding present to Alec Sturrock and Mary Newbery, 25cm. high. (Phillips) £42,000

Rubbish dumps are gold mines for people with an eye for a rarity. They dig up bottles, pot lids, old clay pipes, china, decorated tiles, ironware – every piece somebody's rubbish from the past which is worth money today. Although milk has been sold in glass bottles since the latter part of the 19th century, they did not come into common use until after the First World War. The earliest known example 'The Thatcher Milk Protector', was devised by an American, Dr Harvey P. Thatcher in 1884 and is worth about £150. Unwanted items can always be swopped through the network of Bottle Collecting Clubs which are found all over the country. No matter how odd or unusual a find, there is always someone somewhere who yearns to own it.

Rare early light bulbs, circa 1882, worth from £170 to £300 for the Swan 'Pipless' on the right.

Light bulbs, for instance, date from about 1841 when an inventor named Starr found that a bright light could be produced by sending an electric current through a piece of carbon. The first successful incandescent electric lamps produced in the U.K. were made by J. W. Swan of Newcastle and one of his light bulbs 'Swan Pipless', made in 1882, is worth about £300.

Two 1920's silk dresses by Mariano Fortuny with Delphos pleating and stencilled belt. (Phillips) £3,000 each

The world of textiles is also a good area for the treasure hunter for a Delphos dress by the designer Mariano Fortuny could be worth over £3,000 and even Marilyn Monroe's bra, left in a London hairdressers, fetched the not inconsiderable sum of £500 at auction.

An early 19th century needlework sampler, 51 x 44.5cm. (Phillips) £500

Crazy quilt, New York, inscribed 'Columbus – Gods Fair World 1492-1892'. (Robt. W. Skinner Inc.) *£1,400*

A fine American mid 19th century pierced and applique cotton album quilt with twenty-six pictorial applique blocks depicting trees and flowers, wreaths and birds, houses and pastoral scenes, surrounding a large central clock of embroidered applique flowers in a woven basket inside a floral wreath border, 86 x 99in., worth over £6,000. (Robt. W. Skinner Inc.)

Designed to keep out the cold, bedcovers were made from two thicknesses of cloth with padding sewn between. This developed into an art and before long we had the richly decorated quilts so highly prized by collectors. A rare example by Sarah Anne Wilson, consisting of thirty appliqued squares of floral and animal design was made in 1854 and recently sold for, would you believe, £22,000.

Samplers were produced from early in the 18th century right through until after the First World War as a means of showing how adept a young girl could be at the useful art of embroidery, as well as knowing her alphabet. Most found today are 19th century and worth £100 or so but early North American examples such as one by Lydia Hart dated May 28th 1744 are extremely rare which accounts for the £24,665 it made.

Tin canisters or old biscuit boxes used to be thrown out, disregarded by the hundreds in the years before the last war and even later, but pretty or unusual tins can demand astonishing prices from collectors today. Collectors tend to specialise in unusually shaped tins or in ones with attractive pictures or portraits of the Royal Family, and Princes Diana and Prince Charles tins are already being collected. Some of the most attractive are 1920's biscuit tins decorated with nursery rhyme scenes or tins shaped liked buses, engines or books.

It seems that nothing is too everyday to be worth money – even the labels from cans of food or cleaning materials on sale in supermarkets today are being collected and show a profit for the collector within a very short period of time. Collectors of these items choose labels which are well designed, particularly attractive or which represent a significant advance in the modern way of life. Biological soap powders were a breakthrough when they first appeared and their packets were worth collecting.

A colourful Victorian magazine insert for 'Sunlight Soap' worth about £5.

It was around 1942 that the immortal cry 'Any Gum, Chum', was first heard echoing throughout Britain as the first Bubble Gum was introduced by the American Allied Forces. The British home product didn't get under way until the early 1950's and with new issues appearing every few weeks many of these wax paper wrappers are now quite rare. Most sought after is 'Mars Attacks' issued in 1962 and quickly withdrawn because there were complaints that it frightened children – it's now worth £100.

Fans of the Beatles in the 1960's and '70's who collected records, magazines, programmes and other things relating to their idols are today sitting on a treasure trove because the big auction houses hold regular sales of pop idol memorabilia at which hundreds of pounds can be paid for an unusual record, a fan photograph, a signed concert programme or even a pair of nylons with the magic name 'The Beatles' on them.

One of a collection of twelve previously unpublished colour pictures of The Beatles. (Christie's) £650

Very rare character jug, 'Churchill', designed by C. J. Noke, introduced in 1940, withdrawn by 1942, AS D6170. Wording on the base: 'Winston Spencer' Churchill Prime Minister of Britain 1940. This Loving Cup was made during the Battle of Britain as a tribute to a great leader, worth over £6,000.

An autographed Cavern Club membership book from the early 1960's can sell for as much as £500 and even old copies of Beatles' sheet music sell for £1.50 each. Tens of thousands of printed items are available on the Beatles who dominated not only popular music but also all youth culture for the best part of a decade. Of particular interest are those items more personally identified with the super group such as a signed concert programme for 1964 which sold for £350, but for really amazing money the hand-written lyrics of 'Imagine' by John Lennon, on the reverse of an hotel bill from Majorca, sold for over £7,000. The same enthusiasm applies to Buddy Holly, Elvis Presley and the memorabilia of other more recent stars. There must be drawers and boxes full of dusty papers and magazines forgotten by one time pop fans in houses all over the country which are worth money now.

Doulton produced a limited number of Toby Jugs of Chaplin in 1918. They were inscribed 'Charlie' on the base and his bowler hat formed the lid. The jugs stand 10½in. high and are today very rare because less than ten are known to be in private collections, worth well over £2,000.

These three Doulton figures, 'Wedding Morn', 'Tulips', and 'The Coming of Spring', are all worth over £500.

An extremely rare Royal Doulton character jug, 'The Maori', circa 1939, which never actually went into production. Occasionally, however, a pilot model comes onto the market and it has been reported that collectors are willing to pay around £12,500 for one.

It is generally accepted that a Royal Doulton character jug inscribed 'Winston Churchill Prime Minister of Britain 1940' was withdrawn after less than a year in production because Churchill was not pleased with the likeness portrayed. As such it is an extremely rare and desirable item coveted by collectors throughout the world and is likely to fetch £6,000 at auction.

Even this amazing price has now been surpassed by an even rarer character jug, a pilot edition known as 'The Maori' produced in 1939, which now sells for over £12,500.

Gustav Stickley, the eldest of six brothers who died in 1942, was an American designer of furniture who signed his creations in red script. Just one of his armchairs can be worth a small fortune and even a wastepaper basket by him is worth £1,000.

Duck Decoys are mainly used in estuaries and ponds by hunters; are made of wood and painted in traditional colours with flat paint. Originally fashioned from mud and reeds they have now become works of art in their own right as can be judged by an example of a Black Duck in preening position by A. Elmer Crowell which sold for a mammoth £24,000.

Even radios have come a long way since Mr Marconi harnessed the transmission of electro-magnetic waves back in 1894 and this is the fascination for collectors. The Phillips Mains AC Super Inductance model from 1932 sells for over £100.

Anyone who wants to make a profit out of buying and selling unusual items should cast aside prejudices against 'junk' and look for the indefinable quality in something that really attracts them. They should be prepared to search out their quarry with infinite patience wherever they go and they should also take the trouble to find out as much about their subject as possible. With the growth of knowledge will come greater discrimination and the ability to spot a true rarity that is worth money. Anyone with the ability to spot an unlikely bargain knows that if they ask themselves the question "What's It Worth?" the answer is very often . . . "Far more than you might expect".

Tony Curtis

All types of space age toys are now in demand especially early Japanese tinplate clockwork robots such as this one entitled 'Lilliput' which sold at Phillips for £280.

An Art Deco bronze and ivory figure of a flute player, by Ferdinand Preiss, 42cm. high. (Phillips) £6,500

ADVERTISING SIGNS

There was a time when enamel advertising signs could be found pinned to every available wall surface colourfully proclaiming the purity and authenticity of every imaginable product. Indeed this was such a common practice that companies employed men whose only job was to fix these signs on site.

Now, in the 1980's, these enamel signs are among the most treasured and in some cases the most expensive examples of advertising collectibles. The most rare and desirable of these are the Victorian or Edwardian signs in mint condition. Ideally, signs should be of a size less than one metre square and feature some favourable characteristic such as a shaped edge, a figurative image or quirky period slogan, printing in full colour or advertise a now obsolete product.

Player's Please. (Street Jewellery) £50

An advertising plaque bearing Rowland's Macassar Oil, the reverse impressed T. J. & J. Mayer, Longport, 16 x 22cm. (Phillips) £500

Singer Sewing Machines, 11 x 7½in. (Street Jewellery) £85

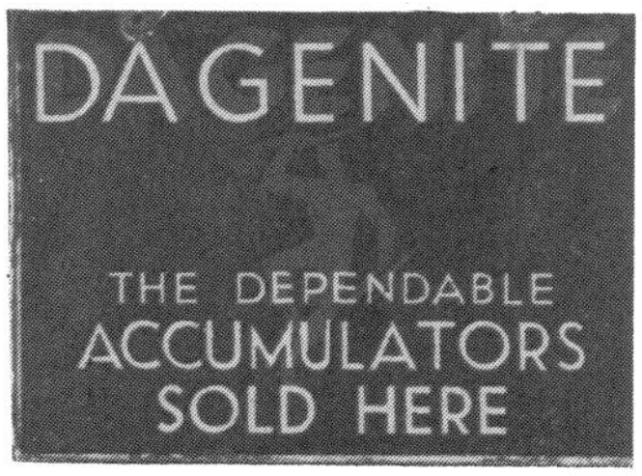

Dagenite, The Dependable Accumulators Sold Here. (Street Jewellery) £40

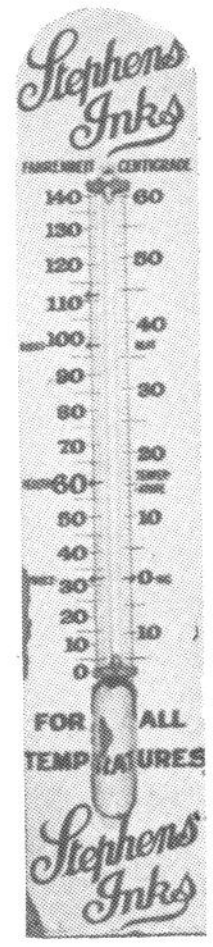

Stephens Inks. (Street Jewellery) £85

Blue Band Margarine. (Street Jewellery) £45

Ovaltine. (Street Jewellery) £80

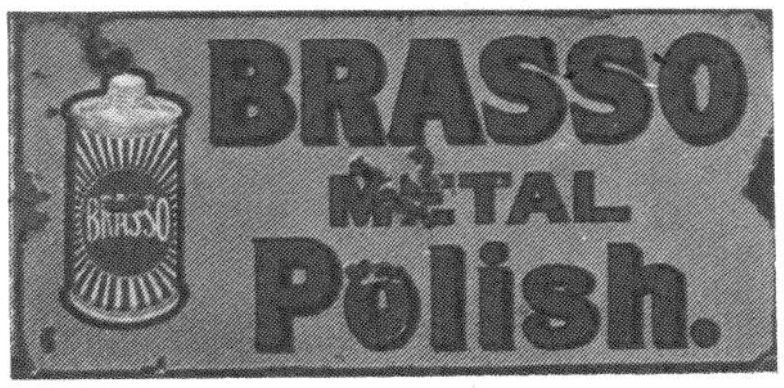

Brasso Metal Polish. (Street Jewellery) £50

Reckitt's Blue. (Street Jewellery) £300

Depot for Norfolk Champion Boots. (Street Jewellery) £75

Chivers' Carpet Soap. (Street Jewellery) £200

Persil, made by Ferro Email, 1930's, 23 x 15in. (Street Jewellery) £80

United Kingdom Tea Company's Delicious Teas. (Street Jewellery) £200

Churchman's 'Tortoiseshell' Smoking Mixture. (Street Jewellery) £175

Rowntree's Elect Cocoa. (Street Jewellery) £40

Depot for 'Swan' Ink. (Street Jewellery) £85

Late 19th century American apothecary sign, 3ft. high. (Robt. W. Skinner Inc.) £810

Patent Steam Carpet Beating Co, Ltd. (Street Jewellery) £250

Fresh Palethorpes Today. (Street Jewellery) £100

W. D. & H. O. Wills, 'Westward Ho!' Smoking Mixture. (Street Jewellery) £75

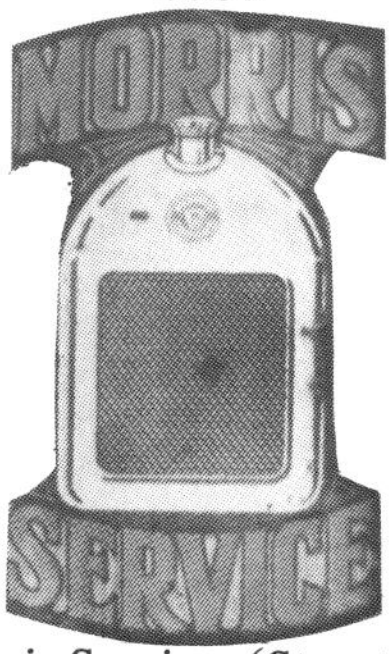

Morris Service. (Street Jewellery) £125

Raleigh, The All-Steel Bicycle. (Street Jewellery) £120

Rowntree's Chocolates and Pastilles. (Street Jewellery) £45

Robin Starch. (Street Jewellery) £175

ADVERTISING WARES

Over the years, manufacturers have advertised and promoted their products by means of 'free gifts'. Based on the premise that it is always nice to be given something for nothing, especially an object that is either useful or decorative, they have stamped their name on a variety of goods ranging from the sublime to the ridiculous.

Goods range from a motor car to a very cheap and nasty key ring with a fascinating selection of interesting items somewhere in between.

Some of the best examples have come to us via the early exhibitions such as The British Empire Exhibition held in 1924/25 at Wembley, and a more modest range from the tradition upheld by door to door salesmen of giving away to customers the tiny sample tins of polish or little gadgets like needle threaders or bottle openers.

Some collectors concentrate on a particular product such as Bovril or Globe Polish while others collect specific items such as fans or needle cases, both of which were a popular give-away with a number of manufacturers.

Sunlight Soap advertising rubber, ¾in. wide. £2

China mug from Rolls Royce. £4

Ogden's 'St. Julien' tobacco advertising weather gauge. £20

Small character jug liqueur flask made for W. Walklate Ltd. depicting 'Poacher', 4in. high. £38

A tea caddy made for 'Twinings of the Strand', June 1953, 7in. high. £65

Four Robertson's Golly musicians, 3in. high. £15

Horlicks Malted Milk beaker, 4½in. high. £3.50

Pot for Holloway's Ointment for Gout and Rheumatism, 1½in. tall. £7

Hudson's Soap handbag mirror, 5cm. diam. £6

Deckers 'Scurf Pomade' beaker, 1930's. £10

A Royal Doulton advertising model of a bulldog, 14.7cm. high. £600

AERONAUTICAL

Although Wilbur Wright and his brother Orvil are credited with making the first powered flight in December 1903, it was another American, Samuel Pierpont Langley, who actually invented the first aeroplane.
After achieving success with a model launched from the roof of a houseboat on the Potomac in 1896, he progressed to a full size machine and was ready to repeat the experiment early in 1903. Unfortunately, the starting mechanism failed and the aircraft plunged into the river. Professor Langley died in 1906 never having achieved his life's ambition.
The postscript to this story is, that in 1914, his former students fitted floats to Langley's 'curiosity' in an attempt to launch direct from the river – it flew like a bird.
All subject material relating to the early events and other important highlights in the history of aviation are keenly sought after by collectors.

A blue enamel oval snuff box, the cover painted with a hot air balloon over the countryside, 2¼in. long. (Christie's) £420

Two of a set of twenty-four coloured magic lantern slides depicting early ballooning and flying scenes, in original box. (Christie's) £150

An openface pocket watch, the white face inscribed 'Shock proof lever, Swiss made' and depicting a monoplane, 2in. diam. (Christie's) £55

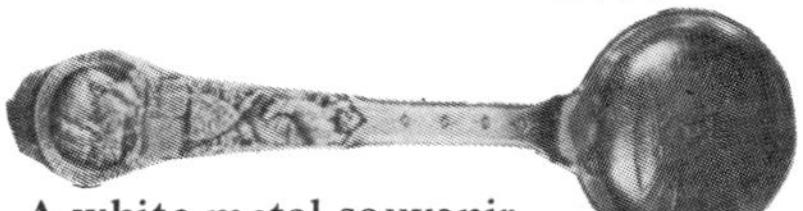

A white metal souvenir spoon commemorating the journey of Norwegian airship 'Norge' in 1926, 5in. long. (Christie's) £40

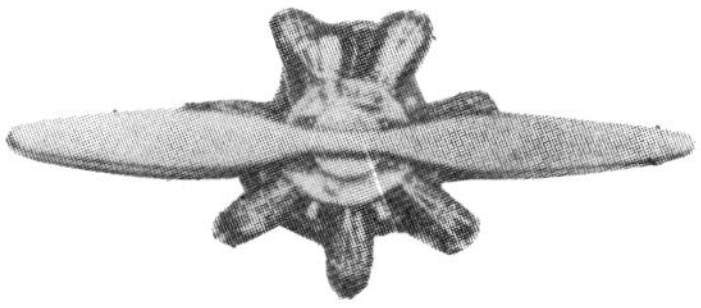

A silver lapel badge in the form of a gnome engine with propeller, 1¾in. long. (Christie's) £55

An ivory paper knife, reputed to have been salvaged from Manfred von Richthofen's aircraft, 12in long. (Christie's) £380

One of four silver place-setting holders depicting a Wright flyer, 1½in. high, in presentation case. (Christie's) £350

A sheepskin-lined U.S. Army flying jacket, type B-3, size 48. (Christie's) £150

A complimentary Season Pass to the London Aerodrome, Hendon, 1914, issued to John F. Plummer, together with a collection of other related material. (Christie's) £130

A pair of sheepskin-lined flying trousers, type B-1. (Christie's) £75

AMUSEMENT MACHINES

Now that highly sophisticated video games and complex electronically operated machines dominate the amusement arcades, attention is wistfully returning to the great mechanical devices of a bygone age.

Fast gaining in popularity with collectors, amusement machines form a fascinating collection and offer an excellent investment potential.

The promise of challenge and entertainment suggested by these evocatively named contraptions is almost irresistible. One may have one's fortune told, test one's grip, take part in a death dive and experience the delights of one pennyworth of the Gay Deceiver – all good clean fun.

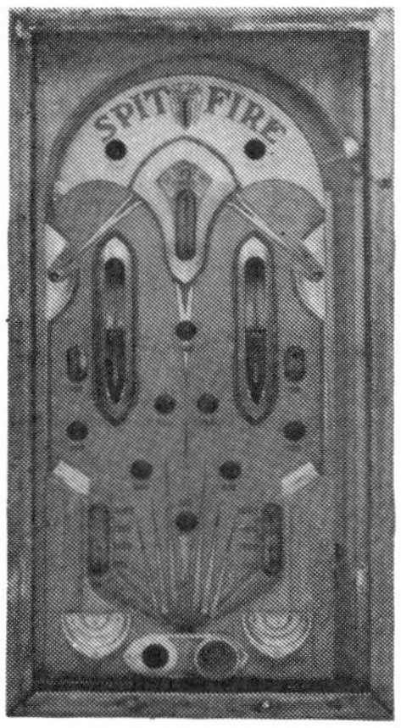

Early Genco pinball bagatelle table with glass top, circa 1935, 39in. long. £300

Ahrens stereoscopic viewer in oak cabinet, circa 1925, 68in. high. £495

'Pussy' Shooter, amusement machine, circa 1935, 76in. high. £308

'Test Your Grip' amusement machine with iron grip handle, circa 1925, 50in. high. £385

Ahrens 'Test Your Strength' amusement machine in painted wooden case, circa 1922, 79in. high. £528

Ahrens '22-Man Football' game, coin-operated, in oak casing, circa 1930, 43¾in. wide. £440

Caillie Brothers grip-test amusement machine in green-painted case, circa 1910, 59in. high. £528

'Laughing Sailor', amusement machine, coin-operated bearing Ruffler & Walker plaque, 68½in. high, circa 1935. £528

ARMOUR

Although full suits of armour are a little bulky to contemplate collecting, quite apart from costing anything from a few hundred to many thousands of pounds, such articles as gauntlets, arm and shoulder defences and particularly breastplates can lead to an interesting and not too expensive collection.
Independent breastplates have been known since the 14th century, and examples of these can of course be on the dear side, but those from later centuries can be found from as little as £50 upwards.
Beware of reproductions, however, for they have been made for the last hundred years. All those I have seen come complete with a suitable hole or dent where the heart is, along with the story about how the ploughman turned it up where the battle of Culloden (or suitable local shindig) took place.

A composite suit of late 16th century cuirassier's half armour £1,250

A 15th century Turkish breastplate, Krug, struck with the St. Irene arsenal mark. (Wallis & Wallis) £190

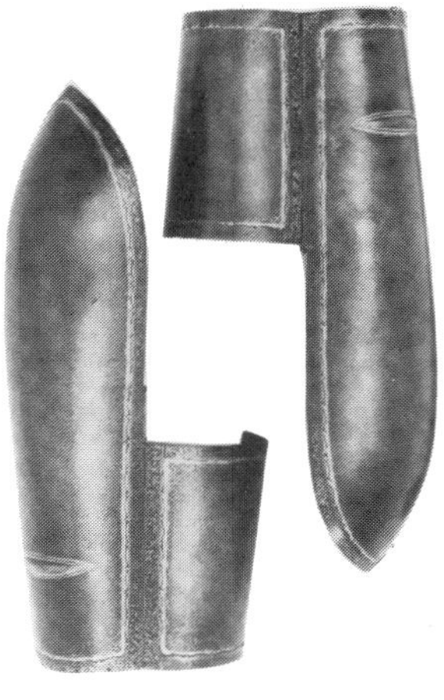

A pair of 18th century gold damascened Indian arm defences Bazu-Band, 12¾in., of solid shaped form. (Wallis & Wallis) £230

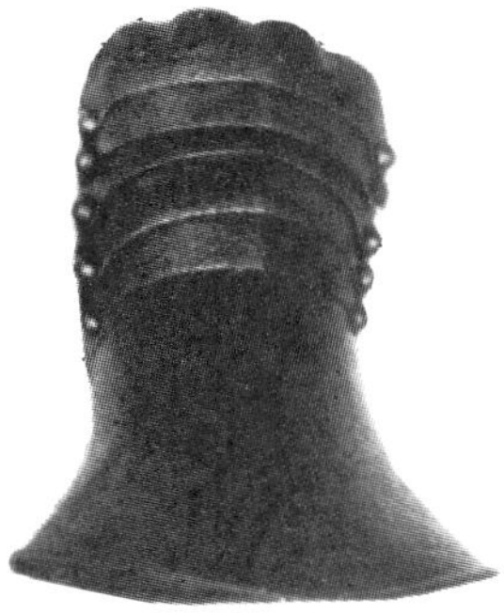

An articulated right-hand gauntlet, circa 1600, with flared cuff. (Wallis & Wallis) £70

A 17th century breast and bullet proof backplate, turned over borders and distinct medial ridge. (Wallis & Wallis) £400

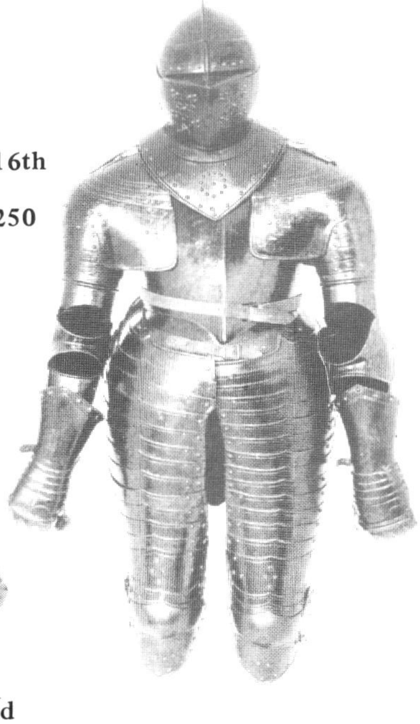

A cuirassier's three-quarter armour, circa 1640, the whole mounted on plastic dummy and wooden base. £5,500

Prussian Regt. of Garde du Corps officer's parade cuirass. (Christie's) £4,500

A suit of armour dated Tenmon gonen (1536). (Christie's) £2,592

ASHTRAYS

Over the years, many thousands of different types of ashtrays have been produced in just about every conceivable material and form. One may find everything from stylised aeroplanes to armchairs in materials ranging from bronze to bakelite.
A popular specialist area is in collecting advertising ashtrays. Clubs, pubs, hotels, large companies and organisations have nearly all, at one time or another, issued a special ashtray decorated with their name and sometimes an illustration of their premises and location. Souvenir ashtrays, produced for the turn of the century holidaymakers, also make an interesting collection. These are quite plentiful and generally inexpensive. There are however, one or two exceptions – and this makes the search that bit more interesting. While most are priced at around two or three pounds, sometimes less, anything from the Goss factory is worth considerably more. Some fine examples fetch upwards of £20.

Victorian horn ashtray on plated feet. £4

Commemorative pewter ashtray, for 'University College of Wales', Aberystwyth. £7

Burns ashtray by W. H. Goss. £20

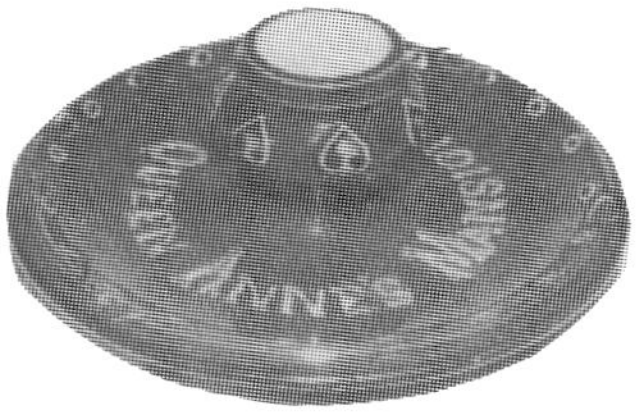

A Doulton Lambeth stoneware ashtray match holder, 'Queen Anne's Mansion'. £30

20th century Indian brass ashtray inlaid with semi precious stones. £8

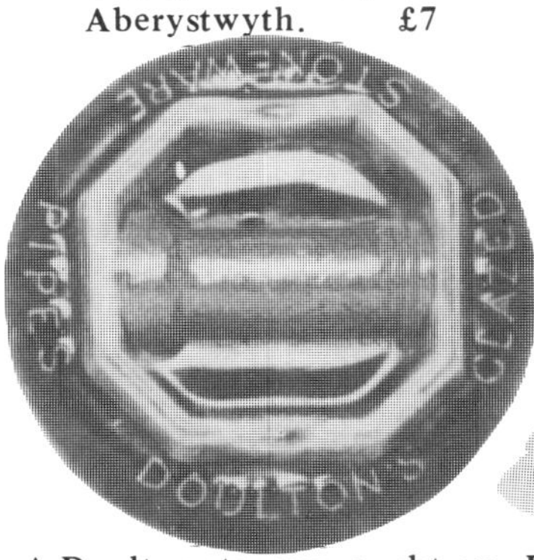

A Doulton stoneware ashtray, for pipes, circa 1900. £28

Pip Squeak and Wilfred ashtray made for The Daily Mirror, Fetter Lane, London, 4in. high, circa 1930 £250

Empire Nut Brown Tobacco ashtray. £15

1930's wooden barrel type ashtray. £4

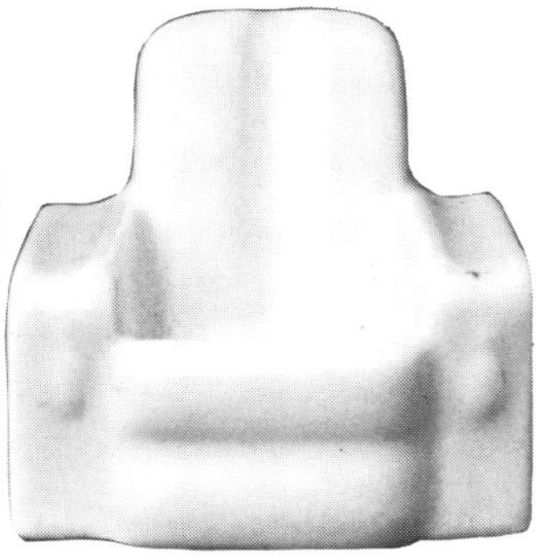

China armchair ashtray by B. G. R. in the 1930's style. £2

Castrol Oil glass ashtray. £4

'Winston Churchill' ashtray by Hammersley & Co., Stoke on Trent. £5

AUTOGRAPH LETTERS & DOCUMENTS

Original letters and documents written or signed by the famous names of history in all fields, from great authors to naval and military leaders. Kings and Queens, scientists, artists and musicians, provide a fascinating field for the private collector, as well as the raw material for historical and literary research. The collector will find himself in competition with the research libraries of the world, but will also have the reward of working alongside historians with a common aim. There is a particular demand for literary letters and for royal documents, but any piece of paper or parchment bearing a famous name is likely to be of some value. The signatures of many of our popular entertainers and recent sportsmen are of little worth, but there is always the chance that they may gain interest in the future.

The value of any letter or document will depend on many factors, most importantly the identity of the writer and the scarcity of the signature. In addition, the contents and condition are significant and must always be taken into account. There are numerous facsimile reproductions, not only of important letters but of routine notes like the acknowledgements sent out by Churchill in response to messages of greetings, and forgery has long been a popular pastime. It is sensible to buy from a reputable dealer who will guarantee the authenticity of everything he sells.

Although most of the examples illustrated are indicative of the upper end of the market there is still a wealth of material from lesser personalities which can be bought at prices well within the reach of most collectors.

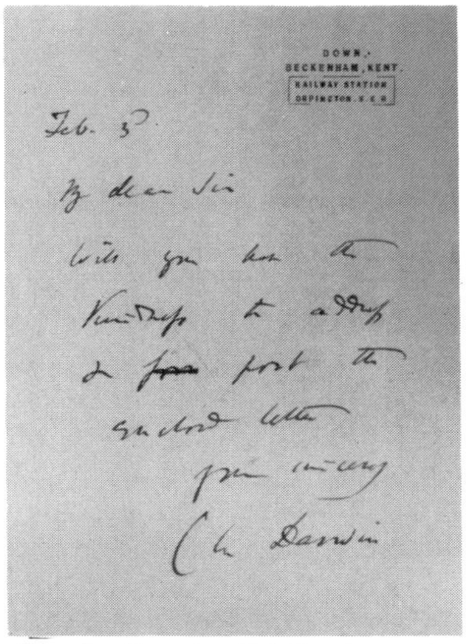
Down, Beckenham, Kent. Railway Station Orpington S.E.R.

Feb. 3

My dear Sir

Will you have the kindness to address & post the enclosed letter.

Yours sincerely

Ch. Darwin

Charles Darwin: Brief autograph letter signed, 1 page 8vo, 3 February n.y. £750

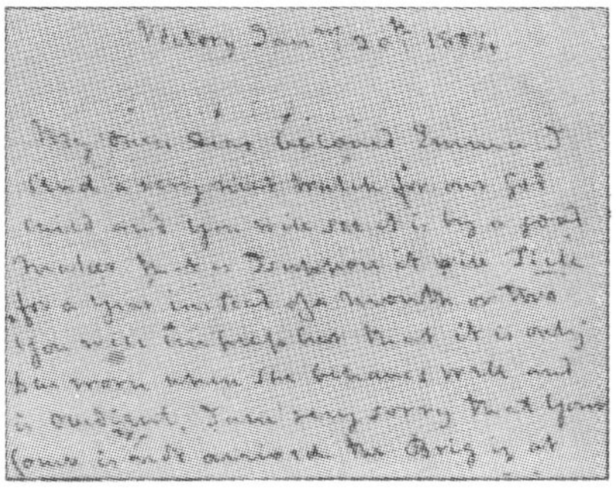

Horatio Nelson, fine autograph letter signed Nelson and Bronte to Emma Hamilton, 4 pages, quarto, sending a watch for their child and mentions that a comb is on its way to Emma etc., Victory, 20 January 1804. £2,500

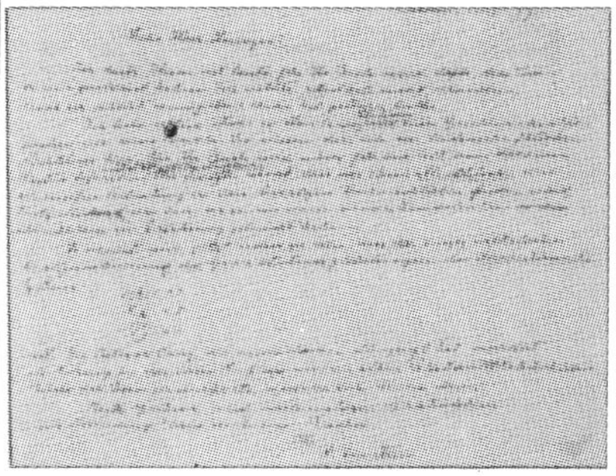

Albert Einstein, autograph letter signed about relevance of Lanczos' work to Einstein's theories on relativity, 1 page, Princeton 1949. £1,050

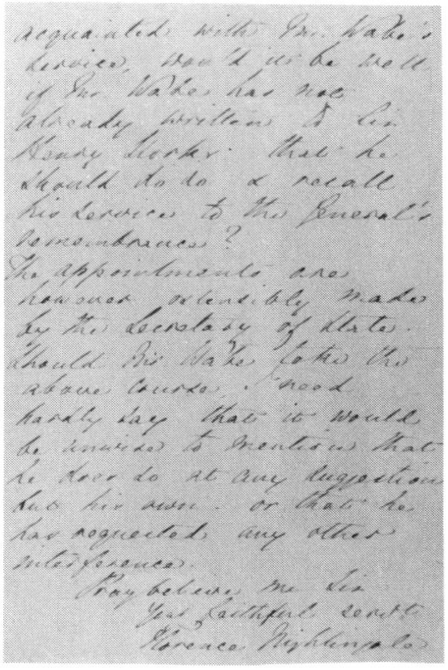
acquainted with Mr. Wake's services, wouldn't it be well if Mr Wake has not already written to Sir Henry Storks that he should do so & recall his services to the General's remembrance? The appointments are however ostensibly made by the Secretary of State. Should Mr Wake take the above course, I need hardly say that it would be unwise to mention that he does so at any suggestion but his own, or that he has requested any other interference.

Pray believe me Sir
Yours faithful servt
Florence Nightingale

Florence Nightingale: Autograph letter signed, 3 pages 8vo with envelope, 29 November 1869, (last page). £350

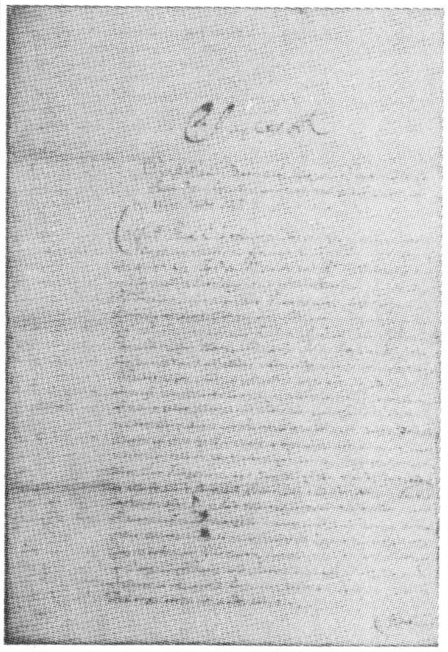

Charles II, King of England, letter relating to plantations in America, counter signed by Earl of Arlington, 1672. (Robert W. Skinner Inc.) £1,000

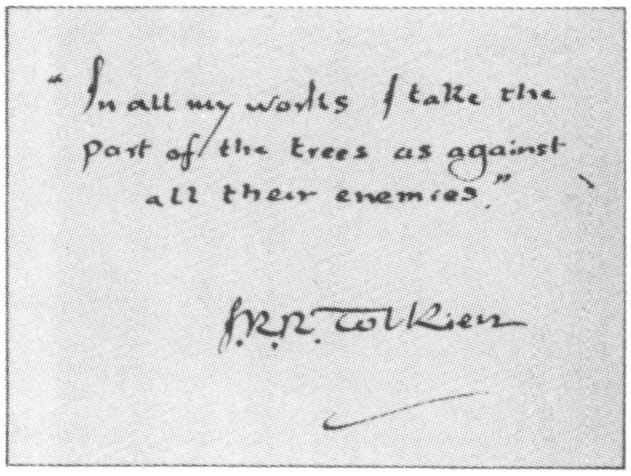
"In all my works I take the part of the trees as against all their enemies."

J.R.R. Tolkien

J.R.R. Tolkien, autograph statement signed 'In all my works I take the part of the trees as against all their enemies', on an oblong slip of paper. £155

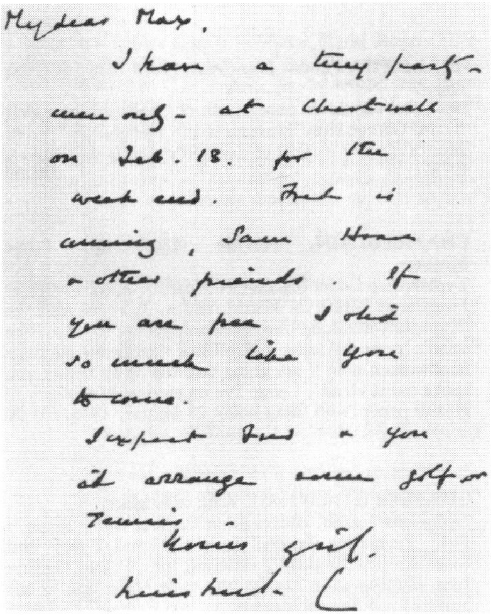

My dear Max,
I have a tiny party coming only at Chartwell on Feb. 18. for the week end. Freddie is coming, Sam Hoare & other friends. If you are free I should so much like you to come.
I expect Freddie & you will arrange some golf or Tennis.
Yours ever,
Winston S.C.

Sir Winston Spencer Churchill: Autograph letter, signed ('Winston S.C.'), 1 page 8vo, Treasury Chambers, Whitehall, 1 February 1926. £320

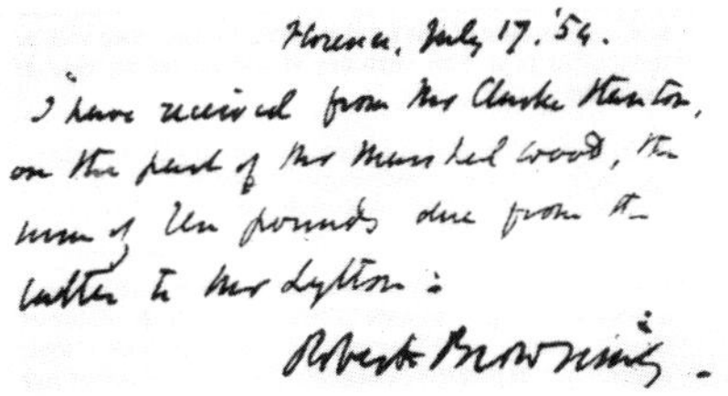

Florence, July 17. '54.
I have received from Mr Clarke Hunter, on the part of Mr Mansfield Wood, the sum of ten pounds due from the latter to Mr Lytton:
Robert Browning.

Robert Browning: Autograph receipt, signed, 1 page 16mo; Florence, 17 July 1854. £125

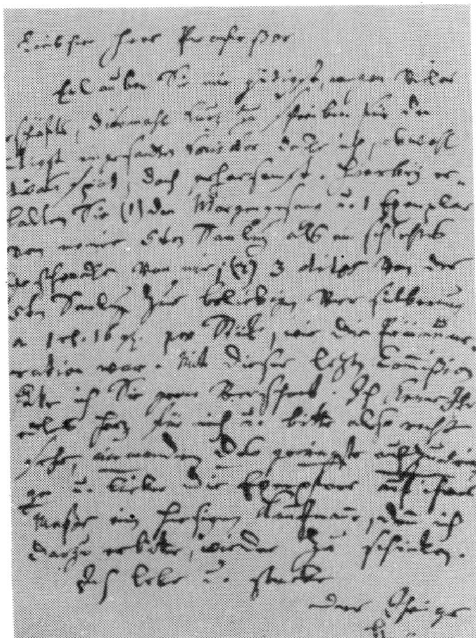

Carl Philipp Emanuel Bach, fine autograph letter signed, 1 page, octavo, Hamburg, 14 December 1785. £5,500

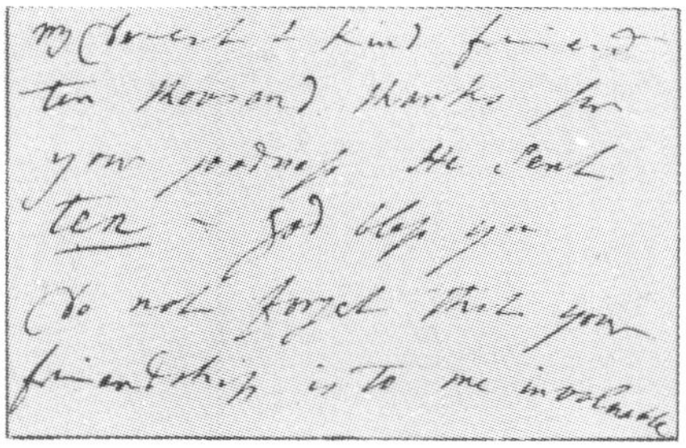

my dearest & kind friend ten thousand thanks for your goodness. He sent ten – God bless you. Do not forget that your friendship is to me invaluable

Lady Emma Hamilton, three autograph letters signed Emma And E.H., 3 pages, quarto and octavo, from 12 Temple Place to Sir Richard Puleston. £280

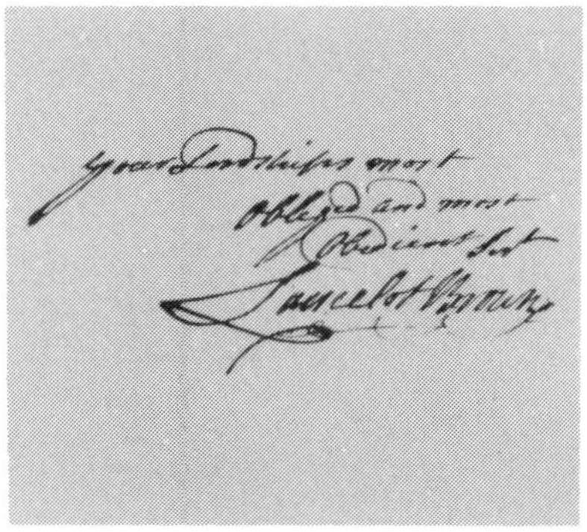

your Lordships most Obliged and most Obedient Servt
Lancelot Brown

Lancelot Brown, 'Capability', autograph letter signed, one page, quarto, to an un-named peer asking him to repay a bond, 16 December 1779. £110

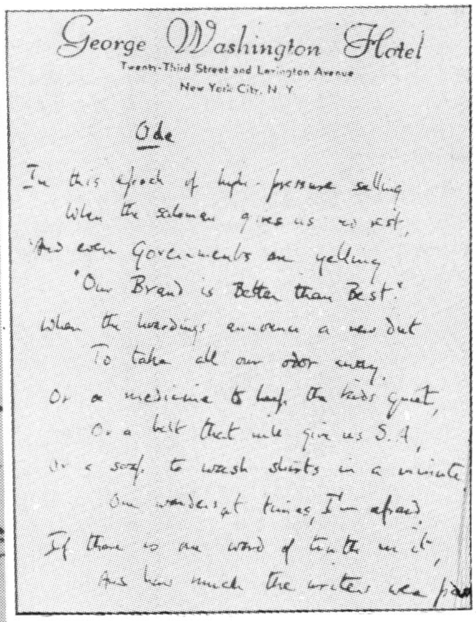

George Washington Hotel
Twenty-Third Street and Lexington Avenue
New York City, N.Y.

Ode

In this epoch of high-pressure selling
When the salesmen give us no rest,
And even Governments are yelling
'Our Brand is Better than Best.'
When the hoardings announce a new Deal
To take all our odor away,
Or a medicine to keep the kids quiet,
Or a belt that will give us S.A.,
Or a soap to wash shirts in a minute
Our wonderful times, I'm afraid,
If there is one word of truth in it,
Ask how much the writer was paid

W.H. Auden, autograph manuscript of his 'Ode to the George Washington Hotel' comprising 60 lines with 2 revisions signed and inscribed to the Manager and all staff, 5 pages, octavo and small quarto. £550

Mary Queen of Scots, remarkable autograph letter written at the age of 11 to her mother Mary of Guise announcing her intention to make her first communion, one page, folio, Meudon Easter 1554. £5,200

I am yours most truly.
David Livingstone
J. B. Horsfall Esq

David Livingstone, autograph letters arranging to procure beads for next visit to Africa, 4 pages, 8vo, to J. B. Horsfall MP, Kensington Palace Gardens, January 1858. £440

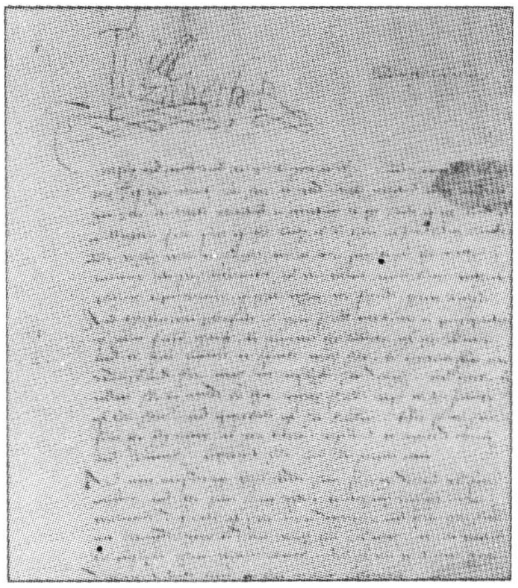

Elizabeth I, important letter sogned Elizabeth R at head, to Sir Nicholas Throckmorton, her ambassador to Scotland, containing a major statement about Elizabeth's policy towards the fate of Mary Queen of Scots, July 1567. £16,500

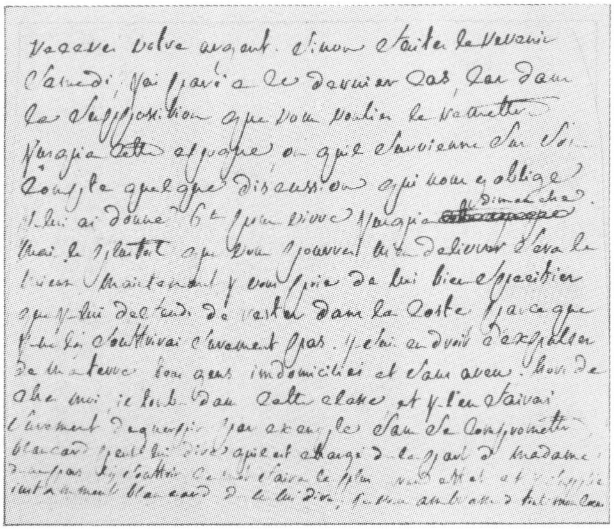

Donathien Sade, autograph letter, unsigned, to his lawyer Gaufridy, relating to the scandal caused by Sade's keeping a number of young girls at his chateaux for his pleasures, 4 pages, quarto, Provence, June 1775. £550

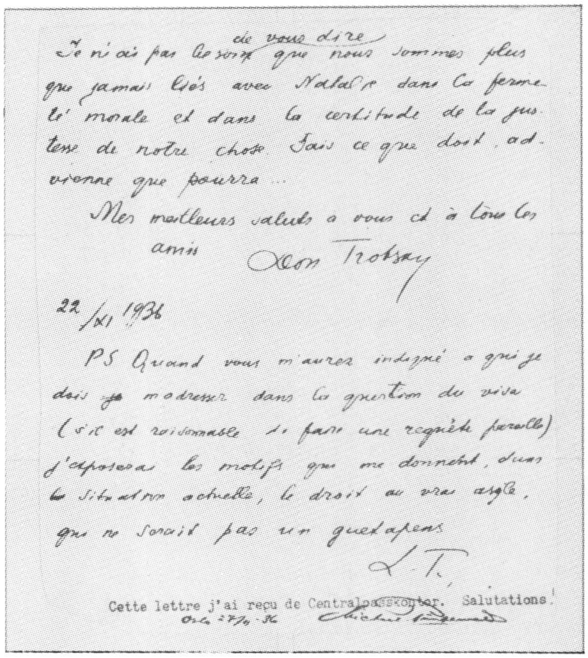

Je n'ai pas besoin de vous dire que nous sommes plus que jamais liés avec Natalia dans la fermeté morale et dans la certitude de la justesse de notre chose. Fais ce que doit, advienne que pourra...

Mes meilleurs saluts à vous et à tous les amis

Leon Trotsky

22/XI 1936

PS Quand vous m'aurez indiqué à qui je dois m'adresser dans la question du visa (s'il est raisonnable de faire une requête pareille) j'exposerai les motifs qui me donnent, dans la situation actuelle, le droit au vrai asyle, qui ne serait pas un guet-apens

L.T.

Cette lettre j'ai reçu de Centralpasskontor. Salutations!

Leon Trotsky, highly important autograph letter signed, written a month before his deportation to Mexico, 4 pages, quarto, 22 November 1936. £1,650

Henry VIII: Document signed, 1 page folio (oblong) on vellum, 1 May 1545. £5,000

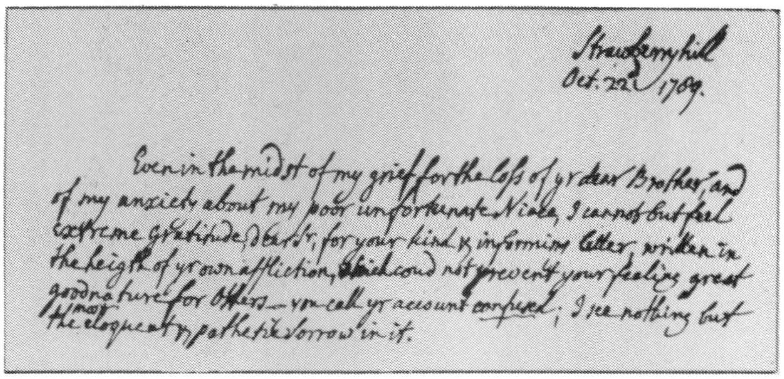

Strawberry hill
Oct. 22 1789.

Even in the midst of my grief for the loss of yr dear Brother, and of my anxiety about my poor unfortunate Niece, I cannot but feel extreme gratitude, dear Sr, for your kind & informing letter, written in the height of yr own affliction, which could not prevent your feeling great goodnature for Others — you call yr account confused; I see nothing but the eloquent & pathetic sorrow in it.

H. Walpole, fine autographed letter signed, to Captain Waldegrave, 2 pages, quarto, Strawberry Hill, 22 October 1789. £480

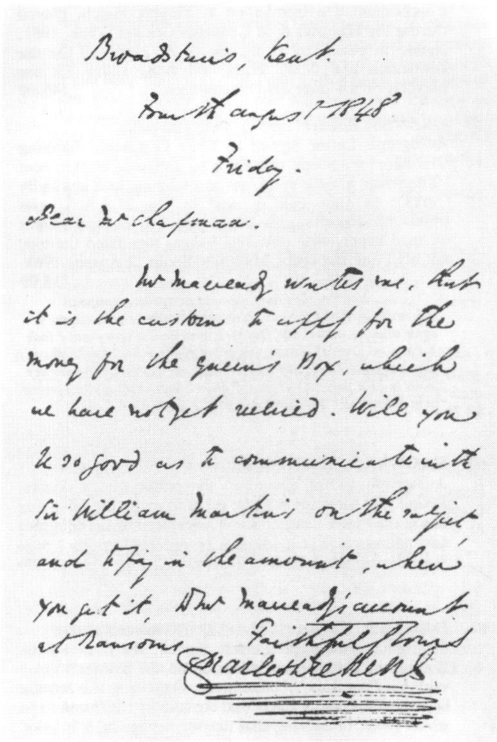

Broadstairs, Kent.
Fourth August 1848
Friday.

Dear Mr Chapman.

Mr Macready writes me, that it is the custom to apply for the money for the Queen's Box, which we have not yet received. Will you be so good as to communicate with Sir William Martins on the subject and to pay in the amount, when you get it, to Mr Macready's account at Ransoms. Faithfully Yours

Charles Dickens

Charles Dickens: Autograph letter, signed to his publisher (Edward) Chapman, 1 page 8vo, Broadstairs, 4 August, 1848. £250

AUTOMATONS

The genius of the 18th and 19th century craftsmen is perhaps best exhibited in his ability to construct the most ingenious and delicate of automatons. Developed by the Swiss Jacquet-Droz family, and later by the French, mechanical toys grew in complexity until the mid-Victorian era, by which time most occupations, from shoe cleaning to piano playing, had been interpreted with mechanical ingenuity to make delightful adult playthings.

Most depend solely on the driving power of a spring, but many inventors propelled their machines by compressed air, water, sand, mercury and steam. The best examples, worth hundreds or even thousands, are by Vaucanson, Robertson and Rechsteiner, particularly writing and drawing automatons, and talking dolls developed by Von Kempelen.

Mass production of mechanical toys reared its head about 1870 with the rising German tin plate industry and, craftsmanship inevitably suffering, they became simply playthings for children.

A thriving trade developed in importing these toys from Germany to England mainly as a result of their popularity with adults buying for young people for it is a matter of record that they held only a limited appeal for children their subject matter being considered somewhat sophisticated and their independence of movement thought to be 'off putting'.

Adults, however, continued to buy most enthusiastically and to preserve these fascinating pieces and it is thanks to them that we have so many good examples to wonder at and enjoy today.

A 19th century bisque-headed Magicienne automaton. (Phillips) £5,500

A German 19th century automaton of an organ grinder with miniature dancers, on a garden stage. (Phillips) £2,500

An Armand Marseille musical/dancing bisque headed puppet doll, impressed 70·20,5. (Lawrence Fine Art) £525

A picture automaton, the timepiece in the church facade activates the clockwork mechanism, probably French, 35in. long. £770

A mid 19th century German portable barrel organ automaton, 52cm. wide. (Phillips) £6,000

A musical automaton of a bisque headed doll beside a dressing table, marked Simon & Halbig S & H 6, the doll 15in. high. (Christie's) £2,000

AUTOMOBILIA

It all started in Britain around the 1890's. In those days cars were bought by the wealthy and driven by chauffeurs. Then 'sporty types' adopted the new hobby of motoring and, becoming owner-drivers, created a demand and a market for new and improved 'extras'.

Of the wide range of accessories including, radiator caps, oil cans, hub caps, steering wheels, mascots, speedometers, fascia panels and other related gadgets, the massive head-lamps once fixed to fast cars such as Lagondas and Alvis are most enthusiastically collected.

Evidence of the increasing nostalgia for the early days before road tax, insurance or speed limits, is clearly demonstrated by the hordes of visitors and traders attending autojumbles, specialised sales and special events such as those held at Beaulieu.

Collectibles range from postcards, petrol coupons and tax discs selling for around one pound to the rare and coveted sales brochures of Bugatti and Ferrari. These exotic productions sell for a considerably higher price as will collectibles associated with M.G., Bentley and Rolls-Royce. Motor racing in general and Brooklands Track in particular are also high interest areas.

Books on most aspects of motoring are collected and range from under five pounds to over one hundred pounds for Laurence Pomeroy's magnum opus on Grand Prix cars. Magazines too are in demand with 'Autocar', 'Motor Sport' and 'Speed' the most popular examples.

Car head lamp with 4in. diam. reflector, 10in. high, circa 1910. £50

Souvenir of the Brooklands Automobile Racing Club, July 6th 1907. (Onslows) £100

Early 20th century Bleriot brass head lamp, 12in. high. £44

One of two photographs of Leyland-Thomas No. 1 Babs, signed by Parry Thomas. (Onslows) £120

Six Brooklands Official Race Cards and Programmes for 1936. (Onslows) £46

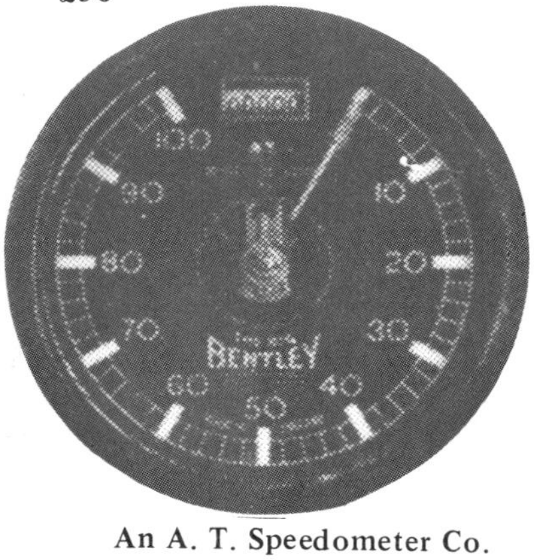

An A. T. Speedometer Co. Ltd. Bentley 6½ or 8 litre speedometer, and a rev counter. (Onslows) £200

De Dion Bouton poster, circa 1903. £100

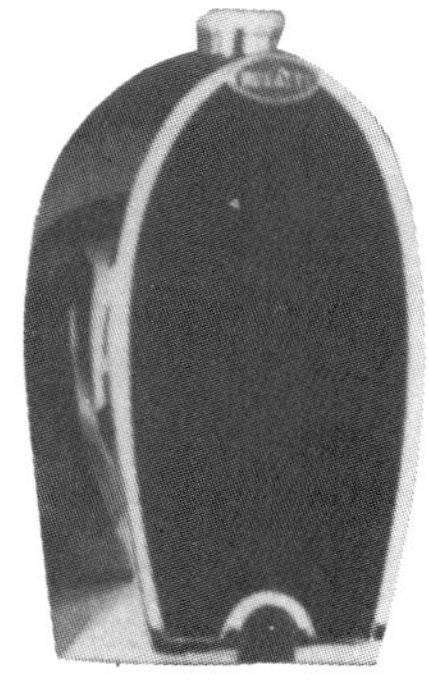

A chromium plated decanter in the form of a Bugatti radiator, by Classic Stable Ltd., 6¾in. high. (Onslows) £260

Mahogany showcase made from a brass Rolls Royce Silver Ghost radiator shell with Spirit of Ecstasy mascot, 35in. high. £200

Smith's tachometer calibrated from 1000 to 2500 rpm, 6½in. diam., plaque inscribed and dated 1933. £200

A chromium plated and gilt desk timepiece modelled as an Edwardian tourer, 8½in. high. (Christie's) £450

Motor Sport, Vol. 5 no. 1, October-November 1928. (Onslows) £140

Peugeot poster 'Le Petit Pouget Montait Une Peugeot'. £65

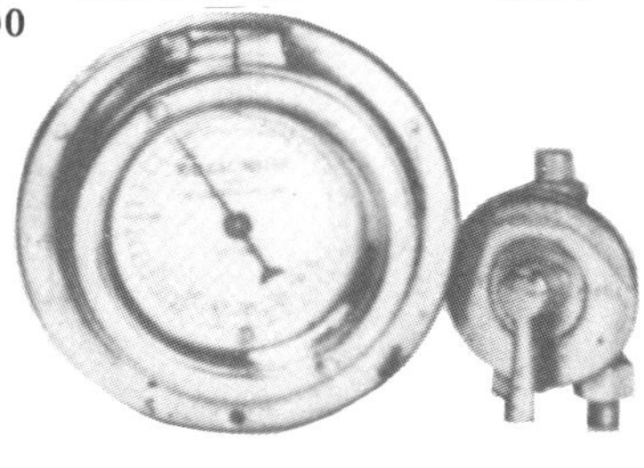

A nickel plated Milegal 'Meter', 4¼in. diam. (Onslows) £50

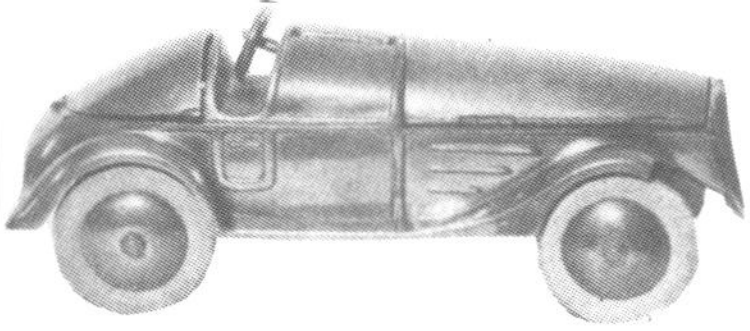

A spelter smoker's compendium modelled as a sports roadster, 9in. long. (Christie's) £300

Six Brooklands Official Race Cards and Programmes for 1937. (Onslows) £40

Harrods Ltd. Automobiles, Petrol Steam Electric Cars, Motorcycles Accessories of All Descriptions, catalogue with prices and text, circa 1903. (Onslows) £130

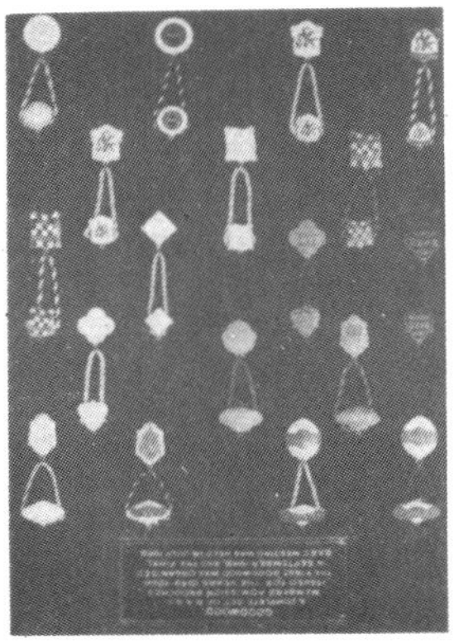

Part of a collection of 62 members' badges and guest brooches, in mahogany display case. (Onslows) £3,200

Five Brooklands Official Race Cards and Programmes for 1938 and 1939. (Onslows) £32

Radiator from a pre war M.G.T.-Type. £70

The Austin Magazine, original artwork for the Christmas Number, December 1937, signed, watercolour, 21½ x 17in. (Christie's) £110

BADEN-POWELL ITEMS

Robert Stephenson Smyth Baden-Powell was the greatest British hero of the early years of the 20th century, long before he started his Scouting movement for which he is best remembered today.

Victorian crowds followed him everywhere because he was famous as the saviour of Mafeking which he had successfully defended in a long siege against the Boers in 1900. To mark his achievement all sorts of souvenirs bearing his image were produced ranging from clay pipes to plates, statuettes, biscuit tins, cigarette cards, badges, Vesta cases and teapots.

These are all collected today as are Baden-Powell's own writings and drawings, for he was an accomplished artist, and artefacts from the early years of the Boy Scout movement which he founded in 1908.

Wedgwood style blue and white coffee pot by Dudson, England, 6in. high. £25

Crystal glass two-handled vase, engraved with a portrait of Baden Powell, on four short feet, 11in. high, slight crack. £12

An unusual teapot featuring Baden Powell in Boer War uniform together with scouts in a camping scene. £35

Tall Staffordshire milk jug with gilt decoration and portrait of Baden Powell. £15 – £20

Staffordshire equestrian figure of Baden Powell, 14in. high. £75 – £100

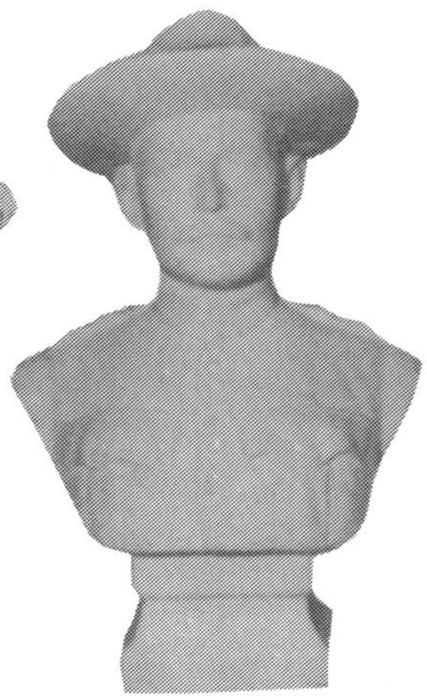

A plaster bust of Baden Powell, 10in. high. £35

Staffordshire oval wall plate with wavy edge featuring Lieut.-Col. R. S. S. Baden Powell. £20 – £25

Staffordshire figure of Baden Powell with cannon, 22in. high. £150

BADGES

There are many interesting aspects to a collection of badges. Through a study of their regimental motifs, numerals, materials and design, one may follow the changes and reforms of the system as well as the history of particular regiments.

A start can often be made on a domestic level. Most families have, at one time or another had a serving soldier in the family and for sentimental reasons soldiers tend to keep their badges.

A cap badge may be identified as such by the fastening. Usually this consists of a prong, a slide or two metal loops designed to be fastened by a split pin. A cap badge is normally larger than those designed to be worn on a uniform collar.

It is a good idea to consult an old Army List for information on who wore what and when. Specialist sales embracing all aspects of military history and interest are held at Wallis & Wallis of Lewes, Sussex.

A Panzer troop's standard bearer's sleeve badge embroidered in silver bullion and black and pink thread. (Wallis & Wallis) £85

An officer's silver Glengarry badge of The Argyll & Sutherland Highlanders, HM Edinburgh 1916, approx. 2½ Troy oz. (Wallis & Wallis) £145

A Georgian officer's silver rectangular shoulder belt plate of The 13th (1st Somersetshire) Regt., worn 1801-16. (Wallis & Wallis) £300

A Victorian officer's gilt and silvered Glengarry badge of The King's Own Light Infantry, (S. Yorks. Regt.). (Wallis & Wallis) £180

An officer's silvered helmet plate of The 1st Northumberland Artillery Vols. (Wallis & Wallis) £90

A Georgian other rank's brass bearskin plate, die-stamped 1801-16 Royal Arms and motto. (Wallis & Wallis) £400

A Victorian hollow-cast gold plaid brooch of the Clan Mackinnon, 1.2oz. Troy. (Wallis & Wallis) £200

A Victorian officer's gilt, silvered and enamel helmet plate of The Border Regt, type 2, worn 1891-1901. (Wallis & Wallis) £160

An N.C.O.'s copper gilt shoulder belt plate of The 96th (or Queen's Own) Regt., worn 1816-18. (Wallis & Wallis) £130

A Victorian officer's gilt, silvered and enamel helmet plate of The Border Regt., first pattern, worn 1881-91. (Wallis & Wallis) £310

An officer's pre 1881 gilt and silvered Glengarry badge of The 72nd (Duke of Albany's Own) Highlanders. (Wallis & Wallis) £355

An other rank's white metal Glengarry badge of The 6th Vol. Bn. (Fifeshire) Black Watch. (Wallis & Wallis) £22

A brass cap badge of The 1st V.A. Bn. Home Guard. (Wallis & Wallis) £40

A Nazi Govt. Admin. official's field grey sleeve badge to the rank of Regierungsamtmann. (Wallis & Wallis) £125

A Turkish Empire official's French silver gilt pin-back shield badge. (Wallis & Wallis) £90

A trooper's helmet plate of The 5th Dragoon Guards. (Wallis & Wallis) £47

A U.S.A. gilt and enamelled sterling silver badge of The Joint Chiefs of Staff, by H. S. Meyer Inc., New York. (Wallis & Wallis) £35

An officer's silver Maltese Cross pouch belt badge of The King's Royal Rifle Corps, HM Birmingham 1917. (Wallis & Wallis) £60

An officer's shoulder belt plate of The 21st Foot, Royal North British Fusiliers. (Wallis & Wallis) £160

A Victorian officer's gilt and silvered helmet plate of The York & Lancaster Regt. (Wallis & Wallis) £90

BAIRNSFATHERWARE

Bruce Bairnsfather was the war artist who created the famous cartoon character 'Old Bill'. The longsuffering, archetypal 'Tommy' of World War I. During and after the war, a vast range of 'Bairnsfatherware' was produced.

These wares fall into seven main categories:
Original paintings, drawings, sketches and letters by Bairnsfather.
Pottery items bearing 'Fragments from France' cartoons and models of Old Bill's head.
Bystander Products. Original 'Fragments from France' cartoons, postcards, (there are 56 available in a complete set) jig-saws and prints.
Metal Ware. Car Mascots of Old Bill, ash trays, etc.
Theatre and Cinema ephemera including posters, advertising postcards, magazines and photographs of the various plays and films made about Old Bill or by Bairnsfather.
Books and Magazines about or by Bairnsfather.
Miscellaneous: Dolls, hankies, badges, glass slides.

The market is still in its infancy and these wares are currently largely overlooked and inexpensive. A boost to the market is assured, however, by publication of the first priced and illustrated catalogue to Bairnsfatherware 'In Search of the Better 'Ole' (Milestone Publications, 62 Murray Road, Horndean, Hampshire PO8 9JL).

Once a collectors' market is established the demand for 'Old Bill' products is self generating the more the interest grows, which indicates good prospects for a healthy investment.

Grimwade bowl with transfers of 'Old Bill'. £30

Grimwade bowl 'What time do they feed the sealions Alf?' £30

Grimwade shaving mug with transfers of 'Old Bill' and Arms of Margate. £40

Metal car mascot of 'Old Bill'. £100

'Old Bill' pottery head, white. £35

'Old Bill', doll in fair condition. £40

Carlton 'Old Bill' with coloured balaclava 'Yours to a cinder Old Bill'. £75

Grimwade pottery plate 'Well if you knows of a better 'ole go to it'. £35

BANK NOTES

As more and more people develop an awareness of the historical and artistic value of paper money the popularity of this subject as a collecting field continues to rise.

Over the years banknotes have been made from a variety of materials including the fabric of a khaki shirt sleeve (Boer War), silk, leather and even seal skin but today, many collectors focus their attention on the beauty of the engraved note.

It is not often realised that top security printing firms reckon on a twenty five year training period for the handful of portrait engravers who make it to the top of their profession. It can take six months to engrave a steel plate yet the collector can buy a piece of 'miniature art' for as little as a pound.

The earliest notes available, at a reasonable price, are those of the Ming Dynasty dated 1368 and worth about £360 but inflation has left the new collector with a wide variety of inexpensive examples to choose from. German hyper-inflation has left notes for collectors at just 50 pence each and French Revolution issues can still be picked up for as little as £3.

An interesting collection can be built around the many emergency issues hand signed by such notable figures as General Gordon, Garibaldi, Louis Kossuth and notes such as those designed by Baden-Powell (Siege of Mafeking) and Benjamin Franklin (War of Independence).

Many modern banknotes of the world have only a short life as leaders, such as Idi Amin or Bokassa, come and go and these will provide a fascinating historical reference.

Bank of Scotland proof £100 note in black and white, by Bradbury & Evans. (Christie's) £150

Government of India, One Thousand Rupees, 2nd June 1913, Bombay, scarce. (Christie's) £180

Paisley Banking Co. One Guinea dated 2nd May 1826. (Christie's) £210

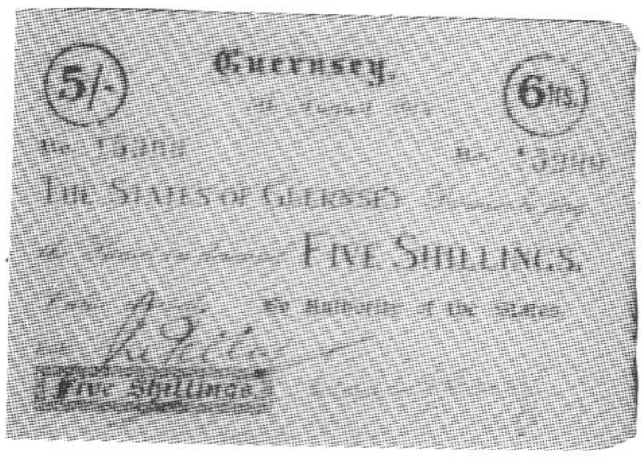

The States of Guernsey Five Shillings or Six Francs, 5th August 1914, rare. (Christie's) £850

John McAdam & Company 5/- note issued in 1763, bearing portrait of George III, damaged, extremely rare. (Christie's) £720

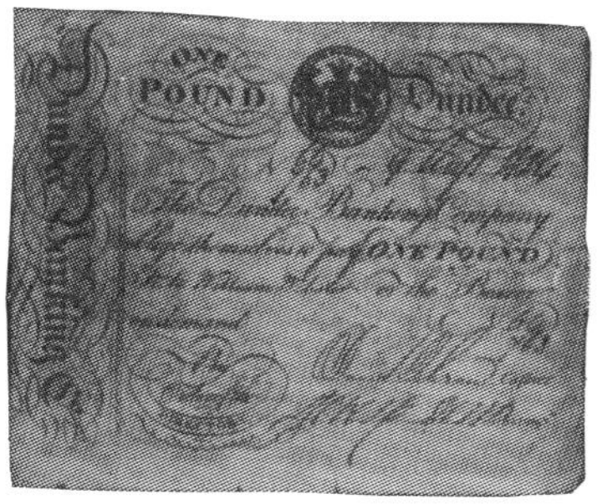

Dundee Banking Company £1 of 1824, torn on right side. (Christie's) £320

Bank of England 5/-, signed K. O. Peppiatt 1941, very rare. (Christie's) £620

Bank of England 2/6, signed K. O. Peppiatt 1941, very rare. (Christie's) £500

New Zealand: 1916 Bank of Australasia £1 issued at Wellington. (Phillips) £200

Greenock Bank Company £1 issued 15th May 1830. (Christie's) £140

Cyprus: 1955-57 Queen Elizabeth II set of 250 mils–£5. (Phillips) £170

Thistle Bank £1 1770, on unwatermarked paper. (Christie's) £820

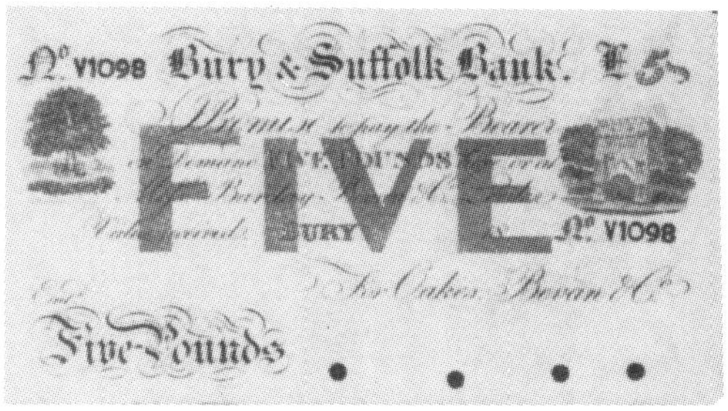

Bury & Suffolk Bank: (Oakes, Bevan & Co.), £5 un-issued. (Phillips) £45

Bank of Scotland proofs of the One Guinea of 1825. (Christie's) £200

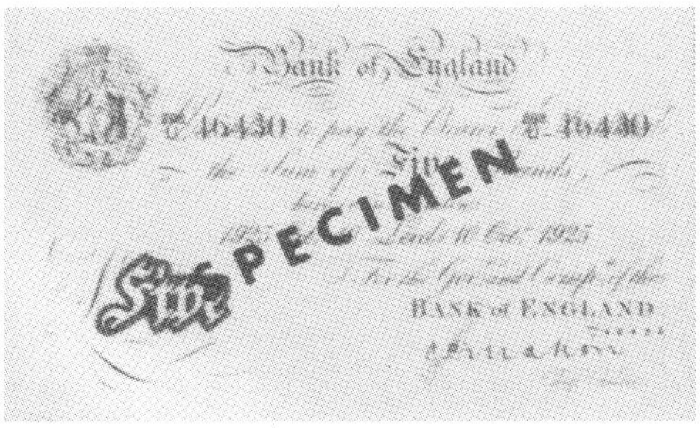

C. P. Mahon: Bank of England £5, 10 October 1925 issued at Leeds. (Phillips) £92

Montrose Bank One Guinea dated 16th December 1814, very rare. (Christie's) £750

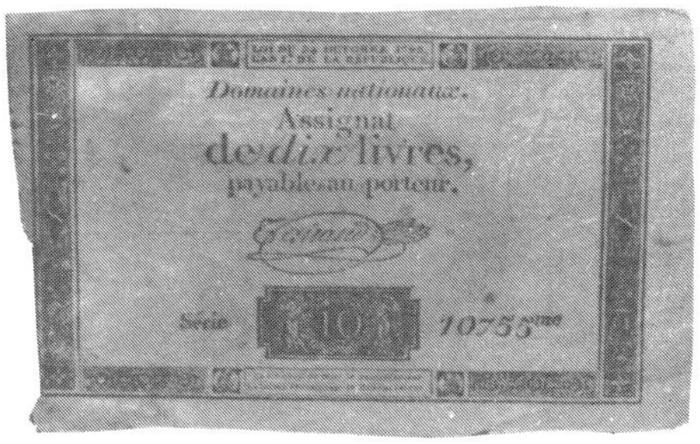

French 10 Livres 1792, a very rare note. £850

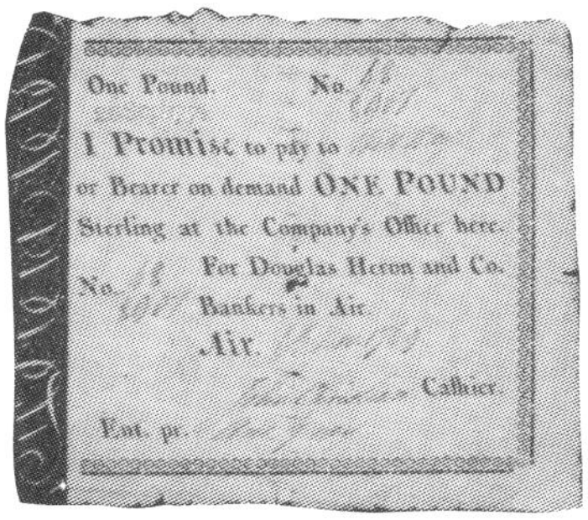

Douglas Heron & Company £1 dated 6th November 1769. (Christie's) £650

Russia: 1819 10 roubles State Assignat. (Phillips) £50

Royal Bank of Scotland £1 dated 9th Feb. 1750, on watermarked paper, rare. (Christie's) £1,350

BAROMETERS

Toricelli, as every schoolboy knows, invented a method of producing the vacuum. In 1660, Robert Boyle adapted Torricelli's technique to the production of a weather glass. Naturally enough, it was not long before the device attracted the attentions of many a notable horologist and instrument maker. Among these was Daniel Quare, Thomas Tompion, John Patrick, Henry Jones and Charles Orme, any of whose works attracts enormous sums of money. As can be seen, however, not all barometers are equally expensive.

By midway through the 18th century, rococo scrolls were often incorporated in the design of barometer cases which, by the final quarter of the century, had evolved into the ever-popular wheel (or banjo) shape. Most have mahogany, or occasionally satinwood, frames with delicate boxwood stringing on the edges and silvered dials enclosed by convex glass. Good examples incorporate in their designs such extras as thermometers, hygrometers, spirit-levels and even clocks – each device adds a bit to the value.

A George I walnut signal barometer, the brass plate inscribed Made by John Patrick in the Old Bailey London, 36¼ x 29½in. (Christie's) £7,020

A brass and nickel plated yacht timepiece modelled as a turret with simulated cannons, 4½in. high, and a matching barometer. (Christie's) £70

Brass ship's barometer, circa 1860. (British Antique Exporters) £53

A Victorian mahogany banjo barometer. (Ball & Percival) £190

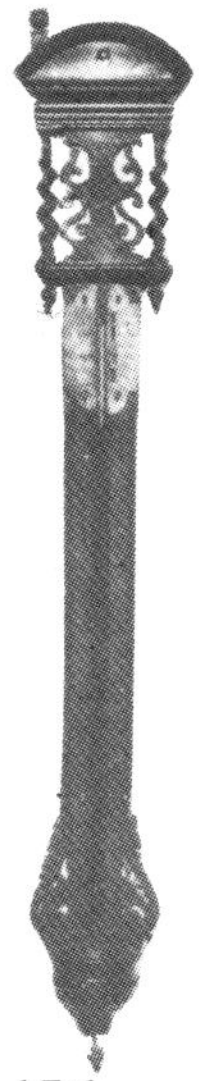

A late 17th century walnut stick barometer, the engraved brass plates for Summer and Winter, 48in. high. (Christie's) £1,700

A 19th century wheel barometer, the 12in. dial inscribed Zuccani, London, 57in. high. (Parsons, Welch & Cowell) £440

A late 19th century oak American Forecast or Royal Polytechnic bulb Cistern barometer, 107cm high. (Phillips) £360

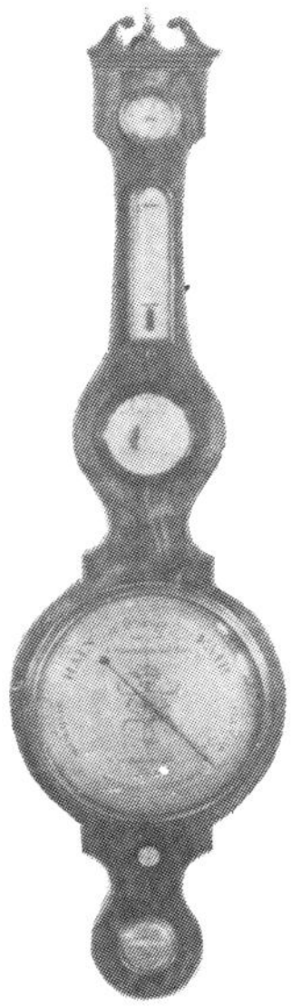

A George III mahogany stick barometer, by J. Somalvico & Son, London, 45in. high. (Christie's) £572

BEER BOTTLE LABELS

Although labels were in use for a number of years beforehand Bass have the unique distinction of having the first three Trade Marks registered after the Trade Marks Registration Act came into operation on January 1st 1876. They were for Bass Pale Ale, Burton Ale and Extra Stout. The Bass triangle itself was not registered until January 16th by which time almost a thousand trade marks had been registered among them a number by Tennents and Ind Coope.

Beer bottle labels were first introduced in the 1850's in the traditional oval shape and have been collected since their inception, the hobby latterly being extended to embrace the bottles themselves either full or empty.

The oval label persisted until the introduction of high speed bottling machines in the late fifties when a variety of shapes came into being.

Some collectors specialise in particular breweries while others concentrate just on these labels relating to special events such as the Victory celebrations after both World Wars or the Royal occasions such as Jubilees, Coronations and Weddings, all of which produced a multitude of interesting and colourful examples. Others collect just new issues, of which there are many, or strive to obtain just one label from as many breweries as possible.

Societies exist worldwide for the advancement of the hobby which is particularly popular in Eastern Europe where some collectors are known to have in excess of 300,000 different labels in their possession. Of the British collectors many have over 25,000 U.K. labels, which although undoubtedly a large number only represents a small fraction of the labels issued over the years.

Three labels from Bernard Ltd., Edinburgh, circa 1899, Brewing ceased circa 1902. £50–£60

Three labels from W. & T. Bagge, King Street Brewery, Kings Lynn, Norfolk, in use to 1929. In excess of £60

Three, pre 1940, labels from Gillespie Sons & Co., Dumbarton, Scotland, (Crown Brewery), which ceased trading in 1953. Up to £10 each label

Anglo-Bavarian Brewery Co. Ltd., Shepton Mallet, labels in use before 1900, but brewery continued to 1939. £65–£70

Four labels used until circa 1899 from Garton & Sons, Bristol, when brewing ceased. £80–£100

Manchester Brewery, Manchester, labels in use around 1909. Ceased brewing 1912. £75

BEER CANS

Beer cans were first produced in 1935. The earlier examples featuring a cone shaped top were superseded in the late 1950's by a flat topped can which required the use of an opener. By the 1960's the ring pull had taken over. It is interesting to note that collectors prefer ringpull cans to be intact and so empty the contents from the bottom of the can. The size of cans in the U.K. is 15½ fl.oz. (440ml.), 9.2/3 fl.oz. (275ml.) and party cans in 4, 7 and, until recently, 5 pint cans. 11.2/3 fl. oz. cans are made for the export market, this being about the most popular size worldwide.

Over 25,000 different cans have been made and many collectors specialise in a particular country, size, brewery or theme. Rarity and design determine the desirability of a can – cone top or flat top cans generally being the hardest to find. Condition is important – badly rusted or dented can is of little interest although restoration can be very rewarding.

Marks & Spencers Bitter, 1976, 9 2/3fl.oz. £2

Harp Lager, 1967, 9.2/3fl.oz. £6

Worthington India Pale Ale, 1969, 9.2/3fl.oz. £4

Hull Brewery Anchor Export Beer, 1969, 9.2/3fl.oz. £12

Felinfoel Prince's Ale, 1969, 9.2/3fl. oz. £20

Aitken's Export, 1958. £20

Tennent's Lager, English Series – Young Lady in Trafalgar Square, 1962. £20

Tennent's Lager, Lager Lovelies – Linda, 1969, 15½fl.oz. £15

Guinness, 15½fl.oz., 1975. £2.50

Tennent's Lager, Housewives' Choice – Thelma (Herring Fritters) 1964. £20

Farrimond's F.B., cone top, 1937, 12fl.oz. £5

Tennent's Lager, temporary can 1975, 11.2/3fl.oz. £20

Hall & Woodhouse Gold Medal Brock Lager, 1972, 11. 2/dfl.oz. £6

Barclay's Export Pilsner Lager, cone top 1955, 12fl.oz. £20

Tennent's Lager – Penny – at the end of the day, 1976, 11.2/3fl.oz. 75p

BEER MATS

From the Latin teges, meaning 'small rug', collectors of beer mats or drip mats, have taken the term Tegestology to describe the subject – a collector being known as a Tegestologist.

The first wood pulp drip mat was patented in 1892 by Robert Sputh in Dresden, Germany but, although used in the rest of Europe from that time, it was not until 1920 that they came into common use in the United Kingdom. It was from these somewhat primitive examples that the beautifully coloured and highly attractive beer mats of today have developed.

With over 100,000 beer mats, Leo Pisker of Austria is thought to hold the largest collection in the world and the largest collection of United Kingdom brewery mats, 28,000, belongs to Tim Stannard of Birmingham.

Vale of Neath Ales. 70p

Cornhill London Dry Gin. 50p

Safir De Gheest. £2

Tom Thumb cigars. £1

Royal Crown, Real American Cola. 80p

Britvic fruit juices. £1.25

Make it a Buckley's. £1.50

Merry Xmas, Happy New Year, Guinness. 30p

Ansells King-Pin mild 'the better keg beer'. £2

Hancocks Barley-brite, A Great Keg Bitter. £1.50

Lamot, its most desirable. 20p

Ansells Ind Coope, Wales 1969. £2

Captain Morgan Jamaica Rum. £4

'Magnet for me', John Smiths, Tadcaster. 30p

Stone's Original Green Ginger Wine. £1.50

Cherapear for a champagne glass. £4

Escort filter tipped 'Big in quality'. £2

Booth's London Dry Gin. £1

For a Hot Tip see over. £9

Chipmunk Crisps, Go on treat yourself. 60p

BELLEEK

One of the most distinctive form of porcelain is Belleek, produced in Co. Fermanagh since 1863.
It is made of a parian paste with an unusual iridescent pearly glaze, which is modelled into a variety of ornamental wares; particularly pieces featuring shells, marine forms and an open basketwork design.

The firm originally traded as David McBirney and Company, and some of the original designs are still in production to this day. Earlier works are often marked "Belleek Co. Fermanagh" with the printed trademark of an Irish wolfhound and harp, while later works, after 1891, usually bear the trademark together with "Co. Fermanagh, Ireland".

A Belleek model of a lighthouse, impressed Belleek and black printed marks, registration mark for 1873, 23cm. high. (Christie's) £700

A Belleek 'dolphin' candlestick, modelled as a putto seated on a dolphin, 19.5cm. high, no. D343. (Phillips) £700

A pair of Belleek candlestick figures of a boy and girl basket bearer, 22cm. high. (Phillips) £3,600

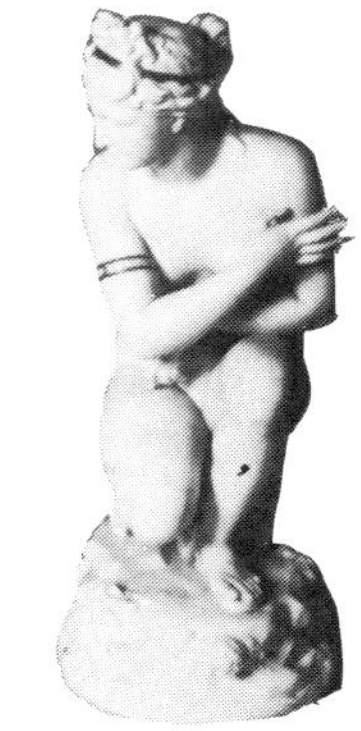

A Belleek First Period figure of 'The Crouching Venus', 18¼in. high. (Christie's) £800

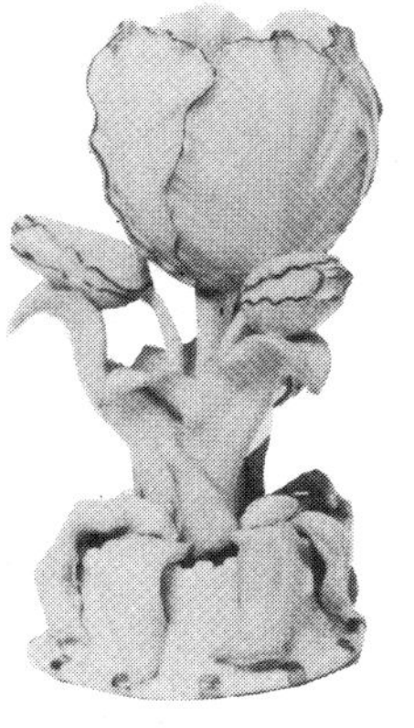

A Belleek 'tulip' vase, standing in a circular basket base encrusted with leaves, 31cm. high, no. D93. (Phillips) £2,200

A pair of Belleek figures of 'Meditation' and 'Affection', 35cm. high, nos. D1134 and D20. (Phillips) £1,800

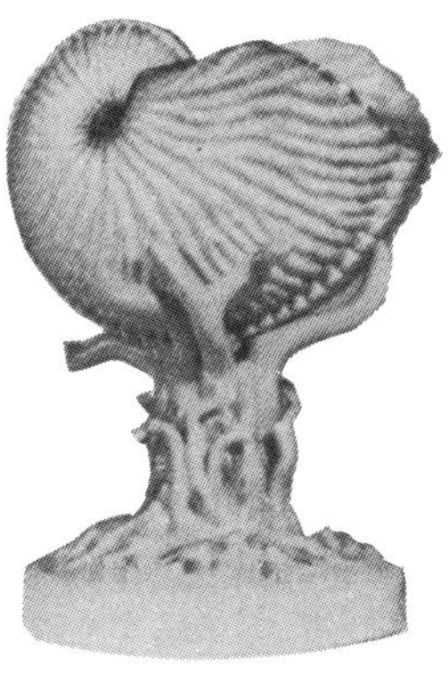

One of a pair of Belleek nautilus vases, naturally modelled and heightened in pink, 21cm. high. (Christie's) £1,000

A Belleek figure of a cooper standing before two barrels forming vases, 21cm. high. (Christie's) £2,000

BERLIN WOOLWORK

Berlin woolwork is a simplified system of embroidery originating in Berlin in the early 19th century and similar in concept to the modern painting by numbers kit.

The designs, usually of exotic birds and flowers or copies of famous paintings, were first printed on squared paper. The needlewoman, working in wools, then transferred these patterns to a canvas most commonly using the tent or cross stitch, and often embellished the work with beads or cut pile areas. The finished product was generally applied to footstools, chairs and firescreens but, if the proud creator was particularly pleased, the work was often mounted in a rosewood or maple frame and hung on the wall of the living room to be admired by all. A popular subject for pictures was the sailing ship and a great number of these were worked by sailors during the long sea voyages.

By the 1830's, designs were being printed directly on to the canvas itself, and as the popularity of woolwork grew in both Europe and America so did the number of patterns available; reaching 14,000 designed for the British market alone around 1840. Early examples are often more subdued in colour than the later which, after the discovery of the purple analine dye became a little bit gaudy.

Berlin woolwork saw its decline in the 1870's, supposedly after criticism that it debased the art of embroidery, but I think its relative frivolity just did not gel with the more austere furniture which was beginning to dominate fashionable taste in the last quarter of the century.

A Berlin woolwork cushion with a large central medallion and sprays of flowers, 18in. square. (Christie's) £972

A large Berlin woolwork bag with leather clasp and brass handle, circa 1860. (Christie's) £118

A Victorian needlework panel, possibly a stool cover, 38 x 27in., together with another. (Christie's) £594

A circular Berlin woolwork picture of an Indian Nabob, in black glass mount framed and glazed, circa 1840, 16in. high. (Christie's) £172

Mid 19th century Berlin woolwork picture of a Turk, 29 x 25½in. (Christie's) £378

An early Victorian mahogany octagonal seat, the hinged lid upholstered in floral needlework, 20¼in. wide. (Christie's) £2,808

BICYCLES

The invention of the bicycle brought a new way of life to many Victorian men and women by making it possible for even the lowest paid workers in that society to experience independence and mobility for the first time and at a very low cost.

Nowadays, pre-1900 bicycles are very much in vogue and fairly expensive. In the seventies, when demand was restricted to a small group of enthusiasts, their value showed only a moderate improvement and it is not so long ago that £500 seemed like a lot to pay for a bicycle. Now we see that some fine examples will fetch thousands.

One does not have to pay that type of money to start a collection however, for there are many examples from early in the 20th century which can be bought for more modest sums.

Ordinary bicycle, circa 1885, driving wheel diameter is 57in. (Christie's S. Kensington) £1,200

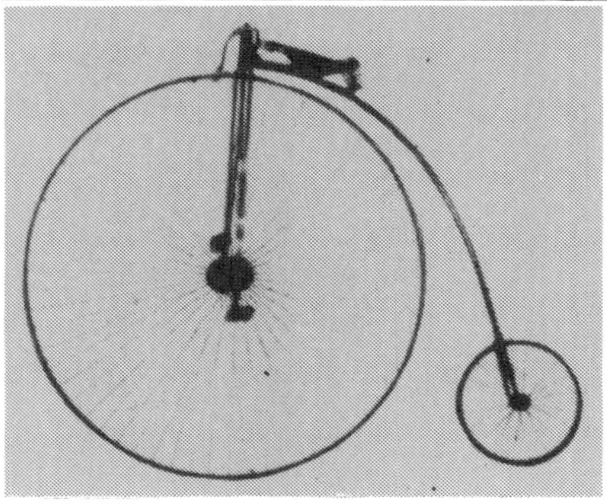

A bicycle with a 52in. driving wheel, the shaped handlebars terminating with wooden knobs. (Christie's) £550

J. Dumbleton 'Lion' ordinary bicycle, circa 1880, built for racing. (Christie's S. Kensington) £800

English B.S.A safety bicycle, circa 1885. £3,300

A 'Pedestrian Hobby Horse' bicycle. (Phillips) £2,000

A late 19th century child's bicycle with 16in. detachable driving wheel. (Christie's) £380

Beck boneshaker or Michaudine, circa 1867-69, built at the Lister Works, Holloway, London. (Christie's S. Kensington) £500

Tandem tricycle, frame no. 189, probably built in Coventry, circa 1888. (Christie's S. Kensington) £4,000

Waltham fixed-wheel bicycle, circa 1890, possibly American and assembled in Britain. (Christie's S. Kensington) £390

BISCUIT TINS

One of the chief delights of Christmas between 1868 and the end of the 1930's was to buy the most delicious biscuits in a decorative tin. The tins, originally designed to keep the product in fresh condition, soon became an important sales feature and manufacturers vied with each other to produce the most inventive novelties.

The idea of printing on tin was pioneered in Britain around 1860 by Benjamin George who patented his many new processes, but it was not until after 1889 that the secrets of simple production methods became available to printed tin manufacturers in general.

Huntley & Palmers who produced some of the earliest decorated tins seem to have been the most prolific manufacturers of these delightful boxes, in a range so vast it became necessary to publish a catalogue informing their customers of available designs.

Rare Edwardian Macfarlane Lang tinplate biscuit tin, with hinged roof, 19.5cm. long. £90

A Victorian biscuit box, in the form of a book, 21cm. long, circa 1870. (Phillips) £300

Jacob & Co., Coronation coach biscuit tin, 1937. £40

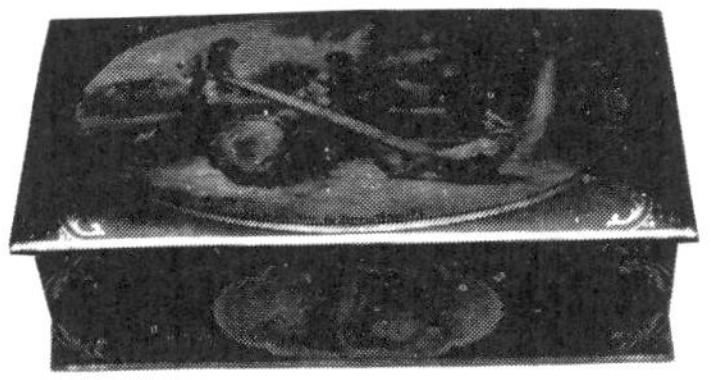

Gray Dunn & Co., Glasgow, tin with pictorial lid. £20

C.W.S. biscuit tin by Crumpsall and Cardiff. £5

Huntley & Palmers book biscuit tin, circa 1903. £50

Huntley & Palmers pedestal biscuit tin decorated with classical figures. £15

Jacob's gypsy caravan biscuit tin, circa 1905. £45

Huntley & Palmers laundry basket biscuit tin, circa 1904. £26

BONDS & SHARE CERTIFICATES

Officially known as Scripophily, this specialised area centres around the collecting of Share Certificates and Bonds issued by Companies and Governments since the 17th century.

Early certificates were printed on vellum (calf skin) which holds a particular appeal for some collectors but there are many other interesting features upon which to base a collection.

For excellence the work produced by the famous security printing firms such as Waterlow, Bradbury Wilkinson and the American Banknote Co., provide us with some beautiful pieces which are always in great demand for their visual appeal. Apart from the artistic appearance of the certificates however, one may decide to trace and record the history of one company in particular or even collect only those bonds and share certificates which have been signed by one of the many famous people connected with their issue. Obviously a collection of the signatures of important personages has a special attraction.

Of the many and diverse branches of industry represented in this field collectors favour those certificates issued by companies involved in mining, the railways and most other forms of transport but all of these factors mentioned-historical interest, artistic merit, significant signatures, will have a bearing on the desirability and market value of a document. It is worth noting that while shares issued in the United Kingdom are generally considered to be the property only of the person named on the document, American and Canadian shares are often made out 'To the bearer' and, if the company should still be in existence and can be traced, these could have a market value well above that of the actual document.

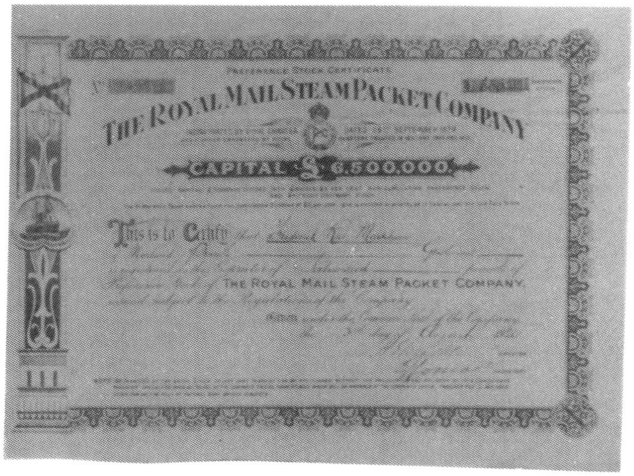

Royal Mail Steam Packet Co., certificate for preference stock, 1920. £5

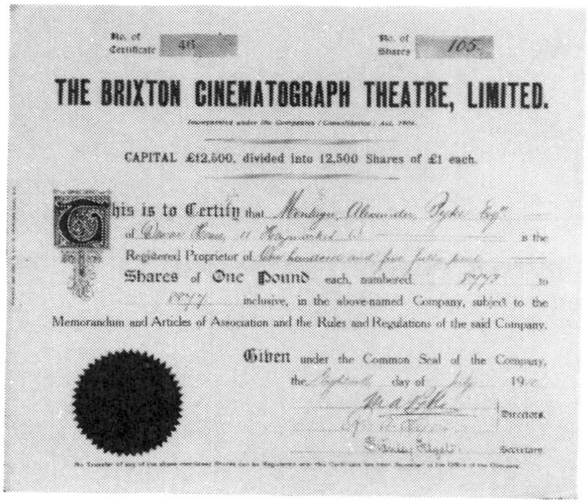

An early **Cinema** share dated 1910. £8

Moscow-Smolensk Railway Co. of Russia, Bond for 200 thalers, 1869. £15

Ramsgate & Margate Tramways Company, Mortgage Debenture for £20, 1888. £15

Central Van Lead Mining Co. Ltd., certificate dated 1877 in this Welsh Company. £20

£20 Bond of the City of Moscow, 1908. £3

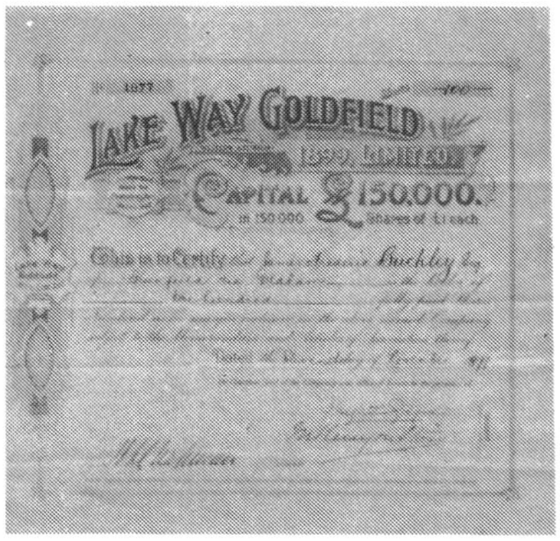

Western Australia, Lake Way Goldfield 1899 Ltd., share certificate, 1899. £10

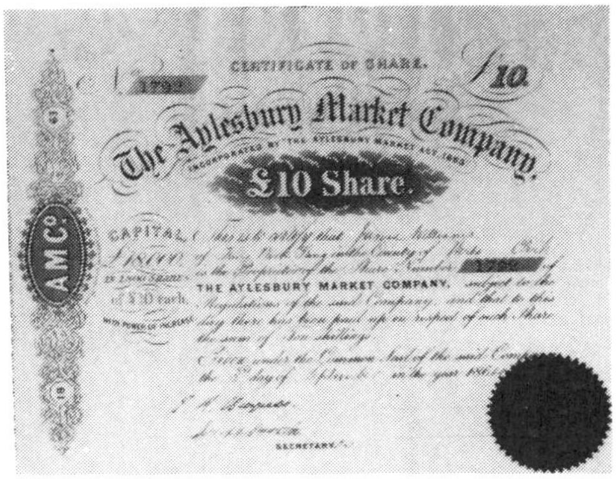

Aylesbury Market Co., £10 share dated 1864. £15

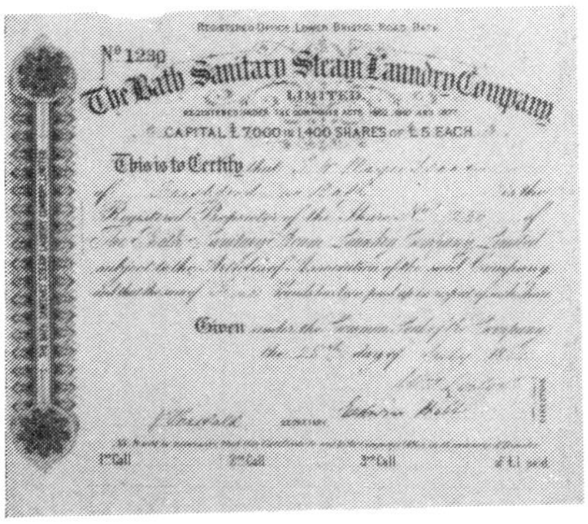

Bath Sanitary Steam Laundry Co. Ltd. share certificate dated 1884. £10

Chinese Government reorganisation loan, 1913, Bond for £20 issued by the Russo Asiatic Band. £8

Perfect Blind-Stitch Sewing Machine Co. Ltd., share certificate 1903. £6

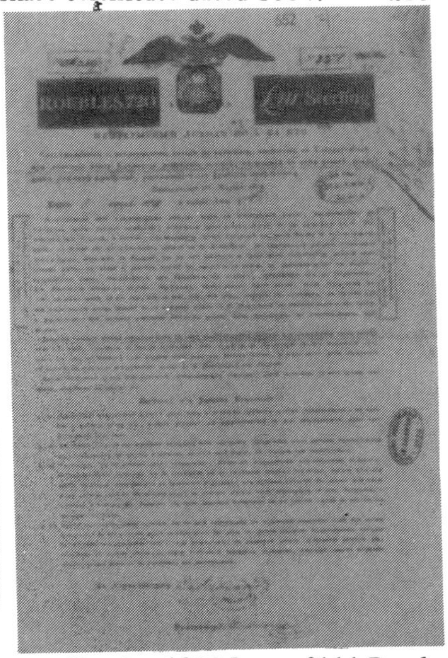

Russian 1822 Loan, £111 Bond handsigned by Nathan Meyer Rothschild. £75

BOOKS

Book Collecting is a growing market which every year attracts new devotees among people who have previously only looked on books as 'good reads' for whiling away long journeys. Now the collecting of books is becoming one of the new 'Commodity markets' and a safe resort for money against inflation. There is fierce bidding at specialised book auctions all over Britain and the days are sadly gone when a box of mixed books which might well contain a first edition could be picked up for pennies at a local junk shop.

For a book enthusiast to buy wisely it is essential to learn something about the subject and then to specialise for this is a huge world indeed.

Some categories are more popular than others – medicine has a dedicated but fairly small following as has war-like subjects and books about British regiments. Books dealing with travel, topography and wild life of every kind come near the top of the popularity poll especially if they contain fine plates and illustrations.

The snobbism that sometimes shows itself in more specialised books is refreshingly absent in the world of modern firsts. Most sought after are Penguin first editions in paperback – especially the first thirty and those brought out during the war when they were printed on thin paper and their fragility made it difficult for them to survive. Rarity is a quality which makes any book collectable.

Binding – Dante Alighieri: La Divini Commedia, some col., green mor. gilt with black overlay abstract design and small gold stars, g.e. by D. Etherington, 4to, Bergamo, 1934. (Phillips) £300

The History of Guy, Earl of Warwick, n.d. (Phillips) £160

Legge (Capt. W. V.): A History of the Birds of Ceylon, 34 hand-col. litho plates, 4to, 1880. (Phillips) £1,050

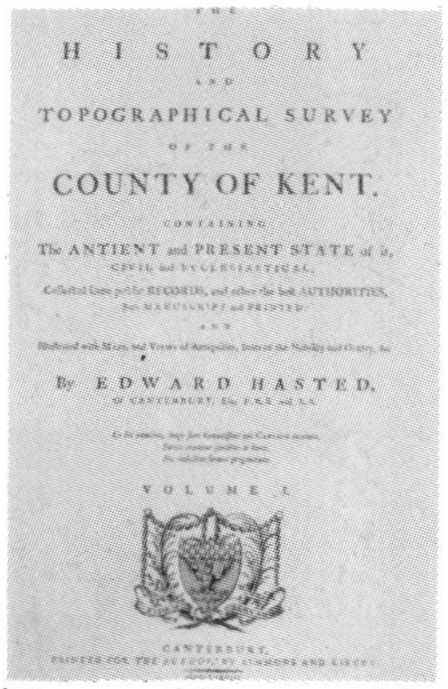

History and Topographical Survey of the County of Kent, by Edward Hasted, First Edition, 4 vols. (Parsons, Welch & Cowell) £1,000

The Iconography, by Sir Anthony van Dyck, seventeen plates, etchings with engravings, averaging 245 x 158mm. (Christie's) £3,024

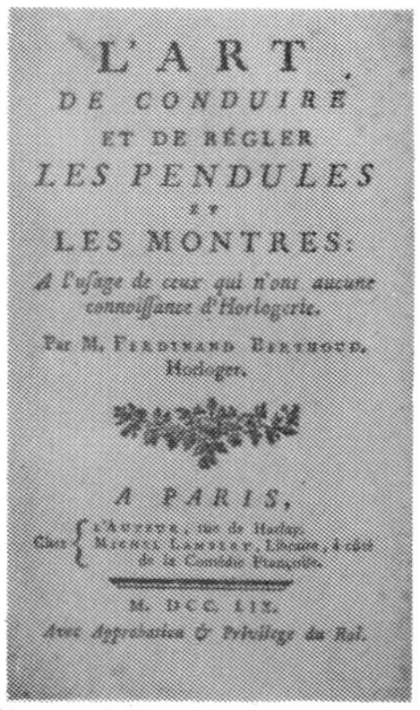

Ferdinand Berthoud, L'Art De Conduire Et De Regler Les Pendules Et Les Montres, First Edition, Paris 1759, 12mo, modern calf. (Christie's) £379

Golding (W.): Lord of the Flies, First Edn., 1954. (Phillips) £150

Edwards (Sydenham): The New Flora Britannica, 61 hand-col. plates, 4to, 1812. (Phillips) £1,050

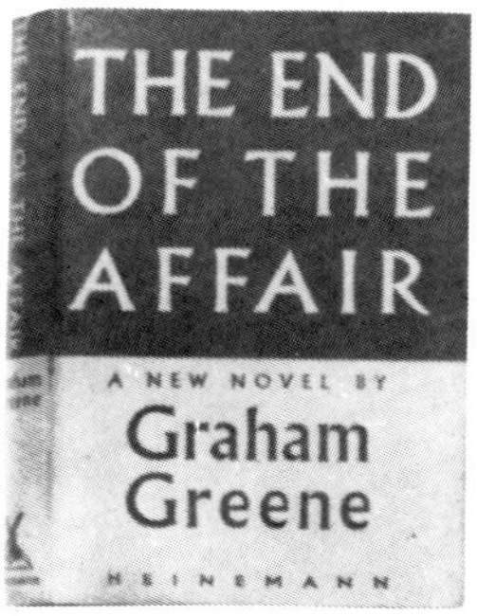

Greene (G.): The End of the Affair, First Edn., 1951. (Phillips) £35

History of The Apple Pie and other stories, 1807-8. (Phillips) £440

Buckskin gilt binding of Hours of the Virgin (Use of Chartres), printed text and miniatures on vellum, France, 1513. (Phillips) £6,800

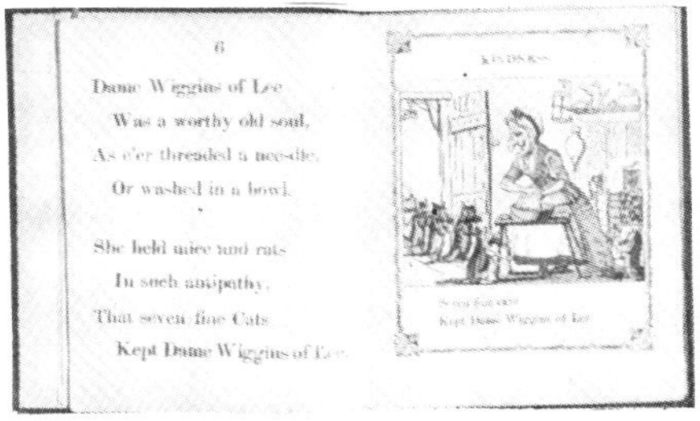

Dame Wiggins of Lee and Her Seven Wonderful Cats, circa 1850. (Phillips) £220

Fowles (J.): The Collector, First Edn., 1963. (Phillips) £90

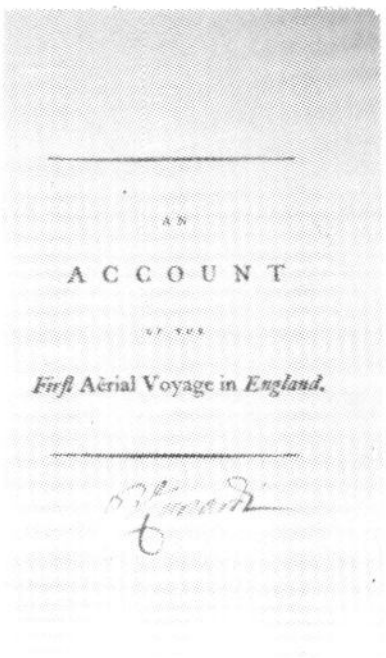

Lunardi (Vincent): An Account of the First Aerial Voyage in England, 2nd Edn., small 4to, 1784. (Phillips) £180

Jeu de la Giraffe, circa 1820. (Phillips) £280

Orwell (G.): Nineteen Eight-Four, First Edn., 1949. (Phillips) £500

Roscoe (William): Monandrian Plants of the Order Scitamineae, from Lord Derby's library with his bookplate, 112 hand-col. plates, 1828. (Phillips) £5,000

Amis (K.): Lucky Jim, First Edn., 1953, and 19 others. (Phillips) £480

Leybourn (William), Cursus Mathematics, Mathematical Sciences In Nine Books, London 1690. (Christie's) £1,138

Spark (M.): The Prime of Miss Jean Brodie, First Edn., 1961, and 18 others. (Phillips) £140

BOTTLE OPENERS

Small and useful objects like bottle openers were, and still are, considered to be the ideal material for advertising purposes.
Usually marked with the company name, a date and perhaps a few words announcing a new product they were generally inexpensive to manufacture and could be given to customers as a token of goodwill.
Some examples produced to commemorate a special event were sold as souvenirs.
Items of 'local' interest as well as novelty pieces will always attract a higher premium.

A Scandinavian Crown cap opener, circa 1860, 6in. long. £17

A Crown cork opener in iron and sheet metal, advertising 'Guinness'. £3

Key-shaped combined bottle opener and cork-screw. £5

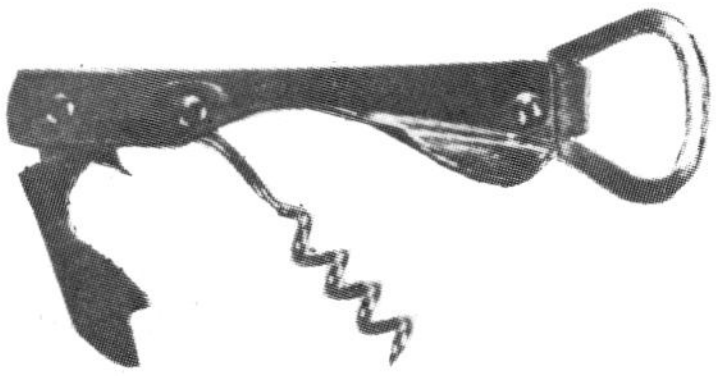

Skyline Bottle Boy, all chrome helical corkscrew with two Crown cork openers, 5in. long. £7

A novelty Crown cork bottle opener, the turned wooden bottle forms the handle, the opener is stamped 'An Tsin Tir Adheanta', 5¾in. long. £18

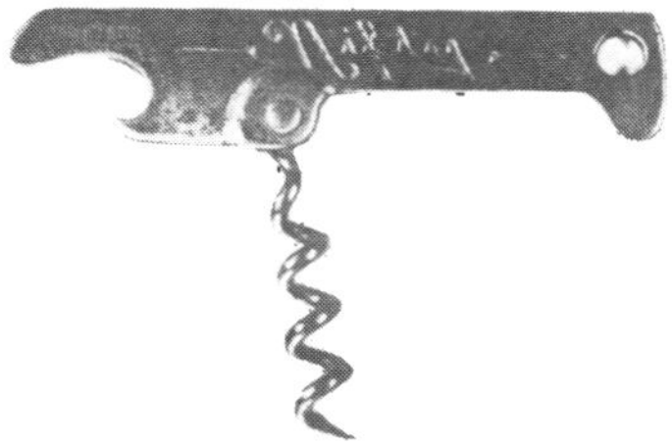

A Crown cork bottle opener and all steel pocket corkscrew, maker's name 'Made & Pat'd. in USA Vaughan Chicago', 3in. long. £23

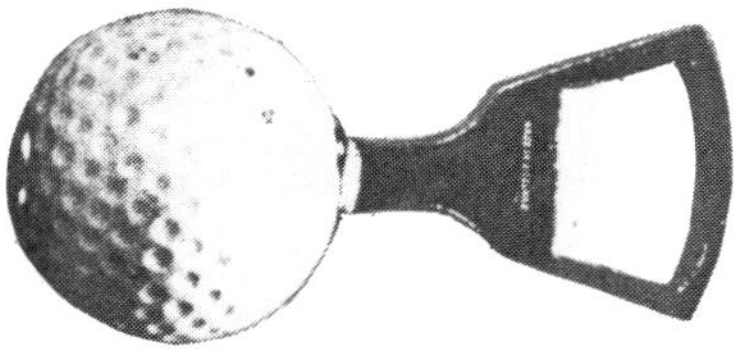

A novelty golf ball Crown cork bottle opener, stamped 'Made in England', 3½in. long. £12

A heavy pewter paperweight and bottle opener, stamped on base 'Ducky' by Kirby & Beard of Paris, circa 1930. £68

An advertising pocket Crown cap bottle opener, on one side the Johnnie Walker gentleman and on reverse is 'Born 1820 Still Going Strong', 1½in. long. £45

An English silver Crown cork bottle opener of Art Deco design, date letter 'D' for 1939 and initials WW, 3½in. long. £35

Combined screwdriver, bottle opener and spanner. £2

A Crown cork opener in cast iron and sheet metal with double sided 'Crown Opener Rd. 702661' and 'Made in England'. £3

BOTTLES

Bottles most popular with British collectors fall into four categories:—

1. Mineral water, beer and other beverage bottles.
2. Quack medicine and 'Cure All' bottles.
3. Glass and stone ink bottles.
4. Poison bottles.

Most collections start with a mineral water bottle, the most popular being Hiram Codd's marble-stoppered lemonade bottle, and the transfer-printed stone ginger beer bottle. Especially sought after are coloured varieties of the Codd bottle. A few years ago they could be bought for under £10, but today, the dark green and amber varieties change hands at about £75 and the cobalt blues well over £100.

The patent medicine 'quack cure' category also shows an indication of some staggering increases in value. Not long ago a Warners Safe Cure Bottle, green in colour could be bought for less than £15. Today you may be lucky enough to pick one up for £50.

The variety of both stone and glass ink bottles to be found is vast, ranging from a simple eight-sided variety to the most sought after of all, the cottage ink, so called because it was moulded in the form of a small cottage with doors and windows. Until recently these were considered to be worth between £10 and £15. Now, because of demand, they average around £40 and certain very rare examples go to overseas collectors at around the £250 mark.

Poison bottles too are becoming a very specialised category with the cobalt blue varieties the most valued. Of particular interest would be a blue poison bottle shaped rather like a submarine or in the figural form of a skull and crossbones which are considered so rare that the price would be negotiable between buyer and seller.

Fishers Seaweed Extract bottle with bulbous neck, 5in. high. £25

A rare mid 17th century green glass sealed wine bottle, 19.5cm. high. £3,000

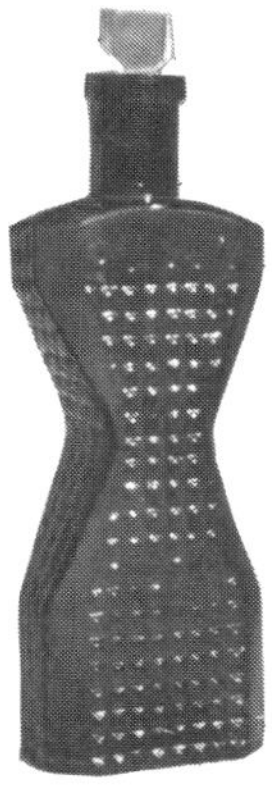

Eclipse patent wasp waist cobalt blue bottle, 8in. high. £175

'Lynaris' Niagara Patent amber glass bottle, 8½in. high. £75

A sealed and dated green glass wine bottle of mallet shape, dated 1738, 8¾in. high. £400

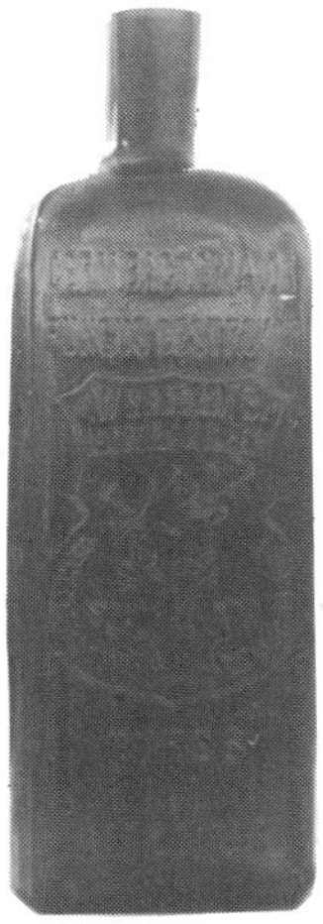

Radam's Microbe Killer bottle, heavily embossed, 10¼in. high. £45

Prices Patent Candle Co. bottle of cobalt blue, 7¼in. high. £30

An early Bellarmine stoneware bottle, 8¼in. high. £250

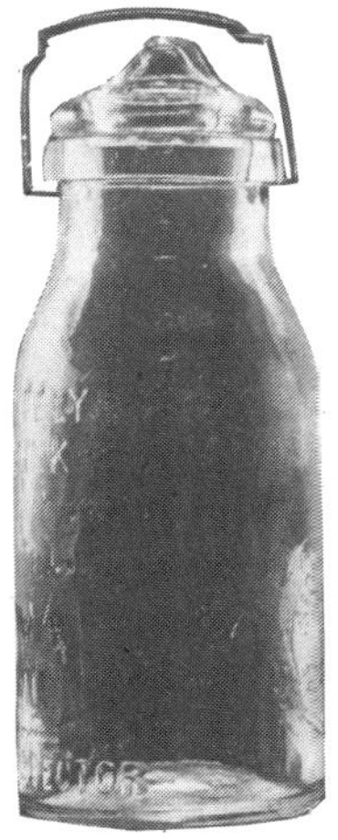

A late 19th century Thatcher Milk Protector. £150

BRONZE ANIMALS

Bronze groups of animal sculpture became a popular art form in the 19th century. When Antoine-Louis Bayre exhibited his 'Tiger Devouring a Gavial' at the Salon of 1831 it caused a commotion in the French art world. The general enthusiasm led to other artists adopting animals as the subject of their work and so a group emerged to become known as – les animaliers.

For the first time, animals were depicted in art as they are in nature: docile, active, resting, feeding, dramatic in combat and always in realistic detail.

Notable artists from this period include P. J. Mene, Isadore Bonheur, Jules Moigniez and Christophe Fratin.

One of a pair of bronze rabbits, signed Tsunemitsu saku, late Meiji/Taisho period, one 19cm. high, the other 21cm. long. (Christie's) £1,404

One of a pair of large 19th century French bronze groups of a setter with a pheasant and a pointer with a hare, signed J. Moigniez, 42cm. high. (Christie's) £7,560

A bronze model of a giraffe, 17in. high. (Christie's) £1,836

A bronze model of a pug dog, signed Tsunemitsu, late Meiji/Taisho period, 13cm. high. (Christie's) £864

A 19th century gilt bronze figure of a sporting hound, 'Tom', signed Barye Fils, 8½in. high. (Peter Wilson & Co.) £180

A 19th century French bronze model of a Shetland pony carrying a dead stag, signed I. Bonheur, 22.5 x 25.5cm. (Christie's) £486

Bronze figure of a pheasant, by Jules Moigniez, French, 20¾in. high. (Robt. W. Skinner Inc.) £1,504

A bronze figure of a stag, the oval base inscribed P. J. Mene, circa 1843, 8½in. high. (Anderson & Garland) £600

A bronze model of a monkey, signed Hidefuji, Meiji period, 25.6cm. high. (Christie's) £594

A bronze group of two tigers attacking an elephant, signed Seiya, Meiji period, 27cm. long. (Christie's) £270

A bronze model of a rat, signed Muroe tancho saku, Meiji period, 14cm. long. (Christie's) £410

A 19th century bronze model of a seated ape, unsigned, 16cm. high. (Christie's) £1,620

Late 17th century South German bronze figure of a lion, on a squared marble base, 9½in. high. £1,155

A bronze model of a stag and a fox, signed Fratin, 22½in. wide. (Christie's) £540

A 19th century bronze spelter model of a camel with saddle, 10½in. high. (Christie's) £594

A late 19th century English bronze model of a wild cat crouching on a rocky promontory, cast from a model by J. Macallan Swan, 23.5cm. high. (Christie's) £1,728

An Egyptian bronze cat's head, probably 6th century BC, 1¾in. high. (Lawrence Fine Art) £440

Bronze group of sheep, by Jules Moigniez, French, 15in. long. (Robt. W. Skinner Inc.) £1,097

A 19th century French bronze group of a ten point stag brought down by two Scottish hounds, cast from a model by A. L. Barye, 39 x 57cm. (Christie's) £4,104

Bronze figure of a horse, by Isadore-Jules Bonheur, France, 32in. long. (Robt. W. Skinner Inc.) £4,065

BUBBLE GUM WRAPPERS

It was around 1942 that the immortal cry 'Any gum chum?' was first heard echoing throughout Britain as we were introduced to the sticky delights of bubble gum by the American allied forces. The British home product did not really get under way until the early 1950's and the big name to emerge from this fiercely competitive field was that of the company A. & B.C.

As part of their promotional campaigns bubble gum manufacturers started to release picture card issues and with each new series a new wrapper featuring art work strongly influenced by topical events in film, television, football and pop music.

Apart from the hardy perennials like Tarzan, Superman and Popeye wrappers depicting The Beatles, Cliff Richard and The Monkees all proved to be extremely popular as did heroes of the Wild West such as The Legend of Custer. The 1957 launching of the satellite Sputnik stimulated an increase in the production of wrappers bearing a space travel theme.

With new issues appearing every few weeks all of these products had a very short 'shelf life' with the result that many of these wax paper wrappers are now quite rare.

The peak of production spans a period of twenty years dating from 1953 to 1973 however, in America, where wrapper collecting is also extremely popular, examples are available from the early thirties onwards.

'Legend of Custer', 1968, A. & B. C. Chewing Gum Ltd. £10

'Football', 1954, Chix Confectionery Co. Ltd. £5

'Mars Attacks', 1962, Bubble Inc. £100

'Superman in the Jungle', 1968, A. & B. C. Chewing Gum Ltd. £15

'Cliff Richard', 1959, Leaf Ltd. £15

'Outer Limits', 1964, Bubble Inc. £20

BUCKLES

Buckles have presented an interesting fashion feature throughout the centuries. Essentially a piece of jewellery, they have been styled for daywear and to sparkle in the evening. They were worn at the belt, on a garter at the knee and on shoes. It is reported that men wore buckles as an indication of their social status and some were so large, they almost covered the whole instep.

Buckles were often included in a parure – a set of matching jewellery – and reflect the changing styles. Examples include those made of precious metals and set with gem-stones and the rather ornate Victorian style of gilt, silver filigree, beads or jet.
Emphasis was placed on the use of metal during the Art Nouveau period and it is buckles from this period that have become most popular with collectors today.

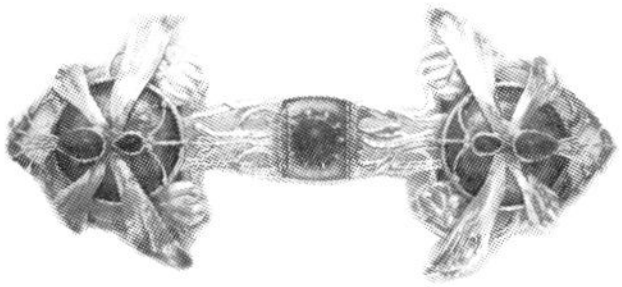

A Guild of Handicrafts Ltd. silver enamel and amethyst buckle/cloak clasp, designed by C. R. Ashbee, circa 1902, 13.75cm. wide. £7,150

Early 16th century German silver gilt buckle and belt end. £1,375

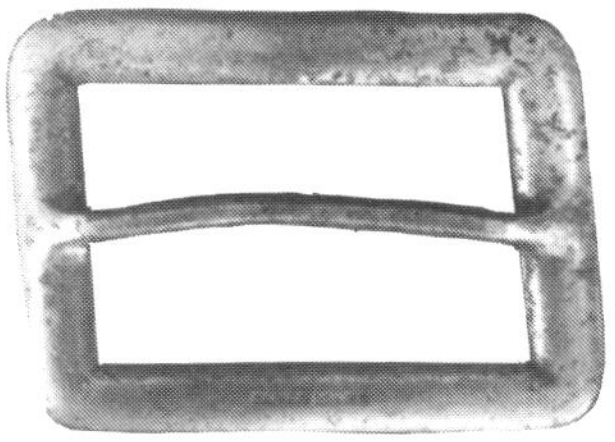

An old large brass harness buckle. £5

18th century iron buckle with fern leaf motifs, 3½in. long. £9

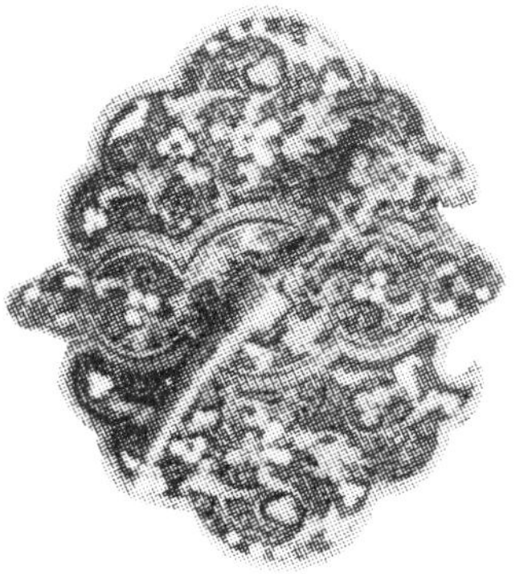

A Russian silver gilt shaped buckle with a dagger clasp. (Christie's S. Kensington) £85

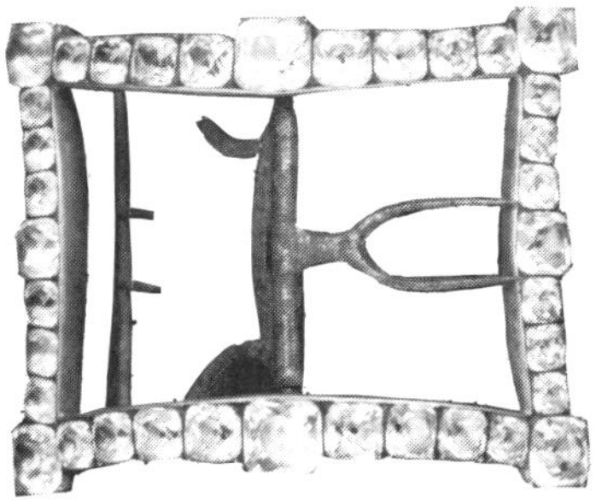

A fine late 18th century shoe buckle of polished steel decorated with crystal stones set in silver. £38

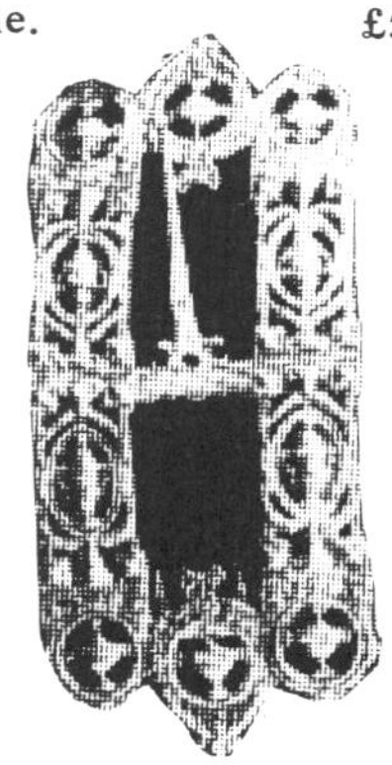

Sterling silver belt buckle by Shreve, Crump & Low, Boston, circa 1900, 3 troy oz., 5½in. long. (Robert W. Skinner Inc.) £95

1930's dress buckle. £1.50

A Lalique gold, diamond, opal and enamel choker buckle, circa 1900, 7.5cm. wide. £17,600

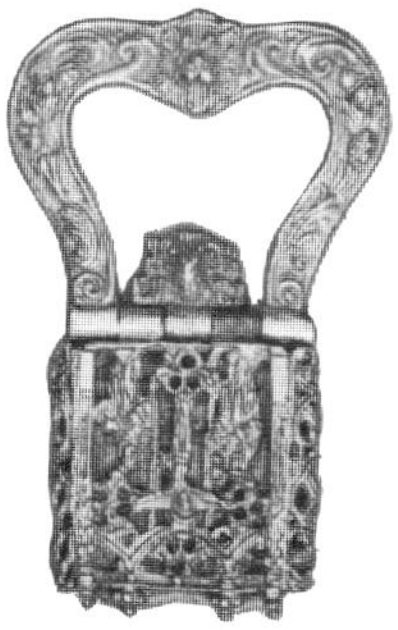

Late 15th/16th century South German silver gilt belt buckle, 4.3/8in. overall. £1,155

1930's brass butterfly belt buckle. £5

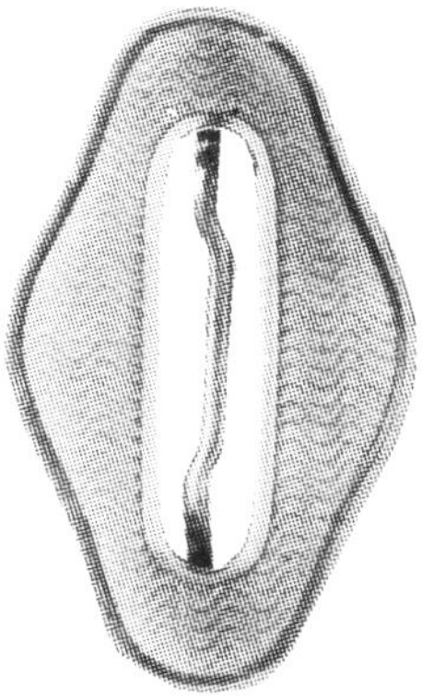

A Faberge silver gilt and enamel buckle, 1899-1903. £721

BUS TICKETS

Putting a price to a collection of bus tickets is not an easy task, for, although the hobby is not a new one, it is practised by a comparatively small and select group. There are a number of dealers but the main source of information and stock is through the Transport Ticket Society.

The T.T.S. has clearly stated its policy in relation to the price of tickets and this is 'that it does not wish to see commercialisation of the subject', therefore the tickets which they have for sale to their members are sold at a minimum cost.

Despite this policy it is inevitable that the value of certain tickets, or types of tickets, will rise according to supply and demand.

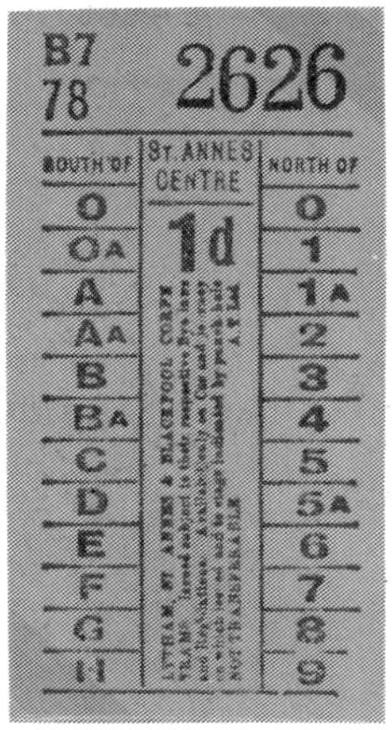

Punch Type – early issue for joint tram services of Blackpool and Lytham St. Annes. 50p

Double Ultimate – Lancaster City. Decimal issue. 2p

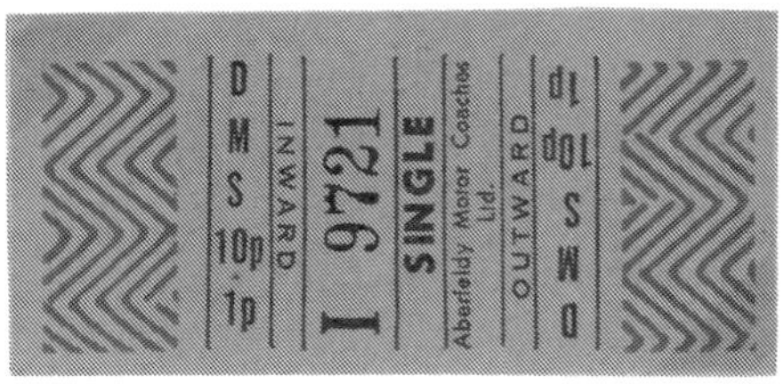

Setright Insert – fare date printed by machine on hatched area. 5p

Edmonson – usually used by railway companies. This is from Leicester trams. 30p

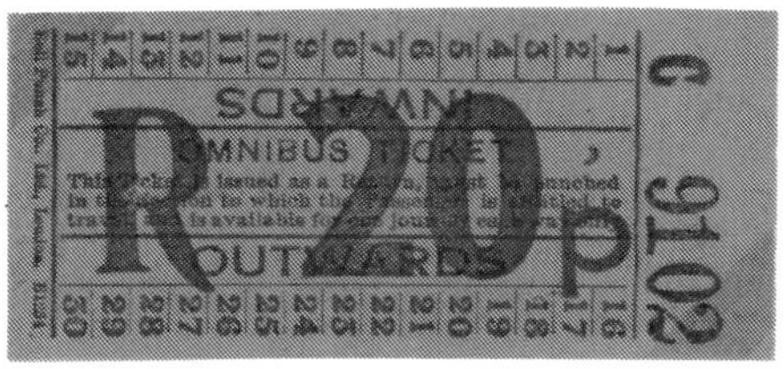

Punch Type – one of the few decimal issues of this type. 'R' denotes Return. 2p

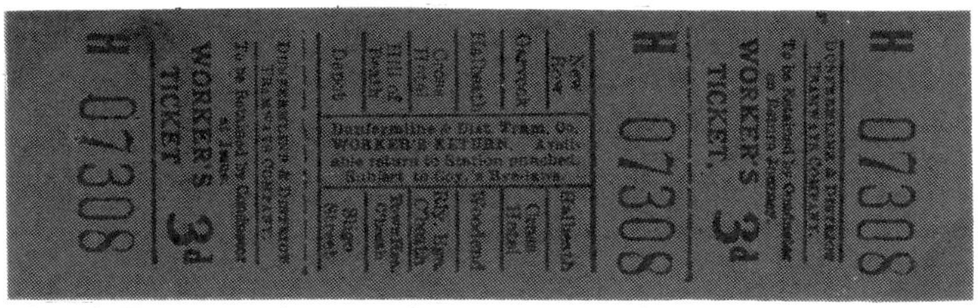

Punch Type – early issue showing principal stopping points tramway route. 50p

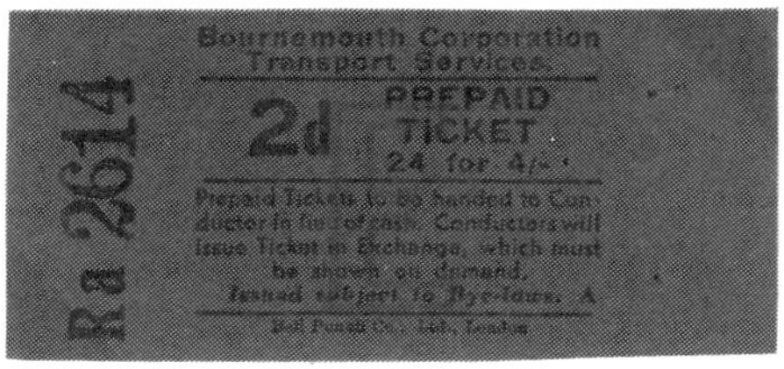

Prepaid – typical prepaid card ticket. This one from Bournemouth. 2p

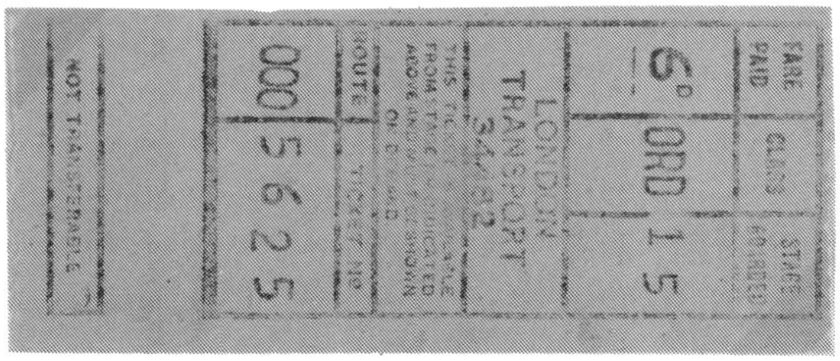

Gibson – these are widely used by London Transport. 40p

Ultimate – single issue is most common version of this type. 2p

Punch type – composite issue covers single or return journeys. 2p

BUTLIN'S BADGES

Enamelled badges were issued at all Butlin's Holiday Camps and Hotels as proof that those wearing them were bona fide guests and were entitled to use all the free facilities on offer. Badges were also issued for special activities such as for the Car Club, Recreation Club and Cycling Club or to denote authority such as for committee members.

Special events such as the 'Festival of Reunion' in 1951 also warranted a badge as did Eric Winstone the legendary bandleader based at Clacton.

Members of staff also sported badges the various colours and designs denoting years of service or seniority.

The rarest camp badges originate from the pre-war period, the first for Skegness issued in 1936 followed by Clacton in 1938, and those from immediately after such as Filey 1945 or the rare plastic variety for Filey issued in 1946.

Apart from the war years they continued to be issued until 1967 although a few special badges such as those for the Beaver Club for children were distributed after this date.

Collecting a complete set of badges would be quite a challenge for most camps had their own designs which often changed from one season to the next and sometimes even from week to week in the same season. As a result there are thought to be about 1,750 different badges, not counting the distinct variations which occur in both enamelling and colour.

The collecting of Butlin's badges was encouraged by the Camps from the beginning for the camper who displayed the most badges was not only presented with a prize but became guest of honour at many of the functions during their holiday.

Travel by Stage Coach with Eric Winstone. £3

Ayr 1964. £1

Skegness 1956. £1

Royal Albert Hall 1951. Festival of Reunion. £3

Butlins Car Club. £5

Clacton 1946. £3

Clacton 1949. £3

Filey 1955. £3

Skegness 1949. £3

Pwllheli 1954. £3

Pwllheli 1947. £3

Skegness 1939. £10

Skegness 1948. £3

Skegness 1955. £1

Clacton 1948. £3

BUTTONS

It is known that buttons date from as early as the 6th century A.D. in the Middle East and from the mid fourteenth century in Great Britain. Can you imagine the quantities of buttons produced in the intervening centuries?

Attention focuses mainly on the buttons known to be worth money. The 18th century sets of silver buttons, the beautiful silver and enamel buttons in the Art Nouveau style and the colourfully decorated cloisonne buttons, all have their devotees – at a price, but apart from these, and a few other types of fine quality buttons, antiques dealers tend to neglect the subject, mainly through lack of available information on pricing.

And that is where the collector comes in. Most people just 'keep' buttons, then realise they have a collection. There is still an enormous variety of buttons to choose from, often by the tinful, and most are very reasonably priced. As soon as some sort of 'going rate' has been established, the price is sure to rise.

Set of twelve French silver buttons. £35

Fermanagh Militia, 1795-1810, gilt. £20

Black Ball Line, gilt, circa 1870. £5

Leicester Yeomanry Cavalry, Coatee, silver plate, 1850. £8

Civil Defence button by J. R. Gaunt & Son, London. 50p

Set of four alloy heraldic buttons. £2.50

North of Europe Steam Navigation Co., gilt, circa 1850. £10

Set of ten decorative brass buttons by Jennens & Co., London. £4

Officer's general pattern, Georgian, gilt, circa 1820. £10

Set of five Islamic silver coin buttons. £10

Co-operative Wholesale Socy. Fire Brigade, brass. £2

A set of twelve George III buttons, possibly by John Orme, London, circa 1780, 1oz.19dwt. £2,310

Set of eight British Red Cross Society buttons of ebonised wood. £12

CADDIES

Of all boxes, chests, caskets and other assorted containers, tea caddies must surely be the most numerous and the most varied with regard to shape and style.

One reason for this is that tea has been drunk in Britain for some three hundred years, at prices ranging from £10 per lb. (at the beginning of the 17th century) down. Naturally, a commodity as expensive as this was neither served direct from the packet nor dumped in just any can on the kitchen shelf.

Early (i.e. 17th century) containers were usually of pottery or porcelain. As the cult of tea-drinking became more widespread during the 18th century, tea-containers of gold and silver began to appear, and these were housed in lockable chests or caddies (the word caddy is derived from the Malay "kati", a measure of tea weighing about 1¼lb.) The more widespread the tea-drinking habit became, the greater the variety of caddies to cater for the demand.

Chippendale, Sheraton and all the other designers and cabinet makers of note produced caddies in their characteristic styles, and ornamentation varied from the simplest, most elegant inlay work to encrustations of brass, ormolu, coloured straw, curled paperwork and every other possible decorative device.

Not too many years ago, it would have been easy to start a collection, for caddies could be picked up almost anywhere for only a few pounds – none but the very best reaching double figures. Nowadays, they are just as ubiquitous but the prices must warm the cockles of any heart who got a collection together at the right time.

They are to be found in a number of materials, including wood, ivory, papier mache, silver, copper, tortoiseshell, china, straw work, Tunbridgeware and with painted decoration.

Walnut tea caddy of hexagonal shape, each side with oval shell inlaid panel. (Butler & Hatch Waterman) £320

An 18th/19th century tea caddy in the form of a boxwood toadstool, 5in. high. £748

An 18th century melon fruitwood tea caddy, England, 6in. high. (Robt. W. Skinner Inc.) £1,527

A George III satinwood, rosewood and fruitwood tea caddy, the crossbanded lid with a silver plaque with initials J.E.R., 12¾in. wide. (Christie's) £1,242

A George III oval tea caddy, the lid centred by a leaf-cast silver handle, circa 1795, 5in. high. £2,860

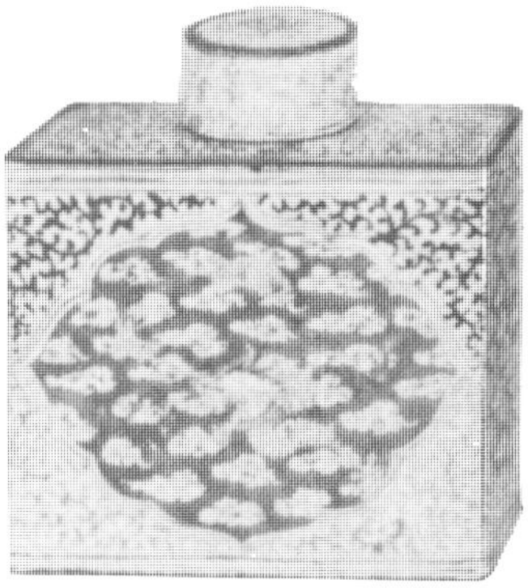

Chinese Peking, enamelled, covered tea caddy, with multi-coloured dragon re serve panel decoration, 4½in. high. (Stalker & Boos) £144

A George III mahogany and scrolled paperwork tea caddy with hinged cover, dated 1789, 17.5cm. wide. (H. Spencer & Sons) £460

A Regency parcel gilt and scarlet lacquer tea cannister, 17½in. high. (Christie's) £864

George III rectangular inlaid tea caddy on a brass edged base on bracket feet, 10in. wide. (Christie's) £308

Three-colour Wedgwood tea caddy, circa 1895, with domed lid, 6in. high. (Robt. W. Skinner Inc.) £310

A George III rectangular tea caddy on rim foot, with blue glass liner, unmarked, circa 1775. (Christie's) £3,240

A Sheraton period cross-banded tea caddy, having two division interior with Bristol blue glass blending bowl, 10¾in. wide. (Geering & Colyer) £280

A George III treen pear tea caddy, the lid with a stalk and enclosing a plain interior. (Christie's) £1,080

A late Georgian tortoiseshell tea caddy of bow shape, 6½in. (Lawrence Fine Art) £770

One of a set of three George II silver gilt, vase-shaped tea caddies, by Samuel Taylor, 1752, 31oz. (Christie's) £5,400

1930's wooden tea box with plated fittings. £5

Late Georgian mahogany tea caddy, sarcophagus shaped with ebony and boxwood cable inlay, 8¼in. wide. (Capes, Dunn & Co.) £42

An ivory veneered Georgian tea caddy with a brass handle and tortoiseshell decoration. (Martel Maides & Le Pelley) £775

CADDY SPOONS

Although it is doubtful if the luck of a Devon farmer will be repeated when he found a 16th century silver spoon worth thousands while rethatching his cottage roof, there are still plenty of prizes to be found in old cutlery drawers.
Most sought after are the early seal top and apostle spoons which have a cast finial joined to the flattened stem with a 'V' joint. Of more unusual form are moat spoons, for scooping the floating debris from the surface of a cup of tea, moustache spoons which have a barrier on the leading edge of the bowl and castor oil spoons designed to administer the beneficial elixir with as little hardship as possible.

The most likely prize to be found, however, are caddy spoons which generally have a large ornate bowl and very short handle, find one of these in the form of an eagle and we are talking about over £1,000.

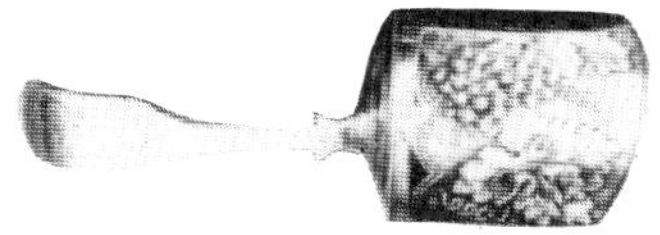

Bright cut caddy spoon, Birmingham, 1798. (Dreweatt Watson & Barton) £55

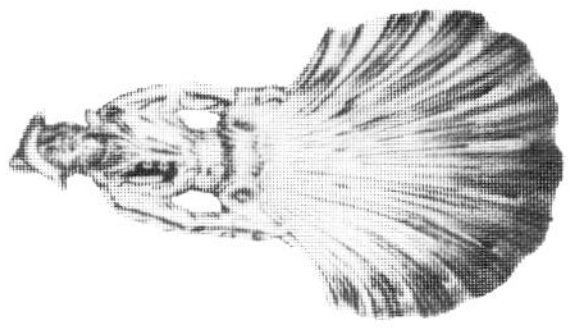

A Victorian caddy spoon, the bowl formed as a shell, by John Foligno, 1854. (Christie's) £561

A Victorian caddy spoon, the bowl formed as a shell, by C. T. & G. Fox, 1841. (Christie's) £972

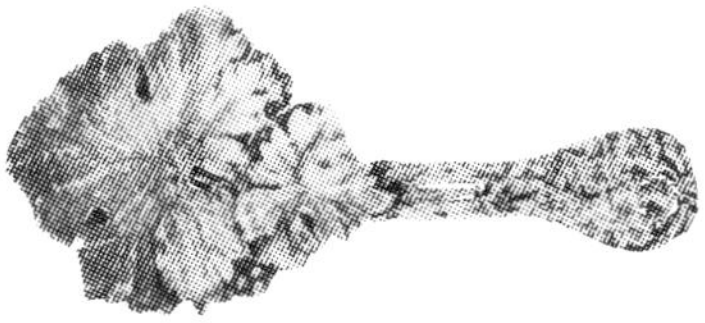

A George IV caddy spoon by C. Reily and G. Storer, 1828. (Christie's) £302

A Regency caddy spoon by Edward Farrell, 1816. (Christie's) £1,242

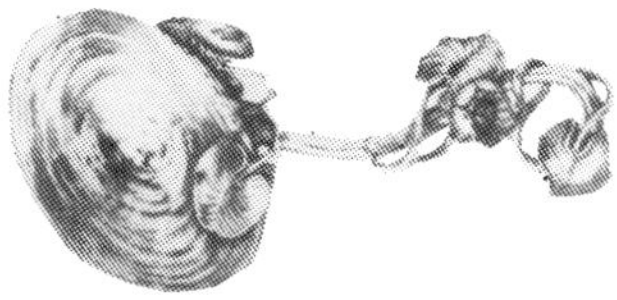

A Victorian silver gilt caddy spoon, the bowl formed as a mussel-shell, by Francis Higgins, 1849. (Christie's) £756

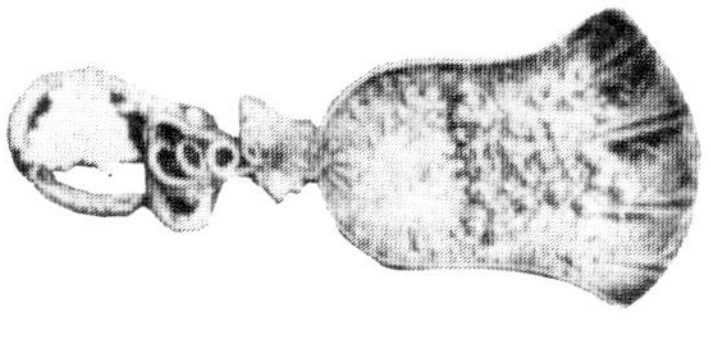

Vine chased caddy spoon, by Hilliard & Thomason, Birmingham, 1852. (Dreweatt Watson & Barton) £80

Jockey cap caddy spoon, by Thos. Willmore, Birmingham, 1798. (Dreweatt Watson & Barton) £175

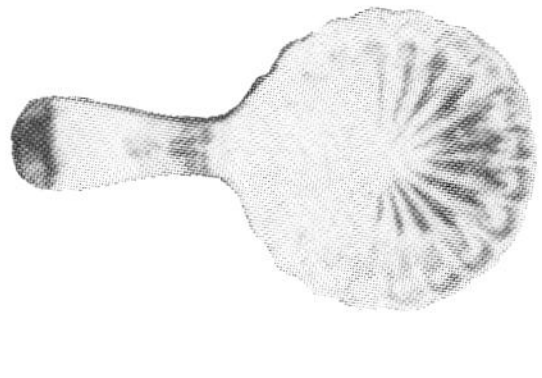

Fiddle pattern caddy spoon, Birmingham, 1814. (Dreweatt Watson & Barton) £62

A Victorian caddy spoon, the bowl formed as acanthus foliage, by John Figg, 1844. (Christie's) £1,296

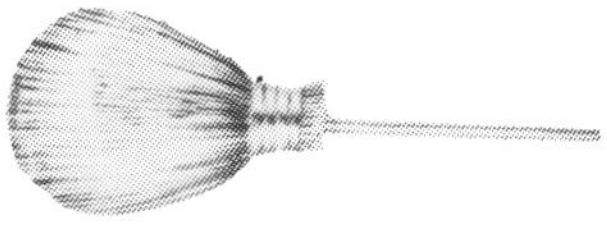

A Victorian caddy spoon formed as a broom, by Charles Fox, 1863. (Christie's) £410

A William IV caddy spoon, the bowl formed as a limpet shell, 1830, maker's mark WT. (Christie's) £702

CAMERAS

Cameras were first produced on a commercial scale at the end of the 19th century and the Victorians quickly developed a passion for the art of photography. Their veritable mania for documentation led them to record all manner of events from the Grand Tour to the day a young man paraded proudly in his first pair of long trousers.

Today, as the race goes on to develope smaller, lighter, slimmer, fully automatic cameras, the trade in old plate cameras and all the paraphernalia of the Victorian studio, is thriving. Made with the precision of scientific instruments most of these cameras are still in usable condition but they have taken on more than a utilitarian appeal and are now treasured for their intrinsic quality.

A few years ago a good Victorian brass and wood plate camera could be bought easily for as little as £10; after all, who wanted old cameras? Then a few enthusiasts began collecting in a serious way and, suddenly, plate cameras were changing hands at ten times as much.

Even some cameras made as recently as ten years ago have acquired a commercial value to collectors – often far in excess of the guide lines worked out by manufacturers for trade-in prices on new equipment.

One of the rarest examples to come on to the market was the Sutton Panoramic Wet Plate Camera which fetched £11,000 at auction, the resulting publicity bringing two more to light which also sold for about the same figure. Although these were exceptional prices, there are many cameras, like the Powell's stereoscopic camera or the Compur Leica, which sell for well over £1,000.

Most, however, change hands for a good deal less than this, but still at prices which would send anybody up into the loft for a search.

A quarter-plate Tropical Model Improved Artist Reflex camera manufactured by The London Stereoscopic Co., with Tessar lens. (Christie's). £200

A 2¼ x 2¼ Redding's Luzo roll-film camera in brass re-inforced mahogany casing, Patent No. 17328. (Christie's) £450

A 45 x 107mm. Ernemann Reflex stereoscopic camera of Jumelle-form with Ernemann Doppel Anastigmat 75mm. f 4.5 lenses, in leather case. (Christie's) £190

A 15 x 10cm. Ica Tropical folding plate camera in metal teak casing with Tessar lens in dial-set Compur shutter. (Christie's) £100

A quarter-plate Gandolfi hand-and-stand camera in mahogany casing, with Aldis Anastigmat lens. (Christie's) £300

A 6 x 9cm. Mentor folding reflex camera with Tessar lens. (Christie's) £160

A tail board folding field camera by Stanley, with Ross 8¾in. wide angle Xpres f4 lens. (Onslow's) £80

A prototype V.P. mono-rail camera in aluminium casing, with Tessar lens. (Christie's) £300

A four-lens multiple-exposure camera, probably by J. Lancaster & Sons, taking four 2 x 1½in. exposures on one quarter plate, in mahogany casing. (Christie's) £1,200

A Lancaster International field camera, with Busch Rapid Aplanat No. 3 10in. lens, in canvas carrying case. (Onslow's) £100

A quarter-plate box-form mahogany survey camera by by J. H. Dallmeyer, London, in mahogany casing with lens, on brass tripod mount. (Christie's) £400

A Thornton-Pickard quarter-plate triple extension field camera. (Onslow's) £170

A Stirn's Waistcoat detective camera, No. 5065, in nickel-plated brass casing, taking six circular exposures on circular plate. (Christie's) £480

An Alpa Reflex 35mm. s.l.r. camera, Mod. 6, No. 38996, with Kern Switar, Schneider and Alpa lenses. (Christie's) £250

A Zeiss Contaflex 35mm. twin-lens reflex camera, No. Z 42268 with a Sonnar taking lens and a Sucher-Objectiv lens, and an exposure meter. (Christie's) £450

CAR CLUB BADGES

The Motor Club Badge is as old as the Motor Car itself. From those early days, the motorist wanted to be identified as belonging to an elite band of priviledged people.
The two most popular themes in badge collecting are the A.A. and R.A.C. types. The earliest style of A.A. badge was produced in either brass or nickel and is worth approximately £100 plus. Fifteen different types of A.A. badges exist today.
R.A.C. badges are available in a variety of different metals and in quite a considerable number of different designs but generally, the earlier the badge, the higher the price it commands. The very first badge produced in 1907 is a very rare badge indeed – now worth approximately £300.

Today the choice for the collector is wide and varied with a few themes listed below:
A.A., R.A.C., Car Clubs, Factory Clubs, Caravan Clubs, Regimental Associations and Sporting Clubs.
The collector must really decide whether to collect all that is offered or to specialise. Obviously the more general the badge, the lower the price with specialised badges costing well into three figures. In this group belong the most desirable badges, mainly those associated with the Brooklands Race Track. A few examples are shown below:

1930's Brooklands Automobile Racing Club	£250 plus
1930's Brooklands Automobile Racing Club with 120 M.P.H. Badge	£700
1930's Brooklands Automobile Racing Club with 130 M.P.H. Badge	£900
1930's Brooklands Flying Club	£700
1930's Brooklands Aero Club	£900
1930's Junior Car Club	£50 plus

It is interesting to note that all these badges could be bought some years ago for considerably less!

'Singapore Motor Club', 1940's badge, chrome plated, scarce. £35 – £40

'Margate & District Car Club', very scarce, chrome badge, 1930's. £30

'Singer Motor Club', very rare badge, from 1934/35, less than 10 known. £90

'A.A.' large type, scarce and sought after, made 1911 to 1922. £40 – £50

R.A.C. Full Member's badge, King's head to front, Union Jack centre on reverse, scarce, 1930's/1940's. £35

B.A.R.C. 'Brooklands Automobile Racing Club', very rare and sought after 1930's badge, chrome/enamel, all numbered. £250 plus

CAR MASCOTS

These decorative symbols introduced around 1905, are usually made of cast metal though sometimes of wood or glass.

Of the wide range of designs, including those issued by car manufacturers, such as, the Rolls Royce Spirit of Ecstasy and the American company Lincoln's greyhound, the magnificent mascots designed by the French glass artists Sabino and Lalique are the most highly prized.

Many car owners had mascots made to their own designs and these offer a great variety of interesting subjects for the collector.

A brass bust of Minerva, stamped, 6in. high, on circular plinth.(Christie's) £140

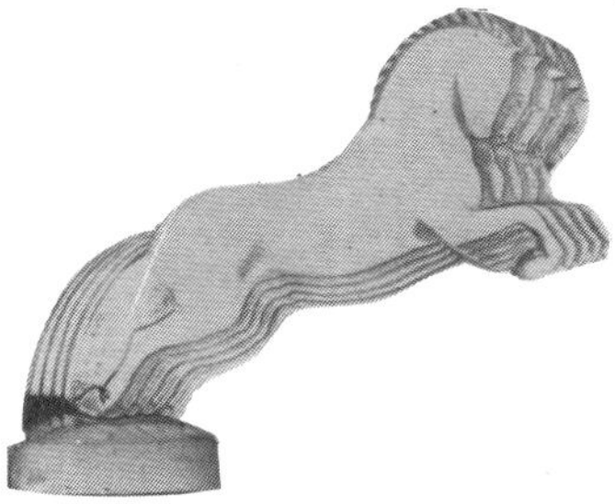

'Cinq Chevaux', a Lalique car mascot moulded in clear glass, etched France No. 1122, 11.5cm. high. (Christie's) £2,376

A brass nymph holding a torch in front with leg raised and trailing scarf, 5¾in. high. (Christie's) £60

A chromium plated stylised cat, stamped Nikolsky No. 14, 6in. long. (Christie's) £95

A nickel plated brass car mascot, caricature figure of an airman with printed porcelain head and moveable helmet, inscribed Hassall, 4¼in. high. (Christie's) £500

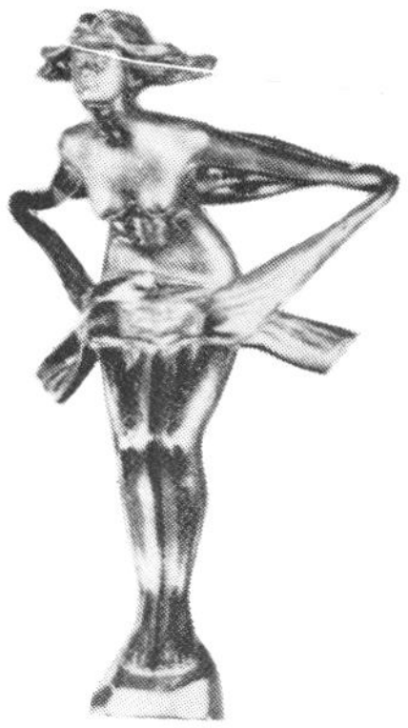

A nickel plated speed nymph clutching a scarf, by Lejeune, stamped Reg. AEL, 6in. high. (Christie's) £150

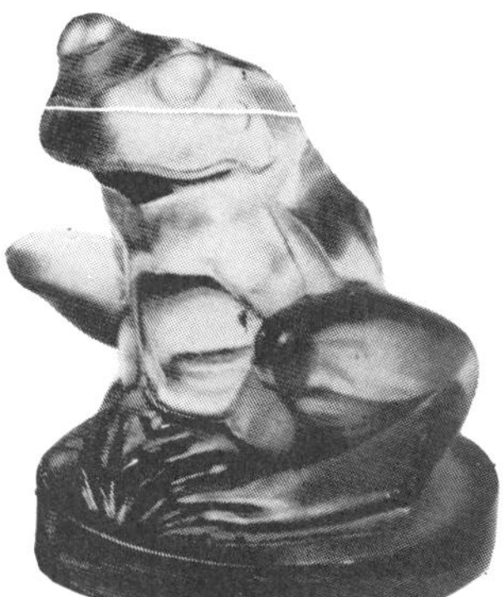

'Grenouille', a Lalique car mascot in clear and satin finished glass moulded as a seated frog, 6.3cm. high. (Christie's) £3,456

A cast silver radiator mascot by Omar Ramsden, 1935, 12.8cm., 21.5oz. (Lawrence Fine Art) £935

CARD CASES

In the days when polite society expected printed notice of an intended visit, the calling card played a vital role. It is said that the fasionable ladies of the 19th century, anxious to impress others with their status, would display cards presented to them by those of considerable social consequence, in a large open dish placed on the drawingroom table. The most important being well to the top.
Cards were often delivered by a footman but the common practice was to carry several personal cards in a case.

Card cases are almost always of slim and rectangular shape and made from a variety of materials such as gold, silver, ivory, tortoiseshell, Tunbridgeware, mother-of-pearl, papier mache and leather. They are often beautifully decorated and sometimes marked with the original owner's monogram or inscribed to commemorate an event.

A Chinese ivory card case, carved in shaped panels with figures and buildings in garden and river scenes. (Lawrence Fine Art) £49

A Victorian shaped silver card case, by Edward Smith, Birmingham 1852, 10.1cm. (Lawrence Fine Art) £264

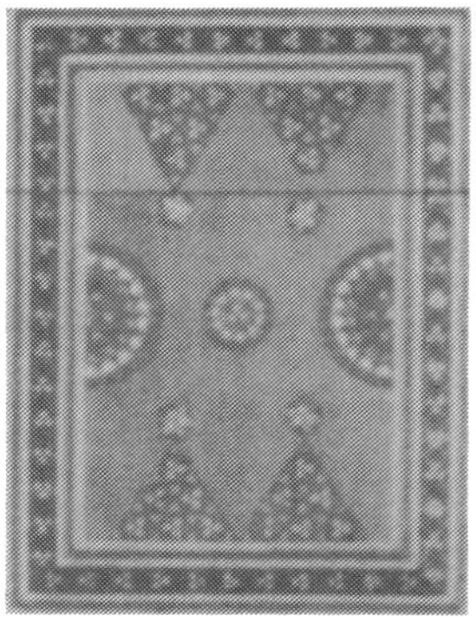

An Indian card case inlaid with mosaic panels and borders of tinted ivory and metal. (Lawrence Fine Art) £11

A Victorian shaped rectangular silver card case, by R. Thornton, Birmingham 1866, 11cm. (Lawrence Fine Art) £55

A papier mache card case, inlaid with mother-of-pearl and gilt with a Chinese river scene. (Lawrence Fine Art) £11

A Chinese ivory card case, deeply carved with numerous figures and buildings in landscapes. (Lawrence Fine Art) £71

A mother-of-pearl card case, inlaid in a trellis pattern with an engraved bird and flowers, with paua shells. (Lawrence Fine Art) £25

A tortoiseshell card case, inlaid in engraved mother-of-pearl . (Lawrence Fine Art) £66

CARLTON WARE

This Staffordshire earthenware and pottery was produced by Wiltshaw and Robinson at Stoke on Trent from 1890 till 1957. From 1958, the firm was re-titled Carlton Ware Ltd. They are best known for porcelain vases produced in the 1920's with bright enamelling and gilded decorations, often on black backgrounds, and painted with flowers or fan motifs. The firm's usual mark is circular enclosing a swallow and topped by a crown. Some pieces are marked Carlton Ware.

Decoration is varied from Art Deco designs of lustrous trees in unusual colours, Kate Greenaway style fairies, fantastic and mythical birds and even traditional Chinese chinoiserie designs.

Egyptianesque jardiniere with frieze decoration and hieroglyphics on a blue ground, 160mm. high. (Goss & Crested China) £950

Vibrant lustrous red 'Rouge Royale' leaf, one of a series introduced after 1930, 220mm. long. (Goss & Crested China) £10

Deep red jug with gold handle and sea-green interior, one of the famous birds series, featuring fantastic and mythical birds, 295mm. high. (Goss & Crested China) £200

Pale pink shaped vase with Art Deco design, 195mm. high. (Goss & Crested China) £125

Oviform vase with dark grey ground simulating nightfall, signed by E. F. Paul, with Kate Greenaway style fairies design, 230mm. high. (Goss & Crested China) £550

Unusual leaf green Art Deco vase with large and small lustrous trees of unusual colours, black inside, 265mm. high. (Goss & Crested China) £250

Standard Carlton Ware vase of pale blue ground with tube lined floral decorations or primary colours, also blue inside the vase, 165mm. high. (Goss & Crested China) £85

'Armand Lustre Ware', vase in streaked brown/green and gilded butterflies, 190mm. high. (Goss & Crested China) £125

CARTE DE VISITE

The earliest recorded mention of the Carte de Visite in La Lumiere, 1854, credits two Frenchmen with – 'an original idea for the use of small portraits'.
The Carte de Visite consisted of a portrait, usually full length and measuring approximately 2½ x 3½ins., mounted on a slightly larger card designed as a calling card, which often carried reference to the photographer on the reverse side. The cost might have been anything up to a shilling.
The idea was promoted by one, Disderi, who, having captured the interest of the people, then applied for a patent.
By 1862, 'cartemania' was sweeping society and Disderi is reputed to have earned as much as £50,000 annually from his studio work.
The bestselling Carte de Visite of all time was W. Downey's portrait of the Princess of Wales (1867), which achieved a sale of 300,000 copies.

Tennyson. (Elliott & Fry). £14

Miss Anderson. £9

King Edward. £10

Queen Victoria – Court size card. (Hughes & Mullins). £8

Mr. W. Terris & Miss Millward in 'The Harbour Lights'. (Theatrical) £6

General Von Moltke. (The London Stereoscopic & Photographic Co.) £11

Mr. Barrington & Miss Jessie Bond in 'Ruddigore'. £6

T.H.R. The Crown Prince & Princess of Prussia with their children. (Hills & Saunders). £14

CAT POSTCARDS

Postcards depicting cats is another very popularly subscribed area of collecting.
One of the most famous 'cat' artists must surely be Louis Wain whose work is most highly prized. His series published by Tucks is particularly favoured and a good example will fetch as much as £16 per card.

Early vignettes by this artist fall into the £8-£20 price range. (It is worth noting that when the front of the cards have been written on they are worth less than those in mint condition.)

Other notable artists in this field are Arthur Thiele, Dorothy Travers Pope and for cats in comic situations we can look to the work of Donald McGill and Lawson Wood.

OGZL Series, 'Kittens At Play', art type postcard No. 638. £1.50

OGZL Series 'Mother And Kittens At Play', art type postcard No. 637. £1.50

ABM Series No. 53 'Cats At Tea', undivided back chromo litho postcard vignette. £4

Cat study by Louis Wain, published by J. Salmon Sevenoaks (middle period). £12

PFB Series No. 7072/A embossed chromo litho study of cats, artist drawn. £6

PFB Series No. 7072/D embossed chromo litho study of cat with bell. £6

'Brown Tabby and Persian' cat study by Ernest H. Mills, Salmon Series P.C. No. 4587. £1.50

Embossed chromo litho Easter card, American, 'Cats And Chicks'. £3

Melissa 'Klasik Kards', 'Cats At The Dentist'. 25p

'Faulkner' Series art type postcard 'Cats In The Sewing Basket', by A. Talboys. £1.75

CHAIRS

Over the years, as rooms have been changed and modernised, many a good chair has been relegated to the attic. It was probably thought at the time that while it was too good to be thrown away it was not worthwhile trying to sell it.
At first glance, an old rickety chair may not strike one as the perfect object for the sitting room but, once restored a transformation can take place.
The Victorian cabriole leg dining chair is probably the nicest chair to have been produced during the Victorian period, dating from about 1850 to the end of the century.
With their full balloon backs and French influenced cabriole legs these chairs achieved a degree of elegance soon to be lost as the popular taste turned towards more ponderous styles. The better made examples of this style were those produced at the beginning of their period of popularity and were usually of rosewood, walnut or mahogany, often with fine floral carving on the backs and knees and the most beautifully carved scroll feet; later chairs were often of beech or oak construction and not so well made or finely carved.
Througout the late Victorian era, dining chairs tended to be heavy and ponderously respectable in style, drawing room chairs being somewhat lighter and bedroom chairs were often positively frivolous. The superabundance of down to earth kitchen chairs in the Windsor style is due to the fact that almost every joinery shop in the country found them easy to produce from whatever wood was to hand. They were produced from about 1830 until the end of the Victorian era and were particularly popular in working class homes and in country districts.
Remember, a pair of chairs is worth more than two singles and a set of four is worth a lot more than two pairs, and so on.

Victorian oak revolving office chair. (British Antique Exporters) £70

A Regency beechwood tub armchair, the back filled with cane and with green leather squab cushion. (Christie's) £1,026

A Regency metamorphic library armchair attributed to Morgan & Saunders, the seat opening to reveal four treads. (Christie's) £3,780

A walnut open armchair of George II style with paperscroll toprail. (Christie's) £2,376

One of a pair of laminated rosewood chairs, attributed to J. H. Belter, circa 1855, 38in. high. (Robt. W. Skinner Inc.) £1,849

A George III mahogany folding campaign chair with arched and hinged leather covered back. (Christie's) £756

A George I mahogany easy chair on cabriole legs with slipper feet, 1720-30. (Christie's) £2,138

One of a set of four Victorian walnut side chairs on French cabriole front supports. (Reeds Rains) £580

One of a pair of George II giltwood open armchairs, the backs and seats covered with contemporary tapestry woven in wool and silk, 41½in. high. (Christie's) £91,800

One of a set of six Regency ebonised dining chairs with bowed seats, four stamped SG. (Christie's) £1,836

One of a set of eight Victorian mahogany framed balloon back dining chairs. (Lots Road Chelsea Auction Galleries) £750

One of a pair of Regency mahogany bergeres, with distressed upholstery in ribbed frames. (Christie's) £3,780

One of a set of six carved hardwood chairs. (F. H. Fellows & Sons) £2,100

A William IV mahogany armchair with scrolled shaped leather upholstered back and seat and ring-turned tapering legs. (Christie's) £2,376

A Louis XVI beechwood fauteuil with cartouche-shaped back and seat frame carved with marguerites. (Woolley & Wallis) £740

One of a set of four Dutch marquetry inlaid dining chairs with drop-in seats. (Worsfolds) £900

A Gustav Stickley willow armchair, circa 1907, 39in. high, 31in. wide. (Robt. W. Skinner Inc.) £277

One of a pair of Regency mahogany hall chairs, the sabre back legs joined by ring-turned stretchers. (Christie's) £4,860

CHAMBER POTS

The chamber pot or 'po' – from the French pot de chambre – was usually supplied as part of a toilet set consisting of a jug, basin, soap dish and slop pail. The quality of material and design varies enormously and includes the simple transfer printed earthenware pot, the better quality and colourful Mason's ironstone pot and the elegant fine porcelain pot enamelled and gilded by a factory such as Limoges. Chamber pots were also made of silver and gold.

Most collectible pots, apart from the obvious, are those bearing some kind of novel decoration like the frog illustrated or those with a portrait of Napoleon or a watching eye painted on the inside on the bottom surface. Early 19th century potters produced many pots bearing an inscription – some amusing, some crude and these too are highly collectible.

A blue and white chamber pot painted with peony and bamboo issuing from rockwork, circa 1750, 18.5cm. diam. (Christie's) £1,489

Child's white china potty, all part of British Rail's Sleeper Service. £4

Sunderland lustre pottery chamber pot with an applied frog and cartoon face in the interior. (Cooper Hirst) £320

An English china chamber pot, by Brown-Westhead, Moore & Co., circa 1870, with polychrome rhododendron decoration on cream ground. £35

A pewter chamber pot, stamped with crown and other marks. (Lots Road Galleries) £80

Floral china chamber pot, 1850. (British Antique Exporters) £32

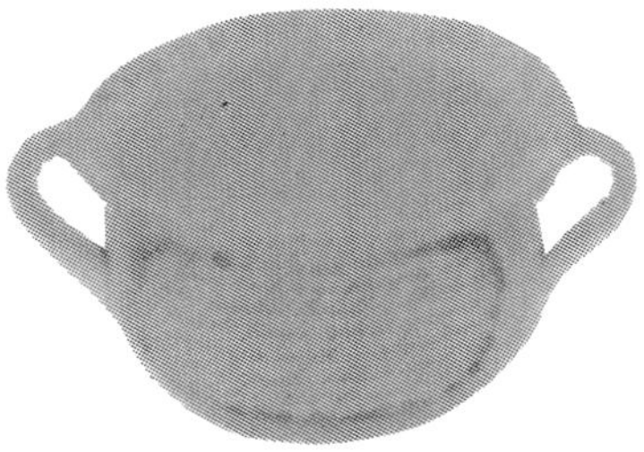

A Victorian two-handled chamber pot, 9¼in. diam. (Dickinson, Davy & Markham) £50

One of two chamber pots, circa 1750, 15.5cm. wide, 12.5cm. diam. (Christie's) £2,438

A late Victorian silver chamber pot, with a scroll handle. (Wolley & Wallis) £480

CHARITY BOXES

Since the mid nineteenth century many of our charitable organisations have promoted a cause and collected for funds through the use of charity boxes. Early boxes were often attached to the end of a long pole so that people deep in a crowd could be canvassed.
In the 1880's the Church Missionary Societies were among the first to use such a box when soliciting contributions for the poor and needy thus giving rise to the popular nickname 'The Poor Box'.
The real boom in the manufacture of charity boxes came in the early twentieth century with fund raising activities on behalf of the various war relief funds reaching a peak.
Boxes are made in a variety of materials and in all shapes and sizes; some in the image of popular characters such as Sooty, Noddy, Basil Brush and other well loved creatures. The well known 'Life boat sliding down the ramp when a penny is inserted in the slot' is a good example of those incorporating a mechanical function.

Collecting box for the Society for The Propagation of the Gospel, circa 1880. £12

R.S.P.C.A. pottery charity box, 8in. wide. £25

Automaton charity box in aid of St. Christopher's Railway Children's Home, in which the pistons are operated by a coin in the slot. £350

An R.S.P.C.A. papier mache 'Puppy' charity box. £25

The Spastics Society 'Tumbling Coin' charity box, modern plastic. £4

Composition R.S.P.C.A. charity box, 2ft.6in. high. £65

A large cast-iron charity box in the form of a seated lion, 3ft. high overall with stand. £400

Composition 'Polio' charity box, 3ft. high. £50

CHEESE DISHES

It is not often realised that throughout the 19th century people were well used to expecting fresh milk, butter and cheese, for cows were actually kept in the centre of large towns for this purpose right up until the First World War.
Most large houses of the period actually had their own dairy set in the coolest part of the house, usually facing north, where they regularly made butter, curds and whey and cheese.

It became fashionable in the 19th century to partake of cheese after dinner and this custom saw the production of vast numbers of decorative china cheese dishes able to grace the diningroom as opposed to the rather plain functional dishes which rarely left the kitchen. Unfortunately some of the larger Stilton cheese dishes have become somewhat redundant for it would cost a king's ransom to fill one.

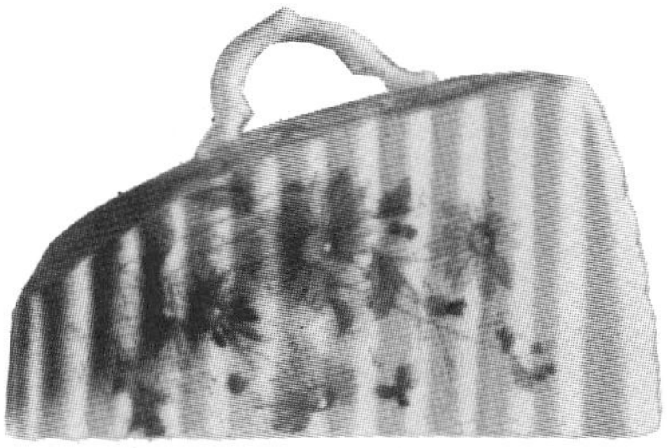

Staffordshire pottery cheese dish with floral decoration. £12

Stilton cheese dish and cover in the style of Wedgwood, circa 1900, 12in. high. (Lots Road Galleries) £100

Wilkinson Ltd. 'bizarre' cheese dish and cover, 1930. £65

A tall Stilton cheese dish and cover with moulded basket weave designs, 12in. high. (Dickinson, Davy & Markham) £65

Booth's blue and white wedge-shaped cheese dish. £20

Late 19th century majolica circular section cheese dish and cover, the lid with a handle in the shape of a recumbent cow, 10½in. diam. £50

Late 19th century majolica cheese dish with domed cover, 10in. diam. (Robt. W. Skinner Inc.) £250

A George Jones majolica cheese dome and stand. (Dreweatts) £360

Early 19th century Chamberlain's Worcester dish. £462

CHILDREN'S BOOKS

As with annuals, the prime motivation for collecting children's books is nostalgia. Some people merely wish to re-read books from their childhood while others wish to amass collections of fine first editions. This means that a 'reading copy', ie. rather worn copy of a later edition of Richard Crompton's William books can be had for £1 while a scarce first edition with dust wrapper of the same book may cost £20. Popular subjects for collecting are early chromolithographed colour books, alphabets, artists such as Mabel Lucie Atwell, and also novels by Enid Blyton, W. E. Johns, Frank Richards etc. There are some artists whose work alone sells a book – Lear, Cruikshank, Tenniel, Ernest Shepherd who illustrated so many of A. A. Milne's books, Arthur Rackham, E. H. Detmold, Jessie M. King and Kay Nielsen (a man, by the way). Fairy story books by Andrew Lang were often illustrated by people like Austen Dobson, Linley Sanbourne, Kate Greenaway, T. Bowick and Randolph Caldecott.

Early children's books like Hornbooks and Chapbooks are of course immensely valuable but they do not turn up every day and when they do the prices they fetch ensure that they will be bought up by libraries or learned institutions.

Every second hand bookshop has its children's section and most collectors combine purchases from these with books bought from specialist mail order dealers.

Condition is all important and because the books were often given rough handling by their original owners those in pristine condition are very rare – and consequently very highly priced when they come up for sale.

Pip and Squeak Annual 1931. £20

Bubbles, Volume 7. £18

Arabian Nights – illustrated by A. E. Jackson. £15

Chatterbox 1907. £7

Peter Pan and Wendy – illustrated by Mabel Lucie Attwell. £25

Alice in Wonderland 1919 – illustrated by Mabel Lucie Attwell. £30

(Lynn Private Collection, Tyne & Wear)

Rover Book for Boys 1940.
£10

Baby's Opera – illustrated by Walter Crane. £40

Greyfriars Holiday Annual 1921. £20

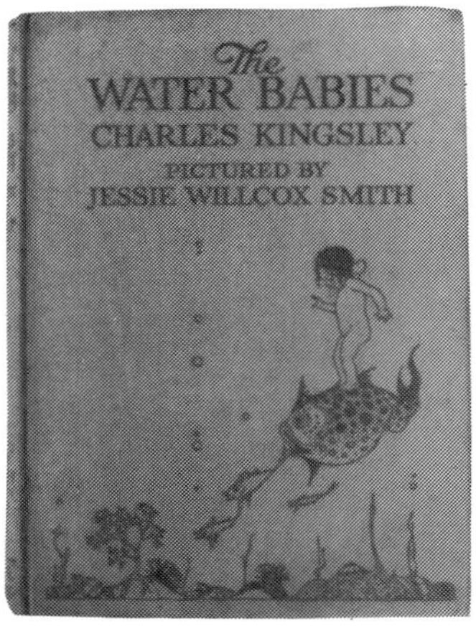

Water Babies 1938 – illustrated by Jessie Wilcox Smith.
£22

The Magic Doorway. £8

Peggy and Joan – illustrated by Honor Appleton. £9

Merry Hearts 1896. £36

The Oojah Annual. £6

Little Wide-Awake 1890.
£24

(Lynn Private Collection, Tyne & Wear)

Mickey Mouse Annual 1945. £10

Treasure Island 1929 — illustrated by Rowland Hilder. £10

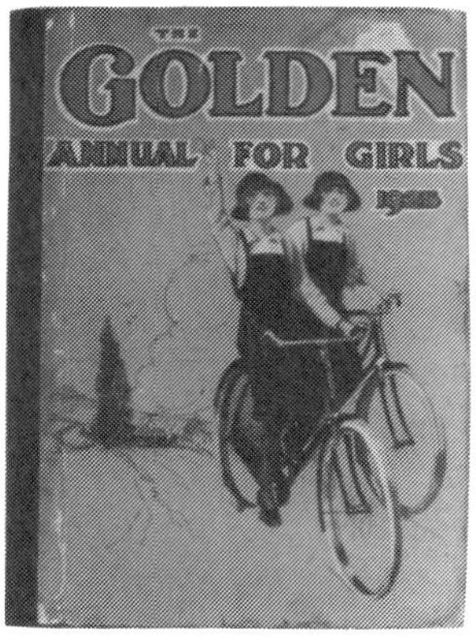

Golden Annual for Girls 1925. £7

Big Book of Mother Goose, has revolving disc of hunt scene in cover. £12

Armchair Story Book 1937. £8

Playbox Annual 1918. £16

My Book of Ships 1913. £5

Wilfred's Annual 1930. £16

My Favourite Annual 1933. £8

(Lynn Private Collection, Tyne & Wear)

CIGARETTE CARDS

Cigarette cards were the 'commercial breaks' of the 1870's until the end of the Second World War. During that time more than 5,000 sets of cards were produced ranging in subject over every possible aspect of life and interests from royalty to railway trains.

Before the arrival of the cardboard slide-action packet, cigarettes were presented in a thin paper packet with a piece of card inserted to protect the cigarettes from damage.

American manufacturers with a keen eye for the promotional main chance were the first to put a picture on the cards and around 1885 W.D. & H.O. Wills of Bristol became the first firm to issue these cigarette cards in Britain. They were an immediate success and soon eagerly collected by youngsters throughout the land.

Many of the cards were of high artistic merit and since most offer some information on the subject illustrated on the other side, a collection soon became an important source of general knowledge on an abundant range of subjects and made up a richly illustrated history of the times. Early cards show a preference for Kings and Queens and famous statesmen but later issues encompass an endless variety of topics – Sports Personalities, Air Raid Precautions, Stars of Screen and Stage, How to Swim, Do You Know and so on.

Nowadays collectors tend to be of more mature years and collections very valuable assets indeed. A complete set of Taddy's Clowns issued early this century in a series of twenty sold recently for the amazing sum of £4,000. It is important always to bear in mind that the condition of cigarette cards has a direct bearing on their value and dog eared, creased or marked sets are worth considerably less than those in pristine condition.

British Warriors – Series of 50. 1912. £75

Cope's Golfers – Series of 50. 1904. £275

Heroes – Series, unnumbered 50 – 2nd 51-75. 1916-17. £80 and £65

Clowns & Circus Artistes – Series of 20. £4,000

Photocards – Rosella Towne – Continuous Series. 1939.£8

Types of the British Army – Series of 50. 1898. £350

Arms and Armour – Series of 50. 1909. £75

Boy Scouts – Series of 50. 1911. £40

Association Cup Winners – Series of 50. 1930. £6

Lawn Tennis Strokes – Series of 30. 1924/25. £14

Household Hints – Series of 50. 1925. £14

With Captain Scott at the South Pole – Series of 25. 1908. £35

Women on War Work – Series of 50. 1916. £80

Boxer's – Series of 125. 1915. £250

Music Hall Artistes – Series of 50. 1913. £75

Broadcasting – Series of 50. 1935. £5

Kings of Speed – Series of 50. 1939. £3

Famous Jockeys – Series of 25. 1910. £100

CIGARETTE CASES

Some indication of the widespread popularity of the smoking habit can be seen in the abundance of delightful cigarette cases on the market today. This is a popular subject for collectors, mainly because they are plentiful, attractive and, although they were designed to house only the smaller cigarettes, in use they re-create the elegance of times past.

Cigarette cases were made from gold, silver, tortoiseshell, papier mache and enamel ware. The box lid was usually a feature of the decoration and here the variety is infinite. They may be inset with precious stones, engraved, painted or inlaid with contrasting materials. The earliest examples are of formal design, demonstrating the skills of the silversmith and engraver, but after it became fashionable for women to smoke, the designs take on the bold and colourful patterns of the modernist era.

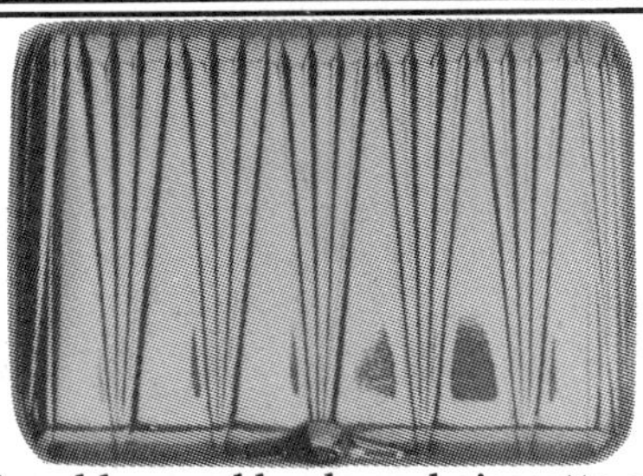

An oblong gold coloured cigarette case with cabochon bluestone pushpiece, with Swedish control marks, 3¼in. long. (Christie's) £810

A white metal and enamel cigarette case, the enamel by F. Zwichl, circa 1920. (Christie's) £1,944

A 1930's cigarette case, silver and two-colour gold coloured metal, with stripes of black lacquer, 11.75cm. wide. £350

A Continental plated cigarette case enamelled with a collie dog on a sky background, circa 1910. (Phillips) £150

An Austrian enamel cigarette case, signed 'Schleiertanz', circa 1895. (Phillips) £500

An Edwardian gilt lined cigarette case, R.C., Birmingham, 1905. (Christie's) £200

A silver and enamel cigarette case by I. Khlebnikov, Moscow, circa 1880, 9.5cm. £690

An Austrian cigarette case applied with two-colour gold and gem set monograms and facsimile signatures, circa 1895. (Phillips) £520

An Art Deco sterling silver cigarette case with black and silver ground and red enamel zigeraut decoration. (Robt. W. Skinner Inc.) £161

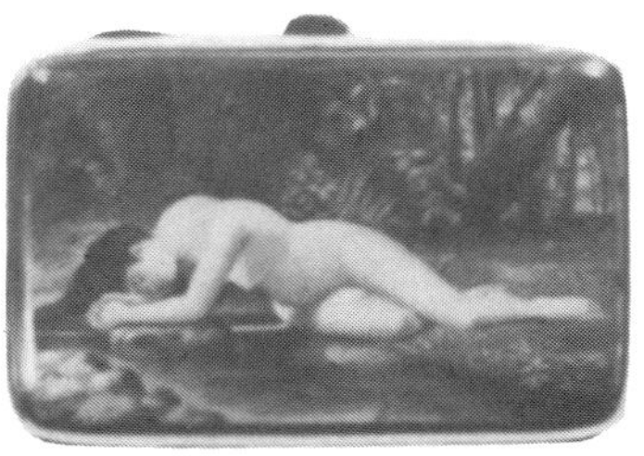

A Victorian cigarette case, the cover enamelled with a nude girl lying beside a stream, Birmingham, 1887. (Phillips) £400

CIGARETTE LIGHTERS

Most of the old cigarette lighters on the market today date from around 1900, and there are still many interesting and unusual examples available at a very modest price.

This is a good area for investment. Particularly in the early experimental types and patented examples which demonstrate a skilful facility in combining ideas to good effect.

There is a combined battery operated torch and petrol lighter, an evening purse cum dance card lighter and a lighter skilfully disguised to conceal a cosmetic compact.
Some of the most interesting lighters date from the period of the first World War when they were handmade from shell cases and other sundry equipment.

'Mondain', a Dunhill patterned 9ct. gold petrol lighter, gold marks for 1950, 4.7cm. high. (Christie's) £259

A Dunhill 'Bijou' lady's 18ct. plain gold petrol lighter, Pat. 143752 Fab. Suisse, 3.2cm. high. (Christie's) £324

A Tiffany & Co. Douglass petrol lighter, patterned yellow metal, stamped 14 Karat Solid gold, 5cm. high. (Christie's) £151

'Mondain', a Dunhill 9ct. plain gold petrol lighter, Pat. No. 143752, gold marks for 1929, 4.3cm. high. (Christie's) £216

Zetron 'Dunhill' style plated lighter. £1

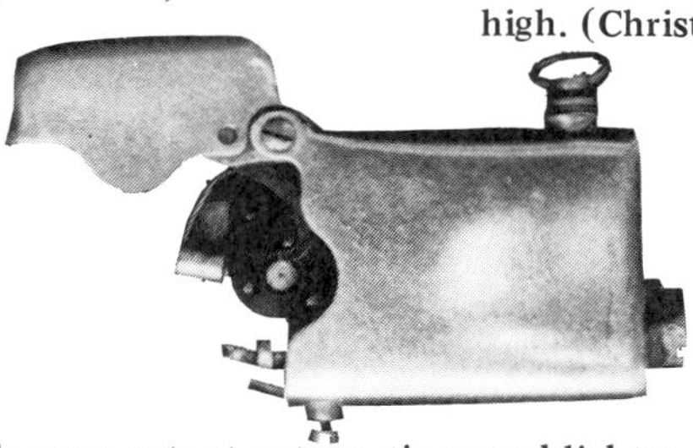

Rare Thorens patent automatic petrol lighter. £12

Osmond alloy petrol lighter in the Dunhill style. £2

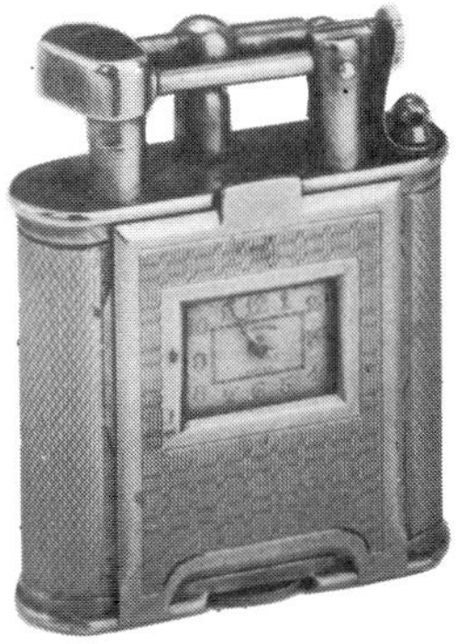

A 9ct. gold combined cigarette lighter and watch by Dunhill, the base stamped Made in Switzerland, 5.3cm. high. (Lawrence Fine Art) £605

Late 19th century spelter table lighter. £28

An Alfred Dunhill silver gilt and enamel cigarette box and lighter, London hallmarks for 1929. (Christie's) £756

An unusual early 'Penny' petrol lighter. £8

CIGARETTE PACKETS

Sixty or seventy years ago small boys used to stand outside tobacconists asking 'Got any fag cards, mister?'. In the late forties youngsters went around picking up empty packets and tearing off the fronts. Cards had been discontinued during the war and the packet front was a sort of substitute.

Things are on a firmer footing now with over 100 serious collectors in this country. There is also a keen following abroad, especially in Brazil, Czechoslovakia, Hungary and the U.S.A.

The formation of the British Cigarette Packet Collectors' Club in 1980 coincided with the publication of the one and only book on the subject of cigarette packet design, Cigarette Pack Art by Chris Mullen, published by Hamlyn. The club was the brainchild of Mr Nat Chait, a retail tobacconist from Richmond in Surrey whose knowledge of the trade over many years is unsurpassed, while his collection of items of pre-1914 vintage is probably the finest in the country.

Collectors ages range between 9 and 69. Collections range in size from a few hundred to tens of thousands.

The current world record holder, Mr Vernon Young, has in excess of 60,000. Compared with cigarette cards prices are low for the hobby is relatively new, and as a consequence the field for research is large. Cigarettes have sold in Britain since 1851. General awareness regarding their packaging did not come about for almost 100 years.

Further information regarding the collectors' club can be had from Mr Hilary Humphries, 15 Dullingham Road, Newmarket, Cambs. CB8 9JT.

'All Gay', packet of five cigarettes at 1d., by W. J. Harris, circa 1900. £5

'Navy Cut', packet of twenty cigarettes, by the Army & Navy Stores Ltd., circa 1935. £3

'Nutcracker', packet of five cigarettes at 1d. by Gallaher, circa 1900. £5

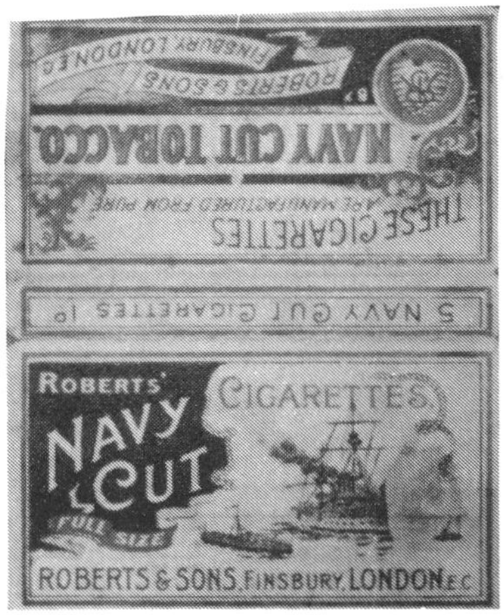

'Roberts Navy Cut', packet of five cigarettes at 1d., by Roberts & Sons, circa 1900. £5

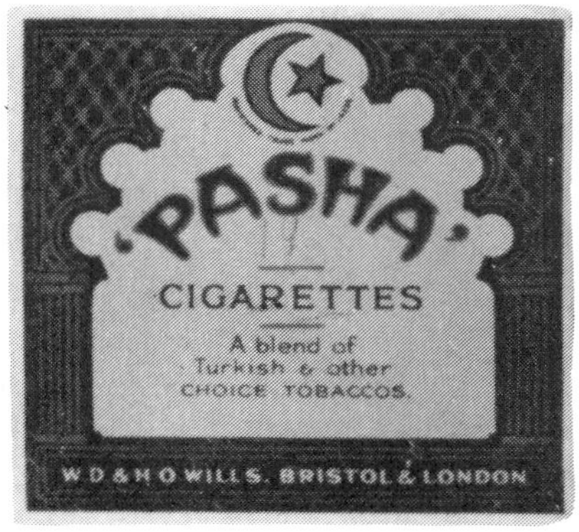

Pasha, packet of 20 cigarettes, W. D. & H. O. Wills, U.K. £1

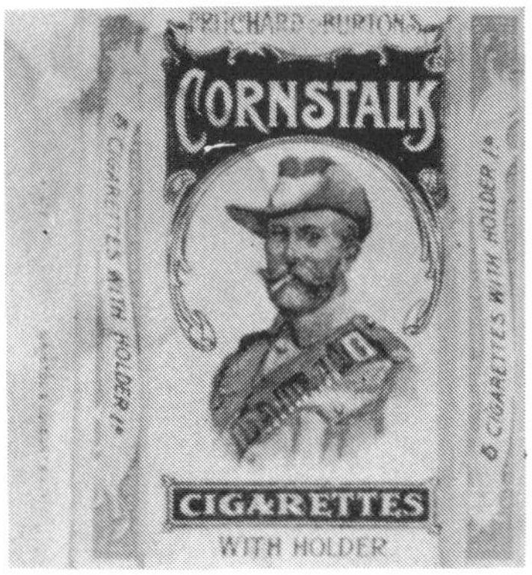

'Cornstalk', packet of five cigarettes at 1d., by Pritchard & Burton, circa 1900. £5

CLARICE CLIFF

Clarice Cliff, who was apprenticed to A.J. Wilkinson Ltd., and later became art director at both the Royal Staffordshire Pottery and a subsidiary company Newport Pottery, produced vases, jars and tableware in a glazed pottery painted in combinations of vibrant yellow, orange and red, or purple, green, blue and orange. These works are distinctive not only in colour content but often in shape. One of the better known examples is a tea set moulded in the shape of corn on the cob and painted yellow.

Patterns to look for include Bizarre, Inspiration Bizarre, Biarritz, Crocus and Fantasque. Although most pieces are easy to identify and there are still many good examples on the market, trade tends to be between collectors and the prices high.

A superb wall plaque by Clarice Cliff painted with a scene inspired by Diaghilev's costume design for The Ballet Russe. (Christie's) £8,000

A Clarice Cliff Bizarre cubist breakfast set painted with geometric designs in red, blue, green and ochre, circa 1931, (Christie's) £500

A Clarice Cliff 'Fantasque' single-handled 'Isis' vase, printed marks, 24.6cm. high. (Lawrence Fine Art) £308

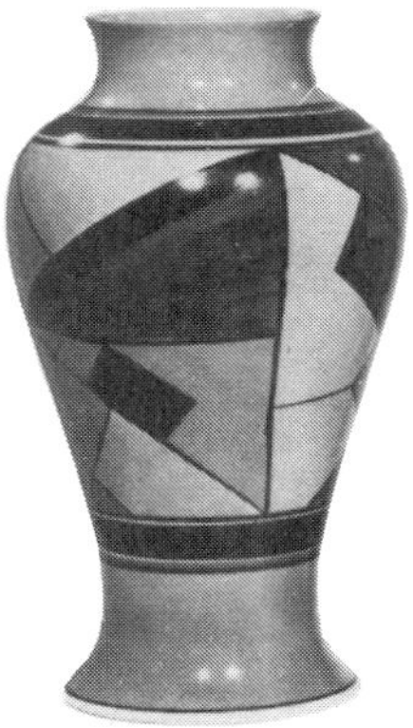

A Clarice Cliff Fantasque baluster shaped vase, 16¼in. high. (Christie's) £1,100

A Clarice Cliff Bizarre oviform jug in the 'Snake Tree' pattern, 6¾in. high. (Christie's) £350

A Clarice Cliff 'Inspiration' vase of tall baluster shape, circa 1930, 41cm. high. (Christie's) £3,240

A Clarice Cliff Bizarre circular wall charger, 45.6cm. diam. (Christie's) £378

BRACKET CLOCKS

Earliest examples resembled truncated grandfather clocks, having square brass faces and plain ebony cases – though they sometimes had a little gilt enrichment. There is a glazed door at the rear, through which can be seen the finely engraved backplate, and a handle on the top enables the piece to be carried from room to room. All English bracket clocks run for at least eight days without rewinding, and nearly all early examples have a fusee movement. This, in the simplest terms, is a top-shaped brass contraption which houses the mainspring whose unwinding is controlled by means of gut, wire or something similar to a miniature bicycle chain coiled round the outside of the 'top'.
Continental clock movements – which can be recognised by the gear teeth set actually on the drum containing the mainspring – are not as sought-after as their English counterparts – whose drums are toothless.

CARRIAGE CLOCKS

Clocks intended for use whilst travelling – with their spring-driven movements – had been used to a small degree since the sixteenth century but they never really caught on until the French clockmakers began to produce them en masse in the 19th century.

Carriage clocks made during the early 19th century usually had quite fine cast brass cases, with thick bevelled glass windows resting in grooves in the frame. The glass at the top was large; later it became much smaller and was let into a metal plate. Carrying handles are usually round on these early 19th century clocks, tapering towards the ends and, because there is often a repeat button on the top front edge, the handles usually fold backwards only.

A red walnut quarter repeating bracket clock, signed on the chapter ring Asselin, London, 19in. high. (Lawrence Fine Art) £935

A George II ebonised grand sonnerie bracket clock, the dial signed Thos. Hughes, London, 9¾in. high. (Christie's) £5,400

A Charles II ebonised striking bracket clock, the square dial signed Hen. Jones London, 16in. high. (Christie's) £3,240

A 19th century French ormolu carriage clock, the lever movement striking on a gong with push repeat and alarm, 8½in. high. (Phillips) £750

Late 19th century French brass repeating alarm carriage clock, the dial signed E. Caldwell & Co., Philadelphia, 7½in. high. (Reeds Rains) £780

A 19th century French gilt brass carriage clock, signed on the back plate E. Dent, Paris, 944, 5½in. high. (Phillips) £1,850

LANTERN CLOCKS

The first truly domestic timepieces were called lantern clocks. Proper old lantern clocks run for thirty hours and only have an hour hand – the minute hand was not introduced until about 1690 – but this is not to say that a clock with only one hand dates necessarily from the 17th century, for the smaller, local clockmakers continued to turn out the less complicated, one-handed timepieces for a further hundred years.

Earliest examples either stood on a bracket or were equipped with an iron ring at the back. This allowed the clock to be hung on a nail driven into the wall and it was levelled and steadied by means of spikes at the base.
Many of the early lantern clocks had a weight supported on a rope.

LONGCASE CLOCKS

At first, faces were eight to nine inches square, of brass, with flowers and scrolls engraved in their centres. These increased to about ten inches square by the 1680's, when the wider cases were introduced. From the beginning of the 18th century, faces were usually twelve inches square, or larger following the introduction of the arch.
This was in widespread use by 1720 and, on early examples, was often less than a semicircle.
After 1750, an engraved brass or silvered face without a chapter ring was often used, and from 1775, a cast brass or enamelled copper face was introduced.

During the last quarter of the 18th century, manufacturers turned their attentions to quantity rather than quality, making such economies as the use of white painted wood or iron faces after 1790.

Wing alarm lantern clock, circa 1700, 15½in. high. £1,500

An Italian brass and iron lantern clock, circa 1700, 35cm. high. (Christie's) £3,000

A brass lantern clock for the Turkish market, signed John Ellis, London, 36cm. high. (Christie's) £808

A lantern clock, the broad chapter ring signed Thatcher Cranbrook, 13½in. high. £1,540

Late 17th century Swiss clock with shaped rectangular iron dial, 40cm. high. (Christie's) £1,500

An early lantern clock, the 7in. dial signed Thomas Knifton at the (crossed keys) Lothbury Fecit, 12in. high. £2,200

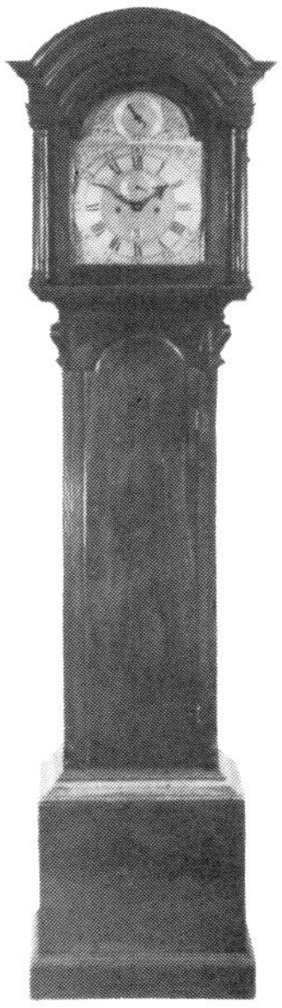

A Georgian mahogany longcase clock, signed on a cartouche John Hart, Yarmouth, 7ft.6in. high. (Phillips) £2,000

A Gustav Stickley oak tall case clock, circa 1902-04, 71in. high. (Robt. W. Skinner Inc.) £5,381

A 19th century mahogany longcase clock, the dial signed Brysons, Edinburgh, 6ft.6in. high. (Phillips) £800

MANTEL CLOCKS

As a basic rule French mantel clocks are nearly all decoration while English models are nearly all clock.

Early French makers to look for are Lepine, Janvier, Amand, Lepaute and Thuret, who started to use a great deal of elaborate scrollwork at the end of the 17th century. If you find a clock by any of these makers you have certainly found a clock. Things to look for are a verge escapement – which is loosely indicated by a horizontally turning crown wheel with sharp teeth just above the pendulum – a painted face or porcelain numerals and a winding hole placed in the face where you least expect it. Pendulums should be pear shaped bobs on brass rods.

By the 19th century, everyone decided they wanted one of these flashy French clocks to add an air of opulence to the lounge. Consequently, manufacturers began doing a spot of overtime.

The word that really matters in any description is 'ormolu' – that is, it is made of a hard metal, such as brass, which is rough cast before being chiselled and engraved by hand and, finally, coated with a thin amalgam of gold and mercury.

Cheaper 19th century mass produced clocks have a similar appearance – at first glance – but they are made of spelter. This is a soft metal which is simply cast and gilded. Clocks with decoration of this kind should sell for about a quarter of the price of the ormolu pieces. The infallible test is to scratch the underside of the clock; if the gold colour comes away to reveal grey metal, it's spelter, if brass is revealed it is ormolu. Another test is to tap the case sharply with a coin. If the sound is sharp and pingy, you have hard metal; if it is a dull thud, you have soft.

An early 19th century ormolu mantel clock, 1ft.9in. high. (Phillips) £680

A French Louis XVI style black marble and ormolu mounted mantel clock, 1ft. 9in. high. (Phillips) £950

A Liberty & Co. Tudric pewter 'Architectural' mantel clock, circa 1920, 7¼in. high. (Robt. W. Skinner Inc.) £520

An Empire carved mahogany shelf clock, by Riley Whiting, Conn., circa 1825, 29½in. high. (Robt. W. Skinner Inc.) £171

A Regency rosewood mantel timepiece, the dial signed Arnold & Dent, Strand, London, 10¼in. high. (Phillips) £650

A Louis XVI white marble and ormolu mounted mantel clock, the dial signed Hardy A Paris, 1ft.2in. high. (Phillips) £850

SKELETON CLOCKS

It is a widely held belief that skeleton clocks – almost all of which were made during the 19th century – were the work of apprentices, made during their final year of study and so designed that examiners could observe the working and workmanship of each part with a minimum of effort.

While this might well have been the practice from which the style originated, its popularity throughout the Victorian period necessitated the masters' involvement in their manufacture. English models are of fret-cut brass, with silvered brass chapter rings, and are usually to be found on wooden bases beneath glass domes – for they are naturally prone to dust damage.

Another variety is the French skeleton clock. This is usually much smaller, having solid front and backplates – often engraved on later examples – and enamelled chapter rings.

WALL CLOCKS

Although wall clocks of a sort had been in existence for quite some time, it was not until Pitt imposed a tax on clocks, in 1797, that the impetus was given for the manufacture of large wall clocks which could be hung in public places for all to see. This is why many large wall clocks are still known today as Act of Parliament Clocks.

By the arrival of the Regency period, wall clocks had reduced in size to about eighteen inches in width, many veneered in rosewood with brass scroll inlay. The larger, Victorian, wall clocks are referred to as Vienna regulators and have a mahogany case and an elaborate pendulum. You will most probably find one driven by means of a spring, but those employing weights are better quality as a rule.

15in. brass skeleton timepiece with strike and chain drive, under dome. (Worsfolds) £230

An English brass striking skeleton clock of York Minster type, on wood base with glass dome, 59cm. high. (Christie's) £1,313

A brass three-train 'Westminster Abbey' skeleton clock, striking on gong and nest of eight bells having mercury pendulum, 24in. high. (Andrew Grant) £4,200

A George III mahogany wall timepiece, the 12in. silvered dial signed Jefferys, London, 1ft.4½in. high. (Phillips) £1,200

A late 17th century Italian day and night clock, signed Jean Baptiste Gonnon a Milan, 20 x 23½in. (Lawrence Fine Art) £2,530

A Georgian mahogany wall timepiece, the 1ft.7in. diam. painted wood dial signed Field, Bath, 3ft.7in. high. (Phillips) £600

CLOISONNE

Cloisonne is a technique of enamelling developed in the 10th century. It consists of soldering fine wires on to a solid base to form a pattern of small cells which are then filled with coloured enamel: the wire acting as a wall to prevent adjacent colours from running together. When fired, the wires remain visible and become an integral part of the design.
This method differs from Champleve enamel where actual depressions are cut into the metal base and then filled with enamel paste and fired as before.
Although a few older pieces are to be found, most of the examples seen today date from the 19th century when enamel was returned to popularity by Alexis Falize. He was a French silversmith who began importing and selling Chinese cloisonne articles while also adapting the technique for his own products.

Late 19th century cloisonne cabinet decorated in various coloured enamels, 14.5 x 9 x 12cm. (Christie's)
£750

One of a pair of 19th century cloisonne enamel figures of zebras.
£56,000

A cloisonne enamel dish, the blue ground decorated with a quail, 18in. diam. (Lawrence Fine Art)
£110

A cloisonne enamel and gilt bronze mounted censer and domed cover with large lotus finial, 18th century, 53cm. high. (Christie's)
£2,800

A 17th century cloisonne enamel pear-shaped vase with taotie and loose ring handles, 39cm. high. (Christie's) £648

A 16th century cloisonne enamel tripod circular dish decorated on a pale-blue ground with a meander of peony and hibiscus, 19.8cm. diam. (Christie's)
£700

Late 19th century cloisonne enamel oviform vase with flaring neck, 61.5cm. high. (Christie's) £3,000

A pair of 19th century cloisonne enamel and gilt bronze cockerels, 17½in. high. (Bermondsey)
£1,500

COMICS, BRITISH

Although nostalgia is the main motivation for comic collecting, an increasing number of people now appreciate comic art for its own sake and a growing amount of research is being carried out by individuals all over the country to identify and catalogue the various artists and authors.

As with any hobby, the most interesting and valuable collections are those which have been built up around a central theme, for example, the work of a particular author or artist, or stories of a particular type. One of the most widely collected artists is Dudley Watkins who drew Desperate Dan for the 'Dandy', Lord Snooty for the 'Beano' and many other comic strips and story illustrations for D. C. Thomson.

Rowland Turner who drew several issues of the 'Super Detective Library' and 'Thriller Picture Library' is another artist whose work is in great demand and any comic containing examples of his art commands a premium price.

The ill-fated boy's magazine the 'Ranger' which only lasted for forty weeks in 1965-66 contained the now legendary Trigan Empire, magnificently drawn by Don Lawrence and printed in full colour. Other artists of note are Eric Parker and Frank Hampson who drew the innovative Dan Dare for the 'Eagle'.

The most popular stories tend to be those of the science fiction/fantasy type. The comic 'TV21' (1965-69) specialises in comic strips, best of Jerry Anderson's TV series 'Thunderbird', 'Fireball XL5', 'Sting Ray' and 'Super Car' and copies of this comic changes hands at up to £3 each.

To bring us up-to-date '2000 A.D.', with its science fiction comic strip, has become something of a cult and early issues, only five or six years old, may bring up to £2 each.

The Magnet, Jan. 15th 1921. £2

The Union Jack. £2

The Dandy, Dec. 21st 1957. £1.50

The Beano Comic, July 30th 1938. £300

Lion, Jan. 17th 1953. 80p

Film Fun. 80p

The Surprise. £2

The Greyfriars Herald, July 17th 1920. £1.50

Lucky Lester's Lone Hand. £2

Radio Fun, Oct. 15th 1938. £30–£50

The Pioneer, Feb. 10th 1934. £5–£15

The Victor, June 25th 1966. 40p

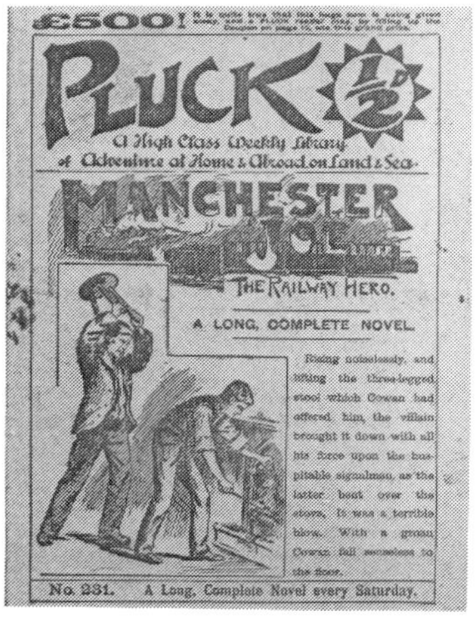

Pluck. £2

The Kinema Comic, Jan. 30th 1932. £2–£4

The Pilot, Oct. 5th 1935. £5–£15

COMICS, AMERICAN

American comics are collected by enthusiasts all over the world reflecting the extensive distribution they have always had. Few collectibles have such a huge range of items available and such a vast range of prices. Action Comics Number 1, if you could find a copy would cost you around £7,500 while at the other extreme scores of titles are readily available at 10 to 20 pence each.

It was in Action Comics launched in June 1938 that the far-famed Superman character made his debut and then only after his creators Joe Schuster and Jerry Seigal had seen their work rejected by almost every major publishing house in America.

Essential reading is the Overstreet Price Guide which lists and values all the American comics ever published in its 350 plus pages.

Detective Comics, No. 28, June 1939, 'Batman'. £1,000

Batman, No. 1, Spring Issue 1940, 'The Batman and Robin'. £2,500

More Fun Comics, No. 47, September 1939. £25

All Star Comics, No. 1, Summer Issue, 1940. £600

Action Comics, No. 1, June 1938, 'Superman'. £7,500

Adventure Comics, No. 72, March 1942, 'Sandman'. £300

Movie Comics, No. 1, April 1939. £30

All-American Comics, No. 1, April 1939. £150

COOKERY BOOKS

Part of the fascination of collecting old cookery books is to notice how taste and ingredients are very much from the period in which the books were written.
Although a few exist from the 17th and 18th centuries they are very expensive for it was not until the latter part of the 19th century when there was something akin to a revolution in the kitchen, that a wide variety were produced, notably by Mrs Beeton and Fannie Farmer.
Of particular interest are those books which still contain colour plates depicting the culinary delights of the period together with hints on how to manage a large household. These often list the uses of all the equipment and pots and pans in the Victorian kitchen which is particularly fascinating.
Occasionally a personal cookery book comes onto the market with hand written recipes and reminders of festivals and important events.

Journey of Discovery, All Round Our House, 1857. £7

Mrs. Beeton's Cookery Book, 1906. £8

Mrs. Beeton's 'Cookery Book', 1930's. £2

'How to Live Well on 5/- a Week Per Head', by L. Rutherford Skey, 1910. £3

'Oxo Meat Cookery! – the Oxo way', by Elizabeth Craig, 1930's. £1

Philip Harben's Cookery Encyclopedia, first edition, 1955. £4

'The Recipe Book of the Mustard Club', by Colman's, 1930's. £4

'Tasty Entrees', by Miss C. L. Howland, circa 1900. £3

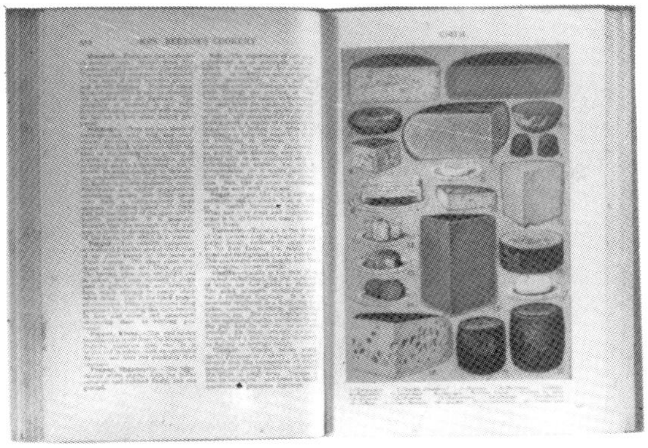

Mrs. Beeton's 'All About Cookery' by Ward Lock. £5

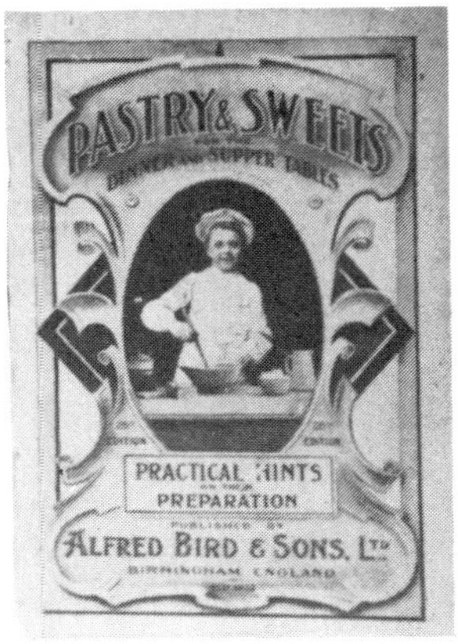

'Pastry & Sweets For The Dinner and Supper Tables', by Alfred Bird & Sons Ltd., circa 1900. £2

Mrs. Beeton's 'Hints to Housewifes', 'Home Running on Labour Saving Lines', by Ward Lock & Co. Ltd., 1930's. £5

Mrs. Beeton's Household Management, by Ward Lock & Co., 1936. £20

'500 Sixpenny Recipes', by Nora Fletcher, 1934. £2

'Cookery for Invalids and the Convalescent', by Herman-Senn, 1910. £2

'The Eat Less Meat Book', by Mrs. C. S. Peel, 1914-18. £3

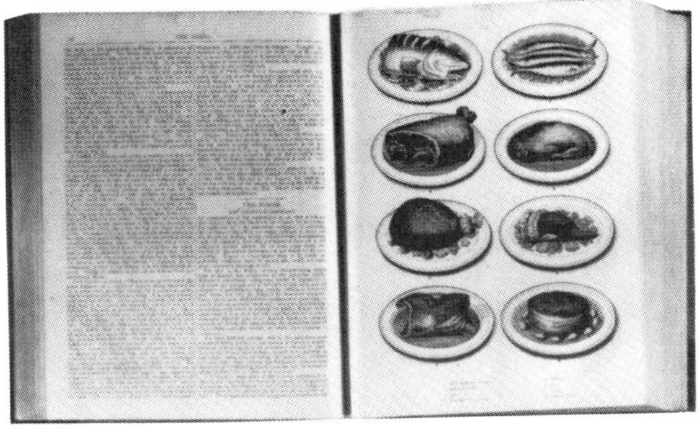

Cassell's Household Guide 'A Complete Encyclopedia of Domestic and Social Economy'. £15

Mrs. Beeton's 'All-About Cookery', New Edition, 1913. £10

COPPER & BRASS

Copper and brass have been used for making an enormous range of generally functional household articles on a commercial scale for over 300 years. Originally there were many flaws on the surface but this was alleviated with improved production methods in the 18th century.

Be it candlesticks or kettles, trivets or jelly moulds, a choice often has to be made as to what to collect but all will enhance the home if you don't mind the cleaning.

With early pieces it is often the patina built up over centuries which accounts for most of the value so care in cleaning is recommended.

There are many reproductions on the market, some very difficult to identify so don't hesitate to ask in antiques shops. Most dealers are willing to pass on the benefit of their experience and knowledge and all are obliged to give an accurate description.

Victorian brass jardiniere on paw feet, 1880. (British Antique Exporters) £41

Late 19th century brass gong with hammer. (British Antique Exporters) £75

Victorian copper kettle, circa 1850. (British Antique Exporters) £49

Victorian brass coal bucket, 1880. (British Antique Exporters) £54

Late 19th century Art Nouveau style brass coal box. (British Antique Exporters) £61

A pair of Federal late 18th/ early 19th century bell metal andirons, 24in. high. (Christie's) £916

A circular embossed brass double ended box, 1.7/8in. diam., with bust of Duke of Wellington on one side. (Wallis & Wallis) £20

An early 20th century Arts & Crafts hammered copper umbrella stand, 25in. high. (Robt. W. Skinner Inc.) £277

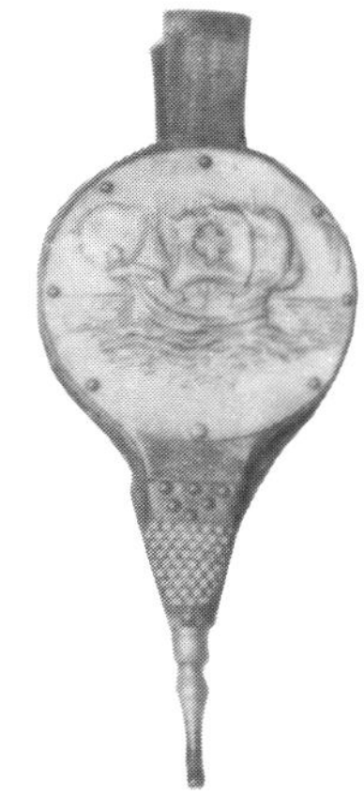

Victorian pressed brass bellows, circa 1880. (British Antique Exporters) £25

A George III brass and steel basket grate, 34¼in. wide, 30½in. high. (Christie's) £4,860

Barlow's patent brass candlestick, Birmingham, England, circa 1839, 7.3/8in. high. (Robt. W. Skinner Inc.) £347

Large embossed brass jardiniere on claw feet. (Ball & Percival) £280

A 17th century brass candlestick engraved 'For the use of ye Company of Joyners and Carpenters', dated 1690, 9in. high. (Gorringes) £6,600

A 16th century European brass alms dish, depicting Adam and Eve in the Garden of Eden, 15¾in. diam. (Robt. W. Skinner Inc.) £207

Victorian copper firescreen with inset mirror, circa 1880. (British Antique Exporters) £32

One of a pair of Anglo-Indian brass jardinieres on later stained oak bases, 41in. high. (Christie's) £2,052

One of a pair of 18th/19th century brass wall sconces, dated 1750, 17¾in. high. £242

A Benham & Froud brass kettle designed by Dr. C. Dresser, on three spiked feet, 24.5cm. high. (Christie's) £324

A Victorian brass and wood paper rack, circa 1880. (British Antique Exporters) £18

Copper milk churn with cover. (Ball & Percival) £66

CORKSCREWS

Most of the corkscrews, or bottle screws, we see around today, date from the middle of the 19th century. Earlier examples do exist, some going back to the 17th century, but these are extremely rare.

The earliest examples were made of steel and consisted of a simple spiral fixed to a wooden handle. It was only later that more complex designs were introduced with handles made of engraved brass, silver, steel, bone, horn and ivory. The handles were often styled in the shape of animals, birds or some more unusual novelty theme.

The Victorian penchant for new inventions ran riot during the 19th century and hundreds of different corkscrew based devices, in all shapes and sizes, were made; many of them patented. Other devices, such as a bottle dusting brush or any number of other small tools, are often incorporated into the handle. Any corkscrew combined with a gadget will be of interest to a collector and this will be reflected in the selling price.

At one time, the corkscrew was one of the essential tools of day to day living. Even miniature scent bottles were sealed with a cork and the ladies often carried small, intricately designed silver versions for this purpose. Sometimes a Victorian housekeeper would attach a small corkscrew, fitted with a hanging loop to her chatelaine, alongside all the other necessary bits and pieces. (The chatelaine being an ornamental bunch of short chains bearing keys, pencil, scissors etc., which is then attached to the belt at the waist. A similar version, in miniature, could be attached to a gentleman's watch chain and, again, a miniature corkscrew was a popular item.)

There was, at one time, a very pleasing custom for a house guest, upon writing to thank his host, to include the gift of a corkscrew, perhaps with some words of praise engraved on the handle.

A nickel plated bar corkscrew 'Original Safety', manufactured by Gaskell & Chambers, 10in. high. £125

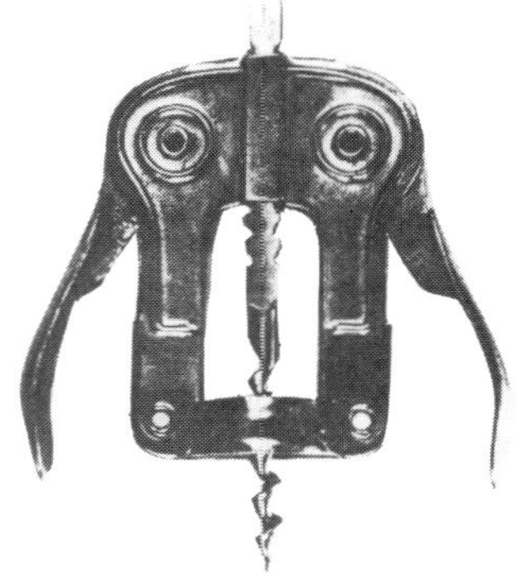

A tinned iron example of a lever corkscrew of the Magic Lever type with perfect 'steep pitched' or 'speed' worm, 8in. long. £38

Pocket folding bow corkscrew in steel, circa 1880, 3in. long closed. £18

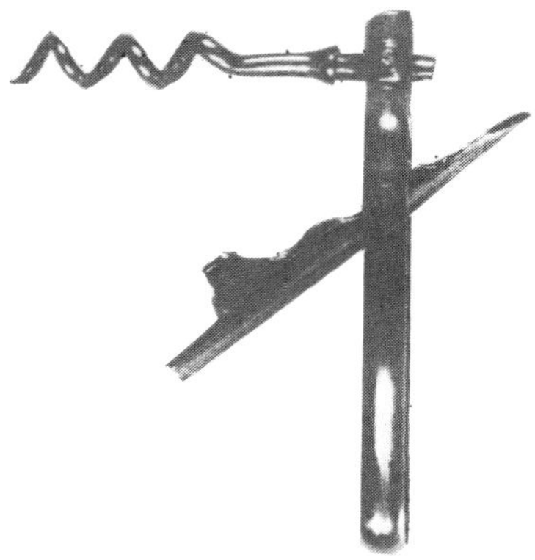

A pocket corkscrew made of steel, stamped Universal Pat. June 27,05 (1905), 5½in. long open. £175

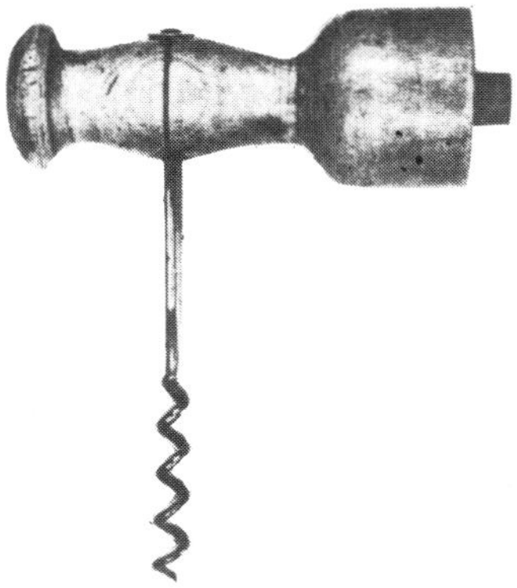

A turned ashwood English corkscrew combined Codd bottle opener with perfect helical worm with 'flat' steel shank, overall height, 5½in. £38

A narrow rack King's Screw corkscrew by Thos. Lund, with perfect turned rosewood crossbar complete with dusting brush inner thread, 7¼in. long closed. £484

COSTUME

Period costume has always held a fascination for collectors so it comes as no surprise when a garment one or two hundred years old fetches a high price.
The current trend, however, shows some astonishing prices paid for clothes from as recent a period as the 1950's.

Elegant dresses of the 20's, 30's and 40's are eagerly sought after by the fashion conscious to be worn today and, all but the rare and flimsy, are likely to be in wearable condition. From the 1900's onward fashionable women were known to change their clothes up to four times a day leaving us the legacy of a multitude of garments showing scant signs of real wear. The named labels to look for are Dior, Cheruit, Chanel, Nini Ricci and Fortuny 'Delphos'.
Clothes that once belonged to well known personalities fall into a category of their own and fetch the high prices of a specialised market.

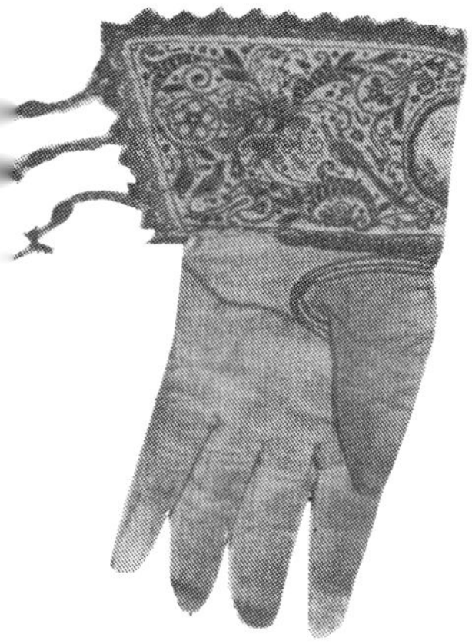

A lady's glove of white kid, the deep cuff of ivory satin lined with pink silk, early 17th century. (Christie's) £280

A Dragon robe, the black gauze ground embroidered with coiling dragons. (Reeds Rains) £620

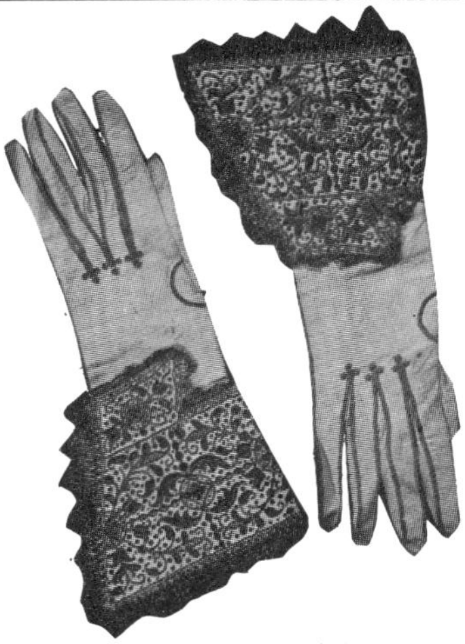

A pair of white kid gloves with deep cuffs of white satin embroidered in silver thread and sequins, mid 17th century. (Christie's) £2,600

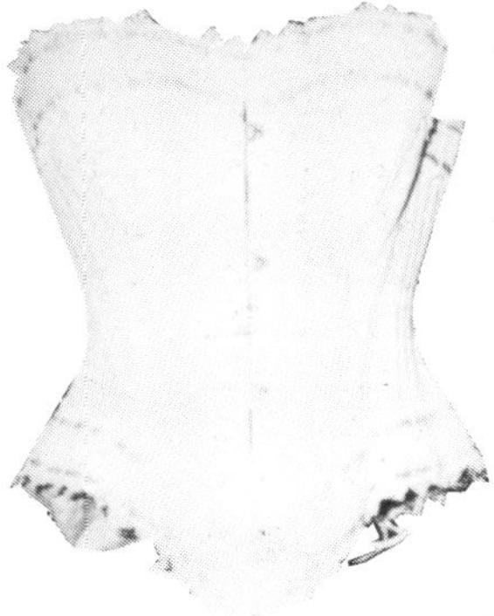

Boned and laced corset in pink cotton with lace trim, French, 1880's. £45

A boy's side fastening tunic of white pique embroidered in red cord with scrolling flowers. (Christie's) £140

A muslin dress with an under-dress of saxe blue silk taffeta, circa 1880. (Christie's) £300

A lady's waistcoat of white cotton quilted in white silk and embroidered in yellow and red wools, English, circa 1730. (Christie's) £2,800

A suit of rust-coloured wool with deep cuffs and wide skirts, circa 1760. (Christie's) £5,000

An open robe of pale yellow silk lustre, the neckline edged with 18th century Binche lace. (Christie's) £1,800

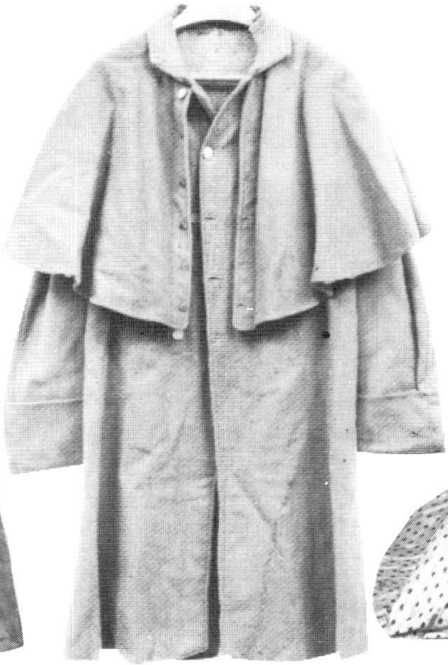

Militia great coat with attached cape, coarse blue wool, Massa., circa 1855. (Robt. W. Skinner Inc.) £530

A mid Victorian orange and purple flowered cream silk dress with boned bodice and slight train. (Dacre, Son & Hartley) £170

A dress of ivory silk woven with satin stripes, the bodice trimmed with ivory satin and with blond lace, lined with silk, circa 1830. (Christie's) £1,400

A dress of pale pink silk figured with sprays of flowers, the sleeves, bodice and hem decorated with pink satin rouleaux, circa 1815. (Christie's) £380

An open robe of cotton printed overall with red and blue convolvulus with red stems against a grey ground, circa 1785. (Christie's) £2,200

A fine full length evening mantle of grey facecloth, by Rouff, 13 Boulevard Hausmann, Paris, 1900. (Christie's) £110

A gentleman's coat of cut velvet woven with patterned pockets, cuffs, collar and trim to front fastening, Italy or France, circa 1760. £260

A jacket and skirt of maroon figured silk brocaded with white stripes sprigged in pink and blue, circa 1770. (Christie's) £2,600

A gentleman's suit of voided velvet woven with pink and black sprigs against a pale blue silk ground, French, circa 1790, together with a waistcoat, circa 1770. (Christie's) £280

A lady's festive jacket with open sleeves, lined with cotton, the couched silver and gold thread embroidery on a red velvet ground, gold braid trim, Albania, mid 19th century. £275

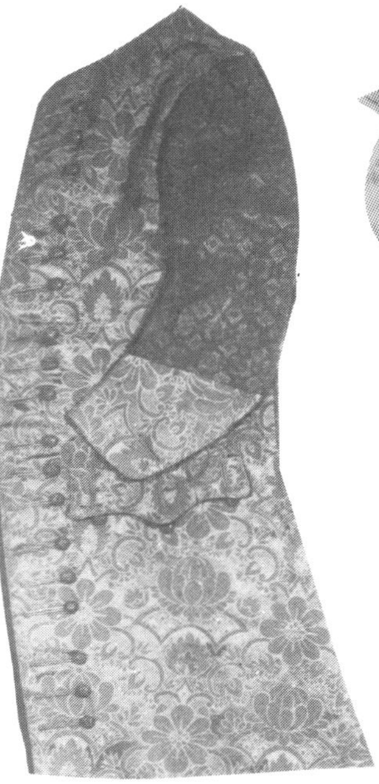

A sleeved waistcoat of emerald green figured, voided silk, woven with sprays of flower heads, English, circa 1730. (Christie's) £900

A dress of ivory satin printed in vertical bands of grey fleck design and a larger pink and grey chine design, circa 1834. (Christie's) £1,200

A gentleman's suit of deep blue satin, French, Lyons, circa 1770. (Christie's) £3,000

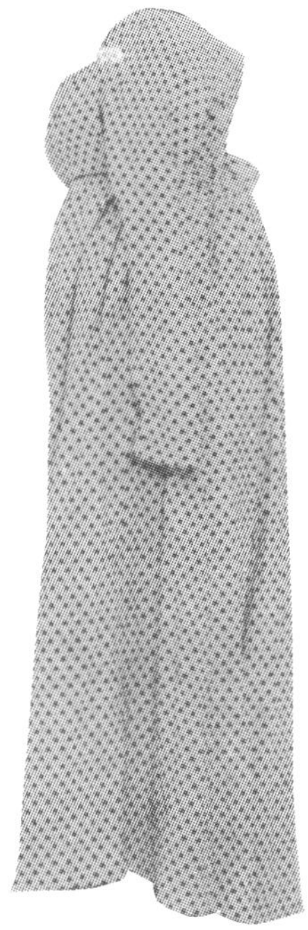

A cotton dress printed with sprigs of brown leaves, with a handkerchief front, circa 1810. (Christie's) £380

CREAM POTS

Cream pots, jars and jugs were used between 1880 and the 1920's for vending different forms of the product including "thick", "clotted", "pure" and "thin" cream. Those of particular interest to collectors still retain the original label printed on the pot – either with an inked rubber stamp or a paper transfer taken from an inked engraved copper plate – before application of the glaze. When fired in a kiln the design was absorbed by the clay and protected by the glaze to give it permanence.
These stoneware containers vary in size from 2in. to 6in. but average about 4in. and were usually rendered airtight by inserting a cork or disc in the mouth of the pot and covering it with a tinfoil seal.

The Ayrshire Market, Galashiels and Selkirk, a grey pot with black printed label of Robbie Burns. £25

Express Dairy, Finchley, a white earthenware pot with blue top and label. £25 – £35

The Ulster Dairy, Belfast, an attractive and desirable pot with sharp sepia pictorial label and high glaze. £100

Bolesworth's Prize Dairy, Loughborough, Leicestershire, an extremely rare pot with a striking black label, although there is a slightly less rare example with a green top.
£250 plus (black)
£200 (green)

Express Dairy, Finchley, a white earthenware pot with dark blue label. Cylindrically shaped pots were tradtionally used for clotted cream. £115 – £140

Strathbogie Dairy, Huntly, an attractive pot with a blue pictorial trade mark. £10 – £12

Minifie's, Weston-Super-Mare, a cylindrical white pot with black transfer, 5in. high. £60

The Imperial Creamery, Glasgow, a rare jar with green glazed top and black label with a pictorial trade mark. £120 – £150

CRESTED CHINA

The value of crested china may be determined by three factors: theme, rarity and condition in that order. The most popular themes are: The Great War, Buildings; Animals (including birds); Transport; Memorials; Statues, Cartoon/Comedy Characters; Comic/Novelty; Sport; Alcohol and Musical Instruments. This list is by no means exhaustive but it does cover the main spheres of interest among collectors. Rarity is self-explanatory; a 'Bomb Thrower' is rarer than a 'Cenotaph' and therefore is worth more. These two factors may be summed up as 'Collectibility', for example a scarce animal would be worth far more than, say, a unique billiken because there is far more demand for the animal from theme collectors. Thus supply and demand play an important part. It should always be borne in mind that even the most attractive and rare crested cup and saucer will never be worth more than a few pounds whereas a rare military piece could command as much as £100.

Condition is the third factor which affects price. Crested china produced by other manufacturers was never as fine as that of the Goss factory. The other producers were not interested in the high standard that Goss set himself, they were only concerned with jumping on the crested china bandwagon and producing wares as quickly and as cheaply as possible for the profitable souvenir trade which was rapidly developing.

Having made the point that crested china factories were not that particular about the quality of their products it follows that many pieces were substandard even before leaving the factory. Such manufacturers' imperfections do not affect value, however, damage occurring in the period subsequent to manufacture such as cracks or chips affect value considerably.

The 'Biddenden Maids', a 12th century pair of Siamese twins. (Goss & Crested China) £40

Carlton 'John Citizen', carrying sack of 'Housing', 'Unemployment' and 'Taxes' probelms. (Goss & Crested China) £70

'Mary Queen of Scots Bed', by Carlton, 90mm. long, a superbly modelled historical piece. (Goss & Crested China) £60

Willow Art cartoon character couple sitting in armchair, Dr. Beetle and Sunny Jim. (Goss & Crested China) £50

Grafton china, 'The Bomb Thrower', 140mm. high. (Goss & Crested China) £110

Carlton child riding donkey, on oval base, can be found inscribed 'This beats going to school'. (Goss & Crested China) £30

CURTAINS

To the untrained eye, a bundle of old curtains in a corner of the attic is precisely that, and no more. If you are having a clear out, and have established that they are the wrong size for the sitting room, wouldn't fit in the back bedroom, then for goodness sake, if they look a bit speculative don't throw them out. Old textiles can be worth money.

A length of fabric designed by, for example, Morris & Co., would be quite a rare find. In 1861, William Morris, along with other well-known painters, an architect and an engineer, set up this company whose aims were, to produce decorative articles of the very finest quality, for 'the people'. His designs, taken from plant and animal forms, are extremely attractive and still very popular today.

The company provided, in today's terms, a complete house furnishing service, supplying everything that could possibly be required within a household, from a stained glass window to a set of teaspoons.

William Morris designed textile in 'peacock and dragon' pattern, circa 1878, 89 x 63in. (Robt. W. Skinner Inc.) £400

One of a set of four Jacobean crewel-work bed hangings, embroidered in coloured wools, 3ft.1in. wide. (Lawrence Fine Art) £2,420

One of a pair of printed plush curtains, 1890's, 130cm. wide. £385

One of a pair of Morris & Co. printed cotton curtains, selvedge with printed Queen Square mark, circa 1876/7, 90cm. wide. £462

One of a set of three wool and silk Templeton's curtains, designed by Bruce Talbert, circa 1880, together with two pelmets. £2,420

A Morris & Co. printed cotton double-sided curtain, selvedge with printed Oxford St. mark, 1891, 181.5cm. wide. £352

One of a pair of Morris & Co. wool curtains and matching pelmet, designed by Wm. Morris, 1880's, 'Bird' pattern, 250 x 240cm. £2,750

One of a pair of early 19th century curtains of cotton, 75 x 64in. (Christie's) £86

DECANTER LABELS

Decanter labels have always struck me as very worthwhile articles to collect, for not only are they small and reasonably plentiful, but there are also rare examples worth hundreds which add spice to the search. They are made in a variety of materials, including silver, enamel, porcelain and Sheffield plate and come in a variety of shapes including oval, shield and rectangular.

Dating from about 1730, they were used in wealthier homes to identify the contents of the opaque bottles of the period, while lesser mortals made do with stuck-on handwritten parchment labels.

Most were individually made until the Victorian period, when mass production took over, but their real demise followed the Grocers' Licences Act of 1860, which allowed wine to be sold in single bottles, provided a paper label indicated their contents.

There are, of course, numerous modern die-stamped reproduction labels to be found, but these are fairly easily distinguishable from the heavier original examples.

A more watchful eye is necessary, however, to spot old labels (usually Madeira) renamed with more saleable titles like brandy or whisky. This practice is indicated by very thin metal on the face, and sometimes old lettering may even be revealed by huffing on the surface.

The rarest labels are those made of Battersea enamel (and I mean Battersea enamel made from 1753 to 1756, not the many other forms of enamel which have attracted the name). The originals are usually quite large, about 7.5cm. across, with a wavy outline, and could be worth hundreds of pounds.

A set of six early Victorian cast swag shape wine labels, by E. J. & W. Barnard, London, 1851, 4oz. (Woolley & Wallis) £380

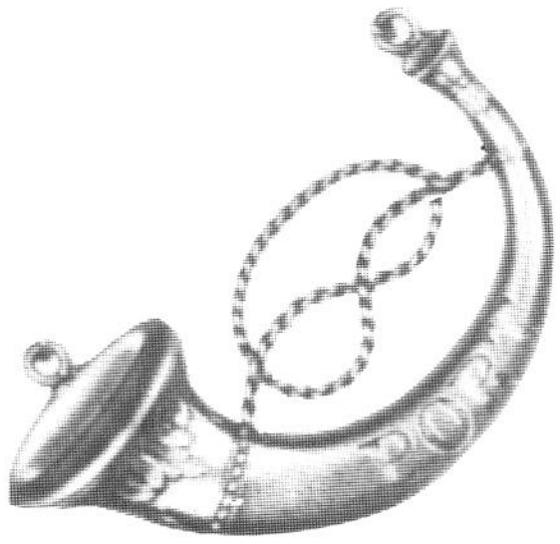

A Victorian stamped-out hunting horn wine label, incised 'Port', by G. Unite, Birmingham, 1857. (Phillips) £300

A Victorian cast wine label, title scroll incised 'Red Constantia', by Rawlings & Sumner, 1843. (Phillips) £380

One of three silver gilt wine labels for Port, Claret and Champagne, by Benjamin Smith, 1808, 3in. high, 7oz.5dwt. (Christie's) £2,484

A George III cast scallop shield wine label, 'Sherry', by Wm. Eley, 1814. (Phillips) £290

A set of three George III cast four-leaf clover wine labels pierced 'Claret' and 'Madeira', probably by B. Smith, London, 1807. (Christie's) £300

DECANTERS

Over the years decanters have changed shape in accordance with styles and a good representative collection will include as many different shapes as possible. The best known are ships' decanters – or Rodneys, mallet shaped decanters, taper decanters perhaps in blue or green, and square decanters – shaped to fit into decanter boxes for fortification during the days of coach travel.

These boxes became less popular when the tantalus with its locking frame system was introduced in the mid 19th century. The tantalus, a case in which decanters are visible but locked up, takes its name from Tantalus, the son of Zeus who, as a punishment, was made to stand in water that ebbed when he would drink, overhung by grapes that drew back when he reached for them!

A cylindrical file-cut decanter and stopper, cut with three rings to the neck, 10in. high. (Christie's) £60

One of a pair of cut glass decanters and stoppers of club shape, circa 1820. (Christie's) £432

A green baluster decanter with lozenge stopper, 9½in. high, and a blue decanter, 9in. high. (Christie's) £160

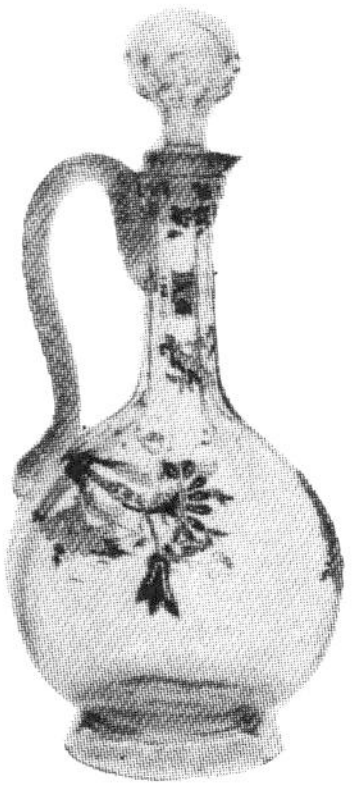

A Galle enamelled glass bottle of flattened flask shape with stopper, 30.25cm. high. £330

A Hukin & Heath 'Crow's foot' decanter, designed by Dr. C. Dresser, electroplate and glass, with registration lozenge for 1879, 24cm. high. (Christie's) £7,776

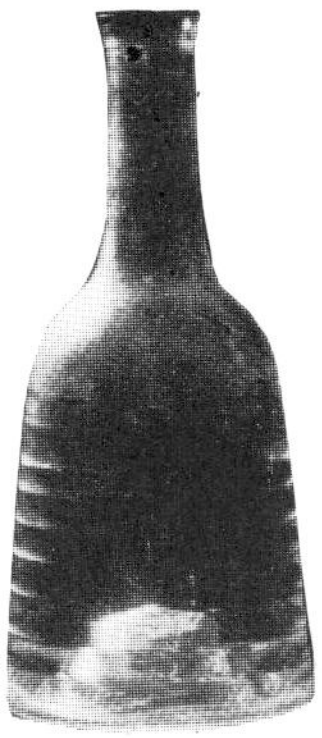

A 'Lynn' decanter of mallet shape, the body lightly moulded with horizontal ribs, circa 1775, 23cm. high. (Christie's) £540

A Guild of Handicraft hammered silver and green glass decanter, the design attributed to C. R. Ashbee, with London hallmarks for 1903, 22.5cm. high. (Christie's) £1,296

A dated enamelled carafe, the opaque white panel inscribed Thos. Worrall 1757, 22cm. high. (Christie's) £6,264

DECOYS

The ancient hunter in search of food, practised decoying by imitating the sounds that animals make. Then, observing that a bird feeding or swimming on a pond represented safety to other birds, he fashioned the decoy.

The first decoys were of primitive style, fashioned from mud and reeds but now decoy making has become the art of professionals.

Decoys are mainly used on estuaries and ponds. They are made of wood and painted in traditional colours with flat paint. They are generally larger than life size; sometimes by half the natural size, sometimes twice as large, for out on the rough water, the larger decoys are spotted sooner.

Decoys of many species may be found. The gulls and crows were often placed on the banks near to where the duck decoy was tethered in order to improve the setting.

A painted cedar hen canvas-back decoy, made by L. T. Ward Bros, 1936, 15in. long.
(Christie's) £2,655

Two late 19th century painted wooden decoys, one 10in. long, the other 11½in. long.
(Christie's) £220

A Canada Goose decoy, by George Boyd, early 20th century, 29in. long.
(Christie's) £1,213

A painted wooden hollow constructed Canada Goose decoy, by Chas. H. Hart, Mass., circa 1890/1915, 20½in. long. (Christie's)
£3,034

A painted wooden Primitive Brant decoy, three-piece laminated construction, 18in. long. (Christie's)
£166

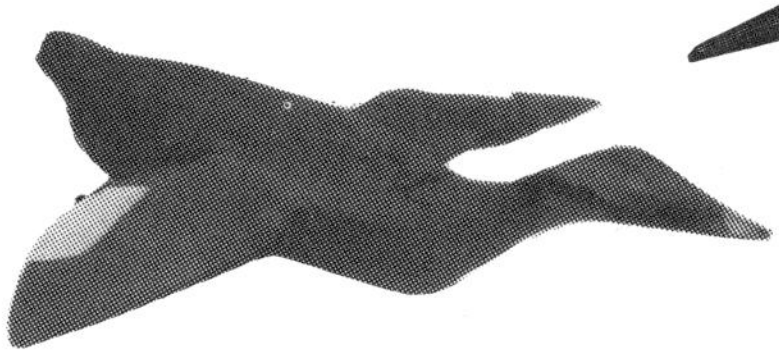

A painted wooden Maine Flying Scoter decoy, by 'Gus' Aaron Wilson, circa 1880/1920, together with two black-painted wooden duck decoys. (Christie's)
£3,136

A pair of painted wooden American Merganser decoys, a hen and drake, by L. T. Holmes, circa 1855/65.
(Christie's) £64,482

A painted wooden oversized Golden Eye decoy, by 'Gus' Aaron Wilson, circa 1880/1920, 20in. long.(Christie's)
£1,213

DOLLS

From the 17th to the early 19th century, ownership of fine looking dolls expensively dressed in silks was generally the prerogative of fashionable society ladies. Some even had two, one clad in the latest haute couture while the other sported a risque negligee. Most children, on the other hand, had to be content to play with dolls made of simply painted wood or rags, very few of which have managed to survive all the loving care lavished upon them.
It wasn't until the mass production methods of the Victorian age that young girls were provided with something a little more lifelike, with bisque china head and limbs and hair that you really could comb. No doubt their popularity was partly brought about by Queen Victoria, who was an avid collector of dolls, dressing many of them herself.

A fine German character doll by Kestner, with original clothes, 13in. high, circa 1915. (Bermondsey) £1,500

A waxed shoulder composition doll with painted closed mouth and fixed blue eyes, 30in. high. (Lawrence Fine Art) £310

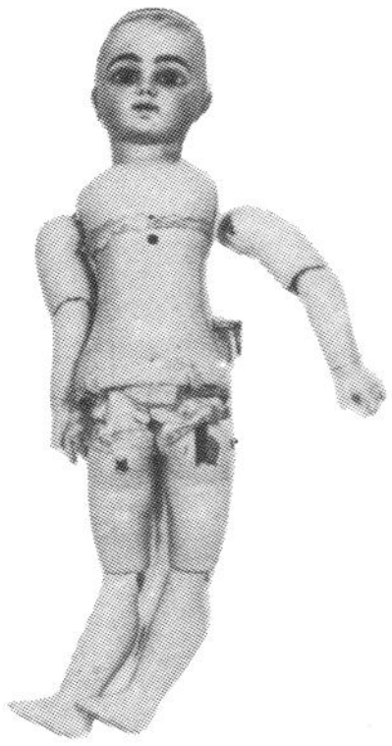

A bisque headed clockwork walking, talking bebe petit pas, marked BRU Jne R 11, 24in. high. (Christie's) £2,500

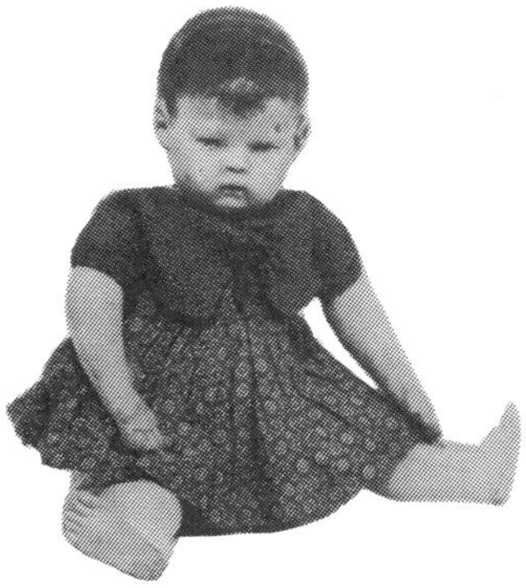

A painted cloth doll with brown painted hair, the stuffed body jointed at hip and shoulder, by Kathe Kruse, 17in. high. (Christie's) £360

A bisque headed doll with composition body, marked Porzellan Fabrik Burggrub Daslachende Baby, 1930/3/ Made in Germany DRGM, 18in. high. (Dacre, Son & Hartley) £430

A Scottish boy doll in Highland dress, with bisque head, in original box marked 'Kelly Boy 306', 12in. high. (Lawrence Fine Art) £110

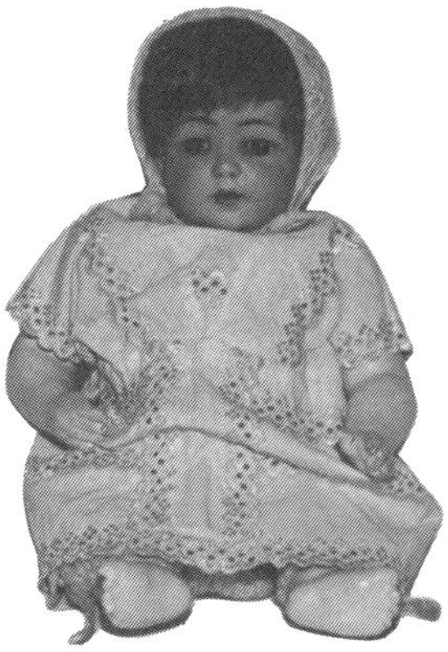

A Franz Schmidt bebe doll with sleeping brown eyes, open mouth and composition body, 9in. high. (Hobbs & Chambers) £125

Early 20th century German character doll by Kathe Kruse, 17in. high. (Bermondsey) £300

A bisque two-faced doll with original blonde wig and with jointed composition body, 11in. high. (Christie's) £900

A bisque headed autoperipatetikos doll with painted blue eyes and brown kid arms, 10in. high. (Christie's) £200

A wax over composition headed doll with smiling painted face, circa 1878, 7in. high. (Christie's) £75

An all-bisque googly-eyed doll's house doll with smiling water-melon closed mouth, 4in. high. (Christie's) £220

A bisque headed bebe with papier mache jointed body, marked 12 by Steiner, 29in. high. (Christie's) £2,400

A Bru Teteur bisque doll, French, circa 1875, 19in. high. (Lawrence Fine Art) £4,400

A William and Mary wooden doll with a wisp of real auburn hair and nailed-on stitched linen wig, English, circa 1690, 16¾in. high. £17,600

A bisque headed doll with jointed composition body, marked Armand Marseille, Germany A9M, 24in. high. (Dacre, Son & Hartley) £190

An English mid 19th century vendor doll of wood and cloth, under glass dome with turned walnut base, 16in. high. (Robt. W. Skinner Inc.) £2,112

A bisque headed bebe, marked J. Steiner Paris, SreA.3, 11in. high. (Christie's) £800

An American 'Shirley Temple' personality doll, 21in. high, circa 1935. (Bermondsey) £475

A bisque headed child doll, marked SFBJ Paris 14, 32in. high, original box marked Bebe Francais. (Christie's) £800

DOLLS' HOUSES

Early 'baby houses' were designed to be a plaything for adults. They were furnished with precious miniature pieces made of silver and other fine materials. Many contain examples of early hand blocked wallpaper and fabrics.

They were thought to have originated from Germany and kitchens complete with all the utensils were being exported from there as early as 1660. The dolls' house, as a toy for children, was kept in the nursery and furnished for play.

A catalogue of the Dolls' Houses at Bethnal Green Museum in London, illustrates houses from 1673 to 1921 and offers an invaluable insight into contemporary life of the times.

The outside of some houses also give a good idea of the lifestyle with carriages, carts and trains set in the landscape.

Large doll's house in the form of a two-storey suburban house, English, circa 1930, 45in. high. £500

English late 19th century interior of an open room in Georgian style, 23in. wide. £495

English late 19th century painted wooden doll's house of Victorian design, 42in. wide. £660

A late Victorian wooden doll's house in the shape of a two-storey villa, with pitched slate roof, 71 x 33cm. £440

Doll's house copied from original family house, with Gothic shaped door, English, circa 1910, 33in. high. £800

Victorian wooden doll's house, cottage style, with working door with brass knob at front, circa 1890. (Theriault's) £1,082

A custom crafted Colonial-style doll's house, circa 1980, with ten rooms of furniture, 28in. high. (Robt. W. Skinner Inc.) £1,200

A wooden doll's house painted to simulate stonework of five bays and three storeys, 46in. wide. (Christie's S. Kensington) £3,800

A large Victorian doll's house with two hinged front sections, mounted on wheels, circa 1890, 40in. wide. £660

DOMESTIC EQUIPMENT

One of the best fields for investment is the early mechanical devices put onto the market as labour savers. As improvements were made, the old ones were almost invariably thrown away with the result that, nowadays they have considerable rarity and curiosity value. After a while, it was realised that many of the old gadgets still actually worked. And worked well. Many will swear that their old Victorian coffee mill grinds coffee far better than the brand new electric jobs, that the heavy iron or copper saucepans are far better than their modern counterparts, that bean slicers, apple peelers and cherry stoners add interest to the most mundane of preparatory tasks in the kitchen.

In saying this, I am referring to Victorian appliances, however, it must be said that it is well worth looking out for the now outdated gadgets of the 30's, 40's and 50's. This is a market still in its early stages and with many intriguing contraptions still modestly priced.

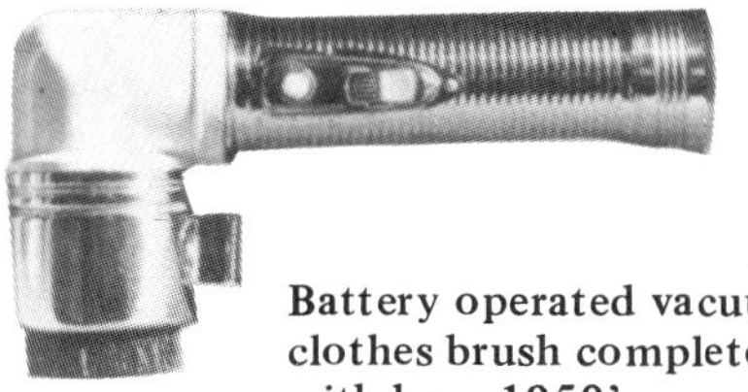

Battery operated vacuum clothes brush complete with box, 1950's. £3

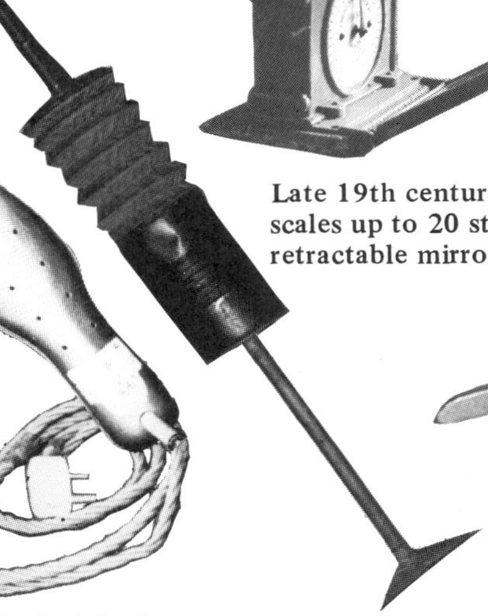

Late 19th century cast iron scales up to 20 stone, with retractable mirror. £50

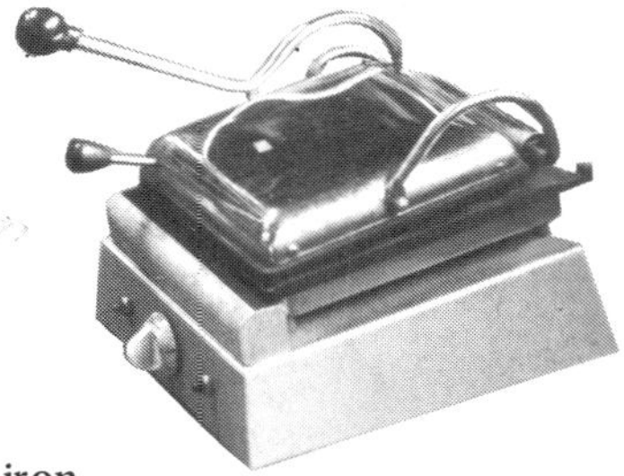

1950's electric toasting machine. £20

An electric kettle, designed by Peter Behrens for AEG, circa 1910, 21cm. £242

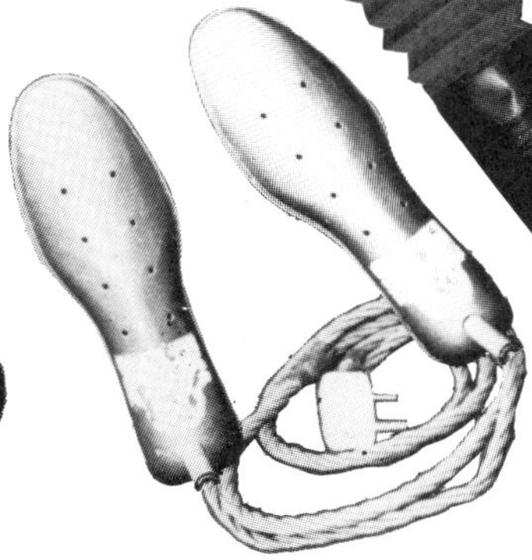

Pair of 1950's electric shoe warmers with original wire. £4

An early 'Star' pump action vacuum cleaner. £30

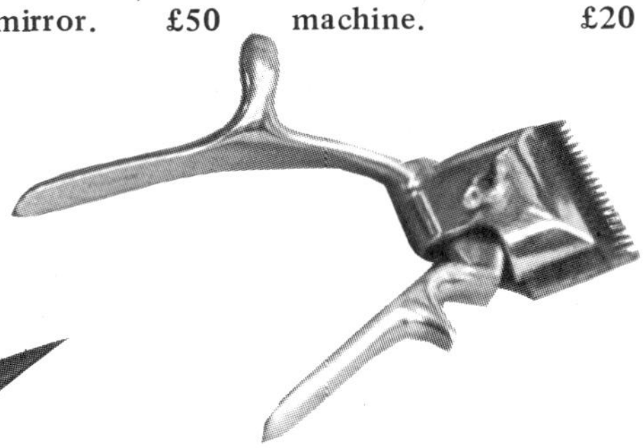

Pair of 1950's hair clippers by Burman, England. £1

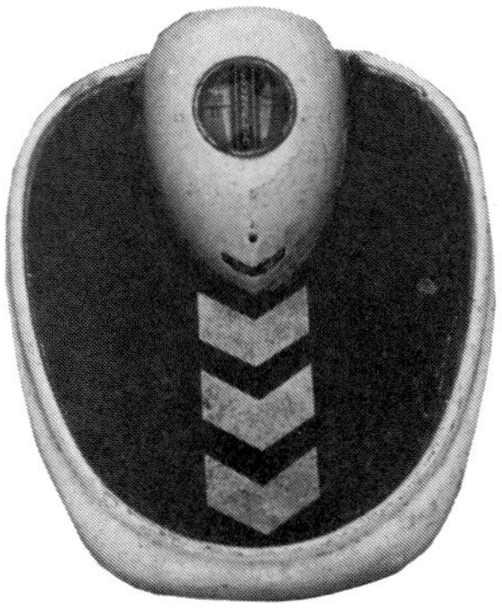

Counselor weighing scales, circa 1937. £22

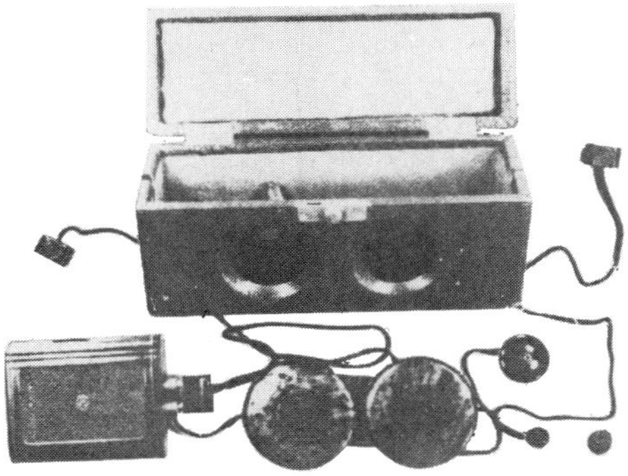

A leatherette covered box containing a battery operated deaf aid, by R. H. Dent, London, circa 1930, box 8 x 2¾ x 3½in. (Christopher Sykes) £35

Valor paraffin heater with brass and alloy fittings. £5

DOOR STOPS

Such is the multitude in variety and composition of door stops, particularly from the 19th century, that one is left to wonder why the Victorians were so keen to keep all their doors ajar.

Due to their function, they are usually heavy and made of cast iron, lead or brass in many forms such as animals, fruit, flowers, fish or in representations of famous people of the day; Wellington, Albert or Victoria. Even Jumbo the notable elephant from London Zoo was immortalised after he was exported to Barnum & Bailey's Circus in America, where he met his untimely death trying to charge a steam train.

Doorstops are also found made of green glass in the shape of a beehive or of Nailsea glass from Bristol with air bubble decoration.

Heavy cast iron door stop of a zebra, circa 1820, 10½in. long, 8in. high. £40

A historical cast brass door stop of King George IV leaning on a pillar, 7½in. long, 8in. high. £50

Victorian cast iron door stop of a Highlander, 9in. high. £24

A solid cast brass standing plaque, stamped on back 'Crowley & Co., Manchester', circa 1860, 9in. long, 7in. high. £20

A 19th century brass dolphin door stopper. £48

Victorian brass dog door stopper, 9in. high. £24

A Victorian cast iron umbrella and stick stand in the form of the young Hercules. £320

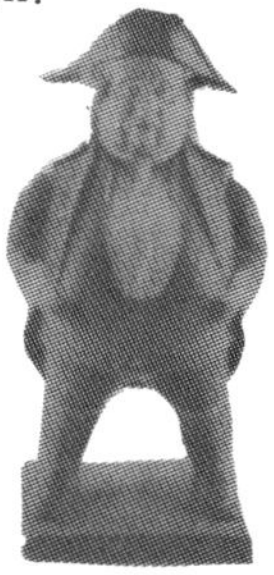

19th century cast iron Toby figure, 14in. high. £233

Napoleon and Princess Eugenie cast iron door stop, 12in. high. £60

'Lion Tamer' cast iron doorstop, 10in. high, circa 1850. £80

19th century cast iron door stop depicting a rampant lion. £35

Victorian cast iron door stop of a horse, on a stepped base, 11¼in. long, 10in. high. £40

DOULTON

So prolific and varied was the output of the Doulton factory in the late 19th century that most households could boast an example of their work, be it a utilitarian piece of stoneware in the bathroom or a fine pair of vases well able to grace any mantlepiece.
Of particular interest, and value, are the works of Hannah Barlow and her sister Florence whose forte was drawing animals and birds freehand onto the wet clay on a wide variety of wares. Musicians and chessmen in the form of mice and frog cricketers by George Tinworth are also well worth looking for.
The most interest recently however, has centred on the Doulton character jugs produced from the 30's to the present day. Find one depicting Sir Francis Drake without a hat and we're talking £3,000 plus, a clown with red triangles on his cheeks is near to £2,000, but the real jewel in the crown is a jug featuring Winston Churchill. Uncoloured, apart from two black handles, this little gem, produced in 1940 and withdrawn because Sir Winston didn't approve of the design, is now worth £6,000 plus.

Gladiator D6550, large, by M. Henk, issued 1961-1967. £270

John Barleycorn D5327, large, by C. Noke, issued 1934-1960. £60

Smuts D6198, large, by H. Fenton, issued 1946-c.1948. £680

Lord Nelson D6336, large, by G. Blower, issued 1952-1969. £160

Churchill (White) D6170, large, by C. Noke, issued 1940-1941. £5,000

Mephistopheles D5757, large, by H. Fenton, issued 1937-1948. £900

Mad Hatter D6598, large, by M. Henk, issued 1965-1983. £35

Clown D5610, large (red haired), by H. Fenton, issued 1937-1942. £1,250

Clark Gable D6709, large, by S. Taylor, issued 1984. £2,200

Gondolier D6589, large, by D. Biggs, issued 1964-1969. £200

Drake D6115, large (hatless), by H. Fenton, issued 1940-1941. £2,000

Maori, large, designer unknown, issued circa 1939. £7,500

'Pirate King', HN2901, designer W. K. Harper, 10in. high, issued 1981-1986. £90

'Sonia', HN1692, designer L. Harradine, 6¼in. high, issued 1935-1949. £275

'Bather', (style two) HN 773, designer L. Harradine, 7½in. high, issued 1925-1938. £300

'Madonna of the Square', HN2034, designer P. Stabler, issued 1949-1951. £450

'Ermine Muff', HN54, designer C. J. Noke, issued 1916-1938. £450

'Wandering Minstrel', HN1224, designer L. Harradine, 7in. high, issued 1927-1938. £800

'Blithe Morning', HN2021, designer L. Harradine, 7¼in. high, issued 1949-1971. £90

'Beggar', (style one) HN526, designer L. Harradine, 6½in. high, issued 1921-1949. £200

'Alchemist', HN1259, designer L. Harradine, 11½in. high, issued 1927-1938. £400

'Coming Of Spring', HN1723, designer L. Harradine, 12½in. high, issued 1935-1949. £800

'Aileen', HN1803, designer L. Harradine, 6in. high, issued 1937-1949. £250

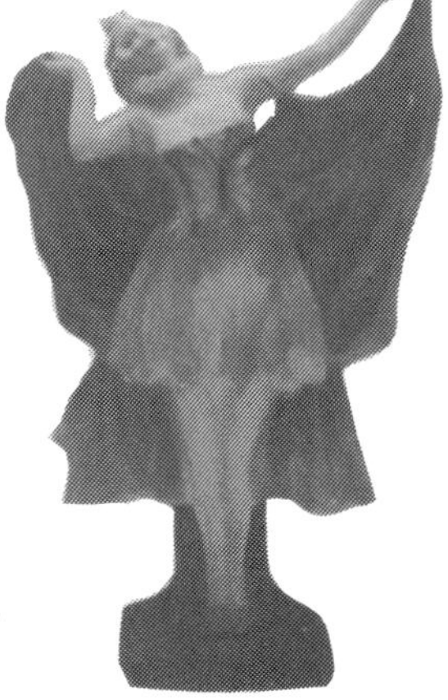

'Butterfly', HN1456, designer L. Harradine, 6½in. high, issued 1931-1938. £400

'Myfanwy Jones', HN39, designer E. W. Light, issued 1914-1938. £1,000

'Mendicant', HN1365, designer L. Harradine, 8¼in. high, issued 1929-1969. £85

'Prudence', HN1883, designer L. Harradine, issued 1938-1949. £200

'Centurion', HN2726, deisgner W. K. Harper, 9¼in. high, issued 1982-1984. £65

'Bo-Peep', (style one) HN1327, designer L. Harradine, 6¾in. high, issued 1929-1938. £400

'Promenade', HN2076, designer M. Davies, issued 1951-1953. £800

'One of the Forty', HN665, designer H. Tittensor, issued 1924-1938. £480

'Fruit Gathering', HN562, designer L. Harradine, issued 1923-1938. £750

'Marianne', HN2074, designer L. Harradine, issued 1951-1953. £220

'Jovial Monk', HN2144, designer M. Davies, 7¾in. high, issued 1954-1976. £110

'Rhythm', HN1904, designer L. Harradine, 6¾in. high, issued 1939-1949. £300

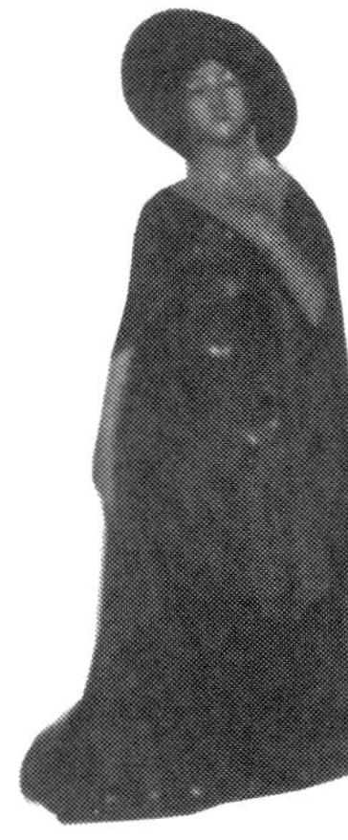

'Gainsborough Hat', HN705, designer H. Tittensor, issued 1925-1938. £350

George Robey, large, designer unknown, issued c. 1925. £3,500

Charlie Chaplin, large, designer unknown, issued c. 1918. £4,000

Squire D6319, medium, by H. Fenton, issued 1950-1969. £90

Cliff Cornell, large (brown suit), designer unknown, issued 1956 in a limited edition of 500. £350

Old Charley D6030, large, by H. Fenton, issued 1939-1960. £55

Sairey Gamp D6263, small, by H. Fenton, issued 1948-1960. £65

Toby XX D6088, large, by H. Fenton, issued 1939-1969. £70

Sam Weller D6265, small, by H. Fenton, issued 1948-1960. £65

Winston Churchill D6171, large, by H. Fenton, issued 1941. £35

The Best Is Not Too Good D6107, small, by H. Fenton, issued 1939-1960. £40

Cliff Cornell, large (beige suit), designer unknown, issued 1956 in a limited edition of 350. £400

Honest Measure D6108, small, by H. Fenton, issued 1939. £20

FAIRINGS

If you had gone to a travelling fair in the 1860s and had proved your prowess on the hoopla stall, chances are that you would have returned home the proud owner of a small china figure bearing a humorous and probably slightly risque legend on the base. These are referred to nowadays as "fairings".

Most are about 4in. high and stand on rectangular bases measuring 2in. by 3in. Subjects include themes like courtship, marriage, politics, war, childhood and animals behaving as people. In all, there are over 400 different types.

With something so typically English as fairings, it comes as a surprise to learn that most were made in Germany, and the two main manufacturers were Springer and Oppenheimer of Elbogen, and Conte and Boehme of Possneck. Of course, it was all a matter of getting down to a price, for the same objects could be bought in the shops for a copper or two, and the German manufacturers had perfected cheap mass production methods without losing on quality.

The manufacturers have obviously borrowed many of their ideas for fairings from such printed materials as sheet music covers. Two, entitled 'Pluck' and 'The Decided Smash' are copies from the cover of a popular song sheet of the time called 'Full Cry Gallop'. In the case of 'Slack' and 'How's Business', these are very good copies of each side of a Staffordshire mug. 'Champagne Charlie is my name' represents George Leybourne making popular the song 'Champagne Charlie' in the 1860s. There are also a few scenes of the Franco-Prussian War which include 'English Neutrality attending the Wounded'.

The Shoemaker In Love £300-£500

Hark Tom Somebody's Coming £70-£90

Some Contributors To Punch £300-£500

The Flower Seller £40-£60

Caught In The Act £150-£200

Before Darwin £20-£30

Baby's First Step £40-£60

Welsh Costume £20-£30

FANS

It is known that Elizabeth I had an interesting collection of fans, as did the richest and most sophisticated ladies of that day, but it was not until the eighteenth century that they became more fashionable, less expensive and more plentiful.

Most eighteenth century fans are either delicately hand painted or those referred to as brise fans, which are composed of overlapping sticks radiating from a pivot and joined with ribbon threaded through slots at the top.

Many of the fans seen today date from the 19th century and, as a rule, do not fetch the very highest prices unless they are made from the finest of materials, incorporate precious metal and stones or are connected with the Empress Eugenie, who was partly responsible for their return to fashion in the Victorian era. Fans became such an important fashion feature that no expense was spared in their design and decoration.

Lace fans with mother-of-pearl mounts were popular from about 1860, until the vogue for all things Oriental popularised large silk fans decorated with birds and flowers in the Japanese style. These were followed by sequinned fans of black and white lace, and large Spanish types with ebony sticks.

The fan, originally a simple and effective gadget, was often modified to incorporate functions other than its original cooling system, e.g. a concealed mirror, peep holes, eye-glasses and even a weapon for self defence – a stiletto!

Particularly popular now are those rich plume fans of Art Deco design made during the brief fan revival of 1925-30.

Spanish cockade fan with inlaid support, made for tourists, circa 1910. £10

A late 19th century French fan with gilded ivory sticks, 35cm. long. (Phillips) £300

An English fan, the serpentine ivory sticks pique with silver and when closed the handle forms a serpent, circa 1730, 10in. (Christie's) £180

An unusually shaped satin leaf fan with finely carved and pierced ivory sticks, circa 1850. £75

Late 19th century silver filigree mounted gold lacquer fan, 39.5cm. high. (Christie's) £1,836

Mid 18th century German ivory fan, the leaf painted with the Continence of Scipio in the manner of Pietro da Cortona, 11in. long. £792

Mid 18th century European framed fan, gouache on skin, on foiled pearl sticks, guard length 11¾in. (Robt. W. Skinner Inc.) £241

Buffalo horn fan from Sumatra with sequinned decoration. £25

FINGER PLATES

Of all door fittings, the finger plate offers the greatest scope for decoration and throughout the ages they have reflected fashionable taste and current architectural design.
The early examples were made from solid brass, steel, cut glass or fine quality porcelain and many were very ornate indeed. As a general rule, the earlier, the better the quality.
Around the mid 1920's finger plates came into more common use and there are some fine Art Deco designs made from bakelite, tin or perspex.
It is clearly demonstrated, by price alone, that the colourful enamel advertising finger plates are the most popular of all. These were designed to be affixed to the outside door of the dealer's shop and, some are still to be found on older properties, often under many layers of paint.
There was also a version made for use inside the shop and, wherever appropriate, this incorporated a match striker.

Spratt's Bird Seeds, match striker and plate. £50

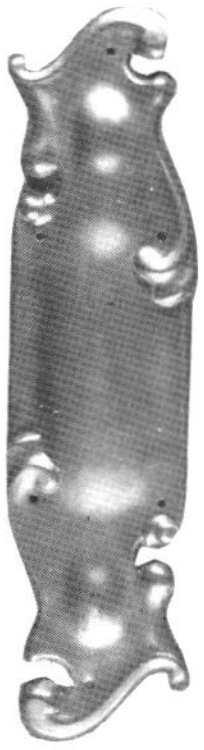

Art Nouveau style pressed brass plate. £5

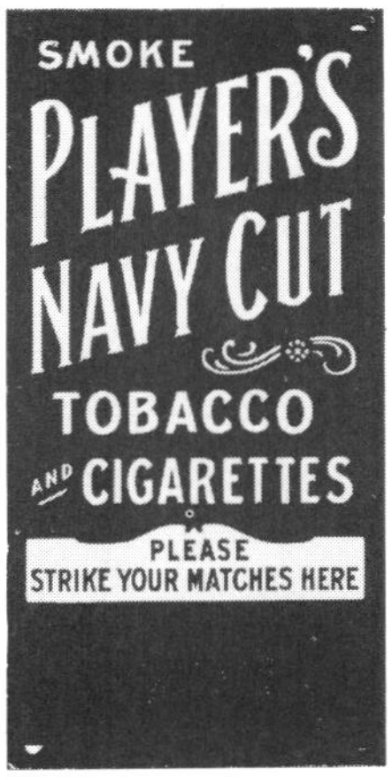

Player's Navy Cut, match striker and plate. £50

Mid 19th century pressed brass plate. £8

Green's Lawn Mower, 'For British People'. £45

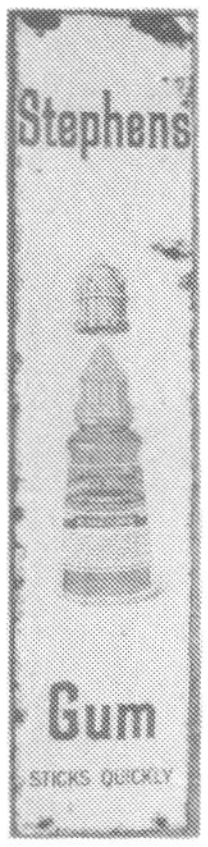

Stephens' Gum Sticks Quickly. £50

French ormolu finger plate, circa 1860. £15

Sunlight Soap, 'Less Labour, Greater Comfort'. £30

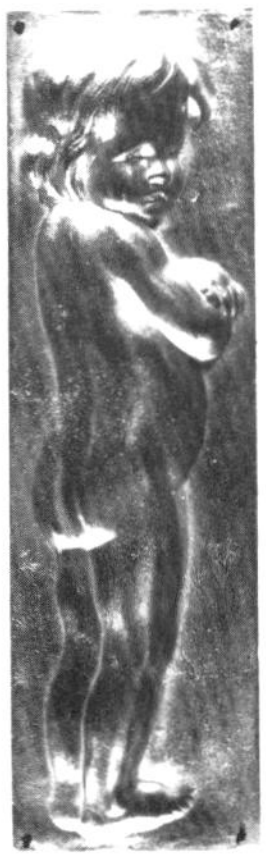

Victorian solid brass cupid finger plate. £12

Thomson's Dye Works Perth. £20

Morris's Blue Book Cigarettes, match striker and plate. £75

Bovril Makes Contented Cooks. £65

FIRE IRONS & FENDERS

An open fire burning brightly in the hearth will tend to monopolise attention in any room and a great deal of expense and attention to detail went into the design and production of the focal point – the fireplace.

Catering for the practicalities of keeping a good fire going without razing the house to the ground led to the production of such necessary tools and accessories as Fire dogs, Fire irons and Fenders. These were produced mainly in materials such as brass, steel, wrought iron, cast iron or copper and fashioned in a variety of designs according to the period and fashion of the day.

A typical set of fire irons may include a shovel, brush, tongs, poker and some sets even incorporate bellows. Long handled irons were produced from the mid 19th century and these were displayed either resting on fire dogs or, where provision was made, in specially designed notches agains the fender. The principal function of the fender was to give protection against burning logs and hot coals tumbling from the hearth but the beautiful designs and good quality materials used in their production soon assured that the fender also became an important feature of the room. One of the most impressive examples, introduced to Britain around 1860, is the Club Fender which apart from a practical function offers quite comfortable seating with its broad, upholstered top running the full length of the hearth.

In recent years there has been something of a revival in the popularity of the open fire with resulting demand for all fireplace furnishings and, while the value of examples once on the market is quickly recognised, these are just the type of pieces that get stashed away in the attic when central heating is installed or the old fireplace removed. They are well worth resurrecting.

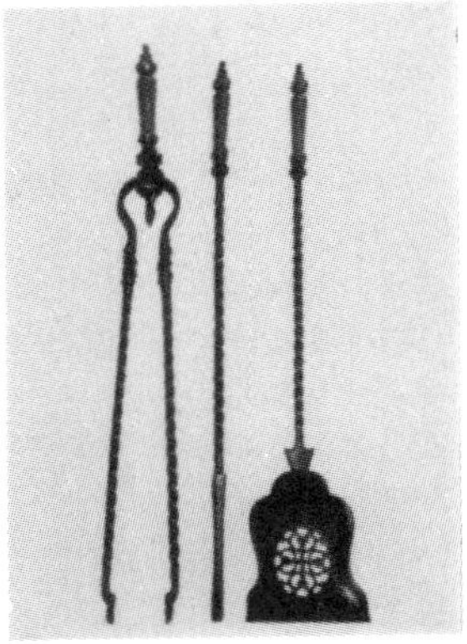

An early set of steel and brass fire irons, 32in. long, circa 1810. £110

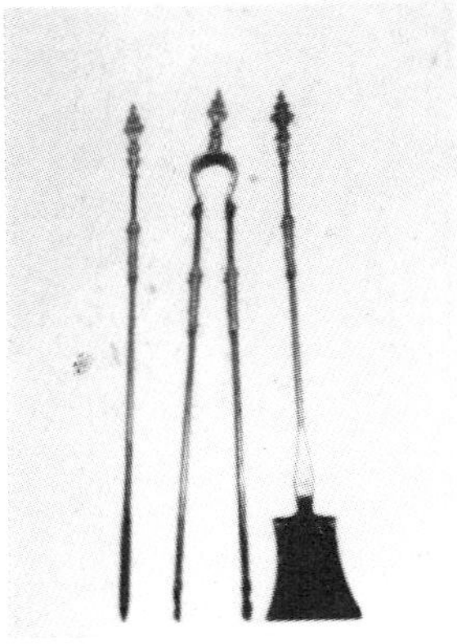

A fine set of Georgian steel fire irons, 32in. long. £145

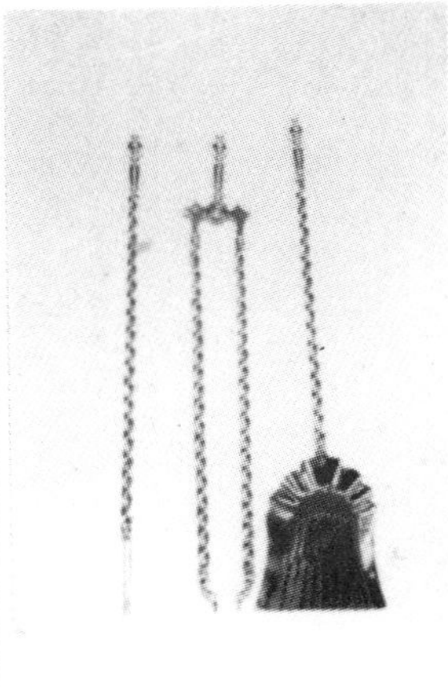

Victorian brass barley twist fire irons, 30in. long. £90

Late Victorian cast iron and brass rail fender, 42in. long. £125

Victorian brass fender with scroll ends, 48in. long. £140

An unusual steel half-moon fender with matching irons, circa 1790. £385

A small Victorian cast iron fender, 24in. long. £60

A very ornate iron fender, 7ft. long, circa 1890. £285

FIREMARKS

If you had been in the unfortunate position of having your "one up and down with outside loo" burst into flames prior to about 1830 you would have been at the mercy of the private fire brigades employed by insurance companies.

If the outside of your house did not display the firemark of the first brigade to arrive, legend has it that their first priority was to sell policies to the neighbours and to blazes with you! It is also rumoured that particularly unscrupulous companies sent runners to impede the progress of rival brigades.

The earliest firemarks were of lead, often bearing the policy number, and these are naturally rare, for I assume they melted if a fire occurred. Later firemarks were of copper, tin or zinc and occasionally of terracotta or porcelain.

Scottish, Commercial Fire and Life Insurance, copper, oval, raised figure of Caledonia.
(Phillips) £220

Liverpool Fire Office, lead, liver bird and torse raised on circular section, 'Liverpool' raised on panel below and impressed with policy no. 426.
(Phillips) £800

Aberdeen Fire and Life Insurance Co., stamped lead, oval, raised arms of the city with motto 'Bon Accord'.
(Phillips) £1,500

Hercules Fire Insurance, cast iron, 'Hercules Fire Office' raised on ornate shield. (Phillips)
£200

West of Scotland Insurance, 1823-38, stamped lead, circular, raised crown in centre.
(Phillips) £220

Royal Exchange Assurance, lead, raised Royal Exchange building, policy no. 570 on panel below, issued circa 1721.
(Phillips) £4,400

Berkshire, Gloucestershire and Provincial Life and Fire Assurance, 1824-31, copper, castle raised on oval.
(Phillips) £160

Westminster Insurance, lead, open portcullis with Prince of Wales' feathers above, policy no. 20867 on panel below.
(Phillips) £350

FISHING REELS

The sport of angling has been a rich source for the collector ever since the days of dear old Isaac Walton. Be it salmon flies, plugs, spoons, spinners, floats, gaffs or even weights there are specialist collectors for all.

Most of the early tackle available dates from the 19th century and certainly very little was made before 1800.

The most notable makers of fine quality fishing tackle was the firm Hardy Brothers of Alnwick, established in 1872, but other well-known makers include Allcocks of Redditch, Farlows of London and Mallochs of Perth all of whom made excellent equipment.

With the exception of lightweight split cane trout rods and other useable items, rods are, in general, not considered to be very much in demand. They tend to deteriorate rapidly, and examples in poor condition are of little value. Rods also have the disadvantage of being difficult to display.

A Hardy Bros. 1896 pattern all brass 'Perfect' reel with ivorine handle, 4¼in. diam. (Christie's) £453

A Malloch's Patent spinning reel with horn handle, 4¼in. diam. (Christie's) £49

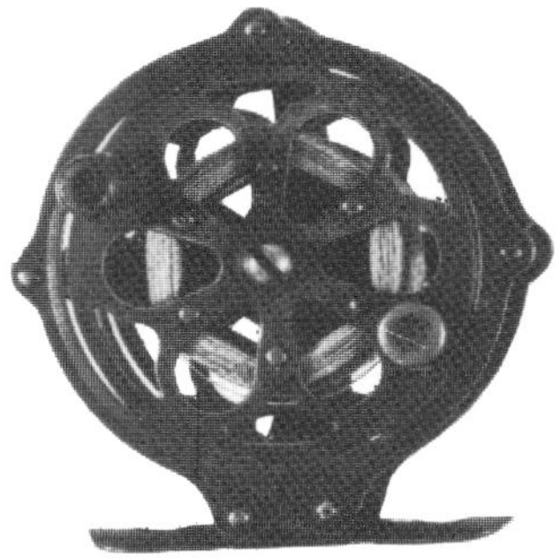

An Allcock's 'Aerial Popular' reel, solid front rim, adjustable drag and optional check, circa 1935, 3in. diam. (N. J. Marchant Lane) £20

A Victorian gilt brass reel with ivory handle, with spring and cog mechanism, 3in. (Christie's) £1,700

A Hardy Bros. Ltd. 'Sea Silex' alloy reel with smooth brass foot, ebonite handles and ivorine check handle, 7in. diam. (N. J. Marchant Lane) £200

A Hardy Bros. all brass 'Perfect' reel with horn handle, smooth foot and oval logo, 2.3/8in. diam. (Christie's) £346

Brass salmon reel with ivory handle and ventilated drum, by Broddell of Belfast, circa 1900, 4¼in. diam. (N. J. Marchant Lane) £80

A large ebonite 'Starback' sea reel by Farlow, with brass star, foot and leather-bound Bickerdyke line guide, circa 1910, 5¾in. diam. (N. J. Marchant Lane) £60

FOOTBALL PROGRAMMES

Football Programmes have been collected for almost as long as the game has been played, but it is only since the late '50's that this has been a recognisable hobby. Now there is a trade association, a monthly magazine and a number of clubs devoted to bringing together collectors, in this most friendly of pursuits.

The earliest examples of football programmes date back to the 1880's and are little more than teamsheets surrounded by advertising.

These early examples can now however change hands for substantial sums of money, but it is worth noting that this is not necessarily a rich man's hobby and it is quite possible to put together an interesting collection without breaking the bank. There is certainly no doubt that a look through any collection brings the memories of famous games and players flooding back to anyone who loves Britain's favourite sport.

1960/61 Burnley v. Aston Villa League Cup Semi Final. £7.50

1922/23 FAC Final between West Ham Utd. and Bolton was the first Wembley Final. £140

1945/46 Scotland v. England (Victory International). £15

1929/30 FAC Final, Arsenal v. Huddersfield, pre-War FAC Finals are amongst the most eagerly sought programmes. £60

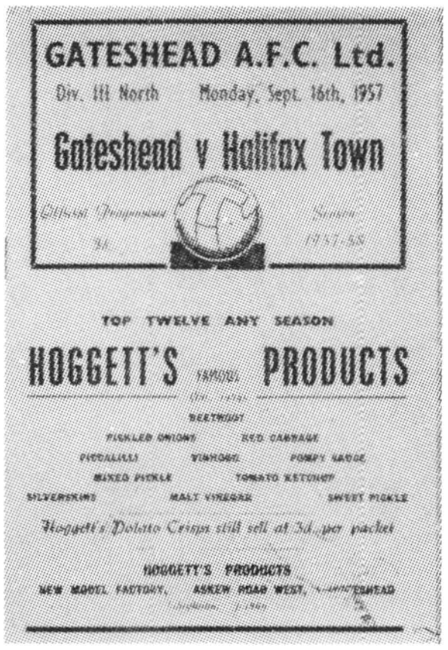

1957/58 Gateshead v. Halifax. Now defunct Gateshead were in Div. 3 North. £8

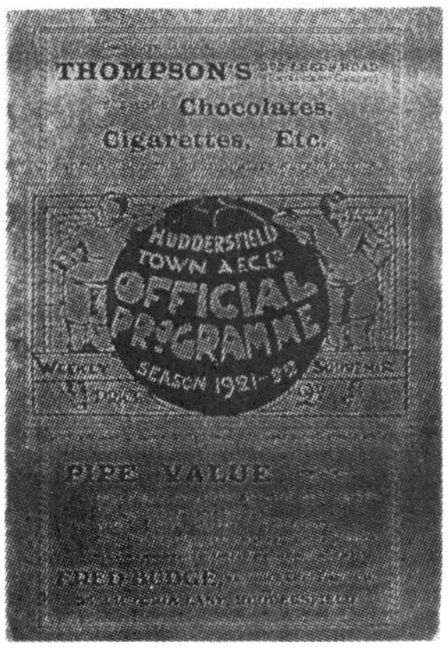

1921/22 Huddersfield Tn. v. Cardiff City. £15

Burnley v. Spurs FA Cup Final 1961/62. Spurs win the Cup for the 2nd year running. £5

1937/38 Queen of the South Reserves v. Falkirk Reserves. Pre-War Scottish programmes are very rare. £10

FURNITURE

The dictionary defines the word 'furniture' as the action of decorating and embellishing and since time began people have wanted to surround themselves with items that please them. Even cavemen painted on the ceilings of their caves.

Everyone collects furniture up to a point but discrimination begins when they look for satisfaction in the design of a piece as well as worrying about how well it carries out its function.

The field of furniture for the collector ranges from chairs and sofas to book cases, armoires, chests and cabinets, Canterburys to tables of all types ranging from Pembrokes to peg-top. Special designers of furniture have been sought out by buyers of taste and men like Chippendale, Hepplewhite, Sheraton and Pugin greatly influenced the living conditions of their day even among people who never heard of them.

The materials used to make furniture range from papier mache, much loved by the Victorians for drawing room pieces, to rare woods like rosewood, tulip wood, satinwood or, more practical and hard wearing, oak, mahogany and teak. Pieces were painted, gilded, upholstered and polished. They were inlaid with marquetry and mounted in ormolu, covered with leather or tapestry and trimmed with tassels but each item of furniture reflects the taste of its time and the skill of its creator which is why we still admire them today.

A late 18th century Anglo-Indian engraved ivory and tortoiseshell veneered table cabinet, 19in. wide. (Christie's) £3,456

An early Georgian oak bureau with double half round mouldings, 38in. wide. (Lawrence Fine Art) £858

A Federal mahogany Pembroke table with two drop leaves, Penn., 1800-10, 49¾in. wide, open. (Christie's) £1,145

A late 19th century black and gold lacquer four-leaf screen, 77 x 26in. (Christie's) £1,620

A 19th century Louis XV-style commode with moulded breccia marble top, 40¼in. wide. (Robt. W. Skinner Inc.) £821

A George III mahogany breakfront bookcase with moulded dentilled cornice, 95½in. wide. (Christie's) £4,104

A French gold and parcel gilt armoire on squat cabriole feet. (Christie's)
£1,600

Oak twin pedestal roll-top desk, 1900. (British Antique Exporters)
£729

1930's oak bureau bookcase with glazed top. (British Antique Exporters)
£118

Early 19th century fruitwood centre table, Austrian or North Italian, 37in. diam. (Christie's) £756

A mahogany latticework waste-paper basket on bracket feet, 14½in. wide. (Christie's)
£3,520

A Charles II black and gold lacquered cabinet on stand, 45in. wide. (Christie's)
£10,800

A Federal mahogany and mahogany veneer server, New England, circa 1815, 37¾in. wide. (Robt. W. Skinner Inc.) £479

A George I black and gold lacquer corner cupboard, 22in. wide. (Christie's)
£918

A Chippendale mahogany blockfront secretary desk, circa 1780, 42in. wide. (Robt. W. Skinner Inc.)
£34,722

A mid Victorian walnut and inlaid side cabinet with glazed door, 34½in. wide. (Dacre, Son & Hartley) £500

A mid Georgian oak tallboy, the base with two long drawers, 46in. wide. (Christie's)
£1,080

A George III two-tier mahogany dumbwaiter with moulded circular shelves, 37in. high. (Christie's)
£864

A William and Mary black and parcel gilt stool with four S-scroll legs, 20in. diam. (Lawrence Fine Art) £6,820

Late 19th century Moorish inlaid occasional table. (British Antique Exporters) £40

A classical carved mahogany drop-leaf table, circa 1815, 38in. wide. (Christie's) £649

A Georgian secretaire bookcase with glazed doors enclosing brocade lined shelves. (Worsfolds) £1,300

A William IV rosewood veneered circular snap-top breakfast table, 4ft.3½in. diam. (Woolley & Wallis) £700

A George III brass bound mahogany cellarette with lead lined interior retaining tap beneath, 19in. wide. (Christie's) £2,808

A mid 18th century oak dresser, the three drawers with brass knobs, 69in. wide.(Dacre, Son & Hartley) £1,000

A Regency rosewood work table by Gillows of Lancaster, 35½in. wide, open. (Christie's) £756

A Georgian style walnut wine table with two tiers of revolving book racks, 30in. high. (Anderson & Garland) £490

A mid Georgian mahogany tea table with D-shaped hinged top and three frieze drawers, possibly Irish, 32½in. wide. (Christie's) £1,944

Late 19th century marquetry secretaire with pull-out secretary drawer, Holland, 41½in. wide. (Robt. W. Skinner Inc.) £875

A 19th century Dutch walnut and marquetry cylinder top bombe-shaped bureau, 36in. wide. (Dacre, Son & Hartley) £1,450

A George III mahogany knee-hole desk with seven various sized drawers, 33in. wide. (Christie's) £1,728

A late Georgian mahogany washstand with gallery back, shelf and single drawer, 18in. wide. (Peter Wilson & Co.) £100

A Victorian mahogany canterbury. (John Hogbin & Son) £540

A Victorian rectangular inlaid burr walnut needlework table with hinged top, 24in. wide. (Parsons, Welch & Cowell) £530

A William and Mary walnut and oak chest-on-stand, 40½in. wide. (Christie's) £1,188

A small George III mahogany chest with a caddy top, the front inset slide with brass knob handles, 31½in. wide. (Woolley & Wallis) £1,500

An early Victorian mahogany chiffonier, the top with a three-quarter galleried superstructure, 40in. wide. (Christie's) £800

A fine quality late 18th century mahogany tray top commode, complete with bowl, 20½in. wide. (Bermondsey) £700

An Edwardian mahogany display cabinet, inlaid with chequered boxwood lines and harewood, 52in. wide. (Christie's) £1,200

A 17th century oak four-poster bed with panelled headboard, 64in. wide, 93in. high. (Christie's) £2,700

A George III satinwood clothes press, the cupboard doors enclosing five slides, 49½in. wide. (Christie's) £3,888

A Regency calamander wood davenport, the turned feet with brass castors, 21¼in. wide, circa 1820. (Woolley & Wallis) £1,100

GINGER BEER BOTTLES

Grocers, chemists, brewers and mineral water manufacturers all produced their own ginger beer and sold it in individual bottles in the 19th and early 20th centuries. The bottles were mostly produced in stoneware by big potteries like Price or Doulton and they were transfer printed with the names of the ginger beer manufacturers or retailers.
The bottles were usually white or brown but they occasionally had blue or green shoulders. Some of them were corked but most commonly they had Galtee More patent closures with stone stoppers held closed by a metal pin through the necks of the bottles.

Ginger Beer bottle from Marsom & Sons, Northill, Biggleswade, white with black printing. £6

Ginger Beer bottle from R. M. Snow & Company, Tea Merchants, South St., Torrington, white with black printing. £10

Galtee More honeyneck Ginger Beer bottle from The Reading Mineral Water Co. with the lion trade mark. £10

Ginger Beer bottle from E. Culverwell A.P.S. Chemist, Exmoor Pharmacy, Minehead, honey coloured, black lettering. £10

A rare ginger beer by W. A. Scott, Montrose, with swing stopper. £200

Rare ginger beer bottles, Pallett & Springwell, 6¾in. high, £100; Spa, 4in. tall, £100; Tuddenham, 2¼in. high, £85; Bourne Denby, ¾in. high, £40.

Hart & Co. ginger beer bottle with blue top and print, 6¾in. high. £150

Coventry ginger beer bottle with transfer printed Bicycle emblem, 6¾in. high. £40

GLASS

Glass is made primarily from a combination of silicic acid and an alkali, potassium or sodium. Added ingredients make possible the huge variety in glass – for example lead, calcium, metallic oxides or gold. Since the Middle Ages people have been collecting glass and today it is one of the most interesting of the collecting categories.

The Venetian glass making industry dates back to the 11th century and in the 13th century the glassmaking ovens were removed to Muran. From the beginning Venetian glass makers delighted in displaying their workmanship by intricate designs, elaborate decorations and colouring.

It was the German glassmakers who developed the skill of cutting glass which was practised with much success in Bohemia. Ruby glass Bohemian goblets are today highly prized by collectors.

Throughout the centuries and in every country there have been skilled and experimental glassmakers. In the late 19th and early 20th centuries, the Art Nouveau and Deco periods produced artists like Galle, Daum, Tiffany and Lalique whose work changes hands today for astronomical prices. Lalique in particular brought the craft of glass moulding to a high art and he did not only create very expensive objects but also produced utilitarian objects like bottles for perfume manufacturers which made his art accessible for a wide range of people and greatly influenced public taste. Collectors also seek out pewter mounted glass articles produced for the London store Liberty's under the trade name of Tudric.

Glass is essentially a utilitarian material and therefore can be found in many guises – flagons, figurines, plates, beakers, goblets and ewers, chandeliers, vases, perfume bottles and of course paper weights. Those made by Baccarat, St Louis and Clichy are among the most beautiful.

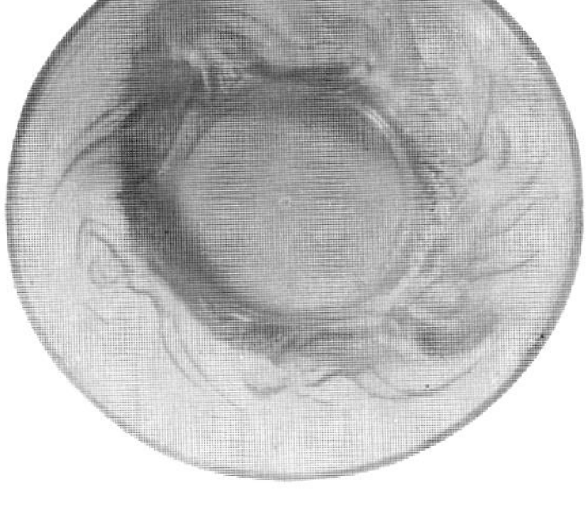

An opalescent 'Ondines' dish, engraved R. Lalique, France, 8in. diam. (Capes, Dunn & Co.) £310

A Bohemian dated, double overlay, gilt metal mounted, rectangular casket for the Persian market, circa 1848, 15cm. wide. (Christie's) £2,160

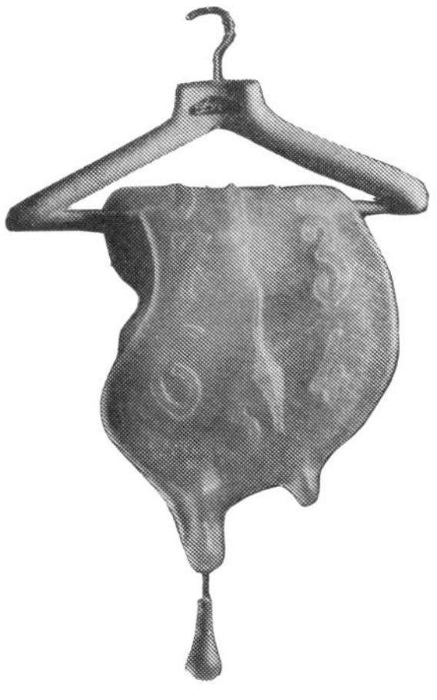

A Daum limited edition pate-de-verre and fibre glass surrealist sculpture by Salvador Dali, depicting a soft clock slumped on a coat hanger. (Christie's) £2,052

A pair of 19th century, blown, colourless glass hanging lamps, approx. 15in. high. (Christie's) £916

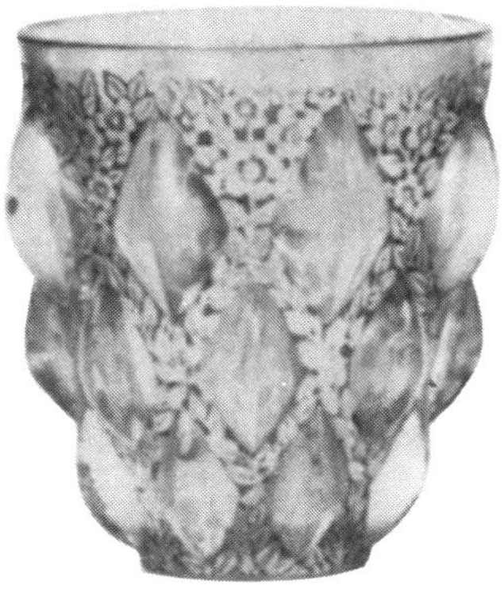

A Lalique opalescent tapering cylindrical glass vase, 'Rampillon', 5in. high. (Christie's) £350

A 19th century glass drug jar with a lid, 24in. high. (Lots Road Chelsea Auction Galleries) £140

A baluster candlestick, the stem with true baluster section above a beaded knop and triple annulated basal knop, circa 1745, 19.5cm. high. (Christie's) £626

A Venini handkerchief vase in blue with a white interior, 9½in. high. (Christie's) £110

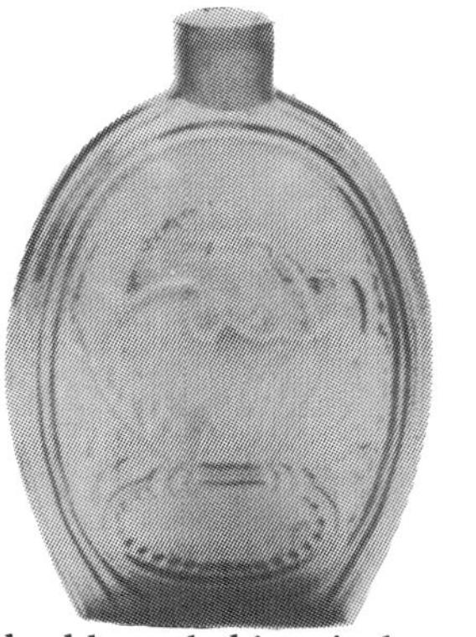

A double eagle historical pint flask, GII-40, bright green, sheared mouth-pontil scar, Kensington Glass Works, 1830-38. (Robt. W. Skinner Inc.) £193

A Nailsea jug, dark green splashed with white, with flared neck, 23cm. high. (Lawrence Fine Art) £77

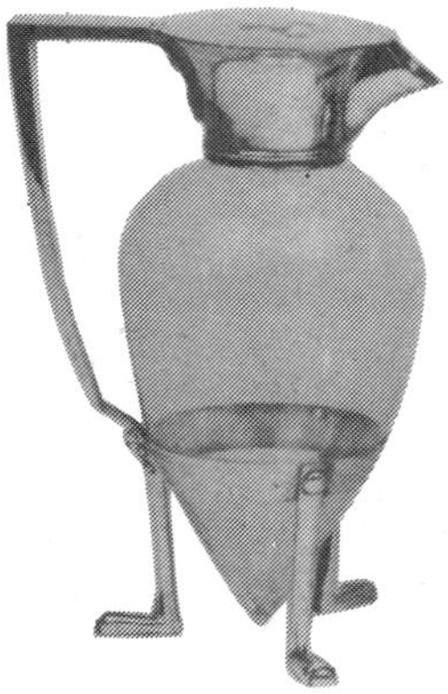

A Hukin & Heath electroplated metal mounted glass claret jug, designed by Dr. C. Dresser, with registration lozenge for 12th November 1879, 23.7cm. high. (Christie's) £6,480

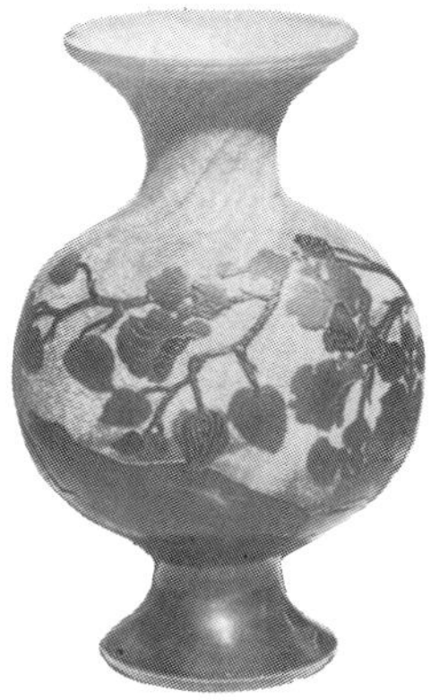

A Galle cameo vase, the flattened globular body on splayed foot, 23.5cm. high. (Christie's) £1,188

One of a pair of Portland clear overshot glass compotes, late 19th century, 8¾in. high. (Robt. W. Skinner Inc.) £335

A glass vase designed by Koloman Moser, the clear glass with gilt loop decoration and iridescent red tears, 17.1cm. high. (Christie's) £1,404

An oak bottle box with thirteen blown glass bottles, late 18th/early 19th century, 13½in. wide. (Christie's) £763

'Three Dahlias', a Lalique blue opalescent circular box and cover of clear and satin finished glass, 20.9cm. diam. (Christie's) £324

A Bohemian ruby overlay engraved tumbler of flared form, circa 1860, 12.5cm. high. (Christie's) £432

A Stourbridge olive-green opaline vase on four gilt feet detailed in white and black enamel, 12¾in. high. (Christie's) £160

A Galle enamelled and green oviform single-handled glass jug, 8½in. high, inscribed. (Christie's) £200

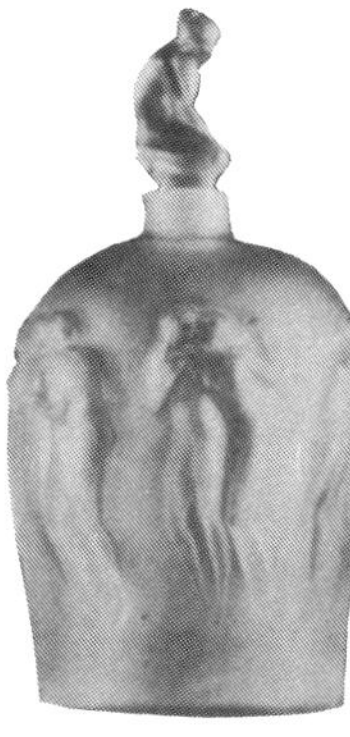

'Figurines Avec Bouchon', a Lalique frosted glass bottle and stopper, 11½in. high. (Christie's) £950

A Steuben crystal-footed bowl and cover, 'The Plains', designed by Lloyd Atkins, 33cm. high. (Christie's) £1,620

A baluster goblet, the thistle bowl supported on a cushion above a drop knopped section, circa 1700, 15.5cm. high. (Christie's) £756

A large Regency ormolu and cut glass vase, the urn-shaped body set with faceted cabochons in latticework frame, 22in. high. (Christie's) £11,340

A Bohemian transparent-enamelled chinoiserie beaker, circa 1835, 12.5cm. high. (Christie's) £1,000

A Ver Centre vase, elongated ovoid shape enamel painted in various colours over a green ground, signature Ver Centre 1927, 29cm. high. (Christie's) £1,080

A Guild of Handicrafts silver and glass box and cover, designed by C. R. Ashbee, with London hallmarks for 1900, 21cm. high, 16oz. 15dwt. gross weight without cover. (Christie's) £4,536

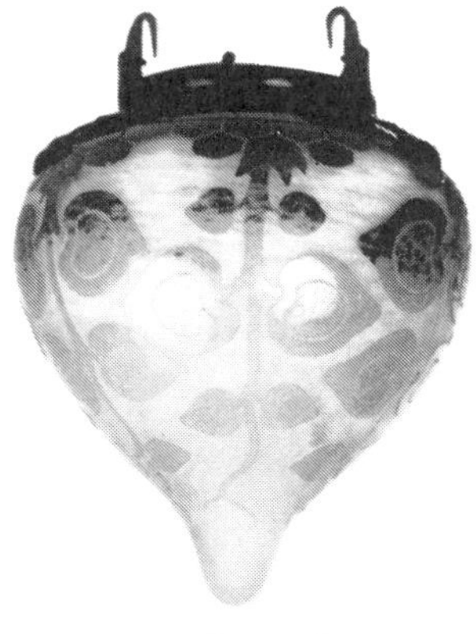

A Le Verre Francais cameo glass hanging lamp shade in the form of a strawberry overlaid in orange and blue, 30.9cm. high. (Christie's) £810

A Bohemian lithyalin, flaring cylindrical beaker, 4¾in. high. (Christie's) £220

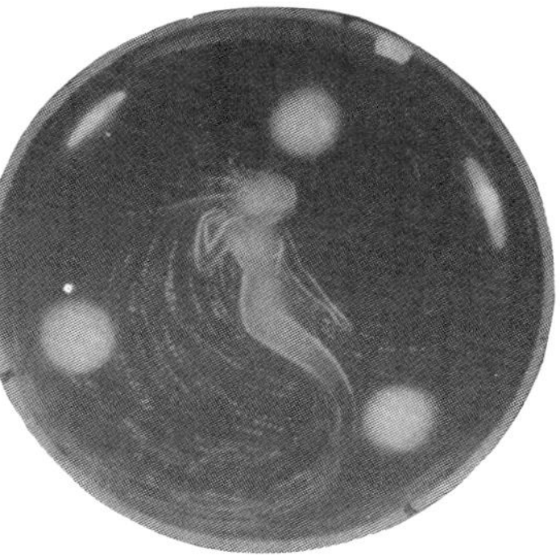

A Lalique opalescent glass dish, 'Sirene', signed, circa 1925, 14½in. diam. (W. H. Lane & Son) £650

A stained glass panel with scene of mediaeval punishment, 18¾ x 15in. (Capes Dunn & Co.) £1,900

GOLDSCHEIDER

The Goldscheider factory of Vienna was founded in 1886 by Friedrich Goldscheider.

Production continued after his death in 1897, under the supervision of his widow and his brother Alois until 1920, when his two sons Marcel and Walter took the business over. Marcel left in 1927 to start the Vereinigte Ateliers fur Kunst and Keramic.

The art nouveau and art deco figures produced from the turn of the century, always incorporate the human form and are the pieces most desirable to collectors.

There are several marks for Goldscheider most including the name and another shows the Imperial Eagle along with the initials F.G.

A china Art Deco figure of a woman by Goldscheider, Vienna, 12½in. high. (Robt. W. Skinner Inc.) £150

A Goldscheider pottery figure modelled as naked young girl with her arms crossed in front of her, 14¼in. high. (Christie's) £420

A pair of Goldscheider pottery figures of a young girl and a young man, made in Austria, 15in. high. (Christie's) £400

A Goldscheider pottery figure modelled as a naked young lady holding a fan, and trailing a shawl behind, 13¾in. high. (Christie's) £350

A Goldscheider pottery mask of a girl looking down, Made in Austria, circa 1925, 23cm. high. (Christie's) £324

A Goldscheider pottery figure of a woman wearing a beaded costume, on a black oval base, 18in. high. (Christie's) £1,700

A Goldscheider Art Deco globular lamp base, decorated in white, orange, black and blue with banding, 25cm. high. (Phillips) £180

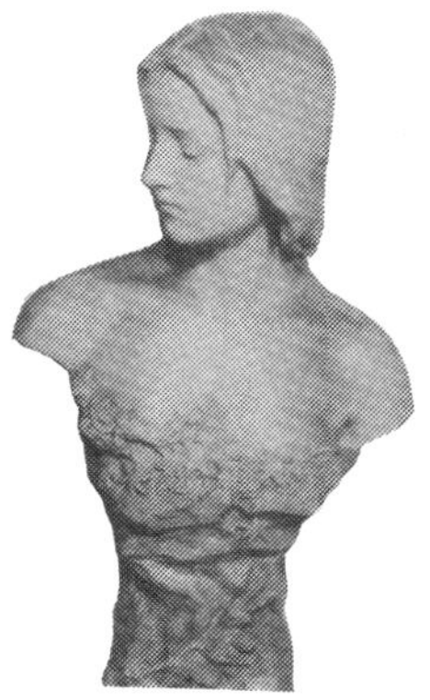

A Goldscheider pottery bust of a young woman in the Art Deco style, signed F. Donatello, 23½in. high. (Outhwaite & Litherland) £350

GOLFING ITEMS

Almost everything to do with the sport of golf is enthusiastically collected; from bags, which made their first appearance around the 1880's, to trophies and other commemorative pieces. Even the most ordinary artefacts, when related by design to golf (like a hatpin in the form of a club), will fetch a much higher price than could otherwise be expected.
The earliest golf balls were made of leather and filled with a concoction of boiled feathers. They were then hammered to a round shape and painted white. In time, these were followed by the 'gutta-percha' balls which were of smooth appearance and patented by a Dr. Paterson of St. Andrews. The balls came into common usage by 1850 and were superseded by the mass produced moulded 'hammered' ball used today.
Golfing items have a particularly strong following for it is a sport with international appeal and early clubs will often obtain hundreds of pounds at auction.

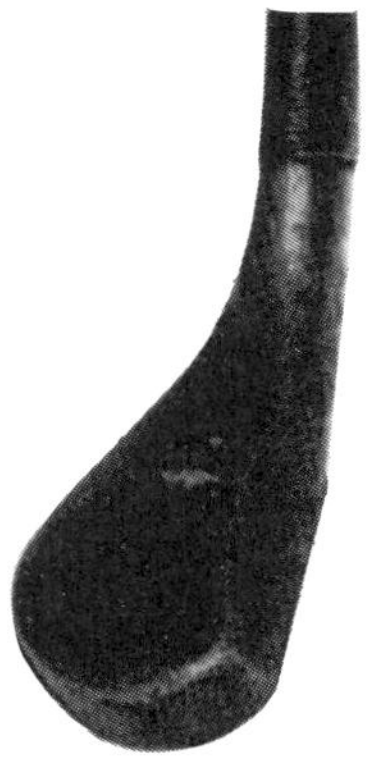

A scared head long-nosed spoon by McEwan, the head so stamped, circa 1875. (Christie's) £886

A Royal Doulton two-handled vase printed and coloured with two golfers and a caddie below a landscape of a golf course, 8in. high. (Christie's) £226

A Gourlay feather ball, size 25, mint condition. (Christie's) £1,350

A scared head long-nosed short spoon by Tom Morris, circa 1875. (Christie's) £702

A composition painted caricature figure carrying a golf bag of clubs advertising the 'Dunlop' golf balls, 17in. high. (Christie's) £226

A Royal Doulton Kingsware mug, the raised decoration of a golfer and his caddie, circa 1910, 5¾in. high. (Christie's) £216

A scared head long-nosed driver by Jack Morris, with greenheart shaft. (Christie's) £540

A bronze figure of Harry Vardon by H. S. Ludlow, cast by Elkington & Co., circa 1900, on oak base, 5in. high, 7½in. overall. (Christie's) £864

GOSS

Had you been a turn of the century holidaymaker, the chances are that, in addition to sticks of rock, you would have carried home an example of the work of William Henry Goss.

A Londoner, born in 1833, he started business in 1858 producing fine china in the Copeland style. He might have gone on forever as just another china man had he not been interested in heraldry, and had his eldest son, Adolphus, not had a passion for archaeology. By combining his manufacturing talent and those two great interests, Goss hit upon a unique and highly successful formula for the holiday trade.

The best china shops of the time had shelves crammed with his miniature models of Roman vases, tombs and lighthouses, together with detailed replicas of famous buildings, which are amongst the most sought after pieces of Goss available today.

He made models of 51 cottages between 1893 and 1929, all of which (bar the Massachusetts Hall and Holden Chapel) were British. The two exceptions, having been made specifically at the request of his Boston (U.S.) agent, are rarely found in this country.

The firm traded under the name of W.H. Goss & Sons and later W.H. Goss Ltd. Printed marks include W.H. Goss, with goshawk, wings outstretched.

A number of factories, well aware of the success of Goss china, went into production with similar models but these are generally of inferior quality but do change hands for the same high price as Goss. Other manufacturers' pieces are quite clearly marked so there need be no confusion between the two.

Wordsworth's Home, Dove Cottage, Grasmere, 102mm. long. (Goss & Crested China) £375

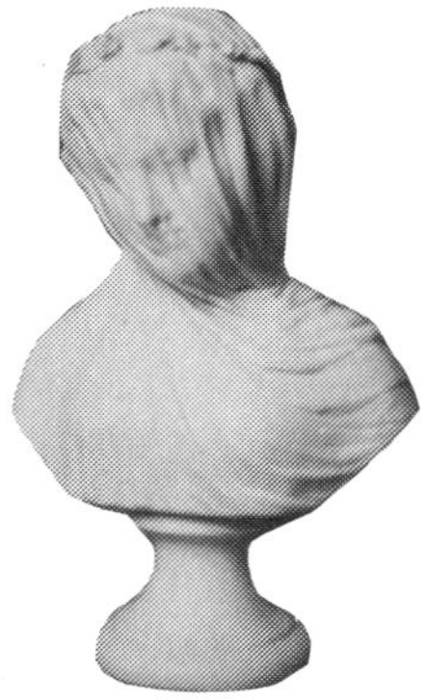

The Veiled Bride, on socle plinth, 270mm. high. (Goss & Crested China) £500

Parian bust of Charles Swain, a colleague of W. H. Goss, 283mm. high, first period. (Goss & Crested China) £600

Kirk Braddon Cross in brown washed parian. $120 £80 Unusually, the white parian example is more valuable at £175

Goss doll, made during the Great War when German products were unavailable. (Goss & Crested China) £350

Ribbed jug with black transfer view of 'Bamburgh Castle'. (Goss & Crested China) £30

GRAMOPHONE NEEDLE TINS

There are many collectors of needle tins throughout the world as the collecting of gramophones and phonographs is a well established international hobby and the collecting of tins developed from this.

The City of London Phonograph and Gramophone Society caters for all these collectors from Australia, America, Holland, Germany and the United Kingdom. Auction houses in London regularly hold sales of all relevant items including tins.

It is only in the last few years that collecting gramophone needle tins, as a distinctly separate hobby from collecting gramophones and phonographs, has developed. The tins used to be found inside the machine or in the lid, so that many machine collectors already had some tins, and these made an ideal side collection as did the cutters, sharpeners and the record cleaning pads.

In their heyday, there were many hundreds of different brands produced and, because initially, each needle was only used once and then thrown away, the need arose to keep buying tins of 100 or 200 needles. The machines had no volume control, the tone being set by the needle, and most popular tones were medium, loud and extra loud.

The common brands were HMV, Songster, Columbia, Decca, Embassy and Edison Bell.

It is possible to build up a collection of 200 tins easily just by collecting variations of these six, and its an ideal start for novice collectors.

Collecting these tins has many advantages: their small size, ease of storage, relative cheapness, so the hobby is growing in popularity all the time.

Columbia Superbe – dark and light blue tin with magic notes. 200 loud needles. 50p–£1.50

Beltona – blue tin and gold writing with face 'trade mark' – Euphonic brand name of tins. £2–£4

Needles for Disc Talking Machines – green and red tin with bird in red cross in centre. 200 sweet and clear full tone needles. £3–£6

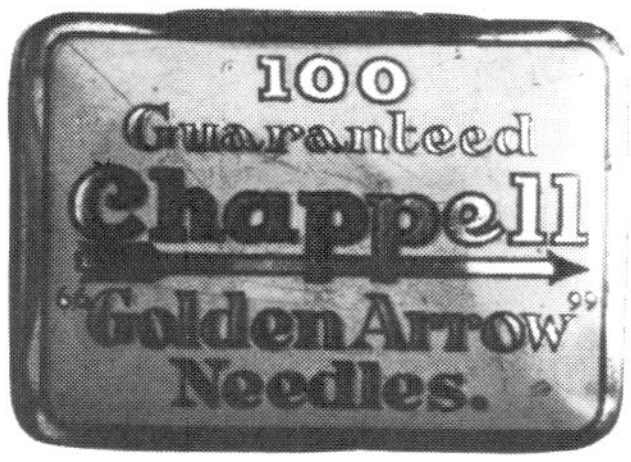

Chappell Golden Arrow – white tin with gold writing and golden arrow. 100 spear point needles. Rare make. £4–£6.50

Lyric – red tin with white writing. Attractive picture of golden harp. 200 needles. £4–£7

Finest Steel Talking Machine Needles – red and green tin with Union Jack. Redditch made. Very rare. £4–£8

Britannia (Minerva) – green, gold and yellow tin, a very attractive British picture tin. Produced in 1911 from The Minerva factory in Redditch, Worcs. 200 disc needles. £2–£4

His Master's Voice – dark blue with world famous trade mark. Many variations and many copies, mainly German and S. African, 200 extra loud needles. £1–£3.50

GUINNESS STOUT BOTTLES

The earliest stoneware stout bottles were produced by the Stephen Green Pottery in Lambeth, the firm that pre-dated Doulton. Stout was a very popular drink in the 18th and 19th centuries because it was believed to have unparalleled nourishing qualities.

When the Guinness family started making their brand of stout, the drink was sold under their name all over the country by various brewers and retail outlets. The sellers did not agree on how the name should be spelt and bottles impressed with the names Guiness, Guinness, Guinnes and Guineas all appeared.

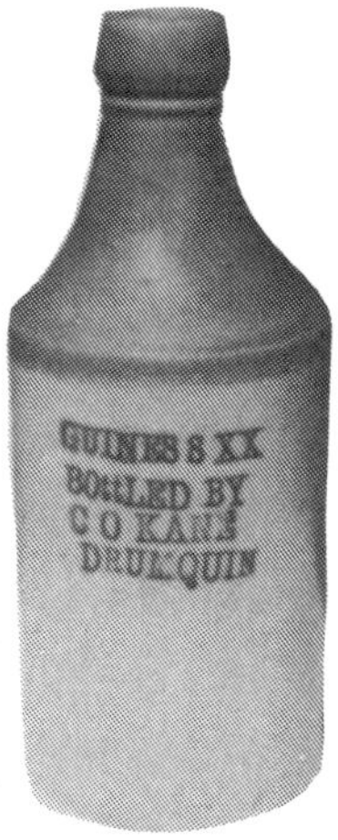

Guiness XX, Bottled by C. O. Kane, Drumquin. £50

Guinness's Extra Stout, bottled by Globe Bottling Co., Dunfermline. £40

Nourishing Stout by O. Bewsher's, Wine & Spirit Merchant, Carlisle. £30

A very rare bottle impressed 'Guinness'XX from George Gordon, Strabane'. £150

Reid's Imperial Stout by J. H. Dewar, Wine Merchant, Glasgow. £30

Guiness's XX Stout by James O'Hanrahan, Commercil Hotel, Graigue. £50

Extra Dublin Stout, bottled by R. Kirkup. The People's Stores, Murton Colliery. £40

Stoneware stout bottle impressed 'London Porter'. £20

HANDKERCHIEFS

The use of handkerchiefs originated in Italy then, gradually, the custom spread throughout Europe.
At first, any old shape was considered suitable and it was only later that the traditional square shape was adopted. It was, actually, more by proclamation than adoption, for it was Marie Antionette, Queen of France, who first suggested the traditional shape and on 2nd January, 1785, a royal decree was announced to the effect that 'Henceforth, all handkerchiefs will be square in shape'.
A collection may follow one of a dozen or more themes such as heraldic, comic, silk, lace, initialled etc., and the price range is wide enough to cater for everyone.

Early 19th century printed handkerchief, printed in red on linen, 32 x 25½in. (Robt. W. Skinner Inc.) £555

'A faithful representation of Her Most Gracious Majesty, Caroline Queen of England in the House of Lords, 1820', a handkerchief on linen, 22in. wide. (Christie's) £400

A printed George Washington handkerchief, probably England, circa 1800, 12½ x 11½in. (Robt. W. Skinner Inc.) £326

Late 19th century handkerchief with central medallion and all-over floral pattern. £4

Royal Corps. of Signals silk and satin handkerchief. £8

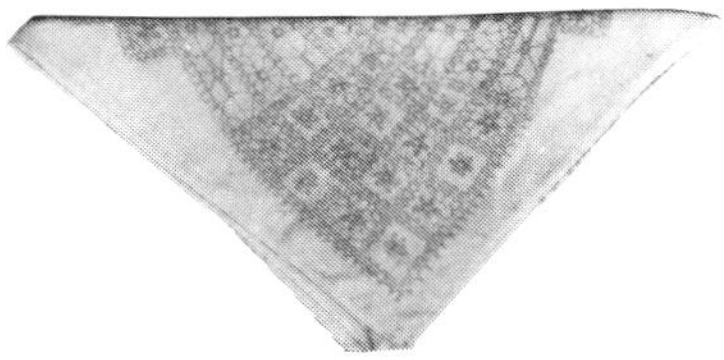

Late Victorian embroidered handkerchief with floral designs. £5

'A representation of the Manchester Reform Meeting dispersed by the Civil and Military Powers, August 16, 1819', handkerchief on linen, 20 x 22in. (Christie's) £350

Early 19th century printed handkerchief apotheosis of George Washington, England, 26 x 19½in. (Robt. W. Skinner Inc.) £634

'The Reformers attack on the Old Rotten Tree – of the Foul Nests of our Morants in Danger', handkerchief printed in colour on silk, circa 1830. (Christie's) £220

HATPINS

Hatpins have been in use to some degree since the 1880's. Originally sold in pairs, or in sets of three or four, they are usually from five to twelve inches long with tops of silver, enamel, glass or semi-precious stones. Designs include butterflies, teddy bears, thistles, flowers, sporting themes, birds, shells and clusters of jewels. Some tops are hinged to give a snug fit close to the hat.

The original function of the hatpin was to anchor hat to hair and as hats got bigger, so did the hatpin. They began to look suspiciously like a dangerous weapon – resulting in a bill being read in America, proposing that, anyone wearing a hatpin more than 9in. in length would be required to carry a licence.

When very short hairstyles became fashionable in the 1920's the hatpin suffered something of a decline in popularity and those made after that date are generally of poorer quality.

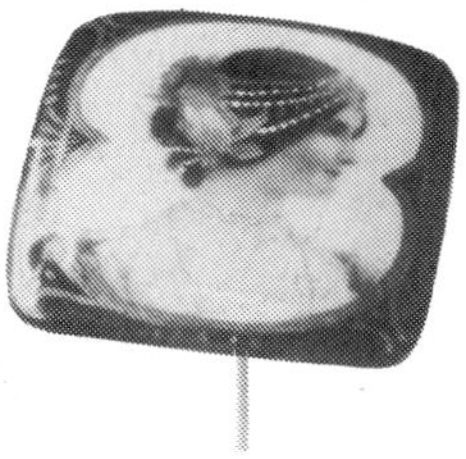

Fine hand-painted porcelain hatpin, early 20th century. £30

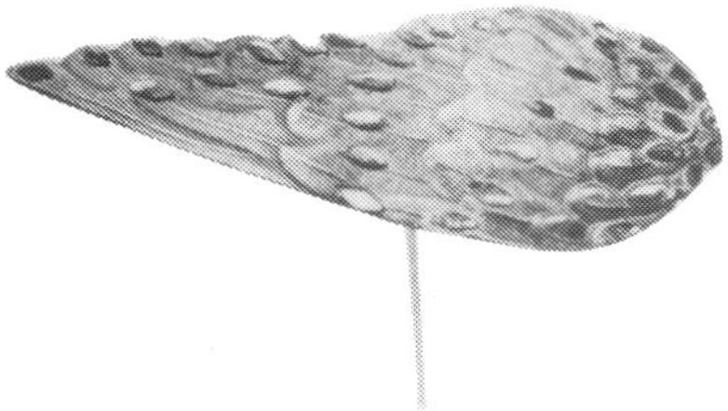

Very unusual Victorian hatpin, a bird's wing in burnished metal set with purple Vauxhall glass. £22

Unusual large and fine silver bear (a popular figure), 1911. £32

Pewter stag-beetle hatpin, circa 1918. £30

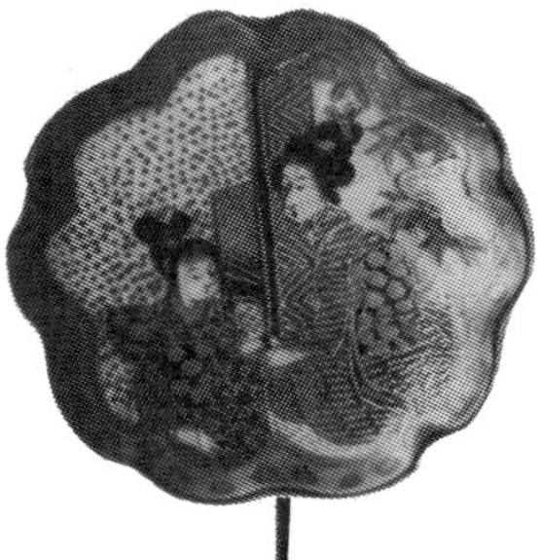

Satsuma hatpin , early 20th century. £35

Silver gilt 'Trembler', which nods as the wearer walks, Victorian. £28

Silver butterfly, set with garnets, circa 1900. £35

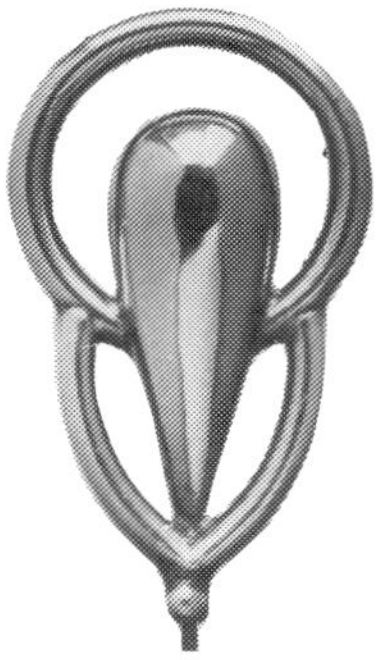

Edwardian silver hatpin, dated 1906. £15

Unusual double-faced pierrot on long pin. £45

Very fine gold and silver pique hatpin, early 20th century. £50

Cut steel swallow with glass eye, on swivel, circa 1900. £17

Carved ivory hatpin in the form of a dragon, circa 1890. £30

HATS

Anyone who has become interested in hats can look forward to forming a thoroughly fascinating collection.
Most hats on the market today date from no earlier than the middle of the 19th century, however, this offers a range including, beautiful Victorian silk bonnets and little richly trimmed hats which were worn perched on top of the head, monumental Edwardian straw extravaganzas, and all of the attractive hats of the 20's, 30's and 40's.

Men's hats also make a marvellous collection and offer examples of the 18th century tricorne which was followed by the top hat made of beaver or felt, then the bowler, checked woollen caps, the summer straw boater and the trilby.
An enthusiastic collector may even attempt to determine the name of the original owner in the knowledge that the hats of the famous can be real collector's items.

Black velvet covered riding hat by Moss Bros. of Covent Garden. £6

1930's lady's felt hat with satin band. £3

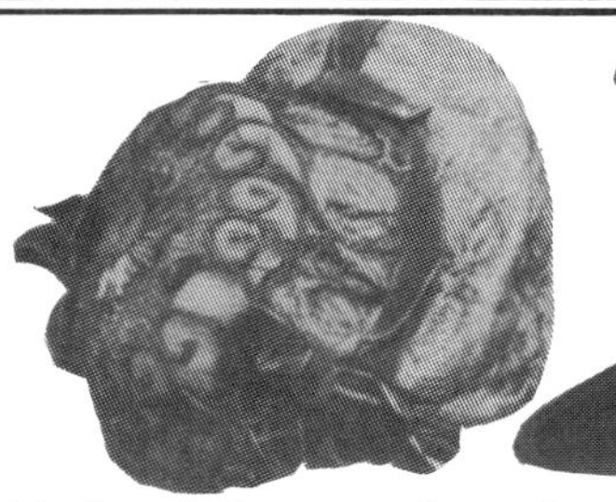

A black satin bonnet trimmed with pleating, circa 1880. (Christie's) £20

Top hat by O. Parsley of Bristol. £6

A lady's flat wide-brimmed hat of black figured silk laid over plaited straw, circa 1770, 15¼in. diam. (Christie's S. Kensington) £600

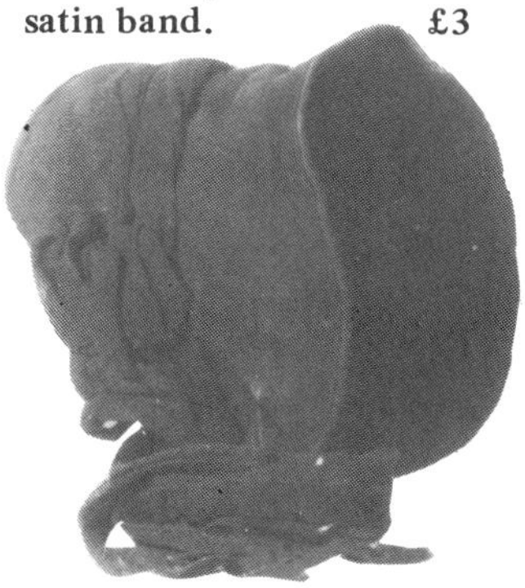

A mourning bonnet of black crepe, circa 1830. (Christie's) £110

A child's or young lady's hat of ivory silk quilted with a scale design and trimmed with a rosette of ivory ribbons, circa 1820. (Christie's) £500

A 16th century man's embroidered cap embellished with sequins and gold lace trim, England, 8in. high. (Robt. W. Skinner Inc.) £6,993

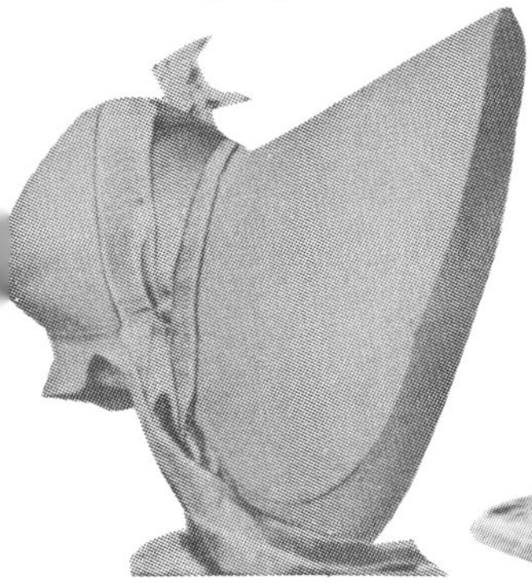

A straw bonnet with deep brim, trimmed later with satin with chine silk ribbon and artificial flowers, circa 1830. (Christie's) £260

A top hat of grey beaver, possibly 1829, labelled M. Strieken, 8in. high. (Christie's) £715

A bonnet of brown striped plaited straw trimmed with brown figured ribbons, edged with a fringe, circa 1850. (Christie's) £50

A top hat of black beaver, with black silk ribbon, 7in. high, circa 1840. (Christie's) £242

HELMETS

It is apparently untrue that Viking warriors wore horned helmets when they went into battle but nonetheless helmets were used to terrify the enemy as much as to protect the head of the warrior. Magnificent helmets have turned up in burial sites as far apart as Greece and northern Scotland and the workmanship and design of them all testify to their function and status.

It is possible today to buy fairly cheaply simple helmets with nose guards such as were used by troopers in the wars between the Cavaliers and the Roundheads and which used to hang on the walls of large houses for the men to grab when alarm sounded. Border reivers were recognisable by their curved 'iron bonnets' and the collecting field extends to recent times with Nazi helmets or war-time 'tin hats' used to protect air raid wardens during bombing raids.

Some of the most impressive helmets, however, are those made by Eastern craftsmen, particularly the Turks and Persians and, even more frightening, the armour helmets turned out by German armourers for mounted knights. The hideously grimacing faces on front of them must have filled the knight's adversaries with terror.

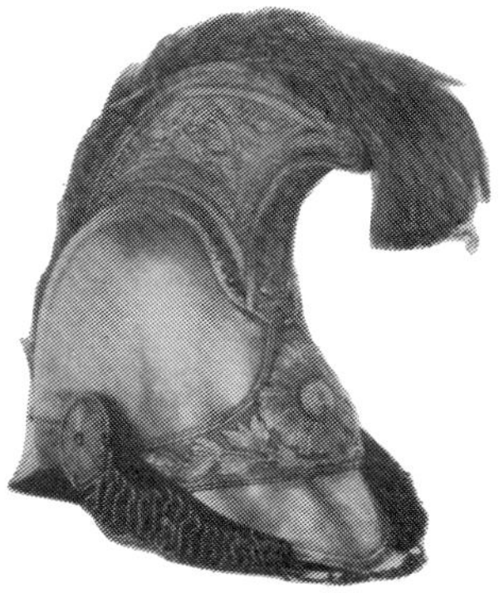

A brass helmet much as for officers of the French Carabiniers, 1856-71. (Christie's) £450

A late 16th century cabasset with brass plume holder. £880

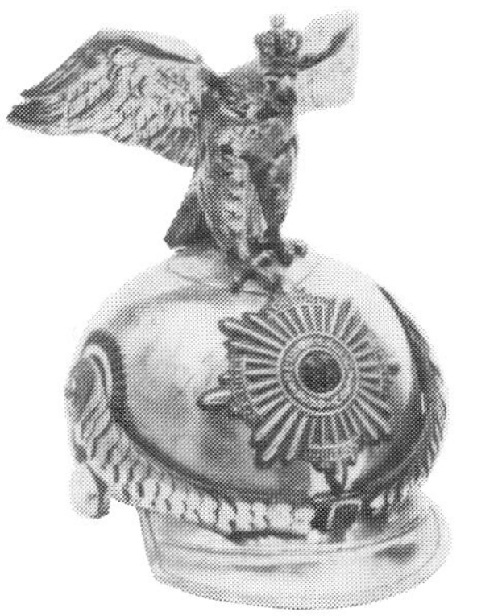

A Prussian Garde du Corps trooper's helmet, with parade eagle to crown. (Wallis & Wallis) £1,150

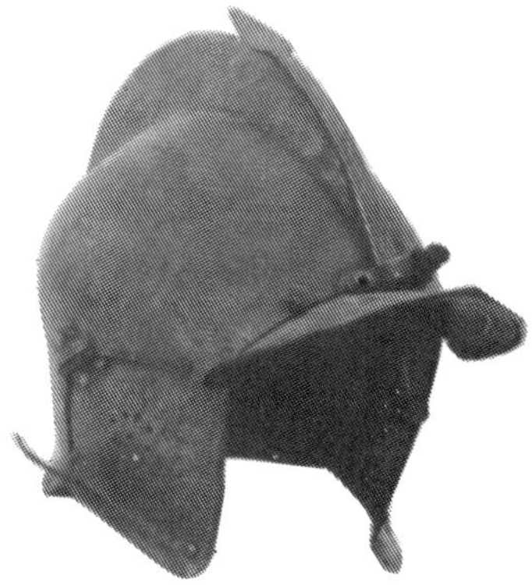

A German burgonet, one-piece skull with tall comb and pierced hinged ear flaps, circa 1600. (Wallis & Wallis) £575

A late 16th century morion, brim with band of foliate decoration and roped edge. £1,430

A Victorian officer's lance cap of The 17th (Duke of Cambridge's Own) Lancers. (Wallis & Wallis) £700

An other rank's composite metal helmet of the Prussian Line Cuirassier Regts. (Christie's) £400

An embossed and parcel gilt helmet, together with two arm guards, Persia, 19th century. (Robt. W. Skinner Inc.) £510

A composite leather pickelhaube of 1842 pattern, bearing an eagle plate of Prussian Garde-Infanterie pattern. (Christie's) £320

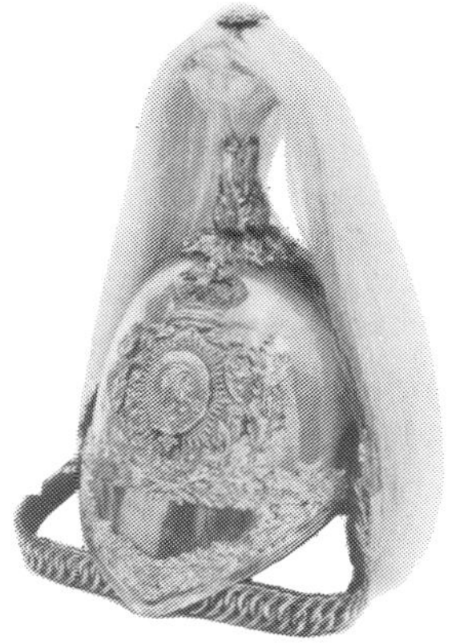

A Victorian officer's Albert pattern helmet of The 4th (Royal Irish) Dragoon Guards. (Wallis & Wallis) £350

A Victorian officer's shako of The Royal Dockyard Bn., contained in its original japanned tin. (Phillips) £420

An officer's composite metal eagle-topped helmet of the Prussian Regimental of Garde du Corps. (Christie's) £1,200

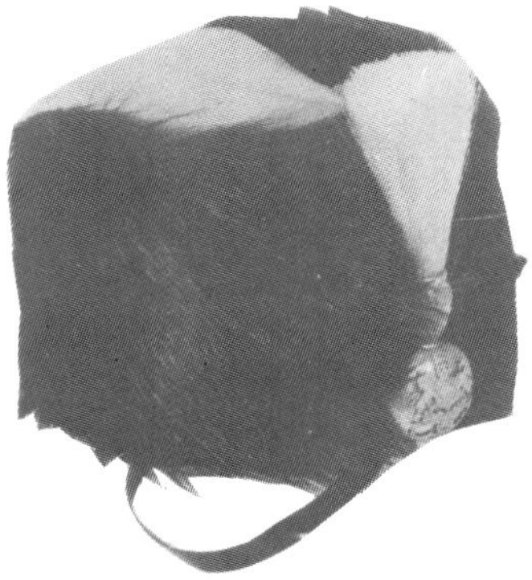

An Artillery officer's busby by Hawkes & Co., the metal case inscribed Earl of Chester's Rifles. (Christie's) £180

The 1st Huntingdonshire Light Horse Volunteers (Duke of Manchester's), black leather helmet. (Christie's) £350

A Baden Infantryman's pickelhaube of The 109th Leib Regt., with German silver helmet plate. (Wallis & Wallis) £260

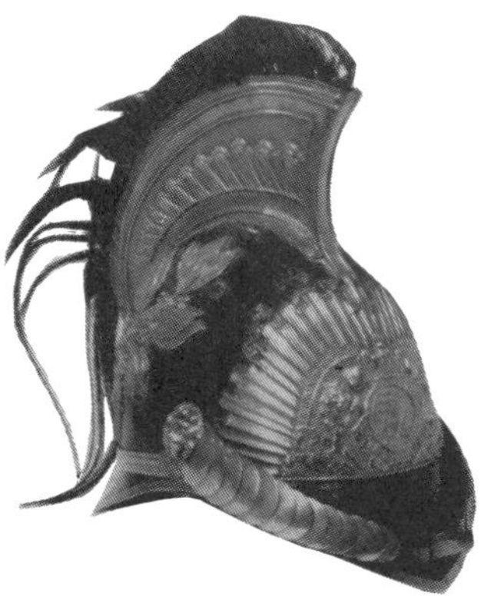

The Blandford Yeomanry Cavalry black japanned metal helmet of early 19th century Roman style. (Christie's) £650

An 18th century Prussian mitre cap, Fusiliermutze, circa 1740-56. (Christie's) £1,900

A 4-plate folding buff, top plate with roped border and pierced sights, circa 1600. (Wallis & Wallis) £625

HORN

Horn is one of those materials which people seem either to dislike intensely or to collect avidly.

The range of objects of horn is almost limitless from spoons to mirror frames, from snuff boxes to chairs, from drinking vessels to chandeliers, and it is in this tremendous versatility that the chief attraction of the material lies.

Dividing horn into three categories we have articles made from treated horn (spoons, combs, shoehorns, snuff boxes, carved drinking vessels), those made of untreated – usually stags' – horn (chairs, tables, chandeliers, cutlery handles) and the grotesquely decorative (heads and skulls with antlers attached which adorn the walls of a few hunters' homes and those of many more would-be hunters).

Combs, spoons, fans, boxes, shoehorns and buttons are fairly widely available at reasonable prices, though spoons dating from the 16th and 17th centuries are rather more desirable and will fetch considerably more. Those having whistles incorporated in their handles are the best.

Powder horns make interesting collections, since many are finely carved and engraved with everything from flowers to coats of arms and hunting scenes.

It is not only the small objects to look for, however, for tables, chairs and chandeliers can also be found, their curiosity value ensuring a ready market.

Early 18th century rhinoceros horn libation cup, 6½in. wide. (Christie's) £1,500

A 17th century pressed-horn plaque with the Raising of Lazarus, 6 x 5cm.. £352

A Bohemian carved staghorn powder flask decorated with three deer moving through a forest, with silver mounts. (Bermondsey) £800

An 18th century rhinoceros horn libation cup finely carved with many travellers walking, on horseback and in boats, 17cm. high, with fitted box. (Christie's) £3,888

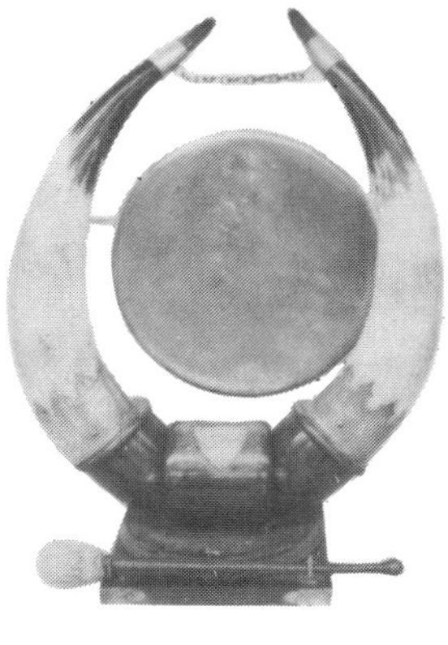

Victorian horn and brass gong. (British Antique Exporters) £75

A late 18th century Scottish horn snuff mull carved with the profile of the Old Pretender, 4¼in. high. (Christie's) £324

HORSE BRASSES

Horse brasses were thought to have originated over 4000 years ago in the near east and their symbolic designs to have evolved from the heraldic emblems on early horse armour. These decorative amulets were thought to have the power to deflect the gaze of the 'evil eye' from the wearer.

Handmade by gypsies and tinkers from sheet brass and sold at fairs up and down the country in the early 19th century they soon became very popular and were often awarded as prizes at agricultural shows and fairs. Demand eventually became so great that a more commercial method of production was sought resulting in the cast brass version making its first appearance around 1830 followed by a mass produced stamped brass as demand reached a peak at the end of Victoria's reign.

Early designs show acorns, flowers, wheatsheaves, trees, stags and fox masks with the later versions of 1840-1860 depicting portraits, county symbols, events and a variety of geometric designs. Of particular interest to collectors are those issued to celebrate Queen Victoria's Jubilee. A most attractive display can be made with Martingales, horse lames and even straps and buckles from Victorian harness.

It is something of a bonus if the brasses are still mounted on their original leather straps.

There is now almost a glut of modern horse brasses on the market but once you have handled and studied early brasses it will become easier to distinguish between the old and the new. As a broad rule, the modern version is much lighter in weight and shows no signs of rubbing on the reverse side.

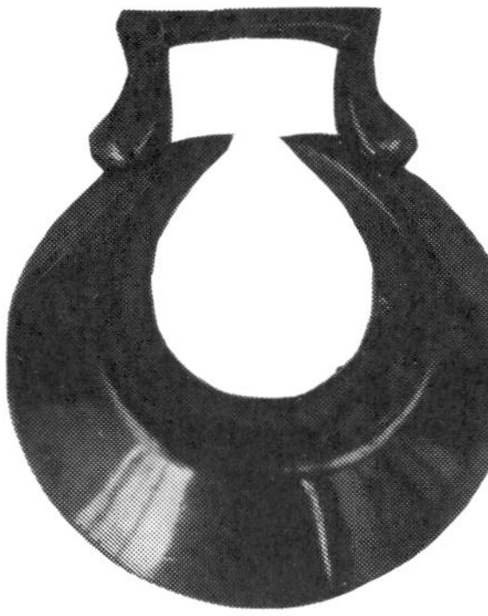

Cast Crescent Brass. £14

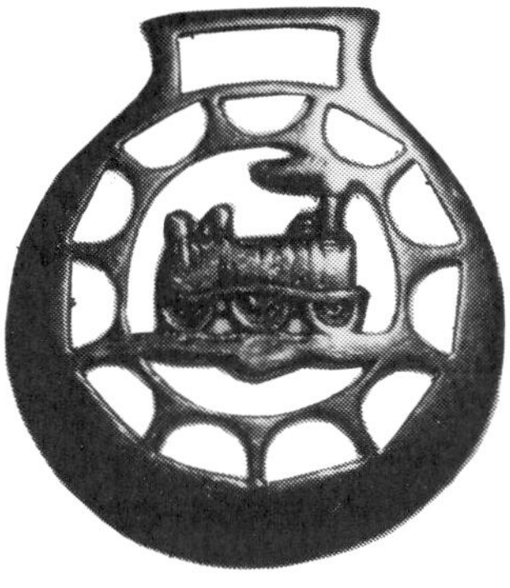

Cast Steam Locomotive Brass. £30

Stamped Brass of Horse Pasant, showing well worn hanger, a good sign of an old brass. £15

Cast Brass, God Save The King 1902. £55

Merit Badge R.S.P.C.A. London Van Horse Parade 1925. £35

Victoria 1870, a rare Cast Brass. £60

HOT WATER BOTTLES

Before the indroduction of the rubber hot water bottle – and long before the electric blanket, 'hotties' were made of a very heavy stoneware material.

The bottle is flat based with an arched top and is sealed by means of a stoneware threaded screw stopper, secured by a rubber washer. Children commonly referred to bottles as 'piggy' bottles because of the squat, flattened nose shape of the handle. Some carry printed trademarks or early advertising slogans.

There are miniature versions designed to be carried within a muff and used as a hand-warmer and a special version designed to be used as a footwarmer for the comfort of coach and carriage travellers.

A decorative two-tone brown stoneware hot water bottle. £5

Late 19th century copper hot water bottle with screw plug, 7½in. diam. £12

Victorian stoneware hot water bottle stamped 'Footwarmer'. £4

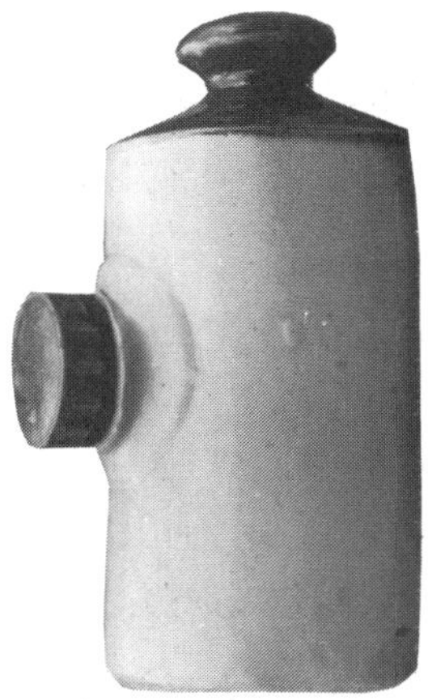

Stoneware hot water bottle, late 19th century. £3

'The Adaptable Hot Water Bottle & Bed Warmer'. £15

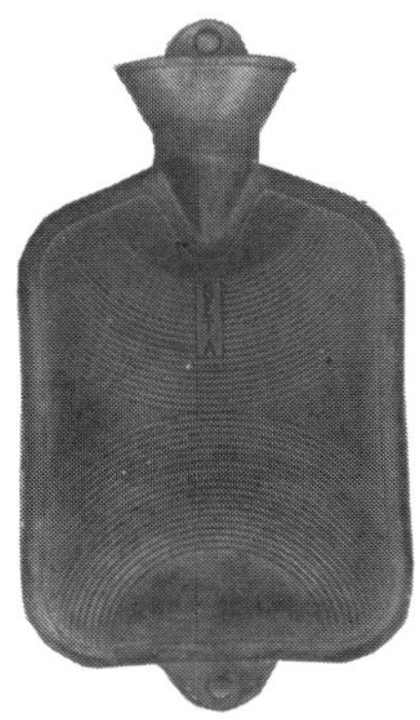

An early example of an English made Beta hot water bottle. 50p

'Handy' stoneware hot water bottle. £8

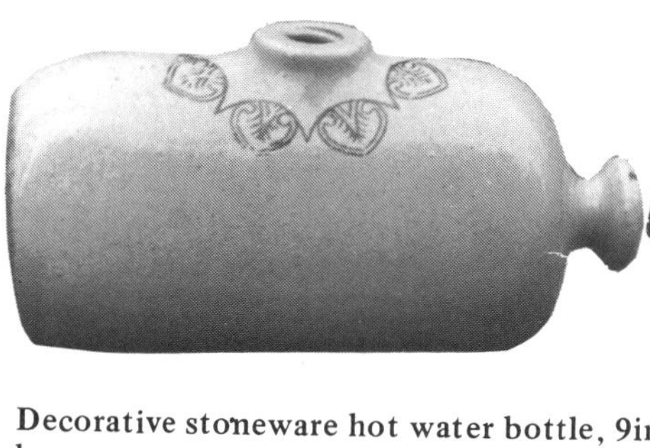

Decorative stoneware hot water bottle, 9in. long. £3.50

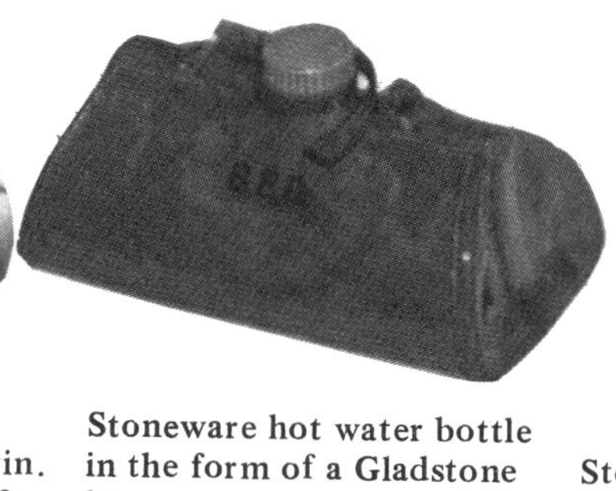

Stoneware hot water bottle in the form of a Gladstone bag. £20

Stoneware 'Sunrays' footwarmer, 8in. wide. £7

ICONS

Russian icons dating from the 10th to the 17th century are extremely rare and precious works of art. However, examples from a later period are more common and the high standard of their workmanship has guaranteed their continuing popularity with collectors.

Usually worked in tempera on wood, the subject is always of a religious or mystical nature showing representations of Christ, The Virgin, The Saints or scenes from a religious life. The majority of icon painters were monks and this work was often produced as part of the discipline of a life of contemplation.

Icons were sometimes set in a folding frame so that they could be carried from place to place. These frames are often of exquisite design and craftsmanship. A three-fold panel is called a triptych.

The Sainted Hierarchs of Rostov, James and Dimitre, late 18th century, 34.5 x 27.5cm. £418

The Virgin Hodigitria, Cretan, 1480-1520, 40.5 x 32.5cm. £5,060

The Tikhvin Mother of God painted on a gold ground, maker's mark A.V., Moscow, 1790, 30.2 x 26cm. £1,100

Late 17th century icon of St. Nicholas, 31.2 x 26.6cm. £550

The Hodigitria Mother of God, inscribed 'through the hand of Nicholas Lamboudi of Sparta', 15th century, 67 x 47.5cm. £19,800

Saints Zosima and Savatii, the oklad with a silvered metal revetment, 18th century, 32 x 26.7cm. £1,210

Early 17th century icon of St. Onouphrios The Great, signed by E. Lambardos, 55.5 x 36.5cm. £41,800

An icon painted in two registers, contained within a repousse and silver gilt oklad, late 18th century, 48.5 x 39.5cm. £2,310

INHALERS

Collectors of medical antiques and memorabilia will be aware of the compulsive interest in health held by the more affluent of our forefathers. This led to an expansive and profitable market for the manufacturers of medications and medical equipment.

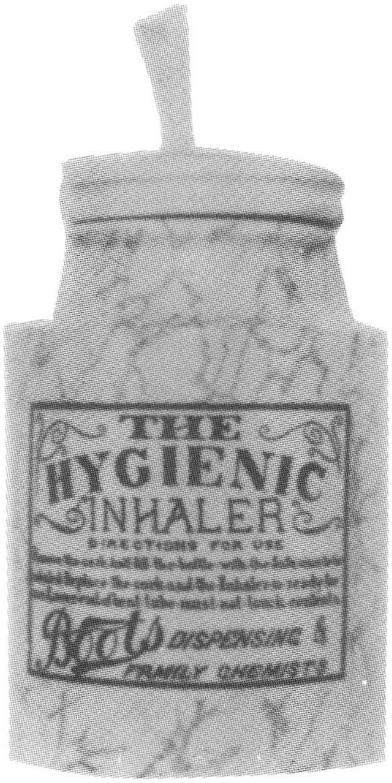

Although relief from coughs and bronchial troubles could probably be obtained effectively by simply inhaling some of the vapour straight from a bowl of boiling water containing some of the prescribed preparation, manufacturers produced a variety of inhalers, some boasting various claims and other bearing attractive mofits.

Small portable inhalers were designed specifically for use when travelling and for convenience, the medication could be introduced beforehand and hot water added when required.

Today, although some searching must be done for the more desirable examples, inhalers can provide a varied and unusual theme for the collector, offering a range from the bizarre to quite beautiful.

Hockin's Acme Inhaler with all-over floral design in sepia and blue colouring. £50

The Bournemouth Inhaler, sepia printed with floral decoration. £60

The Westminster Inhaler, sepia printed with floral decoration. £60

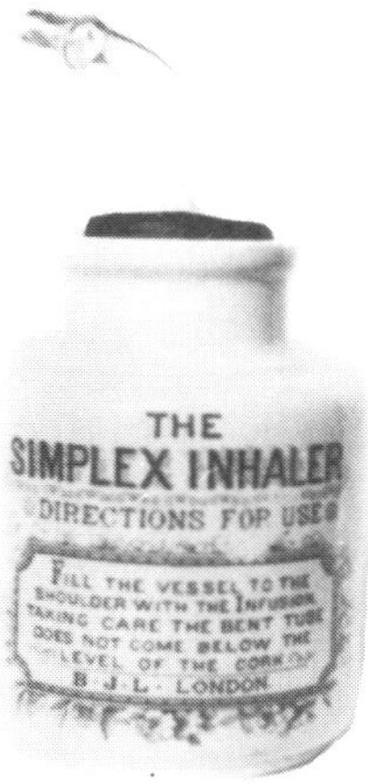

The Simplex Inhaler with white body overprinted with directions in black. £40

Dr. Nelson's Improved Inhaler of bulbous-shape with built-in vent to replace air taken through the mouth-piece, circa 1880. £10

Improved Earthenware Inhaler by S. Maw Son & Thompson with attractive marbled effect. £25

INK BOTTLES

Ink was expensive in the 19th century and to keep the price of their product down in a very competitive market, ink manufacturers made every effort to market it as cheaply – but as eye-catchingly – as possible.
Ink bottles can be found in glass, saltglaze pottery and occasionally porcelain. Among the rarest examples are 'sheered lip' glass bottles in which the glass bottle openings were not polished but only broken off and sealed with a cork and sealing wax.
There were ink bottles in the shape of turtles, cottages, locomotives, Bonaparte, Mr Punch, igloos, bird cages and grimacing clowns. Today there is a strong American interest in ink bottle collecting.

Staffordshire ceramic clown head ink bottle, the open mouth providing access to the ink reservoir and with a quill holder on top of the head. £60

An extremely rare circular cottage inkwell in aqua glass with Registry of Designs diamond embossed on the base for August 1968, 6cm. high. £150–£200

Mid 19th century 'Bonaparte' ink bottle, the hollow body forming the reservoir while the front hole acts as a quill holder and the rear hole as access to the ink. £150

A Whitefriar's paperweight inkwell, from the Bacchus period, circa 1840, 7in. high. £280

One of a pair of white china inkwells in the form of dolphins, with Registry of Designs diamond mark for July 16th 1874 and Perry & Co., London, printed on the base. £150–£200

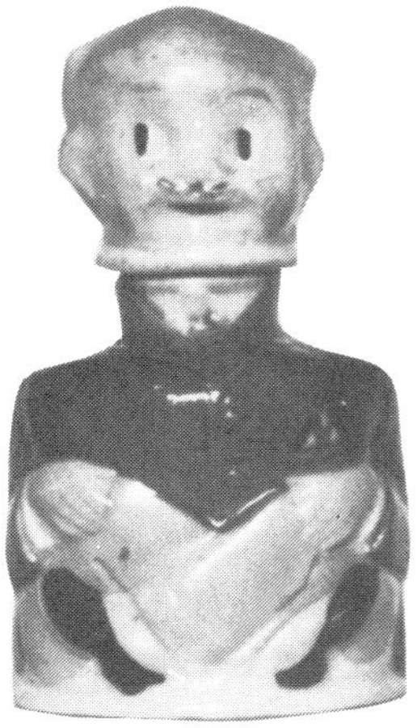

American red and blue ceramic bottles known as 'MA' and 'PA' with removable heads forming the cork stoppers. The 'Mr. & Mrs. Carter's Ink' were patented by C. H. Henkels of Philadelphia for Carter's Ink Co. of Boston and were made in Germany prior to World War I and later in the U.S.A. £100

'Mr. Punch', one of the most sought after saltglaze ink bottles, incised on the back 'Gardeners Ink Works, Lower White Cross St., London', tgoether with the U.K. Registration Diamond mark for 1851, 4½in. high. £120 plus

INROS

Most Japanese inros take the form of a decorative slim rectangular lacquered box. They will usually divide up into three to five sections slotting neatly together and strung on a cord threaded through slots in the sides.

They were used, by men, from the 16th to the 19th century for carrying the family seal, medicine or tobacco and were worn hanging from the belt alongside the sword.

The cords of the inro are secured by a bead (ojime) and attached to the girdle by a netsuke carved in wood or ivory.

Late 19th century three-case hirame inro decorated in takamakie and raden, ivory and other inlay, signed Jushuhan Chohei. (Christie's) £918

Early 19th century three-case inro decorated in gold hiramakie, takamakie, heidatsu and togidashi on a yasuriko ground. (Christie's) £540

An 18th century four-case Nashiji inro, decorated in gold hiramakie, takamakie and hirame, unsigned. (Christie's) £700

A 19th century four-case Kinji inro, signed Hasegawa saku above a red tsubo seal and Shibayama on a shell tablet. (Christie's) £972

A 19th century three-case Kinji inro, with attached black lacquer bead ojime and red lacquered mokko-gata netsuke. (Christie's) £3,200

A small three-case Ginji inro, decorated in gold hiramakie, with wakasa-nuri bead ojime. (Christie's) £1,400

A 19th century three-case silver inro, with attached silver filigree bead ojime and lightly stained ivory netsuke. (Christie's) £6,500

A 19th century Tamenuri three-case inro, with cornelian glass bead ojime. (Christie's) £480

INSTRUMENTS

If ever there was an age of discovery, it must have been the second half of the 19th century when new theories and inventions were being created daily. It would appear that the whole populus was fascinated by science, with hardly a magazine or newspaper not devoting acres of column inches to the likes of Darwin, Eddison and Bell. This has left a legacy of finely made instruments with many, such as the microscopes and telescopes, adequately fulfilling today, the function for which they were designed.
It is not only the scientific instruments such as circumferentors, theodolites, equitorial dials and graphometers which are sought after but domestic instruments as well, such as telephones, typewriters and telegraphs.
All, when cleaned and polished, make an interesting display, a tribute to fine Victorian craftsmanship and inventiveness.

A gilt brass pedometer, German, possibly Augsburg, circa 1700, 65mm. long. (Christie's) £759

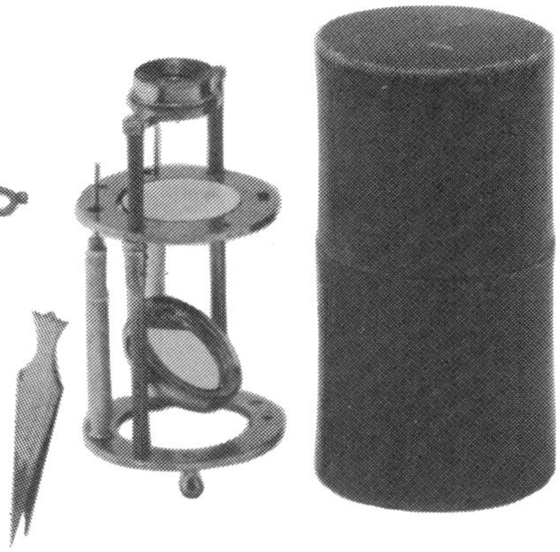

An English Withering type botanical microscope and case, circa 1800, with box, 10.5cm. high. (Christie's) £341

A brass circular protractor with box, signed Blunt, London, circa 1800, 78mm. radius. (Christie's) £288

A 16th century gilt brass miniature armillary sphere, probably German, 55mm. diam. (Christie's) £2,882

A cradle-mounted stereographoscope in black ebonised finish with lens panel, 16in. high. (Christie's) £200

A small 2½in. reflecting telescope, signed J. Watson, London, circa 1800, on folding tripod base, 235mm. long. (Christie's) £910

A brass transit on circular foot with focus levelling screws, signed Troughton & Simms, London, 39cm. high. (Christie's) £493

A small Zoetrope optical toy on wood stand with several picture strips, diam. of drum 5¼in. (Christie's) £100

A German cube dial, the wooden cube with five printed scales, signed D. Beringer, 7in. high. (Lawrence Fine Art) £550

A 17th/18th century brass graduated circle, probably French, 13.7cm. diam. (Christie's) £607

A two-day marine chronometer, the dial signed by Dobbie McInnes Ltd., Glasgow, no. 9615, dial 10cm. diam. (Christie's) £607

A 19th century English brass universal equatorial dial with three levelling screws, 11.5cm. diam. (Christie's) £417

Late 18th century sand clock, the two sand glasses mounted in a brass frame, 5½in. high. £440

An 18in. Malby's celestial globe on stand, 45in. high. £1,012

An Ive's Kromskop colour stereoscopic viewer, in wood carrying case. (Christie's) £700

An American brass and plated brass compound monocular microscope, signed E. Gundlach, pat. Sept. 14, 1878, 29cm. high approx. (Christie's) £288

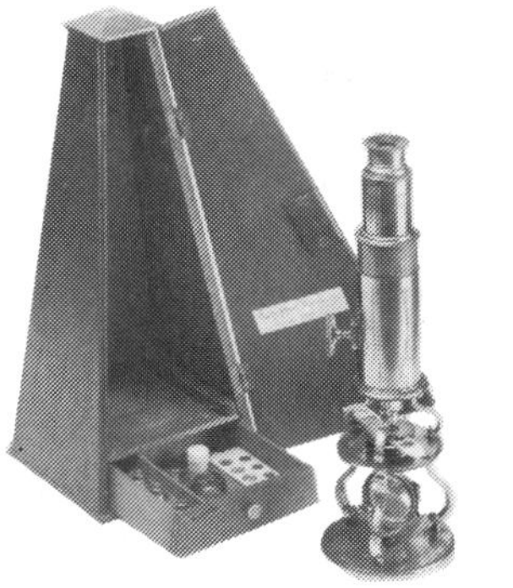

A brass Culpeper-type monocular microscope on three scrolled legs, 10¼in. high, contained in its mahogany case. £440

A cased set of Jacobus Listingh coin weights, Dutch, dated 1659, 3½ x 6¼in., in leather slip case. £3,080

Late 18th century brass transit instrument, signed Lenoir (Paris), on circular base with three levelling screws, the telescope 53.5cm. long. (Christie's) £2,124

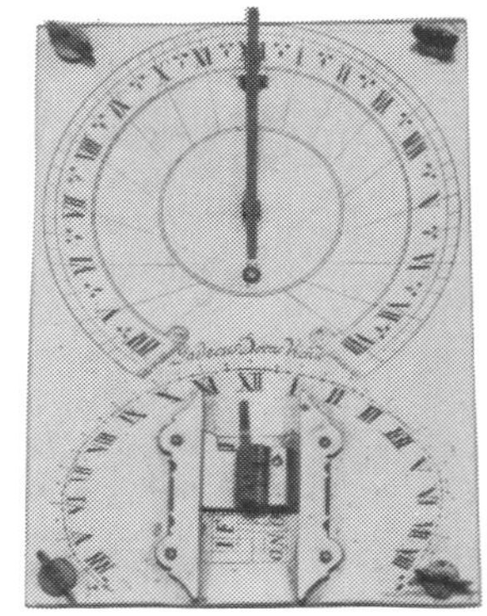

An 18th century brass analemmatic and horizontal inclining dial, signed J. Deens, Vienae, 113mm. long. (Christie's) £606

A French 19th century brass orrery on stand depicting the asteroids, 23cm. diam. (Christie's) £910

A cast iron sundial by E. T. Hurley, circa 1900, 10¼in. diam. (Robt. W. Skinner Inc.) £295

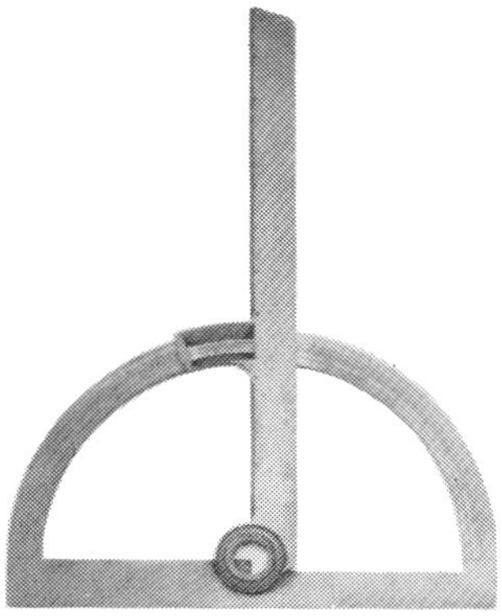

Late 18th century brass protractor, signed Lenoir a Paris, 13cm. radius. (Christie's) £144

A chased silver universal equatorial dial with perpetual calendar, signed Jean-David Beyser, Augsburg, circa 1750, 80mm. long. (Christie's) £758

A London Stereoscopic Co. Brewster-pattern stereoscope with brass mounted eye pieces, in fitted rosewood box, 13in. wide. (Christie's) £380

A Regency mahogany library globe, 28in. diam. (Christie's) £16,200

A Henry Crouch brass binocular microscope, No. 2092, of Lister limb construction. (Lawrence Fine Art) £550

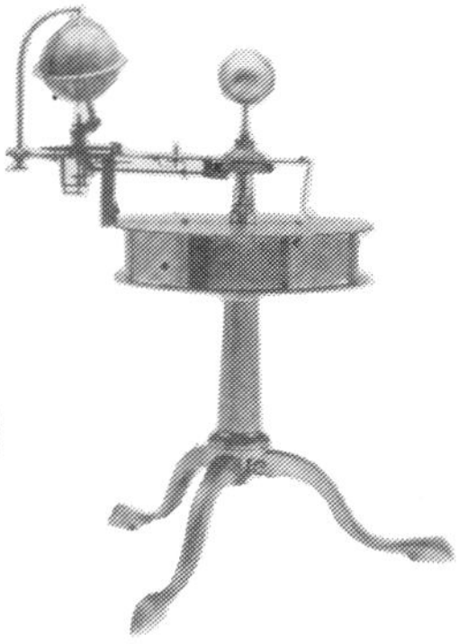

A brass Martin type orrery with tellurium of American interest, signed T. Blunt, London, 22cm. diam. (Christie's) £10,620

A large brass mounted lodestone with bail handle, 20.5cm. high. (Christie's) £2,656

A small brass sextant of T-frame style signed Berge, London, in fitted shaped mahogany case, circa 1800. (Reeds Rains) £1,350

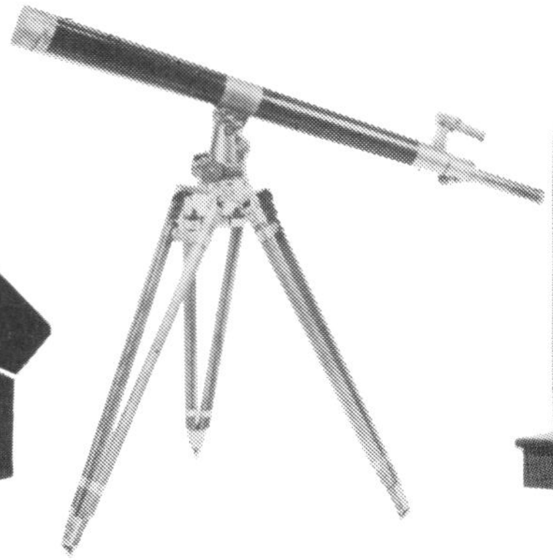

A brass and mahogany 4in. refracting telescope, signed Steinheil in Munchen, no. 2811, the sighting telescope, no. 2886, 171cm. long. (Christie's) £1,137

A mahogany folding Cuminoscope concave mirror photograph/print viewer, by The Cuminoscope Patent Brevetes, S.G.D.G. (Christie's) £180

IRONS

A wise buy for those with the collecting urge, would be old irons. They are comparatively cheap, fairly plentiful, and will form an interesting collection which is sure to increase in value. The variety of different types is staggering; from tiny curved 4in. lace irons to the enormous, professional Tailors Goose which can weigh anything up to 30lb.

It would appear that the practice of ironing clothes was known to the Chinese in the eighth century and introduced to Britain by the Viking invaders, who used a massive smooth stone resembling an inverted mushroom known as a 'sleek'.

Early flat irons were sold in pairs so that one could be reheating either on the stove or placed directly against the fire while the other was in use. They were heavy and the handles hot and awkward to manage. A set of irons with exchangeable handles was patented in America by a Mrs Potts in 1871.

In the 18th century, it was not uncommon for a household wash to be tackled only once every two or three months – an event presenting many challenges with fabrics requiring pleating, crimping, ruffling, goffering and finishing so that by the Victorian period every housekeeper worth her salt was armed with a battery of irons designed to cope with every conceivable task, even one with a tiny base and long handle for ironing hats.

If you keep your eyes open you can find old irons just about anywhere and, a few pounds will buy a simple cast flat (or sad) iron. Raise your sights and you can become the proud possessor of an interesting gas or methylated spirit model – or even a hollow iron complete with heating stone.

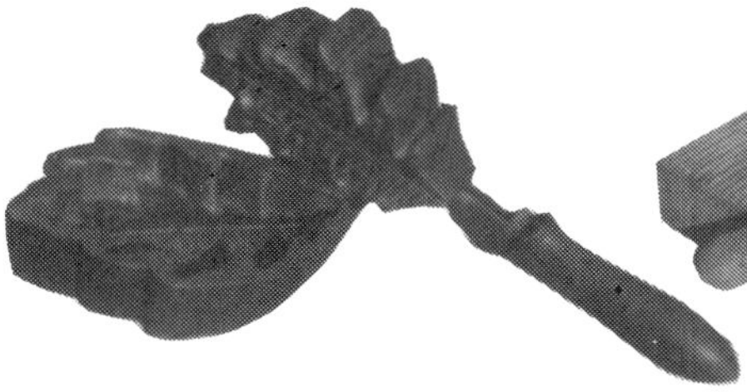

A leaf iron in two parts in which silk is placed to receive an impression before being stitched to bonnets. £40

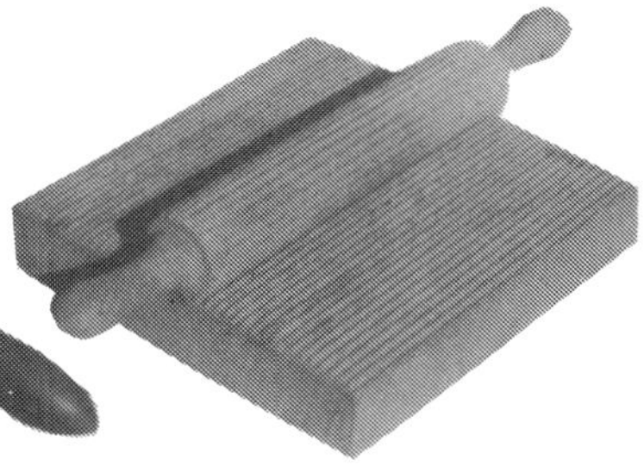

A small wood fluter with a flat base and rolling-pin top. £15

Scottish box iron with ornate brass supports. £65

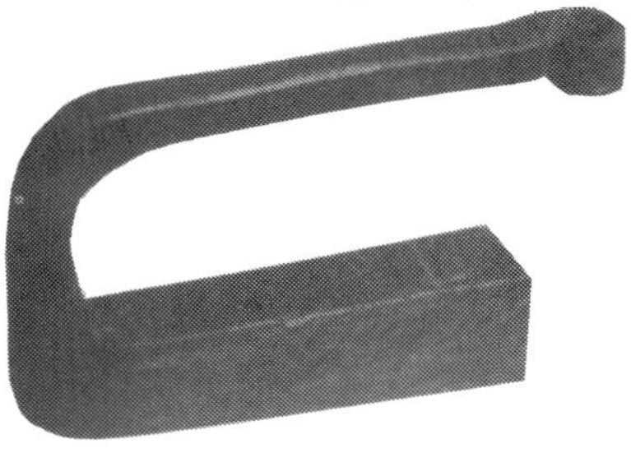

Early 19th century hand wrought goose-iron. £40

Velvet iron complete with stand. £22

Crimping machine with adjustable corrugated rollers, various types. £40–£80

'The Erie Fluter' in two parts with a flat base and rocking top. £30

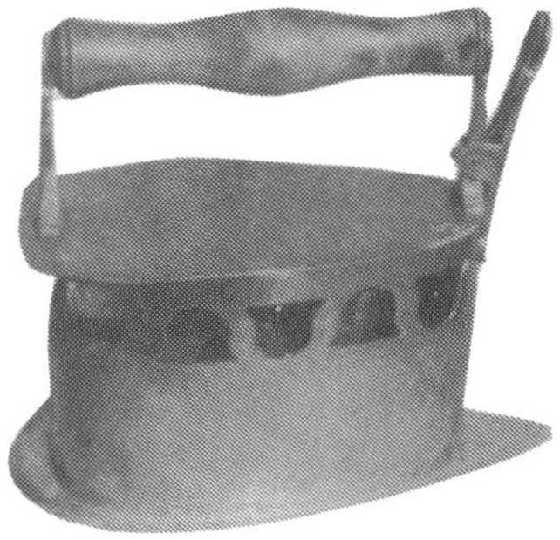

19th century Continental brass charcoal iron. £70

IVORY

Ivory has been recognised as a perfect material for carving since ancient times and the art of the skilled carver has always been well appreciated.

Craftsmen used several kinds of ivory including, elephant tusks (the hard white ivory comes from the African elephant and the yellower from the Indian), and hippopotamus or walrus tusks to produce boxes, jewellery, knife handles, combs, buttons and statuettes and ornamental groups of particular beauty.

Ivory inlaid with designs in fine materials is known as Shibayama, named after the Japanese family Shibayama who excelled in this style of decoration.

There are many well produced fakes made of plastic on the market, but close examination of the surface may show a lack of the characteristic streaking or flecking of ivory. A test, which should be undertaken entirely at your own risk, is to place a hot needle pressed flat against the base of a suspect piece. Plastic will melt!

Late 19th century ivory tusk vase inlaid in Shibayama style, signed, overall height 42.7cm. (Christie's) £540

Late 19th century ivory carving of Kannon, signed Shunyosai Nobuyuki, 13.9cm. high. (Christie's) £540

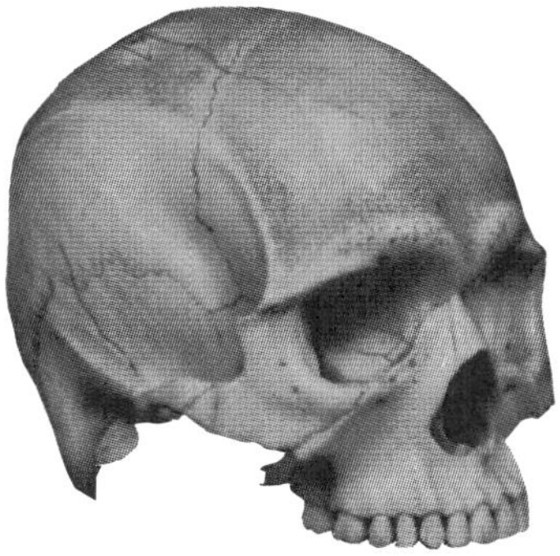

A 19th century ivory okimono of a human skull, signed Shosai to, 13cm. long. (Christie's) £3,672

Late 19th century sectional ivory okimono of a basket weaver and his wife, signed Eitoku, 10cm. high. (Christie's) £561

A large, late 19th century, Continental silver mounted ivory tankard and cover, 16in. high. (Christie's) £7,020

A mid 19th century decorated ivory ink stand, Europe, 3in. high, 5in. diam. (Robt. W. Skinner Inc.) £175

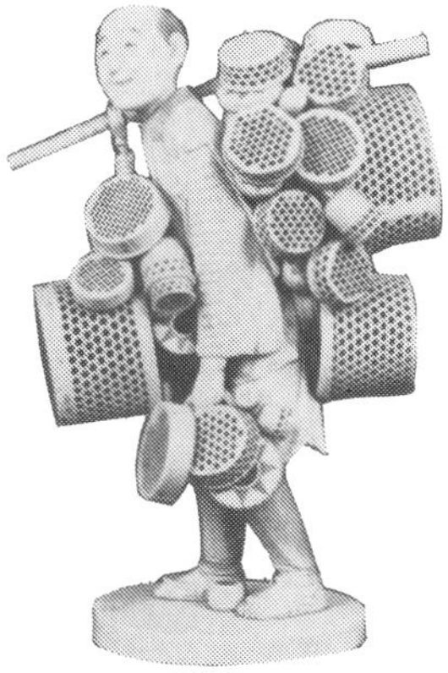

Late 19th century ivory carving of a basket seller, signed Jogyoku, 25cm. high. (Christie's) £1,350

A German 17th century ivory plaque carved with half length figures, 11.5 x 9.7cm. (Lawrence Fine Art) £396

JADE

There are three materials which are called jade – **JADEITE**, the finest, is white with a purple tint or emerald green; **NEPHRITE**, which has been known and used since ancient times and **CHLOROMELANITE**, which is so dark a green that it almost looks black.

These varieties of jade are found in Upper Burma, Central India, Turkestan, Siberia, New Zealand, Silesia and Alaska. Although the people who have always been most fond of jade are the Chinese, none occurs naturally in that country. Chinese jade had to be imported and it was carved into beautiful and delicate objects ranging from religious objects, seals and boxes to vases and jewellery. The skill of the carvers is breathtaking and many beautiful jade pieces can be seen in museums everywhere.

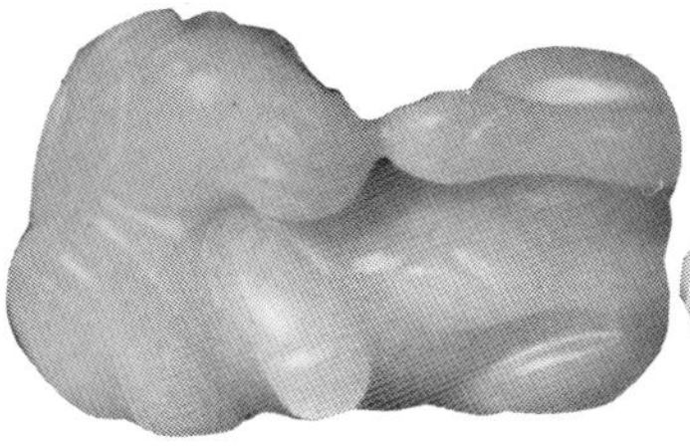

A pale celadon jade figure of a recumbent horse, Yuan Dynasty, 4.6cm. long. (Christie's) £1,458

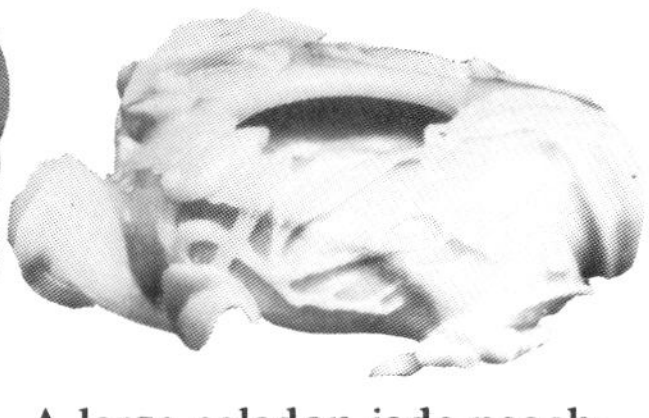

A large celadon jade peach-shaped brushwasher, late Qing Dynasty, 19.5cm. wide. (Christie's) £1,620

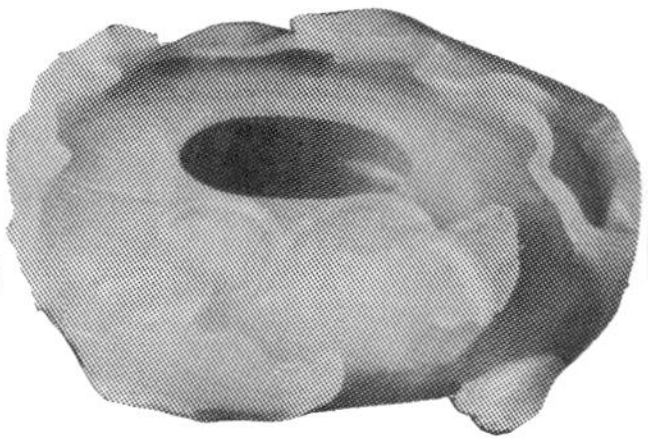

A celadon jade brush washer modelled as a pressed hollowed melon, 3in. wide. (Christie's) £680

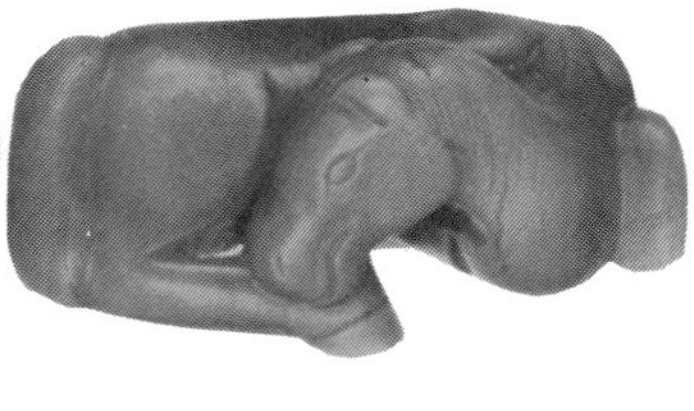

A jade figure of a recumbent horse, Tang/Song Dynasty, 6.5cm. long. (Christie's) £864

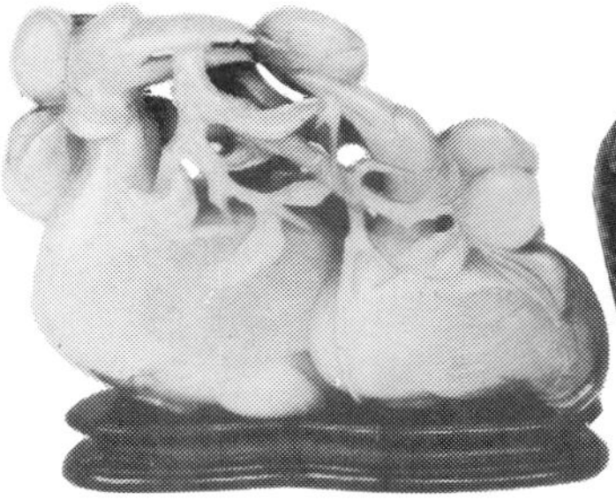

A pale celadon jade model of two mythical birds feeding from a branch of peaches, 6¾in. wide, on wood stand. (Christie's) £2,400

A jade figure of a crouching Buddhistic lion, probably Han/Six Dynasties, 6.8cm. wide. (Christie's) £864

An early celadon jade circular disc, bi, Han Dynasty, 10.7cm. diam., in fitted box.(Christie's) £2,700

A mottled greyish jade square seal carved in the archaic taste, probably Qing Dynasty, 9.5cm. square. (Christie's) £702

A small Longquan celadon jarlet and lotus-moulded cover, 13th/14th century, 7.5cm. high. (Christie's) £1,188

A Longquan celadon yanyan vase, early 14th century, 26.5cm. high. (Christie's) £3,024

A pale celadon and brown jade vase, 17th/18th century, 12.5cm. high, with wood stand. (Christie's) £5,400

A Mogul dark celadon jade ewer of oval octafoil cross-section, 17th/18th century, 15.5cm. high. (Christie's) £5,940

JIGSAW PUZZLES

The forerunner to the modern jigsaw puzzle was invented by a map maker in London during the 1760's and designed to facilitate the teaching of geography.
The puzzle was referred to as a 'dissecting map' and was hand made by mounting a map on a sheet of mahogany which was then cut by a fine marquetry saw. Lines were cut to define areas and the pieces fitted together to form a fairly accurate map. The puzzles were presented in a wooden box with a sliding lid bearing an engraved label.

Early puzzles were hand made and therefore expensive to produce, but their popularity with both adults and children soon led other manufacturers to appreciate their market potential as a learning aid and the range of subjects widened to encompass history, the three R's, religion, mythology and so on. Manufacturers best known during this period were J. Wallis, W. Darton, J. W. Barfoot, W. Peacock, Dean & Son and J. Betts and puzzles by these names are eagerly sought after.

Towards the end of the nineteenth century, boxes began to bear hand-coloured pictorial labels and these have now become collectible in their own right.

The 20th century saw the introduction of mass production techniques and the use of plywood and motorised fretsaws with hundreds of manufacturers responding to the jigsaw 'craze' of the 1920's and 30's. Notable British firms producing during this period are Raphael Tuck (Zag Zaw), Chad Valley (GWR, Cunard/White Star Line), Fredrick Warne (Chandos, Bedford), Victory (Supercut, Artistic), Holtzapffel (Figure-it-out), Salman (Academy), Delta fine cut, Zig Zag, Huvanco and A.V.N. Jones.

'The Romans at Caerlon', one of the series of 43 puzzles made by Chad Valley for the G.W.R. Co. during the 1920's and 1930's. Box of slip-case type from the 1930's, 14 x 14in. £19

'A Labour of Love', Society Dissected Picture Puzzle – The Latest Craze' made for Hamley Bros. to sell during the 1920's, 8 x 6in. £8

A rare Barfoot puzzle, a double sided map dissection, showing the Eastern and Western hemispheres, 12 x 8in., circa 1855. £220

'The Horse', one of a series of 'Graphic illustrations of animals showing their utility to man', by Roake & Varty, circa 1840, 12 x 15in. £70

'Journey into Egypt', probably amatuer cut, all pushfit pieces, typical of its type and style for the period, 1920's, 9 x 7in. £9

'Captain Cuttle', one of a series of twelve Dickens characters made into puzzles and issued by A. V. N. Jones in the 1930's, 10 x 8in. £19

KEYS

These fine old keys come from lock sets which were designed to be both functional and attractive.

The old locks come on the market less frequently than the keys, most remaining united with their original door or chest, but keys are more plentiful and offer an interesting variety of designs.

They are most commonly made of steel, iron and brass though some unusual examples are in gilded wrought iron or pinchbeck. Great attention was given to the design of the 'bow', many are intricately designed and decorated with figures, birds, cherubs and heraldic motifs.

It will add interest to the collection if you know a little about the history of a key and obligingly, they occasionally have faded, written labels attached.

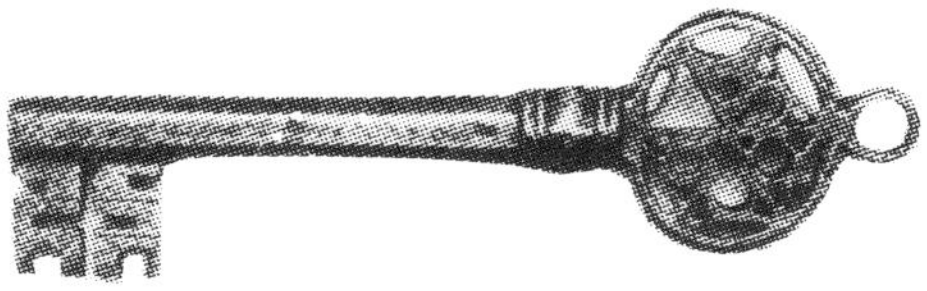

A 15th/16th century Venetian key, 6in. long. £100

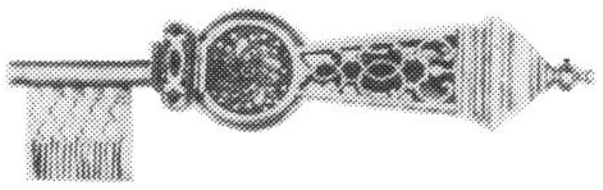

Early 18th century French iron masterpiece lantern key, 5¾in. long. £2,640

Late 18th century iron door key, 5in. long. £7

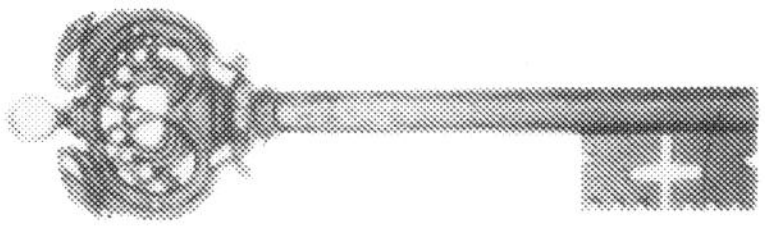

A North Italian key, the bow cast and chiselled with scrolls, circa 1600, 8¼in. long. £308

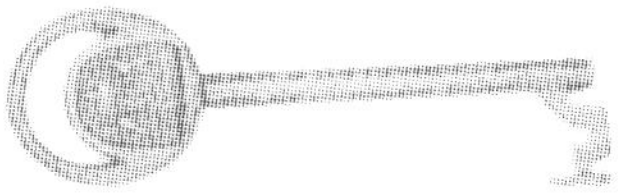

An 18th century Netherlandish key, with circular bow, 4¼in. £165

17th century French Renaissance key, the bow cut with adorned griffins, 5½in. long. £385

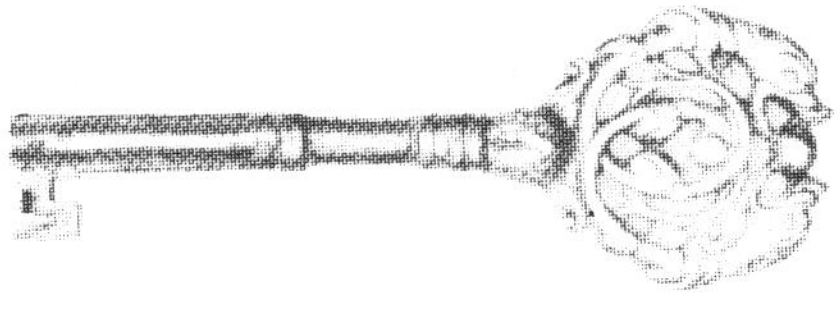

An 18th century French casket key, the gilt bow cast and chased in the form of entwined dolphins. £85

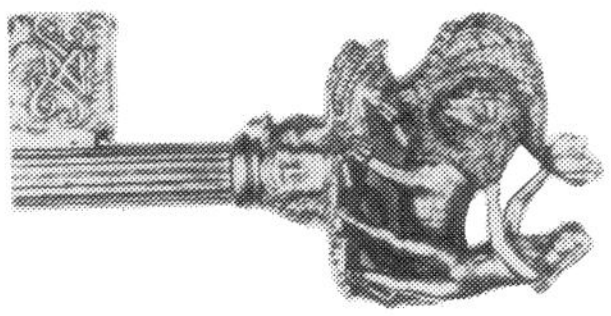

Italian 18th century iron casket key, 4¼in. long. £3,300

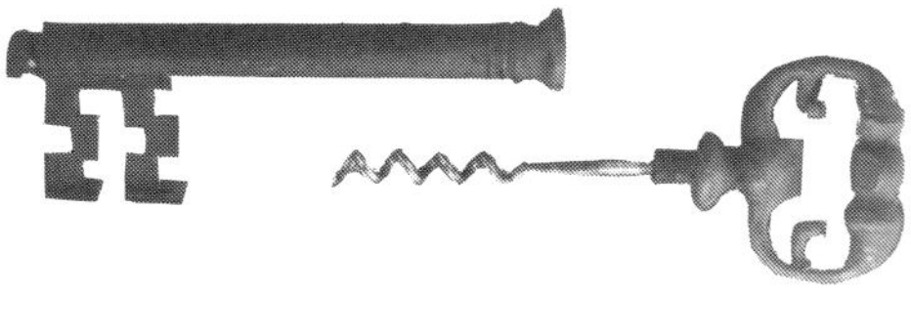

A large iron key converted into a corkscrew. £20

Victorian security lock key in brass. £2.50

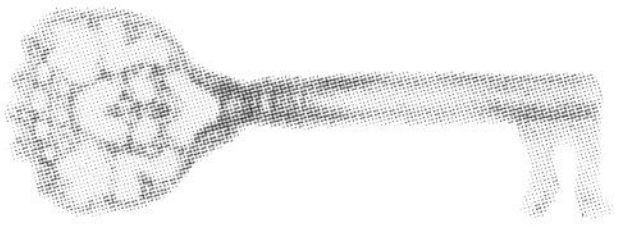

Early 17th century Italian steel key, the bow pierced and cut with scrolling foliage, 3¾in. £198

Late 17th century French Renaissance key, the bow cut as two stylised dolphins, 6in. long. £220

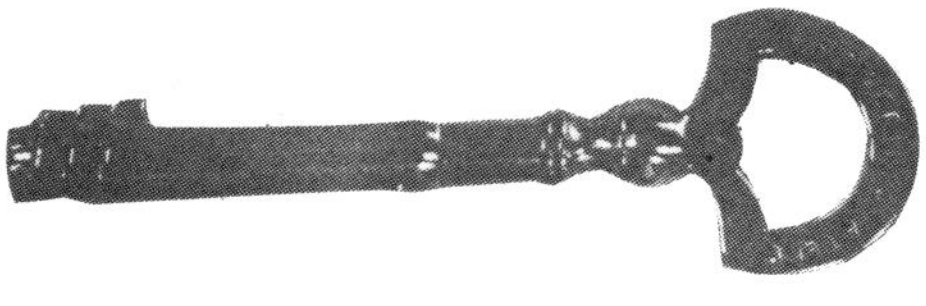

An all steel patent safe key, 3in. long, 'Climax Detector Birmingham'. (Christopher Sykes) £35

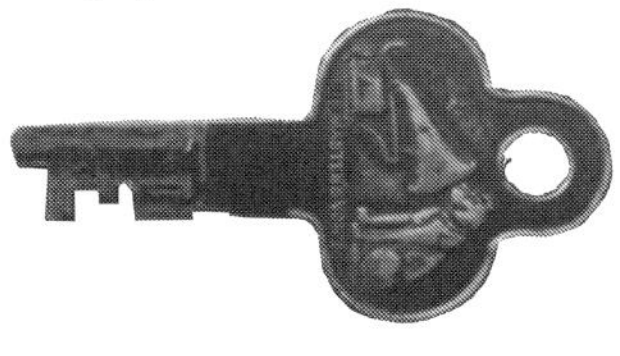

'His Master's Voice' cabinet key. £1.50

Pair of Georgian cabinet keys. £3

KINGSWARE

In 1899 a new method of stoneware production was introduced at Burslem which involved applying colour slips of subdued greens, yellows and reddish browns to the interior of plaster moulds in which a design was impressed. When another brown slip was poured in the colours fused to give a deep and soft effect to the embossed design.

Kingsware was mostly used for the production of pottery flasks to hold whisky and they were produced in enormous quantities, usually in editions of 1,000, for firms like John Dewar and Sons of Perth; Bulloch Lade; Greenlees and Watson and the Hudson's Bay Company.
The glaze was most commonly a dark treacle brown but more unusual was a paler yellow called the 'Kingsware yellow glaze'.

Royal Doulton Kingsware tobacco jar decorated in relief with a gentleman smoking, 8¼in. high. £50

The Leather Bottle, a Royal Doulton Kingsware flask, circa 1918, 6¼in. high, 6in. long. £260

Squire, a Kingsware Toby jug, hallmarked silver rim, 6½in. high. £250

Small fox, head down, a Royal Doulton Kingsware tobacco jar with hallmarked silver rim, circa 1912, 7¾in. high. £260

The Alchemist, a Royal Doulton Kingsware clock, 7½in. high, circa 1913. £320

Dickens' Characters, a Royal Doulton Kingsware water jug, 7in. high. £85

Pied Piper, a Royal Doulton Kingsware water jug with hallmarked silver rim and lid, 8½in. high. £110

Peace flagon, a Kingsware flask with brown border, made for Dewar's, No. 181, 7½in. high, circa 1919. £210

KITCHEN EQUIPMENT

Times change, and fashions with them, but one branch of the antiques business which goes on forever is that dealing in kitchenware – particularly from the Victorian period.

It all began as a reaction against the vogue, some years back, for plastic laminated antisepsis in the kitchen. Doubtless influenced to some extent by the country-kitchen full-colour photographs on the cookery pages, people began to react quite strongly against the characterless rooms in which they were expected to create culinary marvels. Storage jars, pestles and mortars, the odd copper saucepan or two, gradually the demand grew from a trickle to a steady stream.

For centuries, the kitchen in upper and middle class houses was a purely functional room used only by servants for the preparation of their masters' meals. No attention was paid to comfort, decor or labour saving.

As the years passed, meals were no longer prepared by servants but by the mistress of the household who became not only the cook, but nanny and bottle washer into the bargain. And now the wheel has turned still further; the kitchen has become a fashionable room. Food is not only cooked here, but often eaten too, and the kitchen is becoming one of the main living rooms of the house – often being recreated as a place in which to relax and sometimes even entertain.

For this reason alone, the utensils of the great kitchens of the past are much sought after for their decorative qualities. The Victorian kitchens with their copper and brass, their intricately carved wooden implements and their stone and steelware have a lot to offer, particularly since all these things were made in the days when mass production was in its infancy and individual artisan skills were given full rein.

Early 19th century American wire potato boiler, body diam. 11in. (Robt. W. Skinner Inc.) £208

British made alloy juice extractor 'Instant No. 1'. £5

An unusual home canning machine complete with instruction book. £10

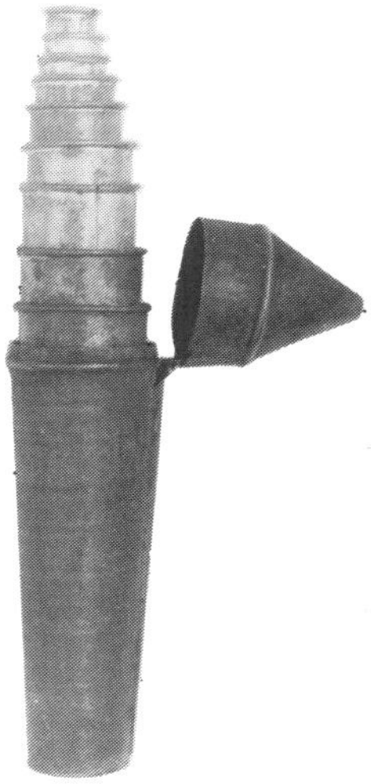

Victorian cased set of icing bag barrels. £18

Victorian turned wood crumpet pricker with steel spikes. £7

Enamelled tin breadbin marked bread. £5

Lister ball bearing cream separator. £15

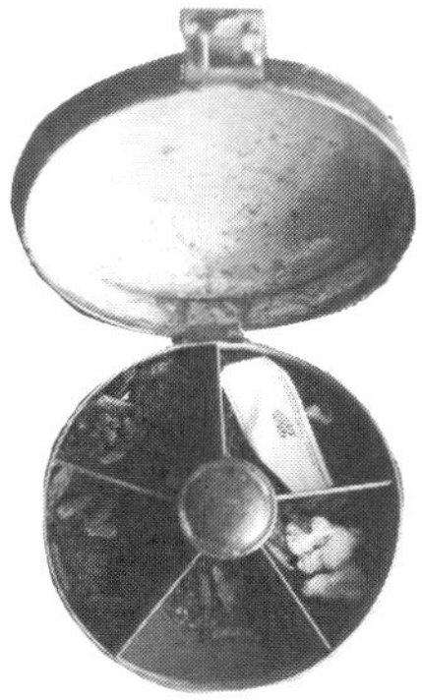

Toleware spice box complete with contents and central nutmeg grater, circa 1835. £28

Plated tin tongue press, circa 1900. £15

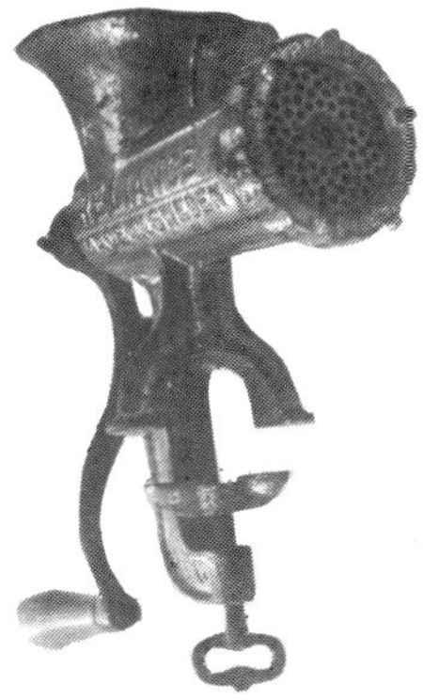

A large Reliance mincer made in Sweden. £4

Early 19th century japanned tin plate warmer with cast metal carrying grips, 27in. high. (Lawrence Fine Art) £1,430

Sheet tin bread board and rolling pin, 11 x 18½in. (Robt. W. Skinner Inc.) £225

Farmhouse individual butter churn, late 19th century. £12

Kitchen grater of tin with three variations, circa 1900. £4

Spong & Co. metal coffee grinder. £14

Late 19th century plated tin milk can, ½ gallon. £8

Beatrice cast iron combined heater and cooker. £7

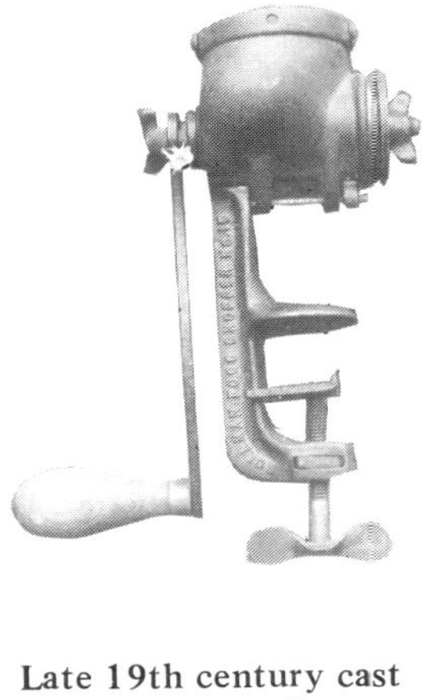

Late 19th century cast iron mincer 'Rollman Food Cropper', No. 15. £3

LAMPS

Although early lamps were operated on little more than an oil supplied candle, by about 1860, the wick and paraffin burning table lamp had been perfected and was in common use. Another popular type was the acetylene lamp, which has a small reservoir of water placed above a container at the base, filled with calcium carbide. Drops of water released onto the carbide would produce acetylene gas which, in turn, produced a brilliant white flame. While most people have some idea of the value of a Victorian brass oil lamp there is a possibility that some of the old brass carbide lamps and tilley lamps may be overlooked. These are collected today and have some monetary value.
A long way away from the basic function of providing a source of light, are the shimmering Art lamps of the late 19th and early 20th century. Lamps are often signed and the names to look for are Daum, Emile Galle, Gustav Gurschner, Handel, Lalique, Loetz and many more. These lamps are traditionally made with a cast bronze stem.

A plated two-branch student's oil lamp with green tinted shades. (Peter Wilson & Co.) £170

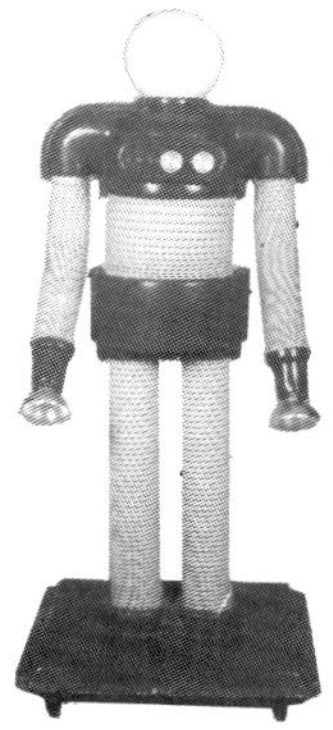

Rudolph, a robot light fitting, designed by Frank Clewett, 149cm. high. (Christie's) £2,420

A Daum Art Deco table lamp, frosted glass with wrought iron, engraved with cross of Lorraine, circa 1925, 46cm. high. (Christie's) £3,240

'Nymph among the bullrushes', a bronze table lamp cast after a model by Louis Convers, 28.1cm. high. (Christie's) £518

A Tiffany Studios favrile glass and bronze ten-light lily lamp, 19½in. high. (Woolley & Wallis) £4,800

A Galle blowout lamp, varying shades of red on an amber ground, signed, circa 1900, 44.5cm. high. (Christie's) £41,040

A Tiffany Studios gilt bronze and glass table lamp, stamped Tiffany Studios New York 590, 48cm. high.(Christie's) £1,728

An early 20th century Handel lamp on Hampshire pottery base, with Mosserine shade, 20in. high. (Robt. W. Skinner Inc.) £625

LEACH

The English potter Bernard Leach was born in 1887. He spent his early years both in Japan and England, returning to Japan to teach engraving and design. His work was influential in the development of the Japanese folk art movement which gained recognition in 1929. In 1920 he started work at St. Ives in Cornwall, producing stoneware from local materials and re-introducing the art of marbled slip decoration.
The work of Bernard Leach and his pupils is noted for the vast range of decorative techniques. Marks include initials BL impressed within rectangle or painted and the work of the Leach pottery at St. Ives is marked with S and I crossed, with two dots, enclosed in circle or square, impressed.
While this is undoubtedly an expensive field of collecting it is one in which knowledge will be rewarded, for the reason that, the work of Leach is not immediately recognisable to the general public as a piece of such potential value.

A stoneware teapot with cane handle by Bernard Leach, circa 1920, 17.2cm. high. (Christie's) £750

A stoneware tea caddy, by Bernard Leach, circa 1970, 16cm. high. (Christie's) £308

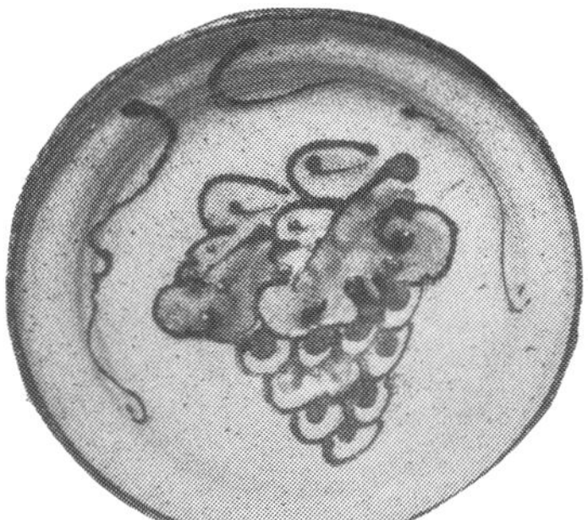

A slip-trailed soft raku bowl by Bernard Leach, impressed BL and St. Ives seals, circa 1920, 23.2cm. diam. (Christie's) £800

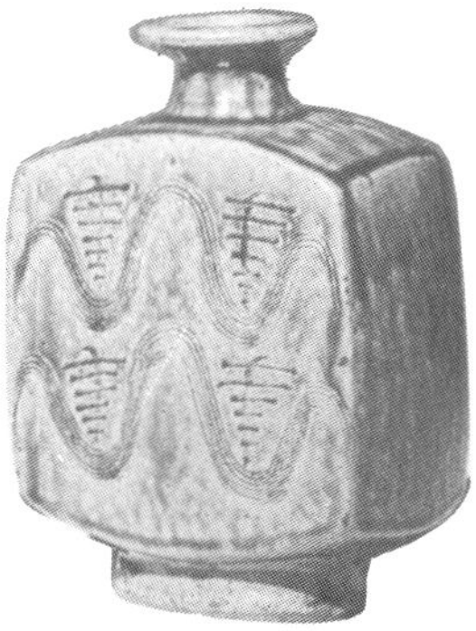

A stoneware flattened rectangular slab bottle by B. Leach, impressed BL and St. Ives seals, circa 1960, 20.2cm. high.(Christie's) £1,296

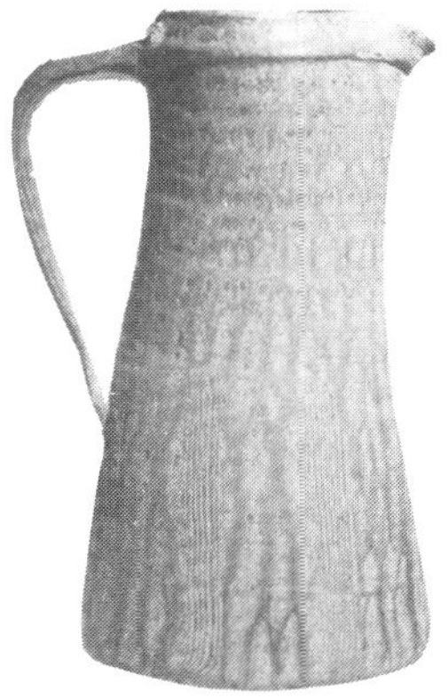

A tall stoneware jug, by Bernard Leach, with ribbed rim and strap handle, 28.8cm. high. (Christie's) £324

A stoneware rectangular slab bottle by Bernard Leach, covered in a rich iron-red glaze, circa 1955, 18.5cm. high. (Christie's) £300

A stoneware large oviform vase by Bernard Leach, impressed BL and St. Ives seals, circa 1958, 34.3cm. high. (Christie's) £700

A stoneware barrel shaped bottle by Bernard Leach, impressed BL and St. Ives seals, circa 1970, 23.1cm. high. (Christie's) £237

LEAD SOLDIERS

In 1893, with the British Empire at its height, the firm of William Britain introduced a series of toy soldiers representing the regiments of the British army.
These were an immediate success and Britain's went on to increase their range, producing an abundance of military models including armies of other nations, tanks, gun units and army bands. Britain's continued to produce new models up until the time of the Coronation in 1953.
Early models fixed to a round base are more valuable than those on a rectangular base, and the stamp on the bottom will help to date the pieces. 'Copyright Wm. Britain' was used before 1912, and 'Britains Ltd.' before 1937. After this 'Made in England' was added.
Although most sets change hands at less than £100, a set of Salvation Army Bandsmen recently made nearer £1,000.

Britains Attendants to the State Coach, including walking outriders, footmen of the Royal Household and Yeomen, in original box. £110

Britains set No. 1470, The Coronation State Coach, including eight Windsor greys, four outriders, H.M. Queen Elizabeth II and Prince Philip, in gold painted state coach, in original box. £160

Elastolin 100mm. scale hand-painted composition soldiers, Coldstream Guards, marching at slope arms in full equipment. £550

Britains early set No. 211, 18in. Howitzer No. 2, with ten horse team, in review order with No. 2 Howitzer and limber, in original box. £900

Britains set No. 1634, The Governor-General's Foot Guards, marching at the slope arms, with officer, in original box. £90

A Britain's boxed set of a Royal Horse Artillery gun team. (Phillips) £6,200

A Britains set No. 434, R.A.F. Monoplane, with two pilots and four R.A.F. personnel, in original box. (Christie's) £1,200

Britains set of South African Mounted Infantry, in its original box.£650

Britains set No. 37, Band of the Coldstream Guards. £200

Twelve German made solid pewter model Boer soldiers, 45mm. high, circa 1900, in original box. £70

Heyde 30mm. hand-painted Indian elephant, with howdah, containing Maharajah and bower, an Indian lancer, 5 palm trees, six 54mm. scale figures and six other figures. £100

Britains set No. 315, 10th Royal Hussars, Prince of Wales' Own, at the halt with swords and bugler, in original box. £250

LIGHT BULBS

One Otto Von Guericke, a contemporary of Robert Boyle, is generally regarded as producing the first light from electricity back in the 17th century when he discovered that by holding the hands firmly against a revolving ball of sulphur, the friction produced a dull glow.

It wasn't, however, until the electric arc was discovered early in the 19th century by Sir Humphrey Davy, that a practical source of artificial light was established.

Light bulbs themselves date from about 1841 when an American inventor named Starr found that a bright light could be produced by sending an electric current through a piece of carbon.

The first successful incandescent electric lamps produced in the U.K. were made by J.W. Swan of Newcastle and subsequently by several other inventors and pioneers including St. George Lane Fox, while in America the market was dominated by T.A. Edison.

All of these manufacturers used carbonised material as the filament, such as a cotton thread (Swan), a fibre of grass (Lane Fox) or a sliver of bamboo (Edison). Such light was regarded with fascination and carbon filament lamps were tremendously popular from 1880 until the turn of the century.

The big breakthrough came in 1906 when the General Electric Company found that by using a tungsten filament sealed in a glass bulb, it not only produced a clear white light but used very little electricity as well.

This revolutionised the whole industry and created a massive demand, though doubts were expressed at the time as to the adverse effect all this powerful light would have on the eyesight of future generations.

Swan 'Pipless' light bulb, English, circa 1882. £300

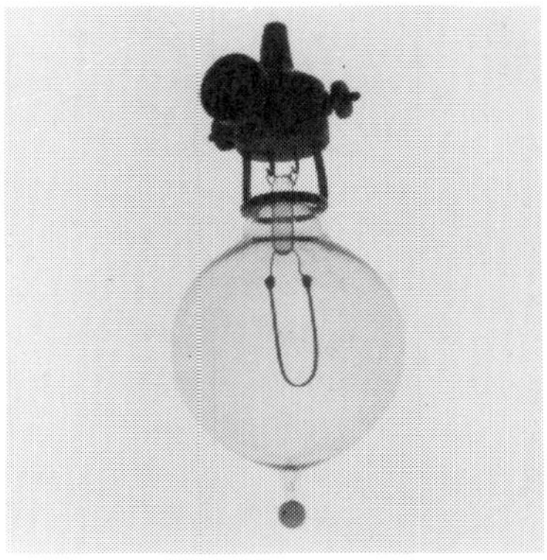

Typical 'Bottom Loop' bulb probably by Swan Lamp, circa 1884. £150

English light bulb by Lane Fox, circa 1881. £250

Nernst Lamp, circa 1900, 6in. high. £35

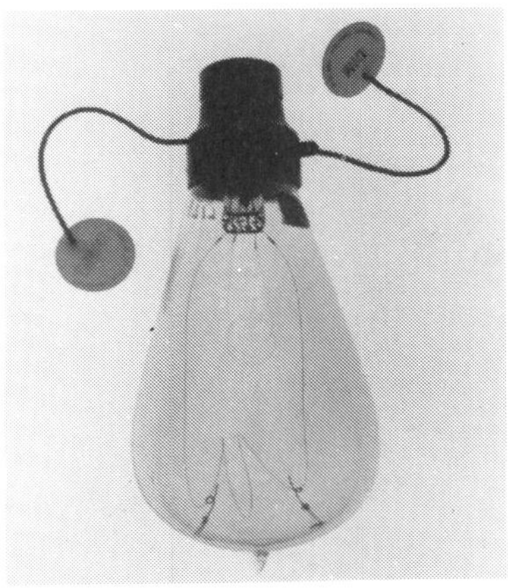

Dual Carbon Filament (dim/bright), circa 1905. £20

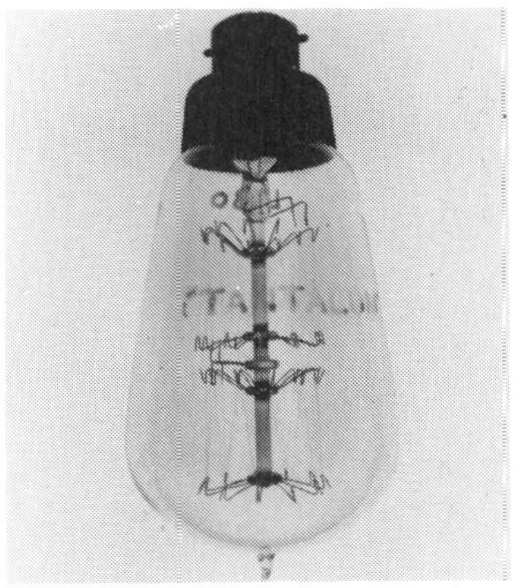

Tantalum Lamp, probably German, circa 1906. £30

LUGGAGE

Travelling 'light' is a modern concept and one which no self respecting traveller of yesteryear would have contemplated. They took their creature comforts with them on long journeys, transported in an astonishing variety of trunks, cases, strongboxes, chests, travelling boxes, carpet bags, hatboxes, picnic boxes and even specially fitted drinks boxes. Because luggage was built to last, we have a legacy of robust and attractive pieces on the market today. A cautionary note to those intending to travel by air – forget about the fabulous old leather suitcases for, even whilst empty, they come very close to the weight allowance permitted for baggage.
Most people nowadays, use the heavier pieces as furnishing features, particularly the old chests. Some were covered in materials such as fine leather or pony skin and decorated with metal studs. Look out for any piece covered in a green, rough textured leathery looking material for this might just be shagreen, a shark skin considered to be very desirable.

Late 19th century travelling chest. £20

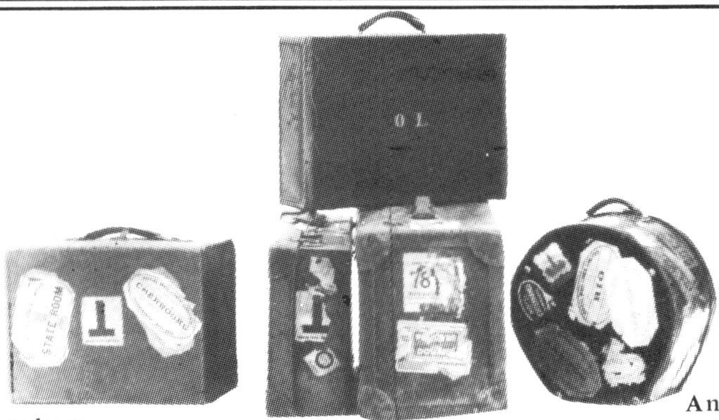

Items of vintage leather luggage, including two trunks, hat box, picnic case and others. (Lots Road Galleries) £250

An 18th century French kingwood coffret forte, 12¼in. (Lawrence Fine Art) £506

1930's leather suitcase with brass locks and fitted interior. £15

Victorian metal uniform case with simulated crocodile skin design. £12

Leather Gladstone bag marked 'Post Office'. £15

A small 1930's leather hand luggage case, 13in. wide. £12

A Louis Vuitton cabin trunk covered in brown hide secured by brass pins and mounted with brass lock plate, 114cm. wide. (Christie's) £918

Early 19th century wallpaper hat box, 'A Peep at the Moon', America, 12½in. high, 17in. wide. (Robt. W. Skinner Inc.) £129

MAGAZINE INSERTS

In the days before cheap colour printing magazines were invariably printed entirely in black and white. In an attempt to give impact to their products advertisers struck upon the idea of the magazine insert.

These small sheets were printed in bright chromolithographed colours and inserted usually at the back or front of the magazine, generally tipped in at the inside edge with glue. At a time when most advertising in periodicals was very visually restrained they stood out with great impact, and then as now, the soap manufacturers lead the way, employing well-known artists such as John Hassall to design their inserts.

With the arrival of cheap colour printing the magazine insert virtually vanished, and the only modern ones tend to be in the form of post cards such as the Butlin's one illustrated.

These attractive little pieces are very collectible today and one can pay up to £3 or £4 for nice images by known artists though these are still cheap compared to advertising post cards at £20 and £30 a time. Look for them, however, in bundles of old magazines in bookshops. Sometimes magazines bought for pence can contain real gems.

Not least of their appeal is the copy on many of the ads. Who could resist such delights as 'Prevents it falling off' for Harlene Hair Tonic or 'Rescue Yourself And Others From Contagion and Disease' for Lifebuoy Soap?

Lifebuoy Soap, 'Rescue Yourself And Others From Contagion And Disease'. £4

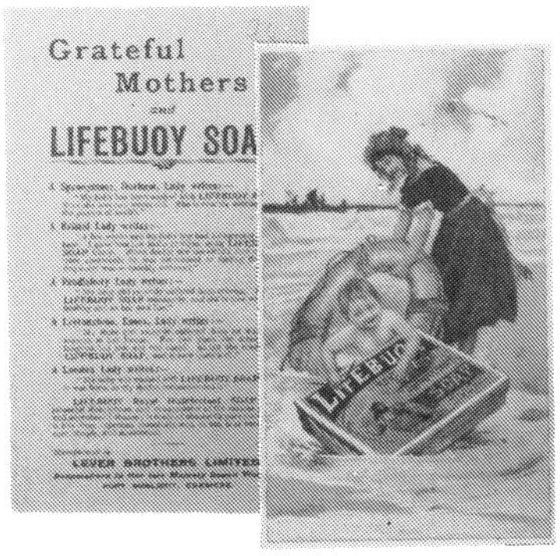

Lifebuoy Soap, 'Grateful Mothers'. £5

Nernstlamp, The Electrical Company Limited'. £5

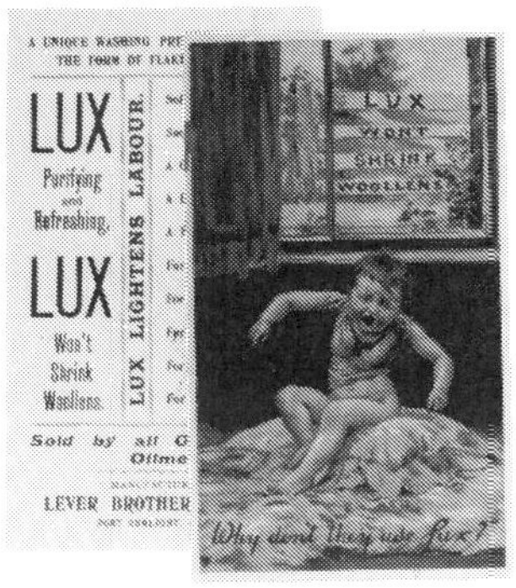

Lux, 'Why Don't They Use Lux'. £4

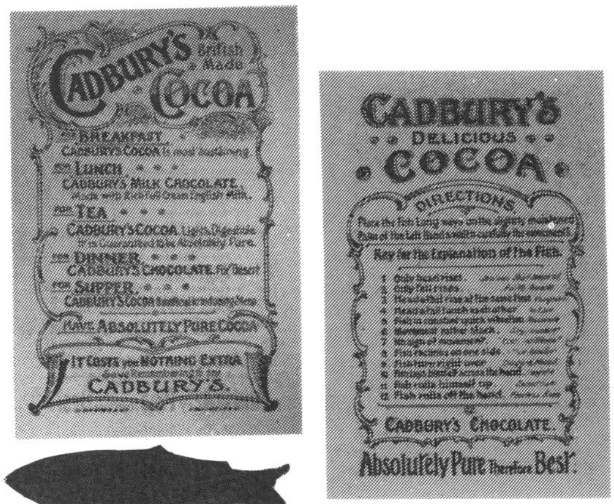

Cadbury's Cocoa, 'Explanation Of The Fish'. £3

Pears' Soap, 'Bubbles', by Sir John E. Millais. £2

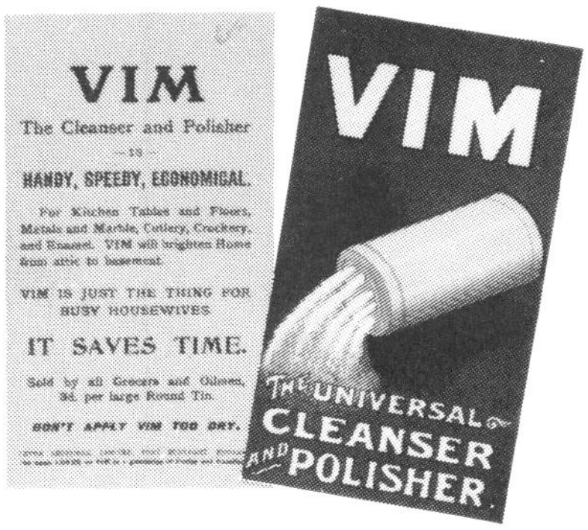

Vim, 'Handy, Speedy, Economical'. £2

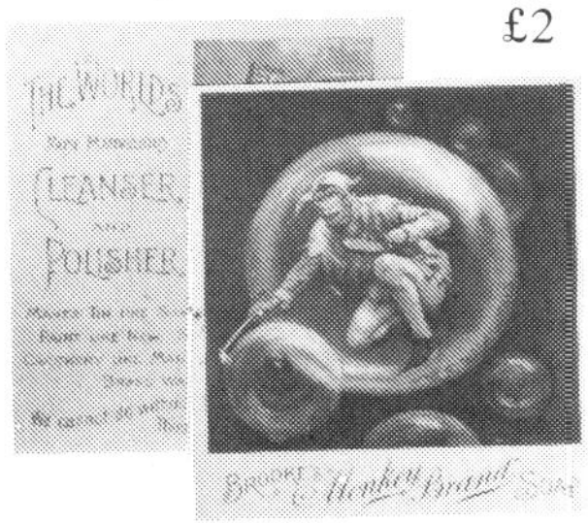

Brooke's Monkey Brand Soap, 'We Cannot Do Without It'. £4

MAGAZINES

There seem to be magazines on every conceivable subject possible, and there seem to be collectors for all of them. Some, such as The Electrical Times, obviously have only a limited appeal and can be bought for 50p or less, while others have a wider collecting public because of the more general nature of their content.

Who can resist a twenty year old copy of Picture Post with its superb studies of the way we used to live. Magazines are often found bound up in annual sets and these often had covers and adverts removed, this seriously devalues them.

In fact it is the adverts which often dictate the value of many magazines for usually they are more suited for framing than the general contents.

Children's Friend 1882. £1.50

Northern Gossip, bound complete copies 1904. £25

My Magazine 1920. £1.50

Health and Efficiency 1935. £1.50

Picture Post Battle of River Plate Special Issue. £2

Chums 1911. £3

Boys Own 1929 £2

Children's Companion 1925. £1.75

Amateur Photographer, bound complete copies July-December 1910. £12

Children's Magazine 1912. £1.50

(Lynn Private Collection, Tyne & Wear)

Film Pictorial 1932. £1.75

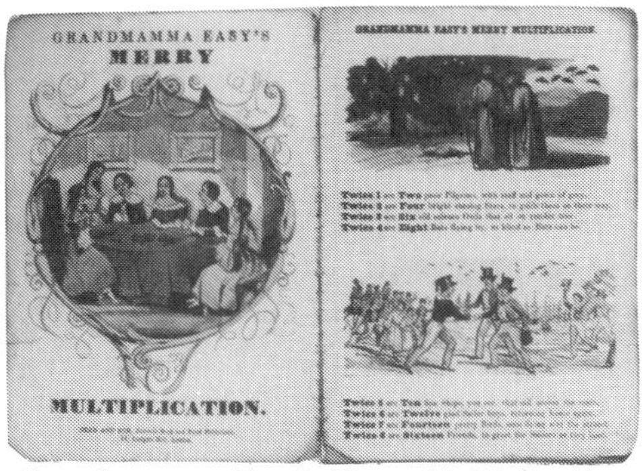

Grandmamma Easy's Merry Multiplication, early Victorian. £5

Picturegoer 1934. £1.75

Film Pictorial Christmas Extra 1936. £3.50

Child's Companion and Juvenile Instructor 1890. £2

Punch 1915. £1

Red Arrow Series 1932 Number 1 of the Swift Story Paper. £1

Everybody's Weekly, bound complete copies, from first issue March-December 1911. £20

Chatterbox 1871. £2.50

Sunshine 1894. £1.50

Courier 1938. £2.50

Under the Union Jack, bound complete copies from first issue November 1899-July 1900. £18

Model Engineer 1929. 50p

(Lynn Private Collection, Tyne & Wear)

MARBLE

The name 'marble' means shining stone and it is a term applied to any limestone or dolomite which is sufficiently close in texture to allow it to be polished.
Greek sculptors worked in marble from their own islands, particularly Paros. The Venus de Milo is a prime example of their art, but the stone most used by the Romans and up to the present day is Carrara marble which is found in northern Italy. India's Taj Mahal is a miracle in marble and the stone for its delicate pierced screens was quarried in Ulwar.
Objects made of marble have always been much coveted and they range from fountain heads to religious objects, fireplaces, vases and statuary. The French were very keen on marble during the 19th century and ormolu mounted vases made at that time fetch high prices.

Fine French marble bust, 1870. (British Antique Exporters) £327

A white marble sculpture of a standing naked Venus, 26in. high. (Lots Road Chelsea Auction Galleries) £380

One of a pair of gilt metal mounted Breche Violette marble vases with fruiting finials, 19in. high. (Christie's) £1,836

A white marble relief of a Roman Emperor in white and gold oval frame, 7½in. high. (Christie's) £432

A Venetian white marble wellhead, the Lion of St. Mark sculptured in relief, dated 1394. (Crowther, Syon Lodge Ltd.) £8,000

A late George III white and sienna marble mantelpiece with breakfront stepped top, 62in. high. (Christie's) £2,782

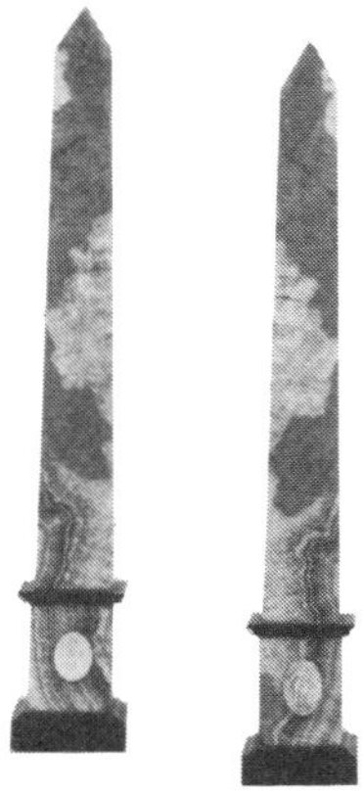

A pair of Breccia and black marble obelisks, 15in. high. (Christie's) £432

Marble bust of Apollo, head turned down gazing to the right, 18¾in. high. (Robt. W. Skinner Inc.) £2,384

MARTINWARE

Robert, Walter and Edwin had all, at one time or another, worked at the Doulton factory in Lambeth but they eventually got together and opened their own workshop at Southall in 1877. It was run by the fourth brother, Charles, who also ran a retail shop in Holborn to sell the wares the brothers produced.

Most of the leering birds and other animal models were made by the eldest brother, Robert, while Walter prepared the clay and made vases, leaving the youngest brother, Edwin, to do all the fancy decoration and, doubtless, make the tea, run round the corner to get the paper and all the other things youngest brothers do. They also produced candlesticks, jugs, clock cases and goblets until the eventual close of the factory in 1914.

A Martin Bros. oviform single-handled pottery jug, in an uneven grey glaze with deeper brown patches, 9¼in. high. (Christie's) £190

A Martin Bros. stoneware jug, the bulbous body suggesting a sea-creature, 21.8cm. high. (Christie's) £432

A Martin Bros. stoneware tobacco jar and cover, modelled as a grotesque grinning cat, 1885, 22cm. high. (Christie's) £7,560

A Martin Bros. stoneware grotesque, double face jug with strap handle, 1897, 22.8cm. high. (Christie's) £1,296

A Martin Bros stoneware spherical vase, London Southall, 1892, 9in. high. (Christie's) £350

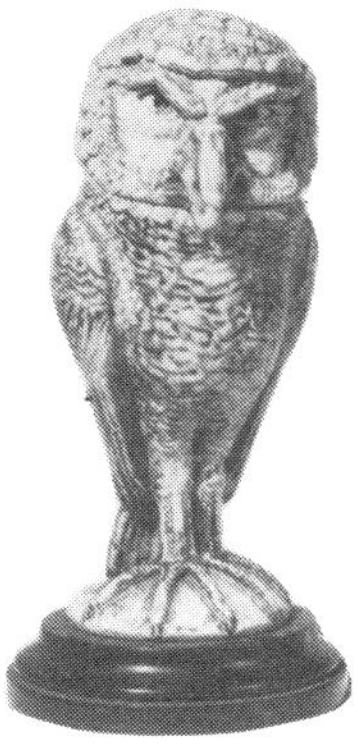

A Martin Bros. stoneware 'judge' bird tobacco jar and cover, London & Southall 4-1889, 25.8cm. high. (Christie's) £2,376

A Martin Bros. face flask with two handles, incised marks dated 1901, 8in. high. (Christie's) £750

A Martinware gourd single-handled lobed pottery jug, London Southall, circa 1900, 10in. high. (Christie's) £380

MARY GREGORY

One of the most distinctive styles of glasswork is that known as Mary Gregory.

Although most of the glass in this style seen today was manufactured during the second half of the 19th century at Jablonec, Czechoslovakia, by the firm of Hahn, the original Mary Gregory worked as an enameller at the Boston & Sandwich Glass Company in the U.S.A.

There she decorated inexpensive blown and tinted glass decanters, jugs and vases with pink or opaque white figures, usually of playful children frolicking, flying kites, fishing, trundling hoops or picking flowers.

The base colours are likely to be red, green, blue, pink, amber or even turquoise, with the earlier examples tending to be slightly 'softer' than pieces made at the turn of the century.

All Mary Gregory glass however, from wherever the provenance, is now eagerly sought after for its appeal is much wider than that normally attributed to glassware.

Cranberry glass, inexpensively produced in Britain in the late 19th century, was often engraved with Mary Gregory style figures. This is a clear pinkish-red glass originally produced for use in the manufacture of chemists' bottles and then adopted in the production of vases, bowls and dishes. A characteristic of Cranberry glassware is the applied clear glass frilled rim.

Mary Gregory amber glass pin tray depicting a boy with a butterfly net. £85

Mary Gregory glass jug, 8in. high. £50

Mary Gregory green glass decanter. £30

Pair of Mary Gregory green glasses depicting a boy and girl. £60

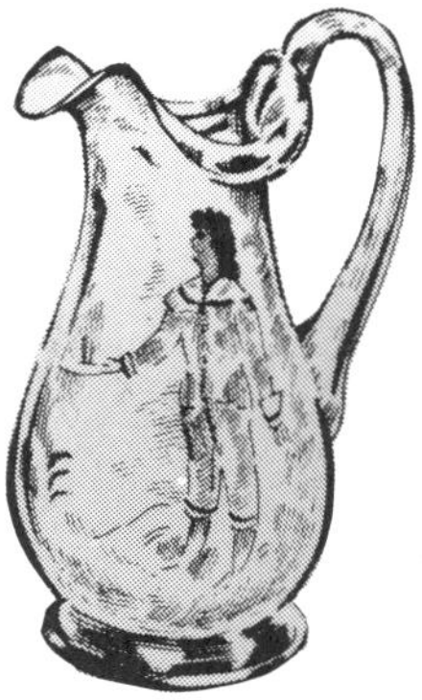

Mary Gregory hand-painted glass cream jug. £25

Mary Gregory enamelled dish with everted rim, circa 1880, 13¼in. diam. £150

MATCH BOX LABELS

At first these little sticks of wood tipped with a combustible substance were sold in plain boxes bearing only the instructions for use. Then, in 1829 along came Mr Jones with the 'Royal Patent Lucifer' presented in a box illustrated with the figures of an Englishman and a Scotsman and the collecting craze began. Now the range is endless, embracing match covers, bill heads, advertising labels even post cards and collectors are forced to adopt a theme in order to keep their collections to a manageable size.

A name associated with early match boxes is that of Sir William Congreve 1772-1828, inventor of the Congreve match – now highly prized labels with collectors.

Today 'phillumeny', is a well organised world wide hobby with its own clubs, magazines and meetings. The beginner will find the range of labels infinite, amounting probably to many millions of different kinds and it need not be an expensive business. A collection can be built up from what is around, exchanging with fellow collectors and of course, from specialist dealers.

Old Bryant & May 'All Round The Box' label, nearly 100 years old. (Issued c. 1888.) £3

'All Round The Box' label from a British Manufacturer no longer in existence, c. early 1900's. £10

From an early British Manufacturer, c. 1863/65. £20

One of a set of Service Rank markings issued during the Second World War. Single label. 20p

One of Bryant & May's early labels, c. 1891. £5

An old label from a British Company no longer in existence, c. early 1920's. £20

MATCH CASES

Matchboxes have not always been the simple card, wood or plastic containers we know today. Originally, they were known as fire boxes, match safes or safety boxes.

Owing to the fact that early matches were liable to flare into life at the slightest knock, or with exposure to not very great heat, it was felt necessary to keep them in containers which, in the event of accidental combustion, would restrict the fire.

As far as is known, the first friction matches were produced in about 1827 and were sold in a tin case to a Mr. Hixon by their maker, John Walker of Stockton-on-Tees. By 1850 the different types of fire boxes were almost limitless, often taking the form of soldiers, historical figures or animals made of iron, brass and other metals. Usually, the heads of the figures were hinged to allow matches to be stored in their hollow interiors.

Very often, there was a small hole somewhere in which a single, lit match could be placed – possibly for reasons of economy in that this allowed the full length of the wooded shaft to burn, and possibly as a means of holding the flame steady when it was being used to melt sealing wax.

In addition to the metal fire boxes, some quite beautiful examples were made of ceramics or wood. Many of these had different provisions for igniting the various kinds of matches. Some merely had roughened patches, others had two roughened discs between which the match head was sandwiched before being sharply withdrawn to effect ignition. There was also a type of match which consisted of a small wooden splint tipped with chlorate of potash. This was lit by dipping the tip into sulphuric acid. Containers for these usually took a cylindrical form, in the centre of which stood the small bottle of acid surrounded by the potash-tipped matches.

1930's enamel matchbox holder. £4

Metal match case in the form of a Gladstone bag. £50

Silver vesta case inscribed Bryant & May's Wax Vestas. (Phillips) £55

Vesta match case showing King Edward, 1901. £75

Vesta match case advertising Otto Monsteds Margarines. £130

Silver match case with floral decoration. £35

French Art Nouveau silver smoker's set, circa 1900. £120

Oval Vesta case in the form of a creel, by T. Johnson, London 1883, 5.7cm. long. £770

A gold match safe, 19th century, with floral and scroll motifs and a gem set clover in central cartouche. (Robt. W. Skinner Inc.) £255

A hammered silver and silver gilt cheroot case and vesta combined, unmarked, possibly American, circa 1890, 4oz. (Christie's) £378

Novelty Vesta case in the form of a clenched fist. £160

A Victorian brass matchbox holder in the form of a book. £10

MATCHSTRIKERS

Before the widespread use of matches in boxes there were numerous little containers designed to house them. Made from a variety of materials including wood, bone, glass, papier mache, Tunbridgeware, enamel, stone and china, their common feature is a lidless compartment for the matches and a grooved or roughened striking surface.

The most numerous and generally regarded as most appealing specimens are those made of porcelain by the German firm of Conte and Boehme, who were also responsible for producing most of the 'fairings' which are so eagerly sought after today.

Many bear a humorous or slightly risque inscription on the base often borrowed from a popular song of the day.

'Present From Canterbury'. £15–£25

'Match, Sir' (also captioned **'Any Lights Sir'**). £45–£75

'I Am Going A-Milking Sir, She Said'. £45–£75

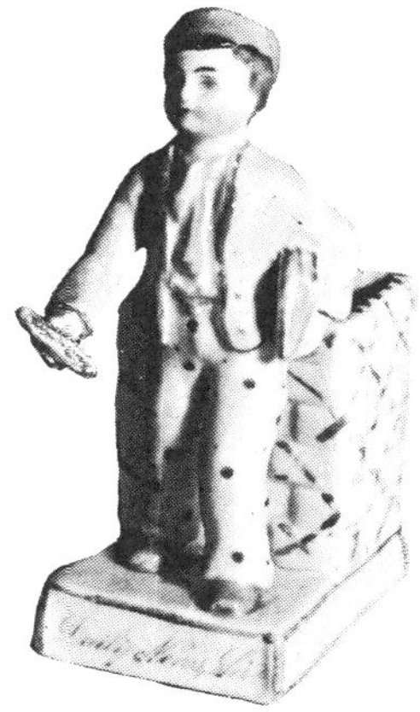

'Daily News Sir'. £75–£100

'A Penny Please, Sir?' £45–£75

'Peau D'Lapin Chiffons'. £45–£75

'Sweet Violets, Sir'. £45–£75

'A Copper Sir?' £15–£25

MEDALS

It may surprise the uninitiated to the field of medal collecting to note the high prices currently achieved. But, for many of the thousands of people who collect, the fascination lies in the historical and personal interest. Most medals bear the name of the original owner along with that of his regiment or ship.
In this extensive field, there is ample opportunity to specialise. Some collectors buy only rare bars or medals awarded for a specific battle or campaign.
Now that medals are fetching high prices, we hear that the fakers are at work – not always successfully I am pleased to say. It may be possible to detect when a medal has been re-named for the rim is usually narrower and slightly rounded where the work has been done.
The majority of medals presented to the troops who fought in the First and Second World Wars, are unlikely ever to reach a high price for the simple reason that millions were issued.

Candahar, Ghuznee, Cabul, 1842, (Lieut. A. MacQueen 42nd Reg. Bengal L.I.). (Christie's)
£200

Six: Companion of the Order of the Bath, (22ct. gold, HM.London 1815), Crimea, four bars, China 1857, 1 bar, Turkey Order of Medjidieh, Turkish Crimea, France Legion of Honour. Together with three miniatures. (Wallis & Wallis)
£900

Waterloo 1815. (Wallis & Wallis)
£950

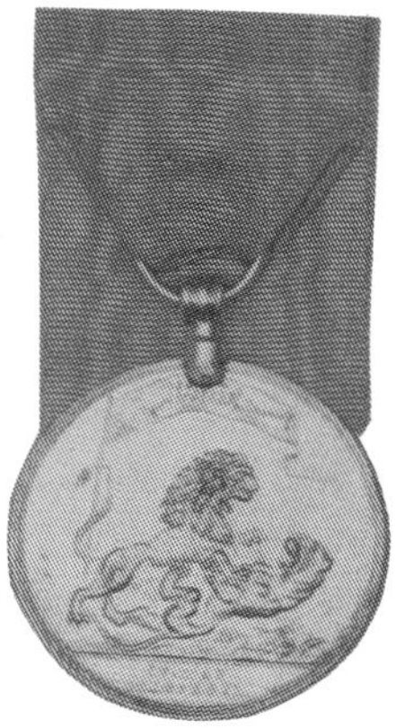

Seringapatam 1799, Silver Medal of the Calcutta mint. (Wallis & Wallis)
£210

Nine: DSM George V Admiral's bust, BEM George VI For Meritorious Service, 1914-15 star trio, 1939-45 star, Defence, War, R.N. George V Admiral's bust, together with a 'diary', press cuttings, photos etc. (Wallis & Wallis)
£385

Indian Mutiny, 1 bar, Defence of Lucknow. (Wallis & Wallis)
£825

Naval General Service Medal 1793, 1 bar Nile. (Wallis & Wallis) £320

Four: M.C. George V, 1914-15 star trio. (Wallis & Wallis) £130

Ashantee War (W. Cook, Asst. Engt., R.N. H.M.S. Druid 73-74). (Wallis & Wallis) £65

The Most Distinguished Order of St. Michael and St. George 1818, in original case from Garrard & Co. Ltd. (Lawrence Fine Art) £451

Ten: Distinguished Conduct Medal Victorian issue, Q.S.A., K.S.A., I.G.S. 1908, B.W.M. Victory, L.S. and G.C. Edward VII issue, M.S.M. George V, Prussia Order of the Red Eagle, bronze medal, D.C.M. dated 21.10.99. (Wallis & Wallis) £1,025

China 1857, 1 bar Taku Forts 1860. (Wallis & Wallis) £75

Three: DCM George V, BWM and the Victory. (Wallis & Wallis) £220

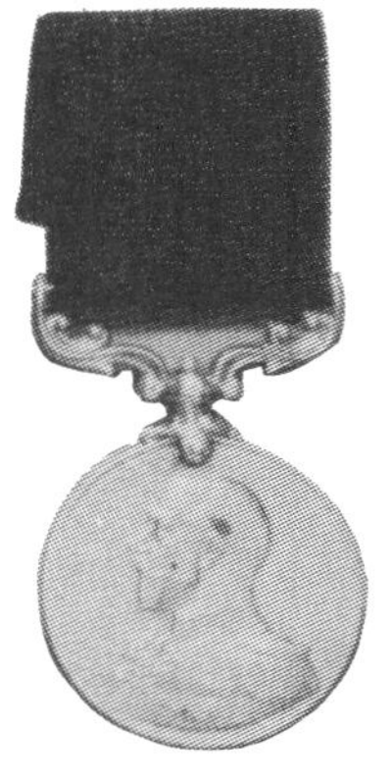

Meritorious Service Medal, George V issue. (Wallis & Wallis) £100

Three: I.G.S. 1854, China 1857, Naval L.S. & G.C. Victorian issue. (Wallis & Wallis) £110

MEDICAL ITEMS

When one surveys the array of medical instruments the Victorians had to endure, it seems a miracle that so many survived at all. And this is the fascination which has given all redundant medical items a ready and eager market.

Cased sets of surgical instruments are particularly sought after by makers such as Hutchinson, A. & S. Maw, J. Milliken and William Pepys. As a rule, wooden, ivory and bone handled instruments are made prior to 1870 and are much more desirable than the later chromium plated examples.

Amputation sets, leech jars, medicine chests and microscopes are all very collectible and can obtain astronomical money for early examples.

Beware, however, of some of the Victorian electrical appliances offered as 'cure alls', for which they had a fascination – try them at your peril.

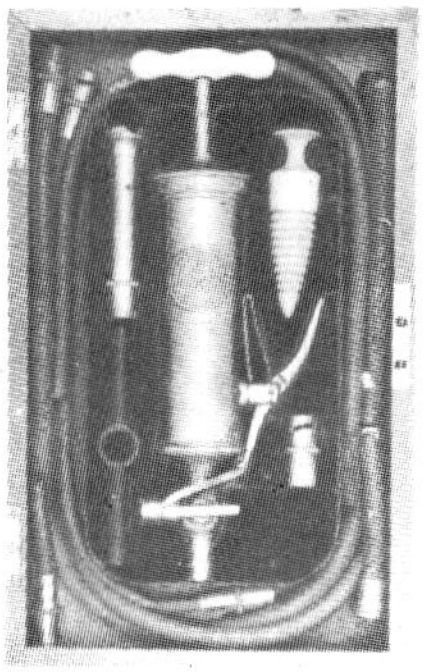

Mid 19th century S. Maw, Son & Thompson enema or stomach pump apparatus, English, 12½ x 7½in. £176

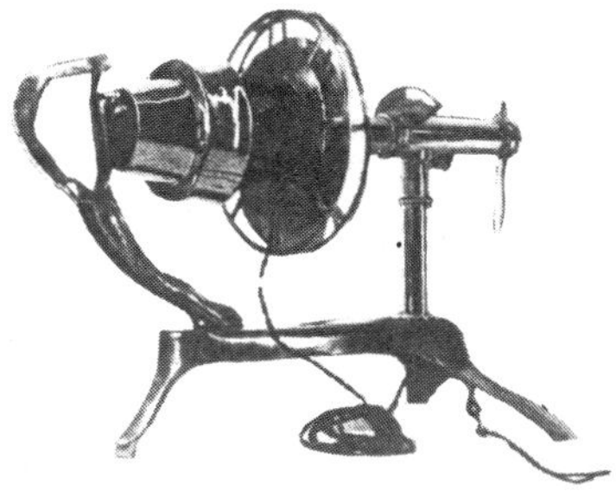

A Keratometer, an instrument for measuring the curvature of the cornea of the eye, made of brass on a cast-iron stand, circa 1910, 24in. long. (Christopher Sykes) £385

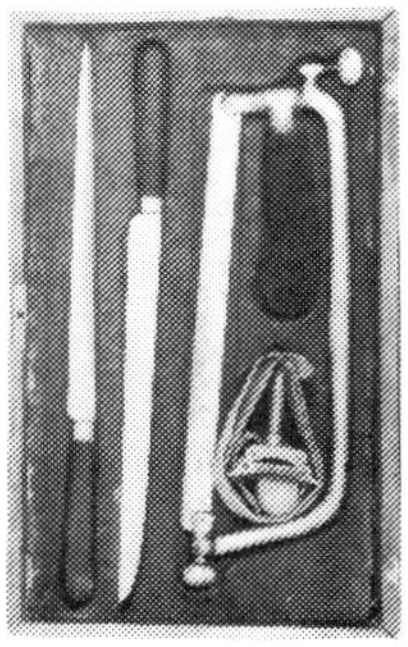

French mid 19th century Charriere amputation set, in fitted walnut case, 16 x 9½in. £605

A Simpson part amputation set, in a fitted mahogany case. £572

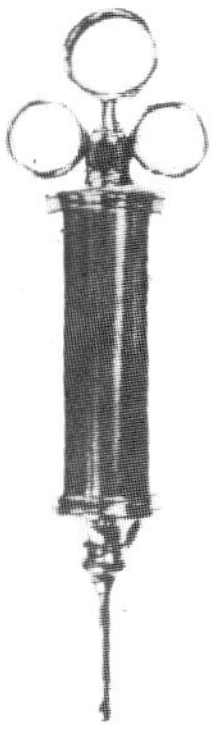

An all brass medical ear syringe with a three-finger pull one end and the hollow tube the other, 9½in. closed, circa 1870. (Christopher Sykes) £48

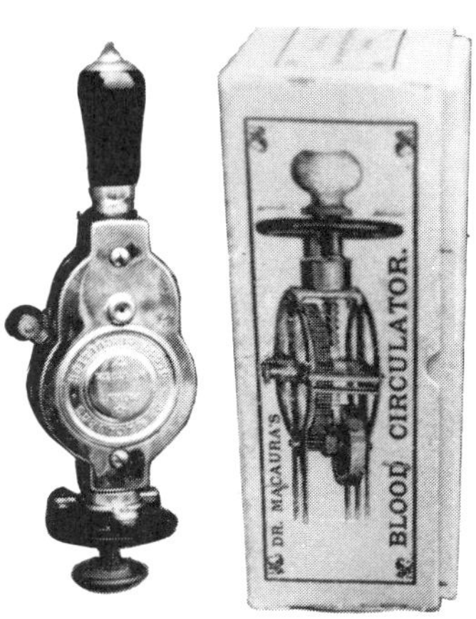

Dr. Macaura' 'Blood Circulator' complete with attachments and original box. £12

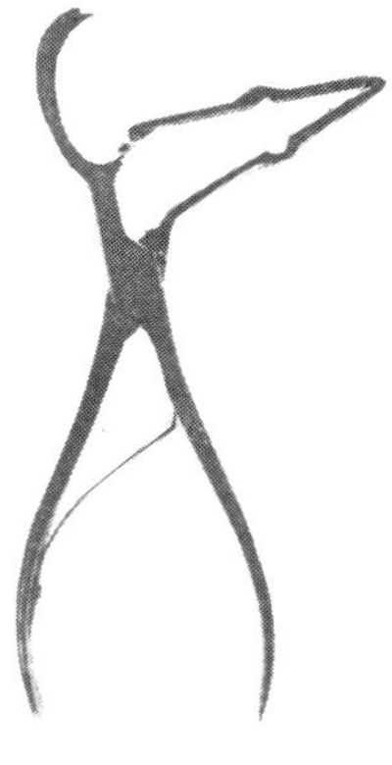

A surgeon's instrument by 'Weiss London', 7½in. long. (Christopher Sykes) £48

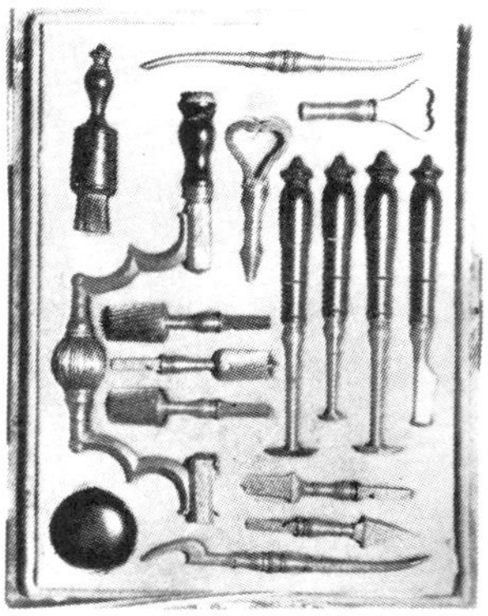

An 18th century set of surgeon's instruments, engraved Ambulance de S M. L'Empereur. (Christie's) £8,100

MEISSEN

The manufacture of china in the Saxon town of Meissen near Dresden began in 1710. During the Napoleonic Wars, the industry suffered a decline but with the appointment of H. G. Kuhn as Director in 1849, its fortunes revived and many of the successful 18th century models were revived as well as new ones being introduced.

Among the most popular pieces of Meissen china are children and the mythological groups produced between 1860 and 1890 as well as models of soldiers and figures in contemporary costume which appeared after 1870. The Meissen mark is a device of crossed swords with the addition of dates in some cases. A dot appears between the sword blades on pieces made between 1924 and 1934.

A Meissen circular snuff box and cover painted by B. G. Hauer, the interior of the base solid gilt, 1725-30, 7.5cm. diam. (Christie's) £19,440

A Meissen group of a scantily draped woman at her toilet, blue crossed swords marks and incised numerals, circa 1880, 15.5cm. high. (Christie's) £345

A Meissen bullet-shaped vase and cover in blue with decorated panels, on stand. (F. H. Fellows & Sons) £420

A Meissen figure of a jay modelled by J. J. Kandler, circa 1745, 39cm. high. (Christie's) £11,880

A Meissen rectangular snuff box and cover with contemporary two-colour gold mounts, circa 1750, 8.5cm. wide. (Christie's) £7,020

One of a pair of Meissen pug dogs modelled by J. J. Kandler and P. Reinicke, one with blue crossed swords mark on base, circa 1745, 15cm. high. (Christie's) £3,240

A Meissen hot water jug and cover, decorated in cisele gold, 17.5cm. high, red lustre mark 11, 1725. (Lawrence Fine Art) £6,820

A Meissen rectangular tea caddy and cover, traces of blue crossed swords mark on base, circa 1770, 12.5cm. high. (Christie's) £1,026

MINERAL WATER BOTTLES

This is a vast field because there were over 1,000 patents issued in the 19th century for internal stoppered bottles alone. The bottles were produced for individual manufacturers and grocers in every town in Great Britain and were usually made of aqua glass. Many of them were embossed with the name of the retailer and they could be closed by marbles, glass stoppers in a wide variety of shapes, rubber balls, pieces of wood or complicated metal and rubber washer devices. They come in a variety of shapes from short and dumpy to tall and elegant and can be found in waste dumps everywhere.

Stone Codd. Brown stoneware standard Codd shape and seal but both bottle and round marble stopper are made of stoneware, 8½in. high. £1,000

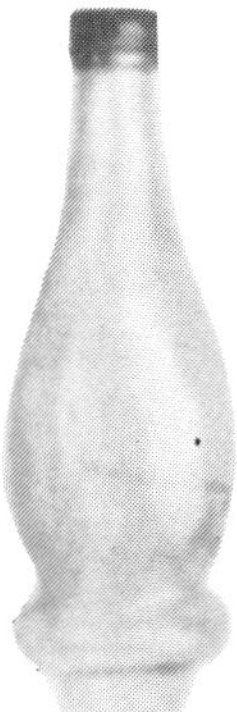

Edwards Patent (1874). Flat-bottomed Hamilton, aqua coloured bottle with wired metal cap over a protruding rubber washer, 9½in. high. £500

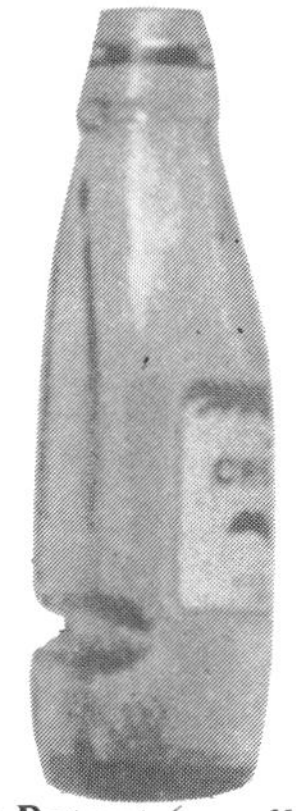

Billows Patent (small size). Aqua coloured, cylindrical bottle, with one flat side which has a groove near its base to retain the round glass stopper, 7½in. high. £300

Barrett & Elers Hybrid. Round-ended aqua coloured bottle with a long wooden stick stopper fitted with a rubber ring, 9½in. high. £150

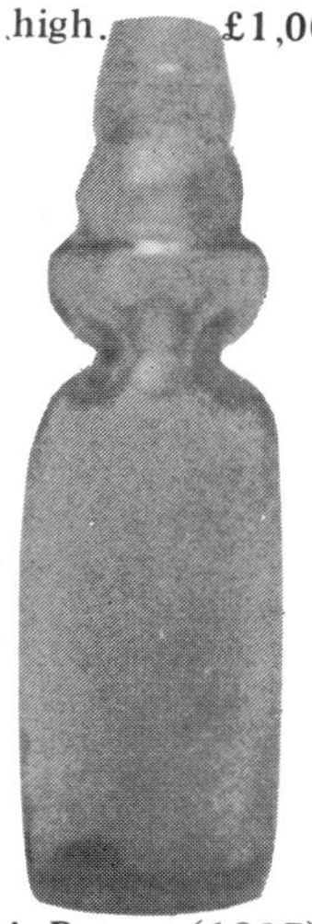

Connor's Patent (1897). Two bulbous cavities in neck to retain a pear shaped glass stopper, Codd Patent washer seal, aqua coloured, 9in. high. £200

Edwards Patent (1874). Internal annular projection to retain a glass marble near the base of the bottle, aqua coloured, 9in. high. £80

J. Lewis Patent, Aqua coloured bottle formed with a double shoulder to retain a long wooden stopper, 8½in. high. £150

Mitchells Patent (1878). A bulbous cavity at the top of the aqua coloured bottle retains a long glass stopper, rubber ring on the stopper to seal bottle. £200

MINIATURES

These miniature pieces fall into three main categories. Dolls' house furnishings, apprentice pieces and simply miniature items which have been crafted to as small a scale as possible in perfect replica of full size objects.

Apprentice pieces, unlike dolls' house furnishings designed specifically for play, were made, as the description implies, by an apprentice, as perfectly as his talents would allow, as part of his final exam before graduating as a fully fledged craftsman. Although most of the furniture today dates from the 19th century, this is a practice which has been in operation since furniture was first made on a commercial scale, with early pieces obtaining the highest prices. It is a practice which would seem to have been fairly widespread for apprentice pieces can be found in all European countries as well as in America.

Miniature 19th century banquet lamp with brown glass shade, 3in. high. £60

An Empire mahogany miniature sofa, American, circa 1840, 19in. wide. (Christie's) £986

An American late Federal mahogany miniature chest of drawers, 10in. wide. (Christie's) £733

A miniature apprentice made marquetry top table. £150

Late 18th century George III mahogany inlaid miniature chest of drawers, 12in. wide. (Christie's) £1,062

A Victorian mahogany miniature work table with silk covered base, 12in. high. (Christie's) £400

An early 19th century miniature Dutch marquetry and mahogany bureau. (Woolley & Wallis) £400

Miniature wicker fernery with high woven handle, 7in. high. £20

MINTON

This Staffordshire pottery began in Stoke on Trent in 1793 and produced a wide range of high quality items including Parian ware, vases in the Sevres style, painted plates, domestic earthenware, tiles, decorated panels and garden ornaments in terracotta and majolica. Some of the famous names to look out for in Minton ware include T. Allen who painted panels and vases; T. Kirkby who decorated items with flowers and fruit; H. Mitchell, painter of animals and R. Pilsbury who painted flowers. Tiles by W. Crane, J. Moyr-Smith and E. J. Poynter are also highly sought after as are the earthenware vases in the Art Nouveau style produced by L. V. Solon between 1897 and 1909.

A Minton double candle-snuffer, modelled as busts of a Medieval pair. (Christie's) £594

A white Minton group of two Amorini pulling a shell chariot. (Worsfolds) £100

A Minton mushroom teapot, with date code for 1862, 14.8cm. high. (Christie's) £440

A Minton majolica game tureen, cover and liner, year cypher for 1860. (Woolley & Wallis) £620

A large Minton 'moon flask' vase with two lug handles, circa 1890, 43.2cm. high. (Christie's) £378

A Minton figure, 'Vintager with basket in each hand', impressed Minton. (Christie's) £648

A Minton 'Palissy' vase formed as a ewer, impressed Minton 900 and date code for 1872, 37cm. high. (Christie's) £324

A Minton lidded 'Tower Jug', impressed Minton 1231 and date code for 1869, 34.5cm. high. (Christie's) £172

A Minton honeycomb dish modelled as a beehive, impressed Minton 1499 and date code for 1877, 18cm. high. (Christie's) £2,160

A Minton jardiniere and underdish with moulded decoration overall of rambling flowers, date code for 1858 on jardiniere, 37cm. high. (Christie's) £1,836

A Minton 'Perforated Garden Pedestal', impressed Minton 451 and date code for 1865, 80.5cm. high. (Christie's) £540

A Minton 'Christmas Jug', the handle modelled as entwined holly branches, impressed Minton 580 (circa 1870), 22.5cm. high. (Christie's) £864

MIRRORS

Since Narcissus admired his own reflection in a pool of water, people have wanted to see themselves as others see them but till the end of the Middle Ages they could only do this in hand mirrors of polished metal.
In 1507, however, the Venetian glassmakers at Murano acquired a monopoly on making mirrors of plain glass backed by an amalgam of mercury and tin. These mirrors were spotted and distorting but the quality improved after 1615 when an Englishman called Sir Robert Mansell patented his mirrors backed by mercury and tinfoil. His factory had over 500 employees and they exported mirrors all over Europe.
The earliest mirrors were small and hand held but when the Duke of Buckingham established a glass works at Vauxhall which could produce mirrors up to three and a half feet long, a revolution in interior decoration was on its way. Owners of fine houses bought mirrors to put on walls between windows and over chimney pieces.

Decorative mirrors are still hugely popular and antique examples fetch high prices. They are found not only as wall hangings but as dressing table and cheval mirrors and come in a variety of styles ranging from the rococo of the mid 18th century to elegant Chippendale gilded pine. This gave way to Chinese Chippendale and the more stately Adam style. Regency oval mirrors still go well with modern decorating schemes as do the larger Victorian gilt gesso framed mirrors.

A Queen Anne giltwood mirror, 47 x 27½in.
(Christie's) £2,160

An ornate Victorian mahogany toilet mirror, 1860.
(British Antique Exporters)
£156

A mirror attributed to Bugatti, various woods decorated with beaten copperwork and copper and pewter inlay, circa 1900, 66 x 61.8cm. (Christie's)
£1,404

A 17th century Spanish parcel gilt and grained mirror, 40½ x 28½in.
(Christie's) £378

A Chippendale inlaid mahogany mirror, possibly N.Y., 1760/80, 43½in. high.
(Christie's) £910

A Irish, George III giltwood overmantel with shaped divided plates, the upper panel painted with a Venetian scene.
(Christie's) £16,200

MODEL BUSES

Collecting toys and models has become increasingly popular over the past ten years and collectors today tend to specialise in a particular area of interest such as buses and trams. No model is too large or small, old or modern, for a good representative collection will cover items ranging in size from 1in. to 8ft. in length like the miniature 1945 Renault and 1949 Harrington coaches.
Prices vary considerably according to condition and while there are many expensive items it is still possible for a new collector to make a start for a comparatively modest outlay. Enthusiasts are well catered for with Collectors Fairs & Swopmeets. It is also worth looking in antique shops, secondhand shops and even in the long established toy shops for old stock. When buying for investment do look out for any signs of metal fatigue on early diecast models and also learn to distinguish between the many replica models being produced today and an authentic item.

Guntermann (W. Germany) tinplate tram, circa 1930, 300mm. long. £130

Johillco (Great Britain), diecast tram, circa 1935. £120

Tootsietoy Greyhound Bus (U.S.A.), diecast, circa 1940. £35

Rico (Spain) tramcar with cut out tin figures in the windows, circa 1910. £200

Guntermann (W. Germany) tinplate General Bus, 1920's. £300

Betall (Great Britain) tinplate trolleybus, 1950's, 175mm. long. £40

Chad Valley (Great Britain) double decker Greenline tinplate bus, circa 1930. £250

Tootsietoy Greyhound Bus (U.S.A.), diecast, circa 1940. £35

Wells Brimtoy Greenline tinplate coach, 1950's. £50

MODEL PLANES

Die cast model toy aeroplanes have been made in numerous countries and have proved to be very popular and highly collectible. Examples made by companies such as Dinky, Corgi, Lone Star (U.K.), Tootsie Toys (U.S.A.), Tekno (Denmark), Schuco (Germany), Solido and Dinky (France), Mercury (Italy), C.I.J. (France), Aeromini and Tomica (Japan) are particularly popular.

Probably the most sought after model to any Dinky collector is number 992 Avro Vulcan. This model of the most famous of the R.A.F. V-Bombers, was produced between 1955 and 1956. The model is quite large and finished in silver. Although it was given the number 992 it carried the number 749.

An original mint and boxed Dinky Vulcan could reasonably be expected to fetch between £1,000 and £1,400 at auction. The original box is extremely rare and adds a great deal to its value.

Frobisher Class Air Liner No. 62R, 1939-41. £45

Post-war Spitfire No. 62A, 1945-49. £10

Vautoor No. 60B, French Issue, 1957-63. £20

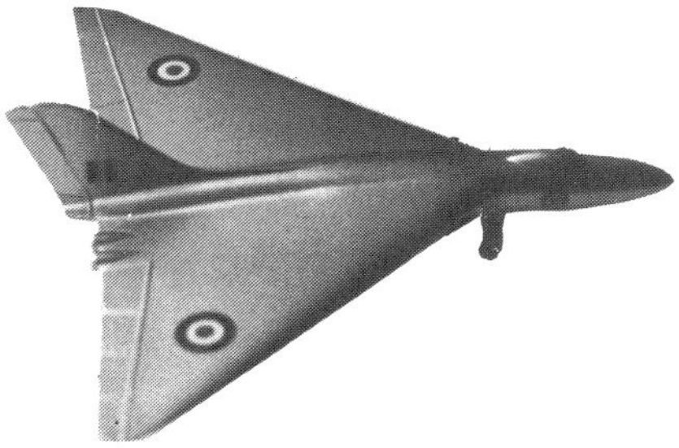

Avro Vulcan No. 992, issued 1955, (not issued in U.K., unknown number released in Canada). £1,200

Ensign Air Liner No. 62P, 1938-41. £40

Iomica (Japanese) F-14A Tomcat, 1978-80. £15

Mayo Composite Aircraft No. 63, 1939-41. £90

Monospar No. 60E, 1934-41. £75

Imperial Airways Liner No. 60A, 1934-40. £75

MODEL SHIPS

Many of the model ships found today could well have originated from a market stall such as that set up on the Esplanade outside Edinburgh Castle by prisoners of the Napoleonic War . They sold wonderfully detailed model ships made largely from left-over bones from the cookhouse, embellished with scraps of ivory, wood and metal bought with the proceeds of other sales. Needless to say, these model ships varied somewhat in size and skill of execution, from two foot long models of 100 gun men o' war now costing many thousands of pounds, to quite small examples.

The Victorians, too, were enthusiastic makers of model ships, particularly those which could be put into glass cases.

A 19th century three-masted ship model, sails furled, approx. 36in. long. (Robt. W. Skinner Inc.) £364

A contemporary early 19th century French prisoner of war bone and horn model man of war reputed to be the French ship of the line 'Redoubtable' of 74 guns, 20½ x 26¾in. (Christie's) £8,000

Early 19th century prisoner-of-war model of a First Class ship of the line, 21in. long. (Christie's) £7,226

A planked and rigged model of a Royal Naval Cutter built by I. H. Wilkie, Sleaford, 36 x 42in. (Christie's) £350

A 19th century carved bone model of a frigate, probably French, 16½in. long. (Christie's) £2,248

A detailed ¼in.: 1ft. model of a twelve gun brig of circa 1840 built by M. J. Gebhard, Tottenham, 36 x 47in. (Christie's) £3,000

MODEL TRAINS

Model trains tend to fall into two distinct collecting fields. Those designed as toys, and these have been made since the last quarter of the 19th century mainly by the German firms of Bing and Marklin, and those superb scale models occasionally as large as 10ft. long, by firms such as Bassett-Lowke.

One of the most prolific British makers was Hornby and occasionally a complete set can be found in its original cardboard box. This adds greatly to the value as does the condition of the train; those with original paintwork and livery obtaining a premium.

Carriages, tenders, stations, bridges and all landscaping features are also eagerly sought after.

Marks to look for are G.B.N. for Bing, G.C. and Co. for Carette and G.M.C. for Marklin.

An exhibition standard 5in. gauge model of the Great Western Railway Dean Single 4-2-2 locomotive and tender No. 3012 'Great Western', 14 x 61in. (Christie's) £7,000

A gauge 0 live steam spirit-fired model of the S.E.C.R. steam rail-car, by Carette, circa 1908. (Christie's) £1,000

A 3½in. gauge model of the 4-4-0 locomotive and tender No. 573 built to the designs of 'Virginia', 11½ x 45in. (Christie's) £900

A 7¼in. gauge model of the Great Western Railway 15XX Class 0-6-0 Pannier tank locomotive No. 1500, rebuilt by F. West, Lee Green, 21 x 55in. (Christie's) £5,000

A gauge 0 (3-rail) electric model of a Continental Doll BLS electric engine, with overhead pantograph, by Bing, circa 1930. (Christie's) £200

A 7mm. finescale two rail electric model of the London Brighton and South Coast Railway Stroudley Class D1 0-4-2 side tank locomotive No. 351, built by B. Miller, 3¾ x 8¾in. (Christie's) £420

A 5in. gauge model of the London Midland and Scottish Railway rebuilt Scot Class 4-6-0 locomotive and tender No. 6154 'The Hussar' built by K. Edge, Peterborough, 16½ x 70in. (Christie's) £3,000

A gauge 0 (3-rail) electric model of a Continental 4-6-2 'Pacific' locomotive and twin bogie tender, Ref. No. HR64/13020, by Marklin, circa 1930. (Christie's) £1,500

A gauge 0 clockwork model of the London Midland and Scottish Railway 4-4-0 locomotive and six-wheel tender No. 5320 'George V', by Bing for Bassett-Lowke. (Christie's) £150

MODELS

The thing which sets models apart from other 'toys' is that most are hand crafted by skilled individuals and in some cases, as with scale model traction engines, this can mean thousands of hours of work involved. As such, it is not unreasonable when some of these intricate models sell for thousands of pounds at auction. The same applies for model steam trains by Bing, Carette and Marklin and some of the magnificent sailor made shipping dioramas from the 19th century.

They are generally found to be in good condition for they were constructed as an adult hobby and never intended for play as with a normal toy.

Engineering models of steam and traction engines tend to obtain the highest prices, but the award for charm must go to the Victorian models of butcher's shops complete with sides of mutton, ribs of beef and a rosy cheeked butcher with striped apron and boater.

An early 20th century model single cylinder surface condensing 'A' frame beam engine, 19½ x 24in. (Christie's) £1,700

An exhibition standard 2in. scale model of the Burrell 5 n.h.p. double crank compound two speed three shaft 'Gold Medal' tractor, engine No. 3846, Registration No. AD7782 'Pouss-nouk-nouk', built from works drawings by P. Penn-Sayers, Laughton, 19¾ x 27¼in. (Christie's) £7,500

An unusual model of a steam driven 19th century twin bore Deep Well Engine House and Pump, built by R. J. Sare, Northleach, 16½ x 18½in. (Christie's) £200

A well presented approx. 1:20 scale model of the Weatherhill Pit Winding Engine of 1833, built by W. K. Walsam, Hayes, 19 x 14½in. (Christie's) £600

A late 19th century glazed and cased model of M. Osborne's – The Butcher's Shop, 46.5 x 43.5cm. (Phillips) £750

Late 19th century model of the three cylinder compound vertical surface condensing mill engine 'Asia', 16¼ x 13¼in. (Christie's) £1,900

A model of a hall with marquetry floor dividing at the landing into stairs on either side going up to a galleried landing, 26in. wide. (Christie's) £300

MONEY BANKS

Most of the early money boxes we see today are made of metal. Many have a mechanical function and most still work. One of the earliest patents for a cast iron mechanical money bank was taken out by J. Hall on 21st December, 1869, for his 'Excelsior' bank.
Magic banks always have a mechanical function. A typical example is where a coin is placed under a magician's hat which, when lowered, causes the coin to disappear. The Trick Dog bank is activated by a lever which causes the dog to leap through a hoop and deposit the coin from its mouth into a barrel. These mechanical banks are fascinating but most are a bit pricey.
Special note: look out for a mechanical bank featuring a young girl skipping. Only recently 'A Girl Skipping Rope' mechanical bank from the late 19th century, sold at auction for £8,250.

American late 19th century Speaking Dog cast-iron mechanical bank, 7in. long. £286

Late 19th century American 'Uncle Sam' mechanical bank, by Shepard Hardware Co., 11½in. high. £220

A mechanical cast iron money box, as a football player with articulated right leg, causing the player to shoot a coin into a goal and ring a bell, circa 1890, 10½in. long. (Christie's) £550

A 20th century English cast-iron 'Dinah' mechanical bank, by John Harper & Co. Ltd., 6½in. high. £104

A cast iron mechanical bank, 'Trick Pony', by Shepard Hardware Co., American, circa 1890, 7in. long. (Christie's) £300

Late 19th century American cast-iron 'Punch & Judy' mechanical bank, by Shepard Hardware Co., 7½in. high. £462

Late 19th century American cast-iron 'Santa Claus' mechanical bank, 6in. high. £495

A late 19th century cast iron Girl Skipping Rope mechanical bank, 20cm. wide. £8,250

MOORCROFT POTTERY

When some bright spark at James Macintyre and Co. decided in 1913 to switch production from pottery to the new-fangled electrical goods, their pottery designer, William Moorcroft, was left a little short of work, to say the least.
So with 15 years of experience behind him, and bearing in mind that life begins at 40, he took the plunge and established his own pottery works at Cobridge, near Stoke-on-Trent, employing many of his former colleagues from Macintyres.
Without any restraints he could give full reign to his ideas leaving a legacy of distinctive pottery now eagerly sought after today.
All his products bear his signature, W. Moorcroft, usually in green until 1920 and thereafter mainly in blue, together with the impressed mark Moorcroft or Moorcroft Burslem.

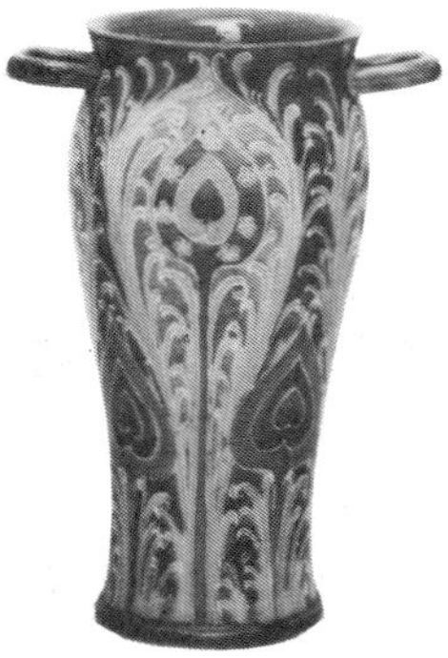

A Moorcroft Macintyre two-handled vase, design no. 360574, signed in green W. Moorcroft, 19cm. high. (Lawrence Fine Art) £308

A Moorcroft globular pottery vase modelled with a swimming fish, outlined in blue on a pale green ground, 6½in. high. (Christie's) £140

A Moorcroft two-handled box and cover, decorated in the 'Claremont' pattern, 6½in. high. (Christie's) £480

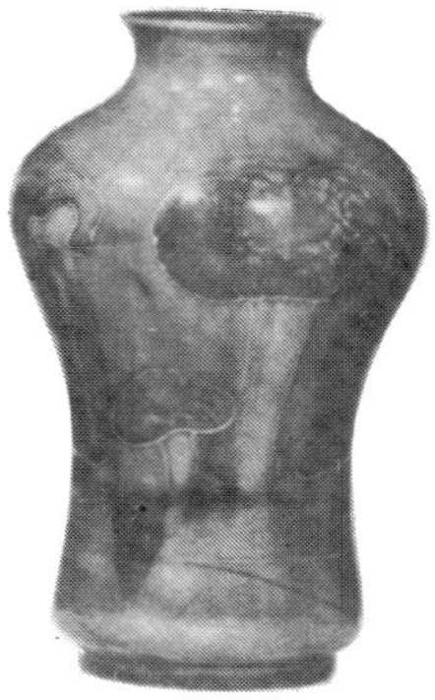

A Moorcroft broad baluster pottery vase made for Liberty & Co., 8in. high. (Christie's) £450

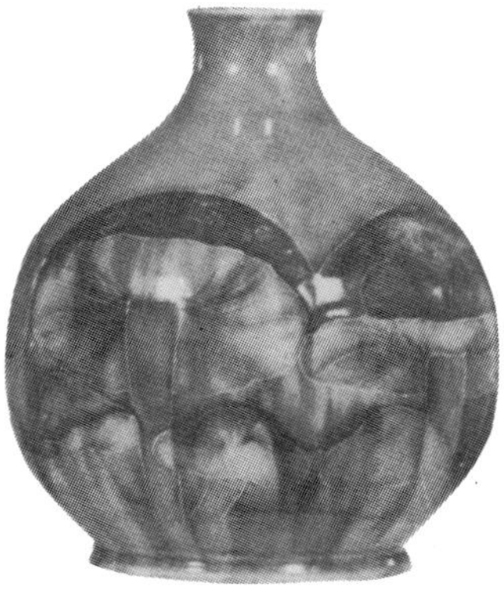

A Moorcroft pottery oviform vase made for Liberty & Co., in the Toadstool pattern, 10in. high, signed in green. (Christie's) £715

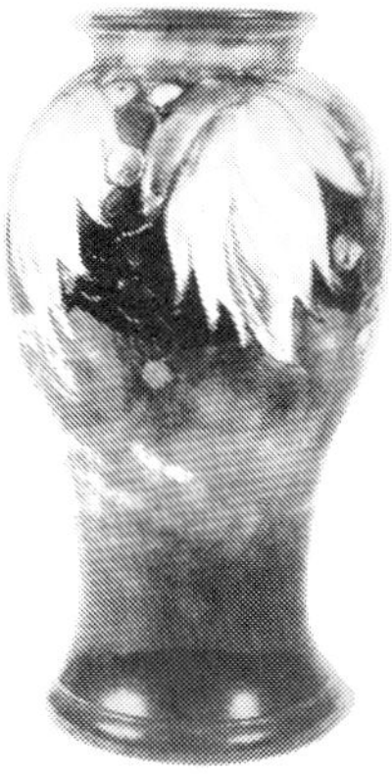

A William Moorcroft grape pattern vase of ovoid form, 16in. high. (Capes, Dunn & Co.) £220

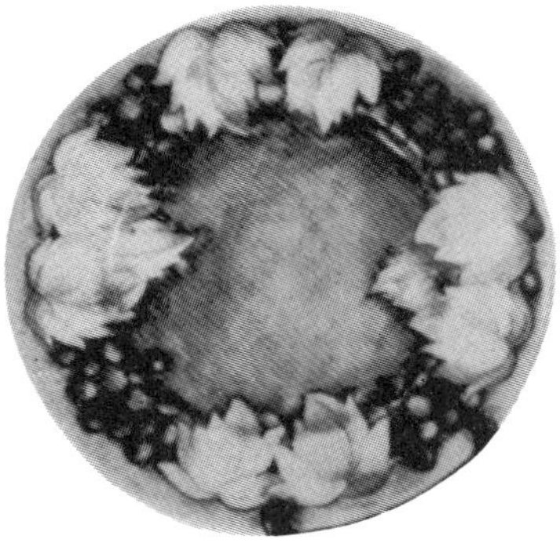

A Moorcroft circular pottery dish painted in the Leaf and Berry pattern, 11½in. diam. (Christie's) £85

One of a pair of Moorcroft Dawn pattern vases of ovoid form, 18.5cm. high. (Lawrence Fine Art) £418

MOTTOWARE

One day in 1867, when a certain Mr. G.P. Allen was dutifully digging in his back garden at Watcombe House, he unearthed, not gold, but what was regarded at the time as the finest red clay in England.

Recognising the potential value of his find he enlisted the aid of Charles Brock, an experienced potter from Hanley. Within two years they had established the Watcombe Pottery, engaging many imported Staffordshire craftsmen.

Most of their products were designed specifically for the souvenir trade, the most popular proving to be modest earthenware pieces with a decoration on one side and a motto on the other – now referred to as Devon motto ware.

The early mark was simply 'Watcombe Pottery' or 'Watcombe Torquay' and from 1875 incorporated a woodpecker seated upon a branch with the sea in the background.

Aller Vale Art Potteries, established in 1865, was a similar firm to Watcombe Pottery, and eventually they amalgamated in 1901. The combined factory prospered until 1962 under the trade name Royal Aller Vale and Watcombe Art Pottery.

Originally the Aller Vale pottery, situated near Newton Abbot, manufactured drain pipes and roof tiles but after the works were severely damaged by fire, John Phillips the owner re-opened and began to produce the popular Art Pottery.

The output from both firms was prolific and, because their products were bought primarily by tourists, pieces can be found in all parts of the country at moderate prices in antique shops and auctions.

A Dartmouth pottery jug, inscribed 'No Road is long with Good Company'. £4

An Aller Vale pottery teapot bearing the legend, 'Ye may get better cheer, But no' wi' better heart'. £15

An unmarked earthenware coffee pot, the motto cut through the white slip to the brown clay. £12,

Torquay Ware shaving mug in brown and cream bearing the motto 'Better do one thing, Than dream all things!'. £15

A Watcombe pottery tile decorated with leaf and flower swirls. £12

An unmarked pottery hot-water jug. £12

MUSICAL BOXES

Music in the home was as common during Victorian times as it is today – the difference being that, in those happy days, at least one member of most families was a more or less accomplished musician who would be happy to entertain the rest of the household at the slightest nod from Papa.

If, however, the said accomplished being was unavailable to perform, the neighbourhood would not necessarily be plunged into an abyss of silent gloom for there was a multitude of cabinets and boxes ready to spring into melodious life at the wind of a handle and the touch of a lever.

Although musical boxes had been fairly widely available during the 18th century, they had been extremely small affairs; novelties produced by ingenious clockmakers who, with wonderful precision, had fitted their tiny mechanisms into small boxes, seals, watches, and even into the handles of walking sticks.

The more widely accepted form of musical box, the antecedent, in its way, of the family record player, didn't put in an appearance until the early 19th century when it was introduced by David le Coutre.

It comprised of a clockwork mechanism powered by a coiled spring. This causes a cylinder, studded with steel pins, to rotate, the pins, pinging against a steel comb with teeth of different lengths to create the different notes.

Other still more exotic examples have drums, flutes, whistles, and even castanets to add a spot of excitement to their tunes.

An HMV Junior Monarch oak horn gramophone with panelled oak case, soundbox replaced. (Christie's) £600

A musical box playing 12 sacredains accompanied by 9 bells with bee strikers, 31in. wide. (Christie's) £1,700

A 19.1/8in. upright Symphonion disc musical box with 'Sublime Harmony' combs, and six discs. (Christie's) £1,700

An Edison Fireside combination type phonograph, Model B No. 89443, with four minute gearing. (Onslows) £470

A lever wind musical box, by Nicole Freres, No. 51725, playing 4 overtures, with tune sheet and rosewood veneered case, 27½in. wide. (Christie's) £2,500

A 15.5/8in. Polyphon in panelled walnut case with double combs and forty-seven discs in circular wood box. (Christie's) £1,600

MUSTARD POTS

Although mustard sauce was in general use by the middle of the 18th century, it is rare to find a mustard pot from before this date.

The earliest silver mustard pots are usually of drum shape with pierced, flowing, scroll designs, which became more restrained towards the end of the century. By this time, they can be found in a variety of designs including oval and vase shaped, a style particularly popular with Hester Bateman.

Victorian mustard pots are generally much bigger. The very largest of all being the most popular for they can also be used as marmalade pots and have a far greater commercial value.

One of a pair of George III vase-shaped mustard pots, by R. Emes and E. Barnard, 1811, 5¼in. high, 42oz. (Christie's) £2,700

George III oval mustard pot, by Hester Bateman, London, 1787, 3in. high.(Bermondsey) £225

George III silver mustard pot, by Edward Capper, London, 1797, 3¾in. high. (Bermondsey) £225

George III silver mustard pot of plain cylindrical form with scroll handle, 3½oz. (Bermondsey) £100

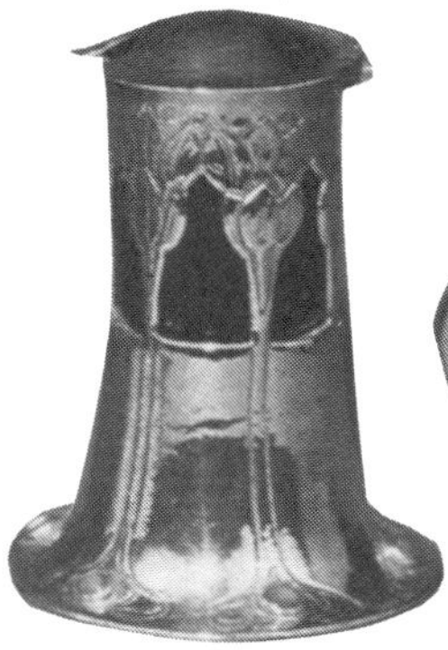

A C. R. Ashbee silver mustard pot, set with six turquoise cabochons, London hallmarks for 1900, 8cm. high. (Christie's) £864

A Guild of Handicrafts silver mustard pot, designed by C. R. Ashbee, with London hallmarks for 1902, 8.5cm. high, 4oz.11dwt. gross weight. (Christie's) £918

A Victorian hexagonal mustard pot, with blue glass liner, London, 1843. (Christie's) £242

A Victorian mustard pot formed as Mr Punch, maker JBH, London 1878, 10cm. high, 6.5oz. (Christie's) £604

NAUTICAL ITEMS

If seafaring is your bag, then it would be easy to turn your home into a veritable nautical paradise – cash permitting.
Items you will find among the many splendid instruments of superb quality and precision are, sextants, log screws, compasses, telegraphs, octants, astrolabes, theodolites, telescopes, and nocturnal dials – any of these items will contribute to an agreeable collection. If it is possible to house something a bit larger, there are binnacles, ship's figureheads or wheels. Nautical furniture will also make an excellent theme for a collection for, almost without exception, all pieces are well proportioned and made from the finest wood set with sunken brass handles.
In fact, one of the main attributes of all nautical items is the quality of the materials used in their production for they were designed for a hard life on the high seas.

An eight-day marine chronometer by Hatton & Harris No. 570, diam. of bezel 133mm. £5,500

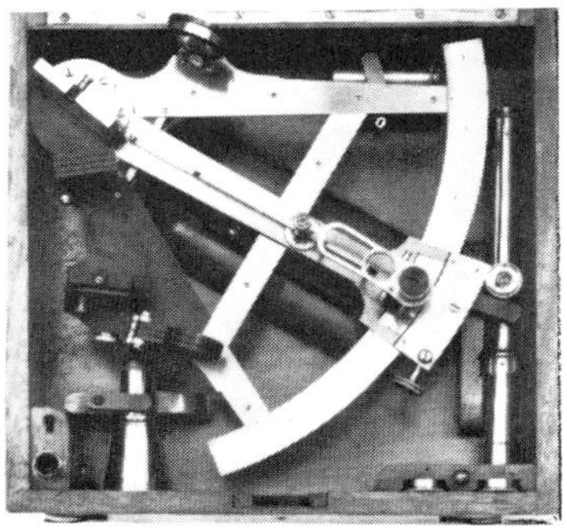

A Cary brass sextant with gold scale, numbered 3856, 11¾ x 11¼in. (Lawrence Fine Art) £1,595

Early 20th century Thos. Walker 'Harpoon' depth finder, English, 6½in. long. £165

Early 20th century Davey & Co. starboard lamp in copper casing. £44

A Kelvin & Hughes Ltd. ship's binnacle compass, English, circa 1940, 53in. high. £748

A Siebe, Gorman & Co. brass and copper diver's helmet, English, circa 1920, 19in. high. (Lawrence Fine Art) £660

Early 20th century White Thompson & Co. ship's binnacle compass, 54in. high. £550

Mid 19th century English ship's wheel with ten turned mahogany spokes, 68cm. diam. £770

NETSUKE

As the traditional national costume of Japan, the kimono, didn't have pockets, objects such as an inro, purse, drinking gourd or tobacco pouch were usually hung from a cord at the waist. The cord was attached to a netsuke (pronounced netski) which was simply slipped under the sash (obi) which fastened the kimono and was held in place by pressure.

Originally netsuke were simple wooden toggles but as attention was given to them they became elaborately carved reaching a sustained peak by the end of the 18th century. They were usually made of either wood or ivory but can be found of bone, rhino, buffalo and stag horn, coral, jet, turtle shell, amber or even metal. The subjects carved are more numerous than the carvers (of whom over 3000 have been identified) but two of the main groups are those depicting characters from Japanese folk history (Mukashi – Banashi) and Sugata – depictions of various craftsmen. Eroticism was also a popular subject and examples not infrequently took the form of young ladies indulging – or being indulged by – sea monsters and mythological characters.

Most netsuke originate from the large areas of population such as Osaka, Nagoya, Kyoto and Edo where the carvers could make a good living.

Their popularity declined when Japan ended her seclusion with the Meija restoration in 1868 and western style dress with pockets became popular. The influx of tourists however, eager for souvenirs of old Japan became a major market for netsuke and vast numbers, of a poor quality compared to earlier ones, were exported to Europe and America.

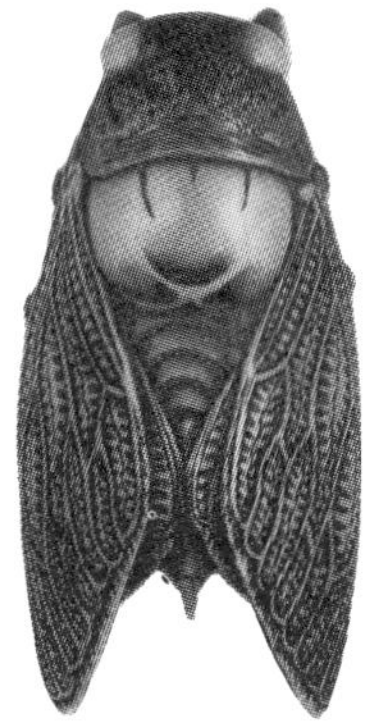

A 19th century ivory netsuke of a cicada, signed Masatsugu. (Christie's) £4,320

Late 19th century ivory netsuke of a monkey and her two young, signed Masatami (Shomin), Yamada School. (Christie's) £1,026

Late 19th century ivory okimono style netsuke of two seated Manzai dancers, signed Fujiyuki. (Christie's) £216

An early/mid 19th century ivory netsuke of a professional sneezer, signed Ryuko, and kao. (Christie's) £475

Early 19th century ivory netsuke of a sumo wrestler, unsigned. (Christie's) £1,512

An ivory netsuke of Nitta No Shiro Tadatsune about to stab the boar, inscribed Masakazu. (Christie's) £756

NEWSPAPERS

Newspapers for the collector fall into two main categories, those which are from library files and those which have been kept individually because of a particular story.

Libraries are now making micro-fiche copies of their copies and large quantities of old newspapers in excellent condition have come onto the market in recent years. These often show signs of having been bound.

Of individually kept copies those to do with Royalty are by far the most common and post-1900 copies should rarely cost more than £1. Look out for aviation 'firsts', notorious murders, disasters etc.

During the 1926 General Strike most newspapers were affected by their labour coming out. Management and strike-breakers then produced emergency editions on a limited scale ranging from the Graphic which was little different to their normal issues to the single mimeographed sheet of the Daily Mirror. Considering that nearly 60 years have passed a considerable number of these newspapers still exist and they present an interesting picture with immediate comment upon one of the most traumatic episodes in recent British labour history.

Most ephemera dealers have selections of these newspaper on offer from time to time and they should not cost more than £2 or £3 each.

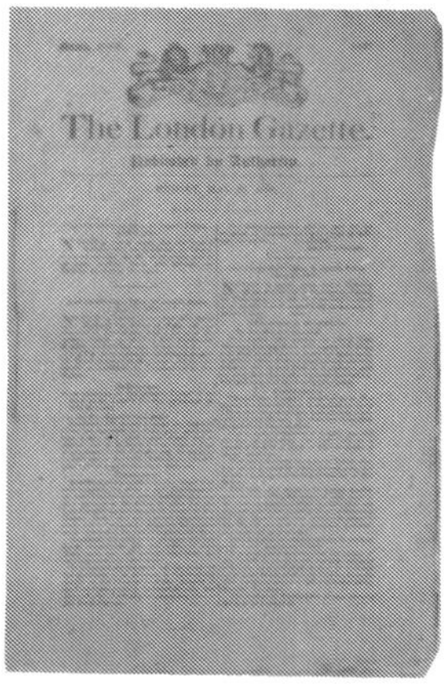
The London Gazette.

The London Gazette, May 20th 1898. £2

The Daily Mirror

The Daily Mirror, January 4th, 1911, Sidney Street Seige. £2.50

Christian Herald
and Signs of Our Times

Christian Herald, 16th October, 1930, R. 101 Airship Disaster. £1.50

The London Chronicle

The London Chronicle, September 1789. £3

Police Gazette

The National Police Gazette, May 26th, 1897. £2.50

Sunday Companion

The Sunday Companion, 28th August, 1908. £1

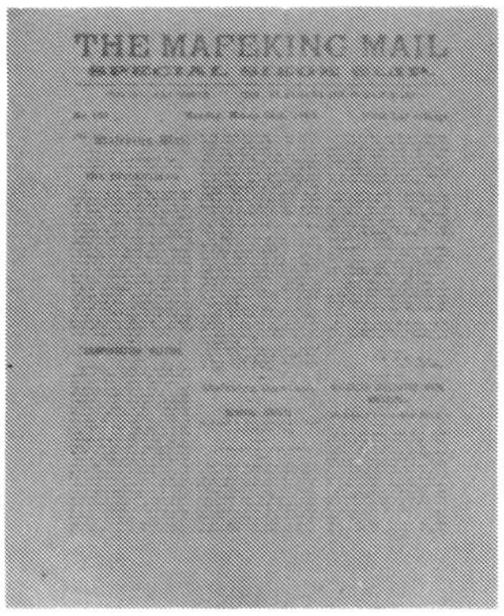

The Mafeking Mail, Special Seige Slip, No. 100, 26th March, 1900. £3

Psychic News, 12th Sept. 1936. 75p

Daily Mail, Midlands Edition, April 25th 1914. £3

The Colliery Guardian, June 19th 1885. £2

The Daily Graphic, Bleriot Channel Flight. £3

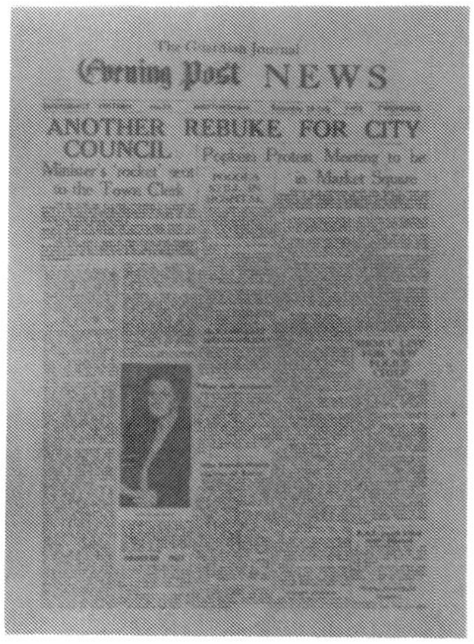

Evening Post News, 18th July 1959, Emergency Edition. £1

Daily Sketch, September 26th 1914. £1.50

The Sunderland Echo, 2nd June, 1953, Coronation Issue. 50p

The Workers' Weekly, Dec. 12th 1924. £1

NUTCRACKERS

It was a Victorian tradition to serve fruit and nuts in their shells towards the end of a meal and predictably, these gadget conscious people had to have the proper tools for the job.

It was not, however, considered sufficient to provide a simple and effective appliance, for, like the nutmeg grater and any other implement which had to be used in the presence of company, a pair of nutcrackers had to compliment the tableware and reflect the status of the household.

For practical purposes, nutcrackers had to be made from a fairly sturdy metal and the focus of attention centred on design. The handles were often decorated with ivory or bone and some were fitted with a scalpel shaped pick, designed to help winkle the kernel from the shell.

Finer examples in silver plated or gilt metal rarely survive intact.

A 17th/18th century box-wood nut cracker of hinged form, 6in. long. £264

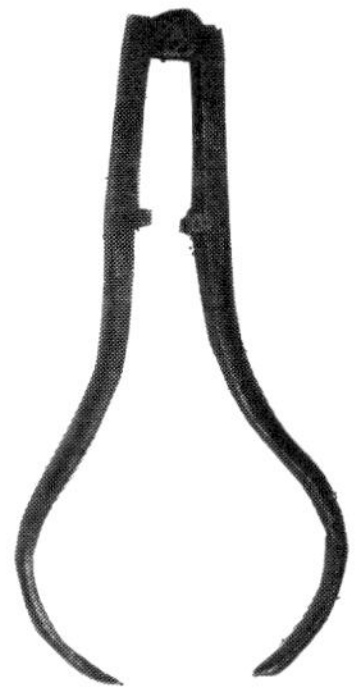

A pair of early 19th century steel nutcrackers. (Paul G. Sheppard) £6

An 18th century yewwood nutcracker of hinged form carved with a man's head, 6¾in. £308

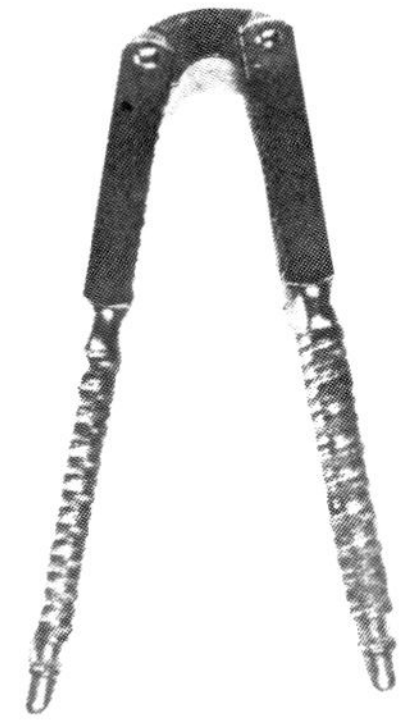

A 19th century pair of steel nut and also lobster shell crackers, circa 1870, 5in. long. (Christopher Sykes) £15

A cast-steel nut cracker in the form of a 7¼in. long alligator, circa 1925. (Christopher Sykes) £22

Victorian steel nut crackers with 'barley sugar' handles, circa 1860, 6in. long. (Christopher Sykes) £18

A 19th century walnut nut cracker of screw type, 8½in. £88

Wrought steel nutcrackers, circa 1820, 5½in. long. (Christopher Sykes) £15

A pair of finely carved Scandinavian treen nutcrackers, circa 1880, 6¼in. long. (Christopher Sykes) £35

A late 18th century wood figure of a sailor his mouth operating as a nutcracker, 9½in. high. (W. H. Lane & Son) £57

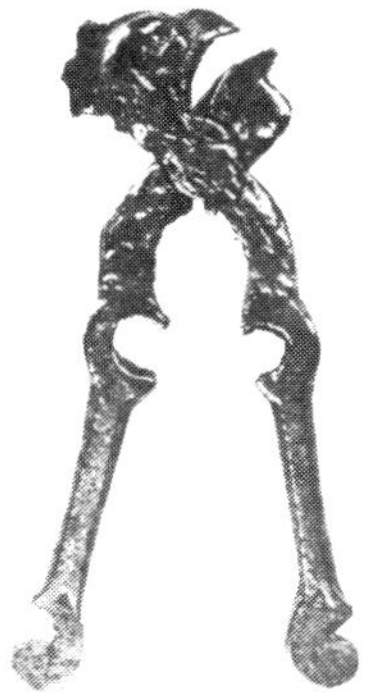

A pair of cast brass 19th century nutcrackers, the top in the form of a cockerel's head, circa 1800, 5¾in. long. (Christopher Sykes) £47

An 18th/19th century walnut nut cracker in the form of an old woman seated, 7¾in. £110

OILIANA

As more and more people become aware of the power of advertising and the influence it has upon their lives, it becomes obvious that, by looking back at company images created at a time when the publicity men must have been more or less working in the dark, some got it right. Shell, Castrol and Mobiloil, and some were not so successful, B.P. and Pratts for example. So, as we move into the present day and take a look at these old pieces of functional advertising in the form of oil cans and pourers, it is the Shell and Castrol examples which are the most sought after and the High Performance Oil containers of these companies 'Aeroshell' and 'Castrol R' which are the most popular.

The Shell company used a variety of shaped enamel signs which now fetch a considerable amount of money.

The Castrol company passed through four distinct design periods. The first can be seen in the Castrol R tin, followed by the style used on the quart Oil Power. There are examples of a pourer in the first style having been repainted and a transfer from the later style applied to bring the pourer up to date. The subsequent style which was employed up to the 1950's can be seen on the quarter and half pint pourers. It was at this time that the present style came into use with the loss of the lower arm on the logo. As time goes by, these modern pieces will almost certainly be collected but as yet they do not really interest collectors.

Remember, you will not be able to find any early Esso items, for the Anglo-American Oil Company used the name of Pratts and, demonstrating the march of progress, all Esso stations are now Exxon in the U.S.A.

Texaco enamel sign made by The Texaco Company, U.S.A. £20

Castrol one pint motor oil tin of conical form. £15

An unusual combined Shell motor oil and petrol can. £35

'Shell' motor oil enamel sign by Shell-Mex Ltd. £80

Castrol motor oil enamel sign. £30

Castrol motor oil quart pourer. £20

PAPERBACKS

Designed as a cheap alternative to the hardback book the paperback only came into its own as a collectible item in the last decade. While there were earlier publishers, indeed Tauchnitz started publishing in 1837, it was not until the advent of Penguin books in 1935 that the paperback became 'respectable'.

Today the collector of paperback books appears in many forms. Some people seek the first 1,000 Penguin books of which No. 1, Ariel, by Maurois sells for around £30. Others may collect a favourite author in paperback first editions where the original hardback 'firsts' are outside their price range, while yet others collect subjects which were often only published in paperback such as the range of teenage gang and drugs novels of the 1950's and 1960's.

Detective and Science Fiction paperbacks also have their enthusiastic collectors while others only have eyes for Mills and Boon romantic novels and those of Barbara Cartland of which there are over 300.

A further field of collecting is based upon the cover art work. Look for American Signet and Bantam books with covers by Avati, the Pocketbook series with McKnight Kauffer art work and the 1950's pulp novels with the lovely ladies by Heade.

Most paperback collectors find the bulk of their books on the shelves of conventional bookdealers who haven't yet realised the desirability of certain paperbacks.

Charity shops and jumble sales are also a happy hunting ground, and even from the specialist paperback dealer most titles are no more expensive than new paperbacks today.

The Weird Shadow Over Innsmouth, Bart House. £25

Tam, by Edgar Wallace. £1.25

Naked On Roller Skates, by Maxwell Bodenheim, Diversey 1949. £15

The Dancing Star, Hodder & Stoughton, Yellow Jacket, 1930's. £2

Ariel, by Andre Maurois, No. 1, 1935. £30

Too Busy To Die, Dell 1947. £5

Gulliver's Travels, 1938, wood engravings by T. Naish. £3

The Amboy Dukes, by Irving Shulman, Avon. £12

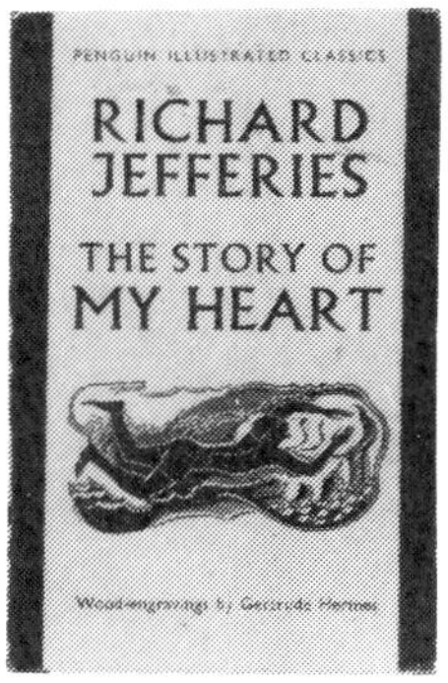

The Story Of My Heart, 1938, wood engravings by Gertrude Hermes. £3

Into Plutonian Depths, Avon Books. £20

Reform School Girl, by Felice Swados, Diversey, 1948. £100

The Sonnets, The Penguin Shakespeare, 1938. £2

The Curse of Cowden by Annie S. Swan, Hutchinson. £2

Kent, Sussex and Surrey, Penguin Guide, 1938. £2

Germany Puts The Clock Back, 1st Special 1937. £3.50

Walden, 1938, wood engravings by Ethelbert White. £3

Rumble, by Harlan Ellison, Pyramid, 1958. £18

Junkie, U.K. 1st Edition of first William Burrough's Novel. £30

PAPERWEIGHTS

Although glass paperweights are reputed to have been used in ancient Egypt, the earliest dated examples of the now familiar shape came from France and Venice in 1845.

They were developed as luxury additions to the popular writing boxes of the period, and the most sought after were produced in vast numbers by three French firms, Baccarat, Clichy and Saint Louis.

American and English glassworks such as the Boston and Sandwich Glass Co. and Bacchus and Sons followed suit a few years later, but their work is somewhat overshadowed by the charisma attached to the weights produced in the first ten years by the French firms.

While the majority of paperweights consist of a heavy clear glass dome, enclosing multi coloured glass rods designed to represent fruit or flowers, weights produced by the French glass artists such as Daum, Almeric Walter, Lalique and Baccarat are to be found in many different shapes including dragonflies, frogs, snakes, birds and nymphs.

It is worth noting that many weights are signed with an initial and a date but usually these marks are so cleverly incorporated into the design as to make them difficult to spot.

Examples by important French makers will naturally be expensive, anything from a few hundred to thousands, but a start can be made with the cheap English variety produced at the end of the 19th century. These usually depict such scenes as "The Esplanade at Hastings" simply stuck beneath a glass blob, but for all their simplicity they do have a certain charm.

A Clichy swirl weight, with alternate turquoise and white staves radiating from a central claret, green and white cane, 8.2cm. diam. (Christie's) £594

A French scramble paperweight with blue, green, white and red canes, 3in. diam. (Robt. W. Skinner Inc.) £291

A St. Louis pink ground pompom weight, 7cm. diam. (Christie's) £1,296

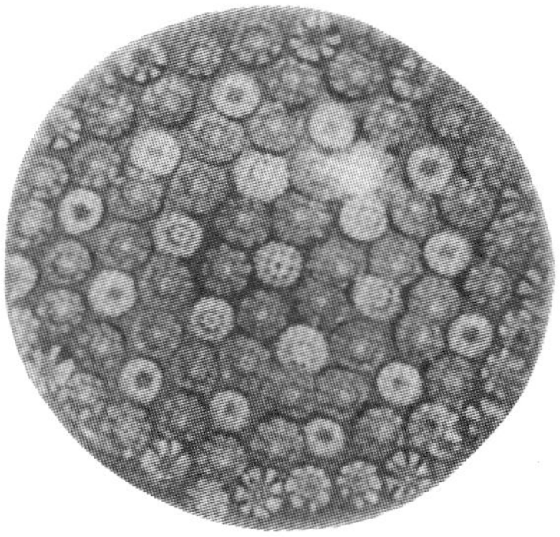

A Clichy blue ground scattered millefiori weight, 8.5cm. diam. (Christie's) £594

A Baccarat mushroom weight on a star-cut base, 8cm. diam. (Christie's) £1,728

A Clichy flat bouquet weight, 7cm. diam. (Christie's) £9,720

PARIAN

The art of parian statuary was first introduced around 1840 and almost simultaneously produced by Copeland & Garrett and Minton; followed in 1848 by Wedgwood.

Parian is a slightly translucent, silky textured, matt white porcelain bearing a strong resemblance to marble but, unlike marble which requires carving, this material could be moulded to reproduce copies of famous pieces of sculpture scaled down to a more practical size for the average home. Manufacturers also commissioned models for their statuary products.

Initially used for the manufacture of figures, groups and applied decoration, the range widened as the production process improved and includes vases, jugs, tea services and other tableware.

A Parian bust of Wellington wearing classical dress, after E. W. Wyon impressed mark, 16in. high. (Christie's) £100

A coloured Parian group modelled as a young girl on rockwork, entitled 'You can't read', 12¼in. high, possibly by Robinson & Leadbetter. (Christie's) £150

A Goss Parian bust of Queen Victoria, for Mortlock's of Oxford Street, 236mm. high. (Phillips) £160

A Minton Parian group of a nude female figure seated on the back of a lion, circa 1847-48, 1ft.3½in. high. (Hobbs & Chambers) £50

A Copeland Parian group, entitled 'Go To Sleep', impressed Art Union of London, J. Durham Sc 1862, 26in. high overall. (Anderson & Garland) £370

A pair of Royal Worcester glazed Parian figures of Paul and Virginia, circa 1865, 33cm. high. (Christie's) £475

One of a pair of glazed Parian figure brackets, allegorical figures in rock-like niches, 9½in. high. (Capes, Dunn & Co.) £110

A Parian standing female figure, probably Belleek but unmarked, 36.5cm. high. (Lawrence Fine Art) £110

PETROL PUMP GLOBES

The inspiration for the petrol pump came from America, and were in use in that country for at least ten years prior to their adoption in Britain. Early American brands included Gilbert & Barker, Bowser and Hammond.
The shape of globes on top of petrol pumps went through significant change in the early years. When Pratts, which was owned by Anglo-American Oil Co., changed its name in 1935 to Standard Oil, the legend on the globe changed to Esso – a clever acronym for S.O. . The characteristic pill-shaped globe of Pratts changed to the now-familiar oval shape of Esso.
Shell globes also evolved. The early Shell globe was globular, dating from the 1930's, but this soon changed to the shell-shaped globe with which we are now familiar. In the 1950's its size was reduced though it retained its distinctive shape.
Some other distinctive globes advertised brands such as National Benzole, V.I.P., Texaco, Regent, Caltex, Lobitos, Mex, Cawoods, M.S., Jet, Globe, Gulf, Mobil and Fina.

Cleveland Super Discol petrol pump globe. (Onslow's)
£100

A National Benzole Mixture, diamond with Mercury head petrol pump globe. (Onslow's)
£150

Esso petrol pump globe. (Onslow's) £70

A Redline Super, pre war petrol pump globe. (Onslow's)
£130

Shell petrol pump bowl. (Onslow's) £100

A post war B.P. shield petrol pump globe. (Onslow's)
£210

A Pratts post war glass petrol pump globe. (Onslow's)
£300

A Shell, first design, pre war glass petrol pump globe. (Onslow's) £210

Pratts petrol pump bowl, pre-war. (Onslow's)
£120

PEWTER

Pewter is an alloy based on tin with the addition of other metals which may be lead, brass or copper. It is thought to have been made by the Romans but was most popular in Britain during Elizabethan times when it was employed for church vessels, domestic purposes and civic functions.

Pewter began to be used for church vessels in the early Middle Ages when it replaced wood for the chalices. Until the 15th century it was customary to bury a pewter chalice with the priest. Pewter chalices, flagons, alms dishes and collecting plates can still be found in many church vaults.

Generally speaking pewter was a makeshift substitute for silver and it was worked in the same patterns and styles as the more precious metal. Some pewter, particularly from Germany, was intricately decorated and cast in relief but such items are rare and pewter is generally spare and workmanlike in design. Artists continue to work in pewter and it appears very successfully in Liberty's Tudric and Clutha designs for serving flagons.

A pewter porringer, by J. Danforth, Jnr., Virginia, circa 1807-1812, 5in. diam. (Christie's) £1,239

A Liberty pewter and green glass bowl, designed by A. Knox, stamped Tudric 0320 Rd, 426933, 20.3cm. diam. (Christie's) £378

A pewter bedpan, by Thos. D. and S. Boardman, Hartford, 1810-50, initial touch struck once on base, 17½in. long, overall. (Christie's) £271

A 17th century pewter charger with reeded rim, 22in. diam. (Woolley & Wallis) £1,350

A Liberty pewter and Clutha glass bowl on stand, designed by Archibald Knox, stamped Tudric 0276, circa 1900, 16.3cm. high. (Christie's) £453

A pyriform teapot, by Thos. Danforth, Conn., 1805-50, marked on bottom, 7in. high. (Christie's) £658

An apple-shaped teapot, by Roswell Gleason, Mass., 1821-71, 7½in. high. (Christie's) £123

An early 18th century North German pewter deep bowl, with scrolled caryatid handles, 9¼in. across handles. £418

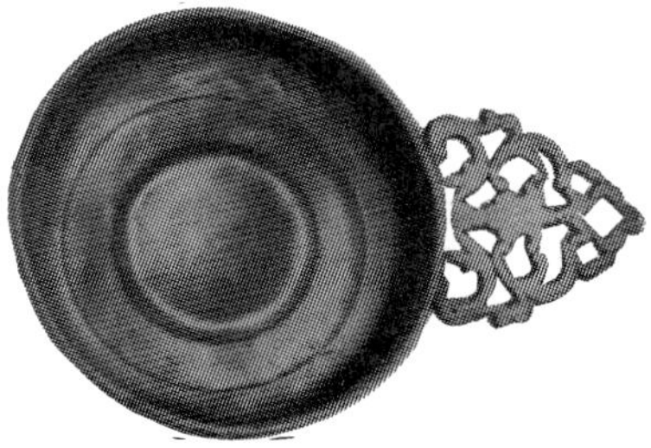

Early 19th century unmarked pewter porringer, with Rhode Ialand flowered handle. (Robt. W. Skinner Inc.) £140

A water pitcher, by Roswell Gleason, circa 1830, 11½in. high, together with a coffee pot and a water cooler. (Christie's) £305

A pewter covered flagon, the flat lid with ball finial and cast C-scroll handle, 9½in. high. (Robt. W. Skinner Inc.) £211

A Jugendstil polished pewter triptych mirror in the style of P. Huber, 32.2 x 53.4cm. (Christie's) £432

One of two similar Italian, late 18th/early 19th century, pewter flagons, 14¼in. high. (Christie's) £371

A WMF rectangular shaped pewter mirror, 14in. high, stamped marks. (Christie's) £480

A lighthouse coffee pot, by Israel Trask, Mass., circa 1813-56, marked on base, 10½in. high. (Christie's) £426

One of two pewter beakers, by James Weekes, New York City, 1820-35, 3.1/8in. high. (Christie's) £216

A WMF silvered pewter jardiniere cast as a conch shell with a salamander, 32cm. high. (Christie's) £486

Mid 19th century pewter flagon, the cast handle with heart-shaped end drop, base marked James Dixon, 13in. high. (Robt. W. Skinner Inc.) £246

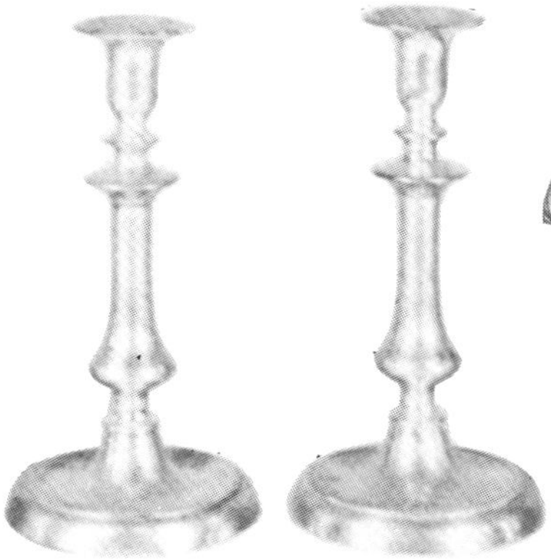

A pair of early 19th century English pewter candlesticks, 9in. high. (Christie's) £50

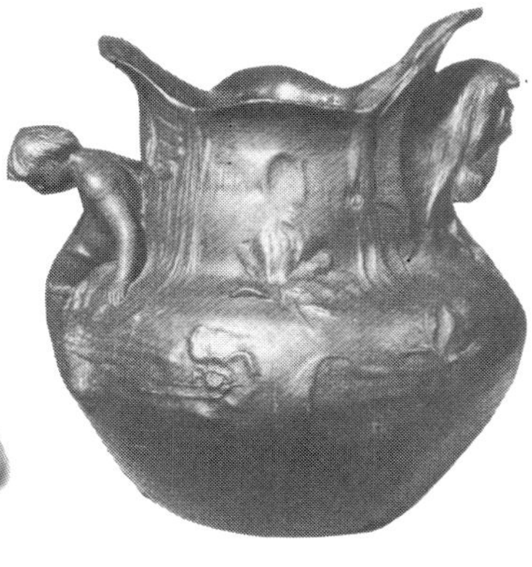

A Kayersinn pewter jardiniere, stamped Kayersinn 4093, 29.8cm. high. (Christie's) £250

An electroplated pewter mirror frame attributed to WMF, circa 1900, 50cm. high. (Christie's) £432

A pewter porringer, by Wm. Billings, Providence R.I., circa 1791-1806, marked on handle with Laughlin touch 346, 4.1/8in. diam. (Christie's) £232

A 19th century pewter leech jar, the pierced lid with carrying handle, 7in. high. (Christie's) £260

A tapering, cylindrical cann, by Robt. Palethorp, Phila., 1817-22, marked inside, 4.1/8in. high. (Christie's) £1,394

One of a pair of late 18th/early 19th century, German, pewter flagons, 17¼in. high. (Christie's) £309

One of a pair of mid 19th century pewter lanterns. (Robt. W. Skinner Inc.) £352

A WMF electroplated pewter drinking set with shaped rectangular tray, circa 1900, tray 48 x 34cm. (Christie's) £648

A lighthouse shaped flagon, by Thos. D. Boardman, marked with eagle touch, name touch and Hartford touch on base, 13¼in. high. (Christie's) £1,316

A tankard with a domed lid and scrolling thumbpiece, late 18th/early 19th century, unmarked, 6¼in. high. (Christie's) £1,084

A pewter covered Church tankard of lighthouse shape with C-scroll handle, circa 1766. (Robt. W. Skinner Inc.) £387

A covered pitcher, by Boardman, Boardman & Hart, 1828-53, marked on bottom, 7¾in. high. (Christie's) £464

A pair of pewter fluid lamps, by James H. Puttnam, Mass., 1830-55, 7¾in. high. (Christie's) £464

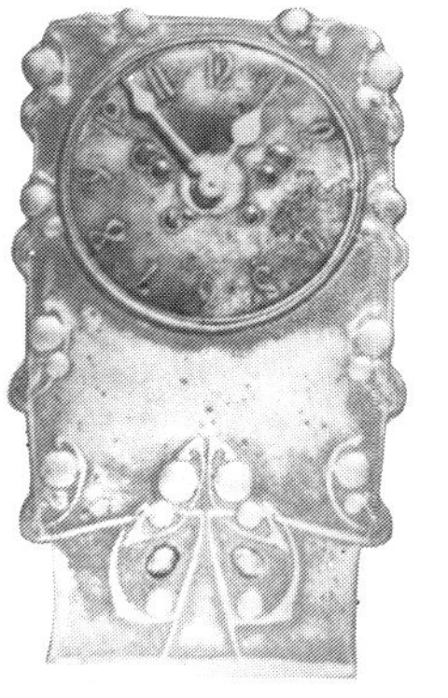

A Liberty pewter and enamel clock, designed by A. Knox, stamped 0608 Rd, 426015, 14cm. high. (Christie's) £1,026

PHOTOGRAPHS

The photographs most popularly collected today fall into two main categories. Those of historical significance in the development of the art and those photographs which are the work of a recognised master. Occasionally the two are combined in one photograph.

Notables of the early days are, William Fox Talbot who patented the Calotype in 1841 and, Louis-Jacques Mande Daguerre who invented the Daguerreotype which, in its early stages of development required over thirty minutes of exposure time. Other early photographers of note are Frances Frith, J.D. Edwards, Roger Fenton, Gustave Le Gray, F.R. Pickersgill and Henry Peach Robinson.

Photographers of importance in more modern times are Man Ray, Bill Brandt and Weegee amongst others.

A gelatin silver print of 'Cyril Ray in Islington', titled in ink on the reverse, by Bill Brandt, 9 x 7.5/8in. (Christie's) £220

Palais du Louvre and Palais des Tuilleries, four albumen prints, approx. 10¼ x 13¼in., 1850's or early 1860's. (Christie's) £160

A gelatin silver print of an 'East End Girl, Dancing The Lambeth Walk', dated in ink on the reverse 1939, by Bill Brandt. (Christie's) £500

A gelatin silver print of Ava Gardner, by Man Ray, 13¾ x 10¾in., signed and dated in pencil on image, 1950. (Christie's) £500

Northern British Locomotive Co. Ltd., approx. 120 gelatin silver prints, from 4½ x 6in. to 10 x 15in., majority 1900-20, all captioned and documented on the reverse. (Christie's) £180

Portrait album of 48 albumen prints, approx. 7½ x 6in. to 13½ x 10½in., by R. T. Crawshay, 1870's. (Christie's) £1,200

A glossy gelatin silver print of 'Carnival Girls', by Robt. Doisneau, 12 x 9½in. (Christie's) £100

A gelatin silver print of 'NYC 1949', by Robert F. Frank, signed in ink in margin, 1949, 10½ x 14in. (Christie's) £550

A gelatin silver print of Cecil Beaton, by E. Blumenfeld, 1940's, 13 x 10in. (Christie's) £480

A 4¼ x 5¾in. daguerreotype with rounded top, of three little sisters in matching dresses, the front of the case embossed 'Prof. Highschool Daguerreotype Institution, 433 West Strand'. (Phillips) £130

'Princess Alice, 1854', by Roger Fenton, albumen print, 5 x 6¾in. (Christie's) £420

'Cathedrale de Mayence, facade sud-est', Blanquart-Evrard salt print, by Chas. Marville, early 1850's, 13½ x 10in. (Christie's) £700

An album of 168 albumen prints of India and Ceylon, by Bourne, Shepherd and Bourne & Shepherd, 1890's, 9 x 11in. (Christie's) £800

A gelatin silver print of 'Mohandas Gandhi', by Margt. Bourke-White, 13½ x 10¼in. (Christie's) £420

An albumen print of Chas. Darwin, by Julia Margt. Cameron, 1868, 12½ x 10½in. (Christie's) £85

PIN-UP MAGAZINES

From the naughty art work of the Victorian era's 'La Vie Parisienne' to the centre-fold lovelies of this month's 'Playboy' magazine the pin-up and glamour magazine has been ever popular. While the early magazines relied upon drawings it was not long before the reproduction of photographs was cheaply available.

Some collectors still prefer the art work pin-up and look for the superb covers of the pre-war American magazines by artists like Dryben and Bolles, others like the photographs, the candid lingerie shots etc found in Spick, Span, Silky but almost all collectors agree that the true pin-up has no need for full frontal explicitness and do not collect beyond the magazines of the late 1960's.

Although a relatively new field of systematic collecting four main areas of interest have emerged They are artists and their artwork, photographers, specific models and subsequent matter.

A magazine to look out for is London Life from the 1920's and 1930's. This apparently innocent journal is devoted to all manner of fetishes, in a very restrained manner of course. Also popular are the works of Pett, the artist who created Jane of the Daily Mirror; his journals turn up from time to time and are very collectible.

Most book shops are a little shy about handling pin-up items, while for naughty book shops these magazines are a little tame. However, they do turn up from time to time, and there are a few mail order dealers who issue catalogues.

3-D Magazines 1950's, Diana Dors. £6 each

Velvet Magazine, 1950's. £2.50

Penthouse Magazine, Volume 1 Number 1. £7.50

Wink, A Whirl Of Girl, 1950's. £6.50

La Beaute, Vol. 3, Paris 1926. £25

College Capers, Reina 1950's. £1.50

Arthur Ferrier's Lovelies, Brought to Life by Roye, 1941. £6

PIPES

The earliest European pipes were made of clay and, because tobacco was so expensive, fitted with a small bowl. The stem of the early pipe was short in length, as in the Cutty, which was followed by a longer stemmed pipe known as the Churchwarden. During the reign of George I the Churchwarden pipe was adapted to accommodate a red wax tip to the mouthpiece and was then referred to as the Alderman.

The best English pipes were made at Winchester and Bronseley. Brier pipes made from the root of the brier shrub are well collected, but the most popular of all is still the Meerschaum. Meerschaum is a material ideally suited to carving and has the added attraction of turning the most beautiful mellow colour with use.

One of the most important, but lesser known pipemakers was Bambier of Paris. His work includes pipes in the form of stylised animals, satirical caricatures of prominent figures and some quite macabre subjects.

Carved burl Civil War pipe bowl, American, circa 1862-63. (Robt. W. Skinner Inc.) £591

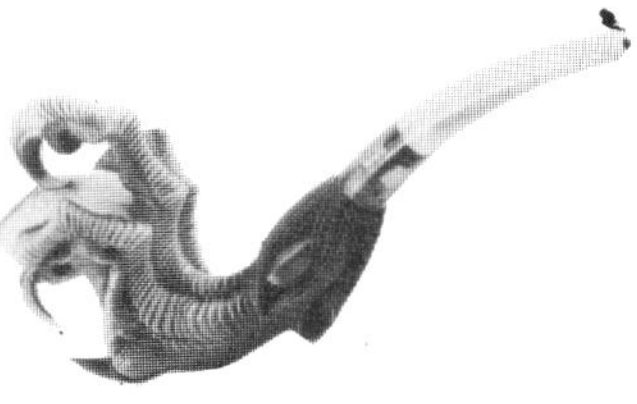

Late 19th century German Meerschaum figural pipe with amber stem, 12¼in. long. (Robt. W. Skinner Inc.) £500

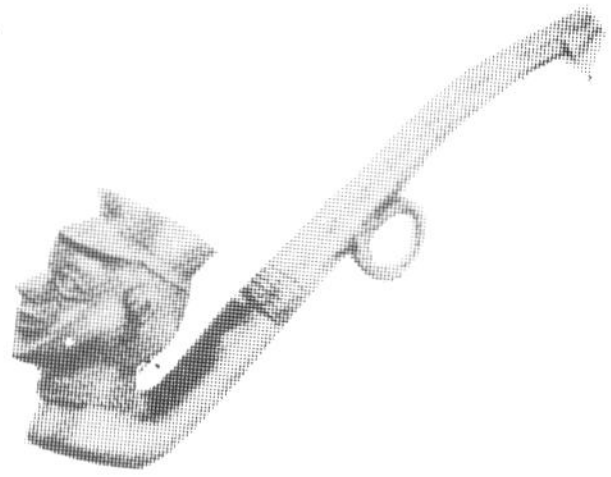

A brass Cameroon pipe. (Christie's S. Kensington) £40

Silver mounted cast iron pipe bowl, probably German, circa 1840, 3¾in. high. £286

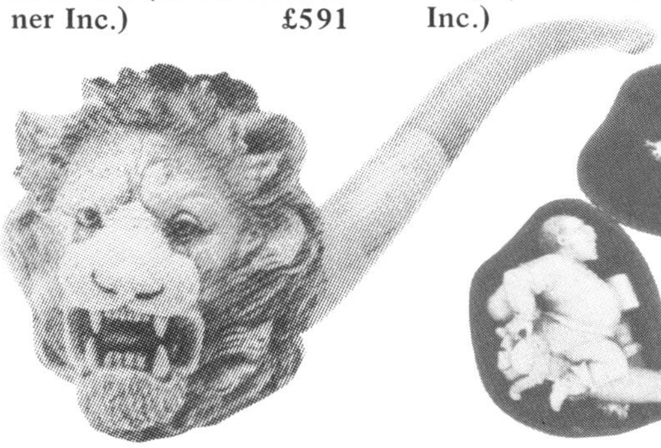

Late 19th century Meerschaum pipe, carved with a lion's head, 7½in. long. (Robt. W. Skinner Inc.) £250

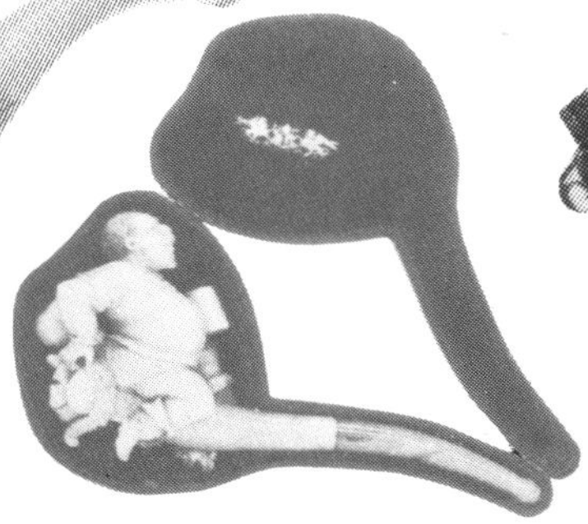

A 19th century Meerschaum pipe, modelled with a figure of a bearded gentleman, 19cm. long. (H. Spencer & Sons) £240

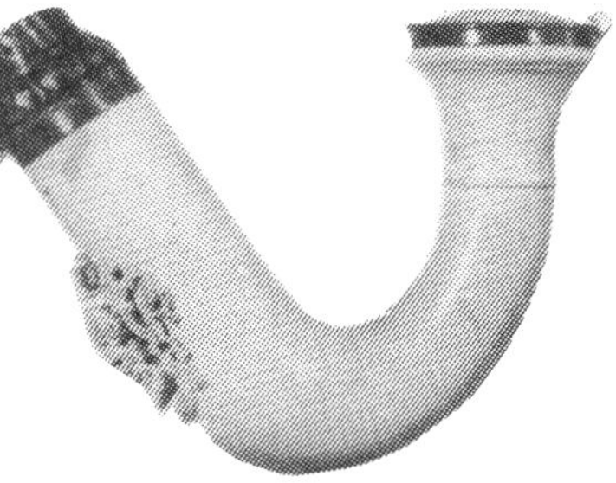

Plain Meerschaum pipe with curved bowl and white metal mounts, carved in high relief with coat of arms. (Christie's S. Kensington) £100

A Zulu wood pipe with a carved female figure. (Christie's S. Kensington) £300

A 17th century Dutch fruitwood pipe, 3.3/8in. long. £1,980

A carved Meerschaum pipe, the bowl in the form of a head of a bearded king, 29in. long. £168

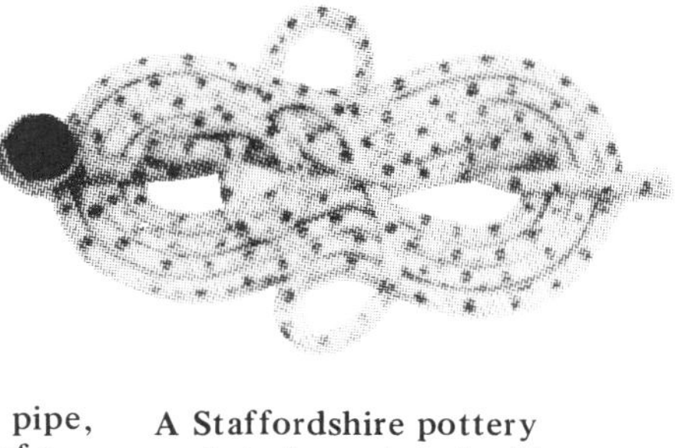

A Staffordshire pottery curled pipe painted with blue and yellow dashes. £220

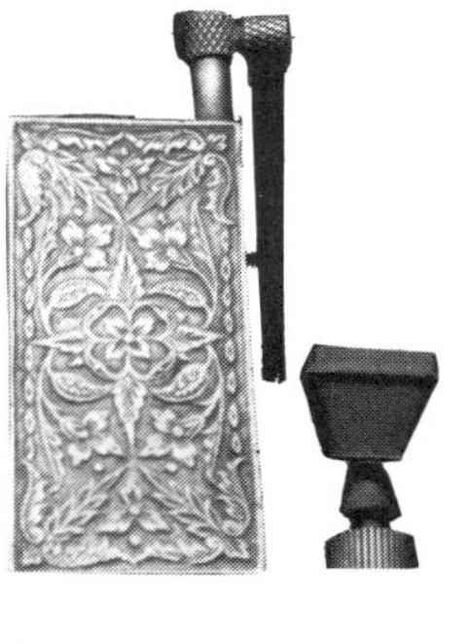

Indian brass pocket 'Hashish' pipe, circa 1960. £6

PISTOLS

Antique pistols are particularly popular with collectors and investors for, as they disappear into collections, their scarcity naturally pushes the value up.

Flintlocks and percussion weapons are straightforward enough, but before purchasing those with a pinfire mechanism, check with the police as they could be regarded as firearms and then certain legislation comes into force.

Always try to buy weapons in pristine condition with no missing or replaced parts, keeping a particular eye for makers such as Nock, Manton, Twigg, Egg, Kuchenreuter and Lepage. Also be on the lookout for pairs of pistols, as they are worth at least three times that of a single – even more if they are in a box complete with accessories.

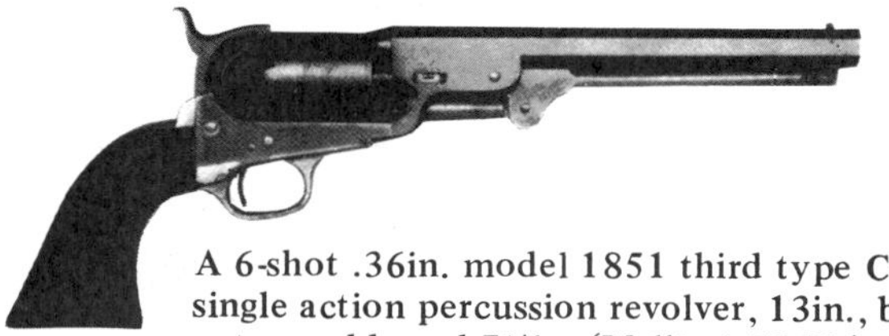

A 6-shot .36in. model 1851 third type Colt Navy single action percussion revolver, 13in., blued octagonal barrel 7½in. (Wallis & Wallis) £2,800

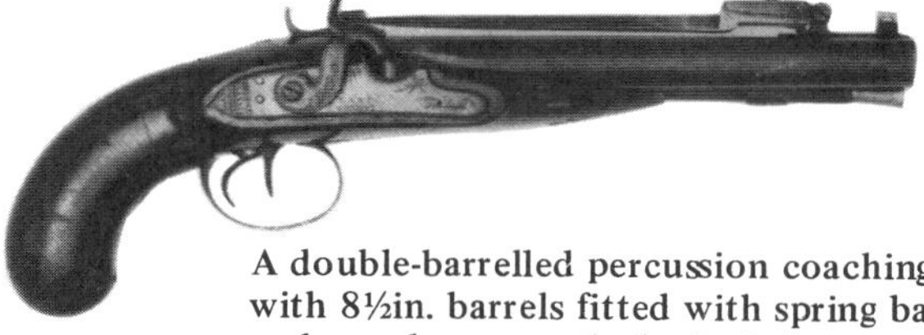

A double-barrelled percussion coaching pisto with 8½in. barrels fitted with spring bayonet and wooden ramrod, the lockplates engraved Enty, London. (Christie's) £300

A 26-bore all steel Scottish flintlock belt pistol by Murdoch of Doune, circa 1770, 12in., barrel 7¾in., foliate engraved, reeded breech, facetted muzzle. Steel fullstock, stock and rounded butt. (Wallis & Wallis) £1,100

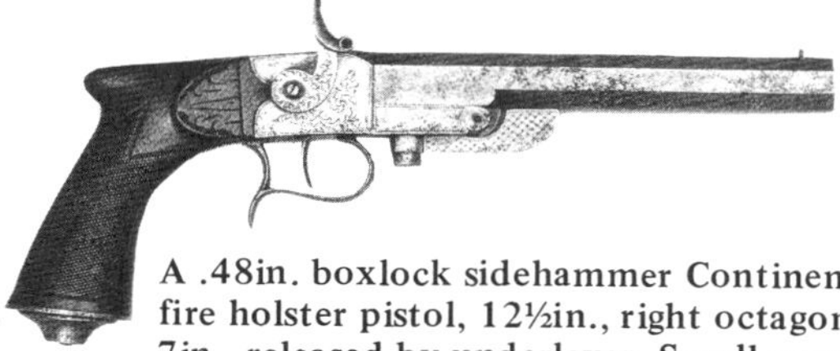

A .48in. boxlock sidehammer Continental needle fire holster pistol, 12½in., right octagonal barrel 7in., released by underlever. Scroll engraved frame side cocking lever and steel furniture, chequered saw handled walnut butt. (Wallis & Wallis) £230

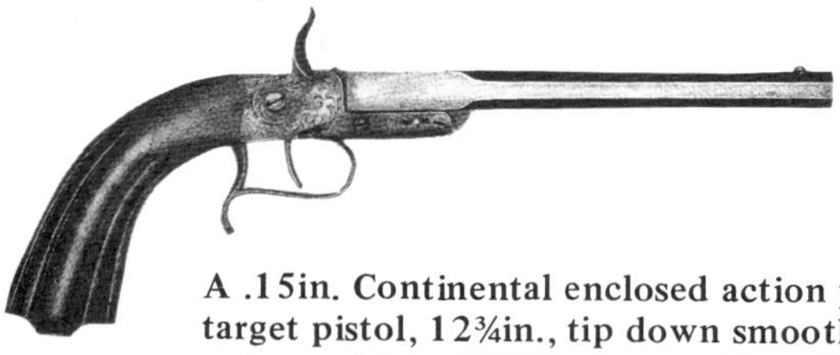

A .15in. Continental enclosed action percussion target pistol, 12¾in., tip down smooth bore octagonal barrel 7½in., secured by side lever and opening merely for capping. Steel furniture and fluted walnut butt. (Wallis & Wallis) £230

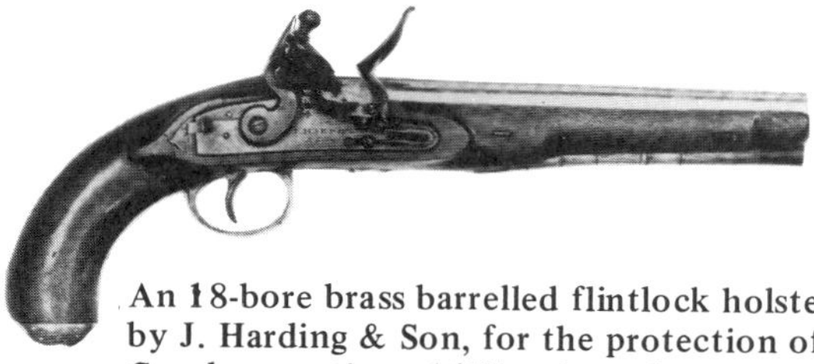

An 18-bore brass barrelled flintlock holster pistol, by J. Harding & Son, for the protection of Mail Coach operatives, 14½in., brass barrel 9in., London and military proofs. (Wallis & Wallis) £700

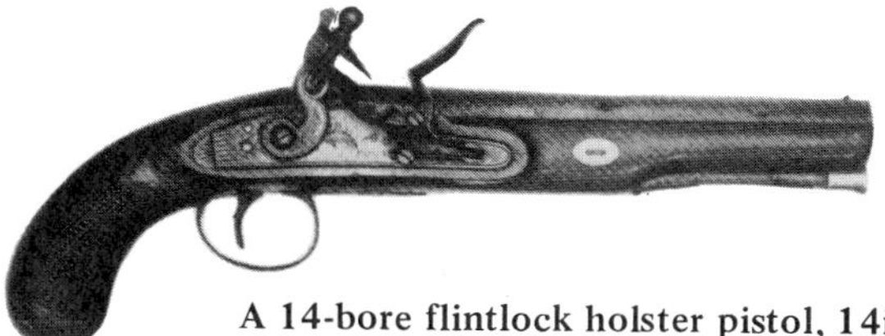

A 14-bore flintlock holster pistol, 14in., barrel 8½in., Birmingham proved. Fullstocked, with stepped lock and steel furniture and rounded chequered butt. (Wallis & Wallis) £270

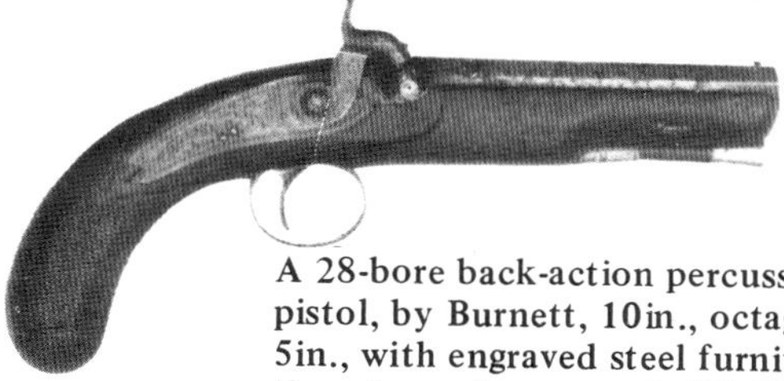

A 28-bore back-action percussion travelling pistol, by Burnett, 10in., octagonal barrel 5in., with engraved steel furniture and brass tipped wooden ramrod. (Wallis & Wallis) £105

PLAYING CARDS

The origin of playing cards is still a subject for speculation, the most widely held view being that they probably originated both in the East and the West independently and simultaneously. The earliest record in Europe is a decree of 23rd May, 1376, issued in the City of Florence, prohibiting their use.

The earliest decks, now of course out of reach of most collectors and to be found only in museums, were hand-drawn and painted packs commissioned by Royalty and the wealthy aristocracy of the period. The earliest pack a collector can hope to possess dates to the end of the 17th century when a series of playing cards in England were used as general information for the public. These early engraved packs are priced at around £500 and above. The range for the collector is otherwise very wide indeed. Cards of the last century can vary dramatically in price range with rarer packs fetching as much as £1,000 whereas some of the common ones are priced at below £10. There also is a very wide range of modern cards with unusual designs produced in the past decade which are priced well below £5 per deck and are undoubtedly the collectors pieces of the future.

Collectors will only be interested in 'non-standard' decks, that is ones that have unusual designs, mainly of the Court card and in game packs which are card decks without suit signs. The English suit signs of spades, hearts, diamonds and clubs (which are derived from the French packs) are not universally in use and even today, the Germanic countries still use the hearts, leaves, dumb-bells and acorns and the Spaniards and Italians still use the coins, cups, swords and sticks. The subject matter of Tarot and fortune-telling cards is an additional and effectively separate branch within the overall picture of playing cards.

Popish Plot 1679 by R. Walton, London. £800

Russia — A Slavic costume deck unknown maker, circa 1935.£60

France — 'Cartes a Rire' — transformation pack attributed to Baron Louis Atthalin 1819 (Courts represent Paris newspapers). £950

England — Transformation pack by Maclure, Macdonald and Macgregor, Manchester, circa 1870. £220

A complete set of fifty-two playing cards, illuminated on pasteboard, each card made up of 4 layers of paper pasted together, South Flanders, possibly Lille, circa 1470-85. £99,000

England — Victoria Diamond Jubilee deck by Goodall & Son, London 1897, all portraits of British Royalty. £85

Italy — Playing cards by E. Dotti, Milan, circa 1870, hand-coloured. £160

POISON BOTTLES

Poison bottles were produced in distinctive shapes, designs and finishes so that they were instantly recognisable and could not be confused with other medicine bottles by someone who may be dosing themselves in the night or in dim light. The first English poison bottle was patented in 1859 and during the rest of the century, hundreds of thousands of them were produced in a staggering variety of designs. Most of the bottles were made of glass coloured cobalt blue, green or amber. Cobalt glass disappeared as the usual container for poison in the 1950's when it was replaced by plastic.

Bottles with embossed labels are the most valuable and among the rarer items are those shaped as skulls, wasp waisted bottles, six sided bottles, bottles shaped like binoculars, submarines or with a sharp U-bend in their necks.

Martins Patent bottle 1902, with the rare type having 'Poison', 'Not To Be Taken' embossed on side, in amber and cobalt blue. £150

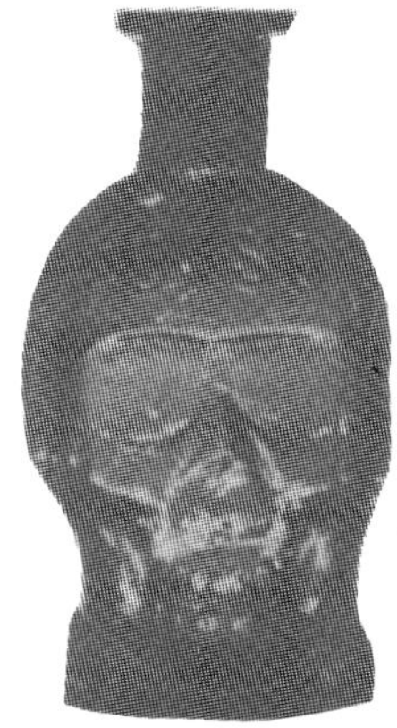

Skull Poisons, Patented by Carlton H. Lee, 1894, in America, cobalt blue glass. £350

Quine's Patent, aqua glass bottle with 'Poison' embossed on the side, patented 1893. £75

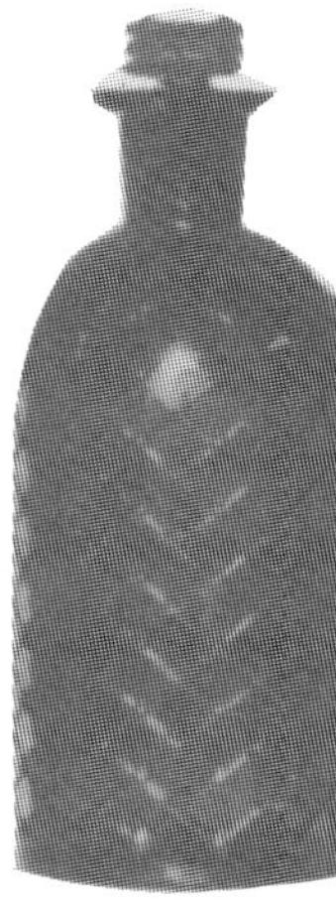

American, 'Quilt Poison', with cross hatching around the sides of the bottle. £100

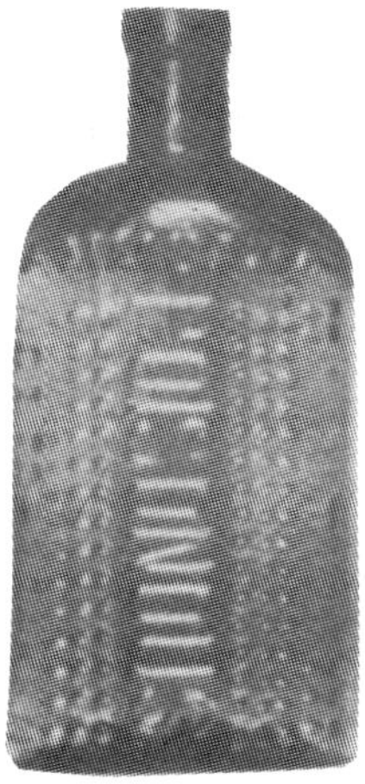

Ammonia Poison bottle in amber glass, embossed 'Ammonia' across top. £10

Very rare 'Wasp Waist' Poison with rows of diamond points embossed on the front and side panels, patented 1894. £450

O'Reilly's Patent, known as Binoculars Poison, embossed on the base 'O'Reillys Patent 1905', only two of these bottles are known. £800

Wilsons Patent emerald green, triangular bottle with notched edges, patented in 1899. £75

PORTRAIT MINIATURES

Before the days of photography, the only way to carry a true likeness of someone was in the form of a miniature portrait; an artform which reached its peak in the last quarter of the 18th century.
Even small towns boasted their own miniaturist and fashionable resorts, such as Bath, supported whole colonies.

Their charges varied from a couple of guineas up to twenty-five guineas for the work of a master such as John Smart. Other names to look for are Richard Cosway, Henry Spicer, Horace Hone, Richard Crosse, Ozias Humphrey, Jeremiah Meyer, Charles Bestland and George Engleheart. Most miniatures from this period are painted on ivory with water-colours used to produce flesh tones and opaque colour for dress.
More reasonably priced examples can be found from the 19th century, though the skills involved seem to decline with the onset of the camera.

A nobleman in crimson coat and lace jabot, by Christian F. Zincke, 1.5/8in. high. (Christie's) £756

Francois Courtier, later Madame Navarre, by Jean Marie Voille, signed and dated l'an 1e (1793), oval, 2.5/8in. high. (Christie's) £2,808

A Lady called Elizabeth, Lady Willoughby D'Eresby, by Isaac Oliver, 2.1/8in. high. (Christie's) £4,320

A gentleman facing left in blue coat, by Sampson T. Roche, signed and dated 1811, oval, 3in. high. (Christie's) £218

A gentleman facing right, by Wm. Marshall Craig, the reverse with gold monogram HW on plaited hair, oval 2.5/8in. high. (Christie's) £486

A lady facing right in decollete white dress, Circle of Engleheart, signed with monogram, 3in. high. (Christie's) £486

Frederick V, Elector Palatine, King of Bohemia, enamel, by Henry Pierce Bone, 3.5/8in. high. (Christie's) £453

A girl facing left in a white dress, the reverse with locks of hair, by Andrew Plimer, oval, 3in. high. (Christie's) £1,206

POSTAL SCALES

The earliest postal scales were made by the manufacturers of scientific instruments such as S. Morden and Co. who had a tradition of using fine wood and brass. As a result many of the early scales are true works of art with mahogany and ebony bases and fine fret cut brass-work. Later models are often made of cast iron and are purely functional items with little aesthetic appeal.

Apart from the weight most scales also display the actual postal charges, enabling the collector to date them fairly accurately for there were frequent changes by the Post Office.

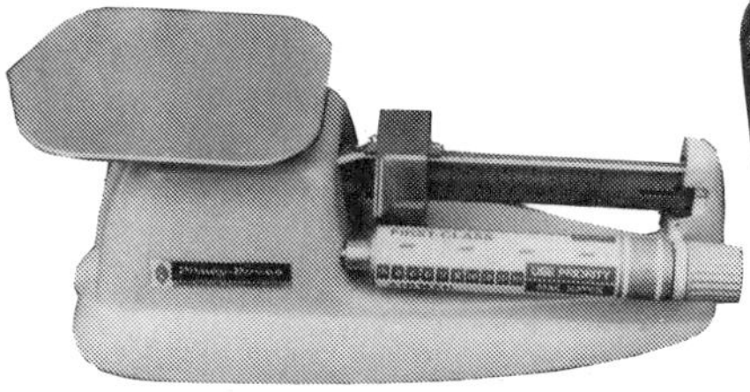

Pitney Bowes scales made in U.S.A., 1970, 10in. wide. £15

Pocket scales by Salter 1923-40, 2in. high. £10

Cast iron scales by Howe, U.S.A. 1932, 19in. wide. £30

19th century painted tin scales, 9in. high. £20

Salter parcel scales with cast iron frame, 1957-61, 11in. high. £7

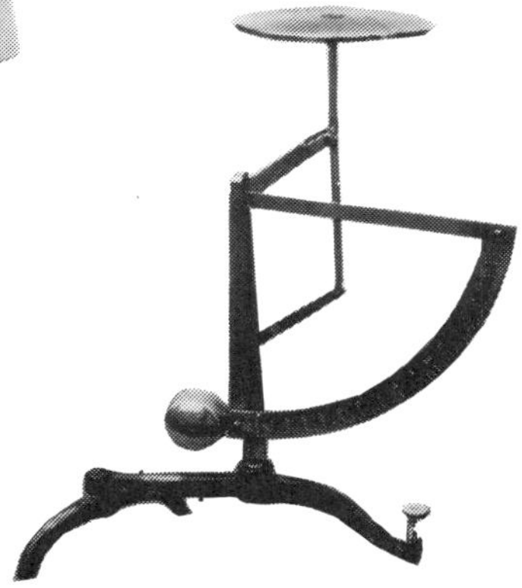

Brass and painted metal scales, 1906-15, 11in. high. £20

Painted metal and brass scales by Triner Scale Co., Chicago, made for the U.K. market, 1935-40, 8in. high. £20

Brass and mahogany scales, 1915-18, 6½in. wide. £30

Brass and mahogany scales by S. Morden & Co., 1906-15, 15in. wide. £150

All brass scales, 1897-1915, 7in. wide. £45

POSTCARDS

When one postcard, delivered on 20th September, 1902 after a trip from Manchester to Haslingden by Balloon Post, sells for £1,675 at auction, postcard collecting needs no further justification for its popularity.

The first British postcards issued by the G.P.O. in 1870 were designed to take the address only on one side and the message alongside the illustration on the other side. This card came complete with a printed half penny stamp and it was not until 1894 that independent companies issued postcards for use with an adhesive stamp. An Act of Parliament in 1902 allowing the message and address to be written on the same side leaving the other side free for a picture gave rise to the popular trend as we know it today.

There is absolutely no limit to the variety of themes from which a collection can be formed and special interest areas include cards depicting Film Stars, Glamour Girls, Humour, Advertising, Transport, Topography and many more subjects.

Some sets of cards are particularly pleasing such as those by C.W. Faulkner and the Tucks Record Card demonstrates the high popularity of cards with some special feature. These always get between £5 and £10 although the record itself is usually disappointing. Cards incorporating moving parts will also get between £5 and £10 and will make an interesting collection. The much sought after Shell Aviation cards sell for about £35 but, beware of reproductions. Obviously, a used, stamped postcard is the best guarantee of authenticity.

Occasionally pictures of tram cars, fire engines and motor cars will fetch a surprisingly high price when sold to specialists to complete a set and only very, very, occasionally a card turns up like the one bearing a little sketch by Picasso – this glittering prize sold for £500.

Raphael Tuck 'oilette' Series No. 9793 'Teddy Bears at the Seaside', artist Wm. Henry Ellam. £3

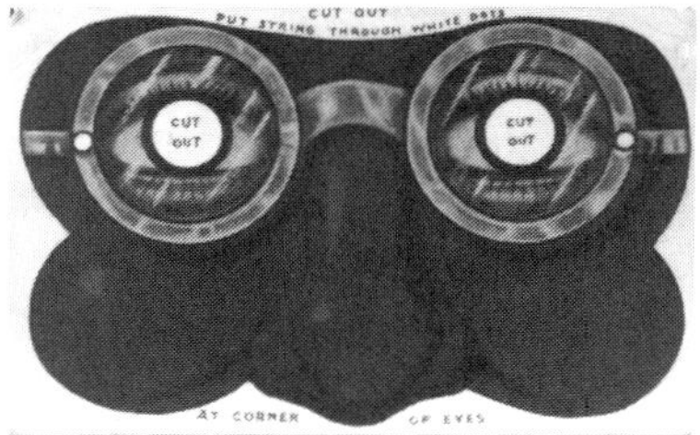

Cut-out mask, circa 1928, it is rare for postcards such as this to survive intact. £17

Real photograph of Hitler by Hopemann of Munchen, 1935. £5

The S6 at Calshot, winner of the Schneider Trophy, later developed into the Hurricane fighter. £15

Victory Day Souvenir card May 8th 1945. £3

LNWR 'Three horse brake bus, Lime St. Station and Landing Stage Liverpool', official postcard 1905. £15

Fry's Cocoa, designed by Maud Fabian, published by Hancock & Corfield Ltd., London, circa 1910. £20

'The Disastrous fire at Mr. Somervelle's house, Harrow School, April 3rd 1908'. £8

James Stuart, film star, real photo in colour. £1.50

I. Benghiat & Son, Aden, A real mermaid? £5

Holdfast Boots, published by James Walker & Co., Dublin, circa 1908. £18

'Bubbles' Pears Soap advert by Sir John Millais, plain back – 75p; advert back £2.

Sing Fat Co. Inc., the famous Oriental bazaar in Chinatown, Los Angeles. £4

Belgian Soldiers Fund official card 1916, 'The Late Nurse Cavell', shot by a German firing squad. £2

Wilfred Westwood, tallest, heaviest boy in the world, aged 11 years, weight 20st. 6lb. £1.50

H.M. Queen Alexandra, Rotary Opalette Series, patented 1908, real photo postcard. £2

'Hold to Light' card, illuminates holly, berries, moon and windows when held to light, 'Tobogganing in the snow'. £4

Much sought after cards, real photos of theatre, this one the Palace Theatre Doncaster in 1915, by J. S. & S.) No. 434. £12

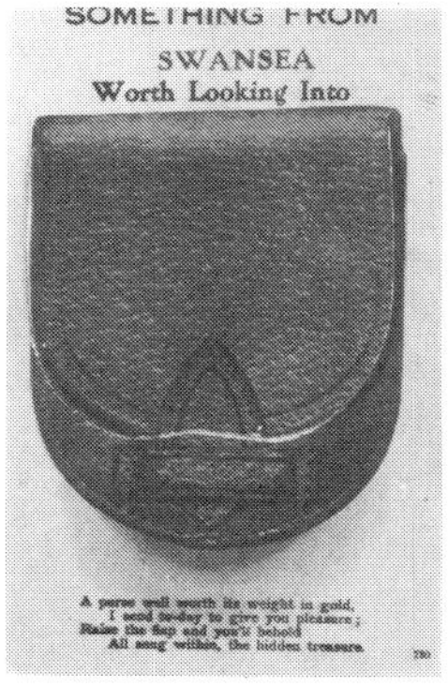

Novelty card from Swansea, purse opens up to reveal multi-view, Valentine Series 'mailing novelty', shape passed by G.P.O. for ½d stamp, 1910. £2.50

Germanic Humour/Fantasy chromo litho card SB Series, notice mouse in mouth. £8

'Silvox' Beef Extract, published by C.W.S. Ltd. £15

Real photo postcard of the clock 'Greenwich Observatory'. £2

Embossed 'frog' New Year card 1906/07, artist drawn Erika Series. £6

Salon de Paris, study by Pereira da Silva, titled 'Salome'. £5

Wheeler & Wilson, 'High Class Sewing Machines are the best', circa 1905. £18

Cook's Lightning Soap poster type advert with verse. £12

Anita 'The Living Doll' aged 30 years, the smallest adult the world has ever seen (signed postcard). £6

Concours De Byrrh, one card by Maurice Denis, in good condition. £100

Greta Garbo, born in Stockholm. First film was an advertising film about Hats. MGM Pictures star. Best films 'Romance', 'Grand Hotel', and 'Queen Christina'. £3

The Rt. Hon. A. J. Balfour (Wolverhampton), Lafayette photograph autographed on reverse. £9

Lifeboat Saturday, a card delivered by air from Manchester to Haslingden on Sept. 20th 1902. £1,675

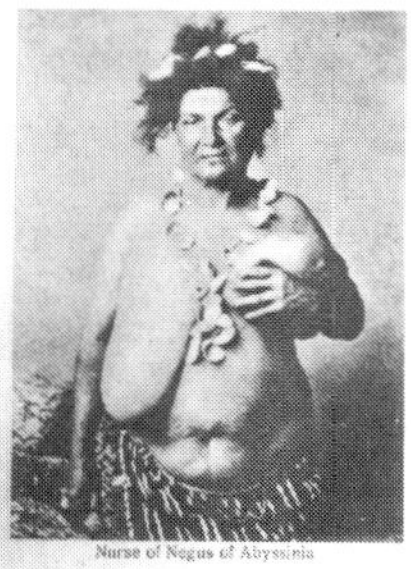

Nurse of Negus of Abyssinia, purchased from the Turkish Shop Hotel l'Europe, Aden. £6

POSTERS

Originally designed to be displayed in public places the function of the poster was to inform by advertising goods or publicising events. Competition in the market place led to a high standard of art work and the production of beautifully coloured and highly decorative items which, unlike some printed collectibles acquiring significance to the collector only with the passing of the years, have been enthusiastically collected since their introduction at the end of the 19th century.

In fact, a monthly magazine 'The Poster', which gave information on how to keep abreast of the trend became an instant bestseller.

The now famous Alphonse Mucha poster announcing Sarah Bernhardt in the new play 'Gismonda' demonstrates the quality of early productions. He went on to design all her publicity material on an exclusive basis for a period of six years and any of his works will command the highest of prices today.

Subjects most favoured by collectors include Motoring, Theatre, Circus and, of course, posters in the Art Nouveau style from that period.

Film posters too have their devotees with Humphrey Bogart, Mae West, Greta Garbo and James Cagney all keenly sought as are the early Rock 'n Roll posters particularly of Elvis and 'super groups' such as the Beatles and the Stones.

While condition and rarity factors are important when evaluating investment potential a collection may be gathered around the work of a particular artist, style, period, range of goods or a specific product with examples spanning a price range from only a few pounds to many thousands.

Poster, 'Dolomiten Ski-Schule Val Gardena (Grodental) m.1300-2200'. (Onslows) £75

Peugeot, by Rene Vincent, lithograph in colours, printed by Draeger, 1170 x 1540mm. (Christie's) £800

Absinthe Robette, by Privat Livemont, lithograph in colours, 1896, on wove paper, printed by J. L. Goffart, Bruxelles, 1105 x 806mm. (Christie's) £750

G. Marconi, Le Maitre De La Radio, by Paul Colin, lithograph in colours, printed by Bedos & Cie, Paris, 1578 x 1130mm. (Christie's) £220

Steinhardt, Unter Den Linden, by Hans Lindenstaedt, lithograph in colours, 1912, on wove paper, 710 x 945mm. (Christie's) £300

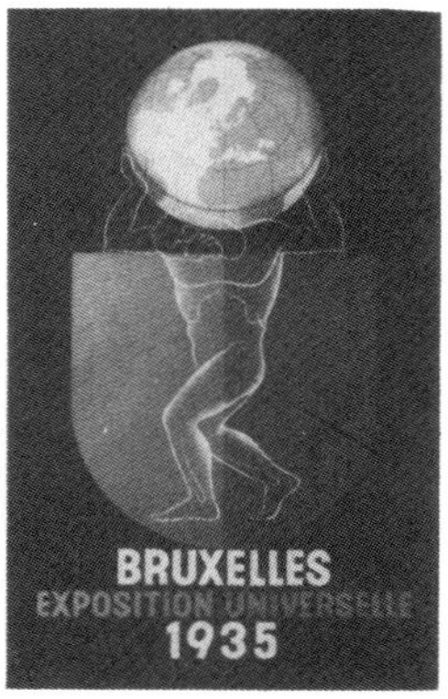

Bruxelles, Exposition Universelle, 1935, by Marfurt, lithograph in colours, printed by Les Creations, Publicitaires, Bruxelles, 1000 x 620mm. (Christie's) £70

Camp Romain, Vin Rouge, Rose, Blanc, by L. Gadoud, lithograph in colours, on wove paper, 1600 x 1200mm. (Christie's) £160

Pierre Stephen, lithograph in colours, on wove paper, printed by Bauduin, Paris, 1538 x 1175mm. (Christie's) £420

Poster, 'P & O Cruises'. (Onslows) £95

Ein Rausch In Rot, Maskenball Wilder Mann, by C.M.I., lithograph in colours, 1928, on wove paper, 920 x 612mm. (Christie's) £150

Alcazar Royal, by Adolphe Crespin and Edouard Duych, lithograph in colours, 1894, 1010 x 775mm. (Christie's) £280

Raphael Tuck, Celebrated Posters No. 1501, Ogden's Guinea Gold Cigarettes and another. (Christie's) £35

Nord Express, by Adolphe Mouron Cassandre, lithograph in colours, 1927, on wove paper, 1048 x 752mm. (Christie's) £1,300

XXVI Ausstellung Secession, by Ferdinand Andri, lithograph in colours, circa 1904, on wove paper, 920 x 602mm. (Christie's) £8,700

Job, by Alphonse Mucha, lithograph in colours, 1898, on wove paper, printed by F. Champenoise, Paris, 1500 x 1010mm. (Christie's) £3,500

David Hockney at the Tate Gallery, lithograph in colour, 1980, on wove paper, signed in pencil, 760 x 505mm. (Christie's) £45

La Revue Des Folies Bergere, by Jules Alexandre Grun, lithograph in colours, 1905, printed by Ch. Verneau, Paris, 1246 x 880mm. (Christie's) £150

Raphael Tuck, Celebrated Posters No. 1501, Rowntree's Elect Cocoa, and two others. (Christie's) £45

POT LIDS

In the mid 19th century many things were sold in small pots with decorative lids. One of the most notable producers of these earthenware pots was the firm F. & R. Pratt & Co., of Fenton in Staffordshire who issued well over three hundred differently decorated containers designed to hold such delights as a hair dressing of bear grease and, later, preserves.
Pots are usually circular in shape, though a few are rectangular, and consist of a shallow undecorated base made of the same material as the loose fitting lid.
In most cases it does not matter too much if the base is missing since it is the underglaze transfer printed lids which have been collected since their first appearance around 1840.

Pot lid by Mayer Bros., circa 1850, 12.7cm. diam. £2,700

Medium pot lid, 'England's Pride'. £45

Pot lid 'Our Home', one of only two known examples. £2,600

A pot lid, 'Hauling the Trawl', with rope twist border, 4in. diam. £42

A medium pot lid with laurel leaf border, 'The Allied Generals'. £65

The 'Garden Terrace', a medium small lid with raised floral and beehive border. £260

A medium pot lid with chain border, 'Embarking for the East'. £55

A large pot lid with double line border and title, 'Napirima Trinidad'. £75

A pot lid, 'The Picnic', Vitruvian border, 4¾in. diam. £80

Medium small lid depicting bear hunting. £340

World record price for a pot lid, 'Eastern Lady and Black Attendant'. £3,600

A pot lid, 'The Buffalo Hunt'. £700

POWDER FLASKS

A 17th century German powder flask made from an antler horn, the surface engraved with foliage, could cost hundreds of pounds but the metal variety by Batty, Hawkins, Ames, Dixon, or The American Flask & Cap Company among others, are fairly plentiful and therefore more reasonably priced. Most are decorated in some form, from simple fluting or basket weave designs to Coats of Arms, deer or even horrendous battle scenes. Of particular interest are the Old Colonial powder horns, which are nearly all engraved or carved by the owners themselves, often complete with personal mottos and beliefs.

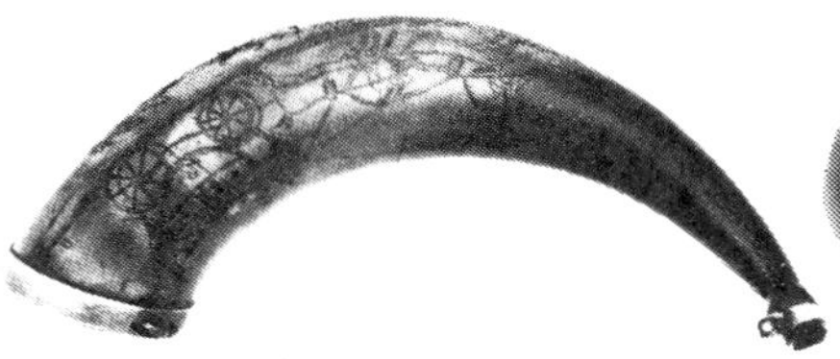

An early 19th century engraved powder horn, the body incised with a thistle encircling John Davis Royal Mail 1815, 12in. overall. £220

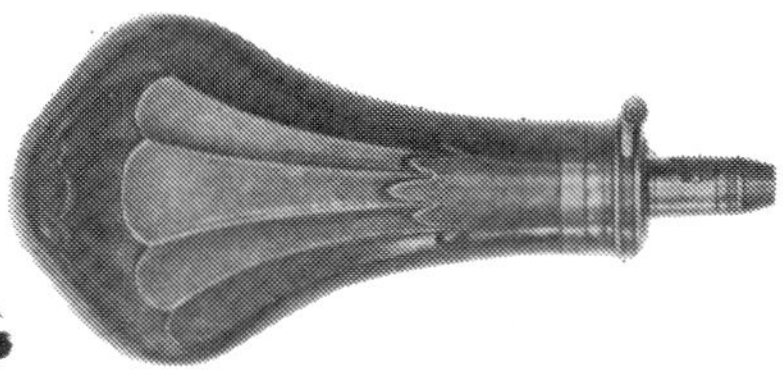

A gun sized fluted copper powder flask, 7¾in., patent brass top stamped James Dixon & Sons, Sheffield. (Wallis & Wallis) £35

A 19th century Scottish dress powder flask with single suspension ring, 11in. £242

A 17th century powder horn, body of flattened cow horn, 11cm. £1,100

A brass mounted priming horn, 7½in., wrap around spring to fixed charger, with twin brass hanging rings, brass end cap and green hanging cord. (Wallis & Wallis) £20

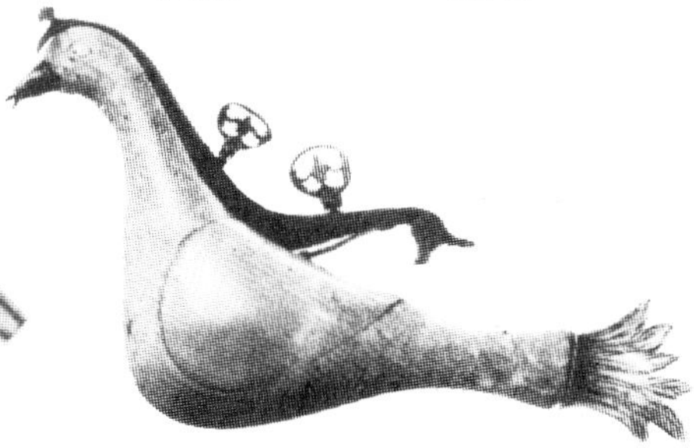

An 18th century Persian priming powder flask, 5in. overall. £682

A 17th century powder horn, body fashioned from section of antler, 12½in. £440

A shell embossed copper powder flask, 8in., common white metal top stamped Bartram & Co., with graduated nozzle. (Wallis & Wallis) £70

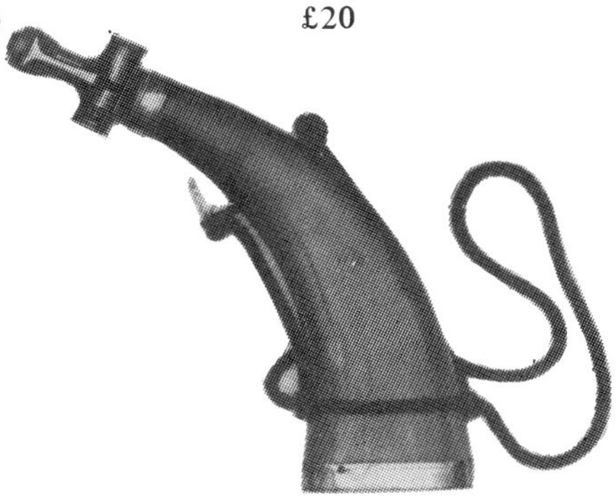

A German flattened cowhorn powder flask with Boche charger, 13in., brass mounts and horn nozzle. (Wallis & Wallis) £80

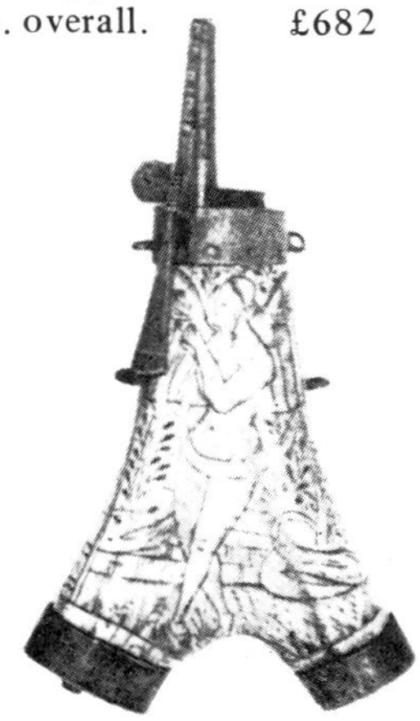

Late 16th/early 17th century powder horn with four small suspension rings, 23cm. £330

PRAMS

The earliest known baby carriage in Britain was made in 1730 (for the children of The 3rd Duke of Devonshire), and designed to be pulled along by a small animal. The first of the baby carriages manufactured for public use was made in 1840. This was a three wheeled version with iron tyres and it still had to be pulled along. About the mid 19th century, a handle was fitted to the back so that the pram could be pushed and this version was called the perambulator. The three wheeled perambulator remained in popular use until about 1880 when it was displaced by the new four wheeled bassinette. The early four wheeled prams were, at first, categorised by the authorities as road vehicles but as they became more popular, this was rescinded.

The pram has always been something of a status symbol and the early prams were no exception. They were coachbuilt with bodies made of wood, sometimes of leather, and dressed with fittings of brass. They were lavishly trimmed and the interiors were often upholstered in soft skins or a leatherette, some deep-buttoned for effect. Safety features such as brakes and strappings were not introduced until after 1900.

An early safety feature perhaps worth noting, is the pram fitted with two handles, one at each end. This was not merely a fashionable 'extra' but a necessity for the safe-keeping of the infants who were trundled around the treacherous roads of the early perambulating days. Pavements were either very narrow or non existent and traffic regulations for coaches and carriages still a bit sketchy, which made turning a pram for the return journey, a hazardous business. With a handle fitted at both ends, the prampusher only had to pass alongside the pram to reverse direction in safety.

1930's simulated leather doll's pram with folding hood and brake. £35

1930's Stella doll's pram with plywood body, leatherette hood and umbrella holder. £40

1920's Acme pram with wooden body and 'C' springs, reg. no. 465485. £80

An early Star Manufacturing Co. round-head pram with leather trim and porcelain handle. £250

A rare Bassinett two handled double pram with painted leather body, circa 1860. £250

The 'London' baby coach with wooden body and fabric cover. £55

A large 1960's Silver Cross pram with metal body and fabric and leatherette upholstery. £35

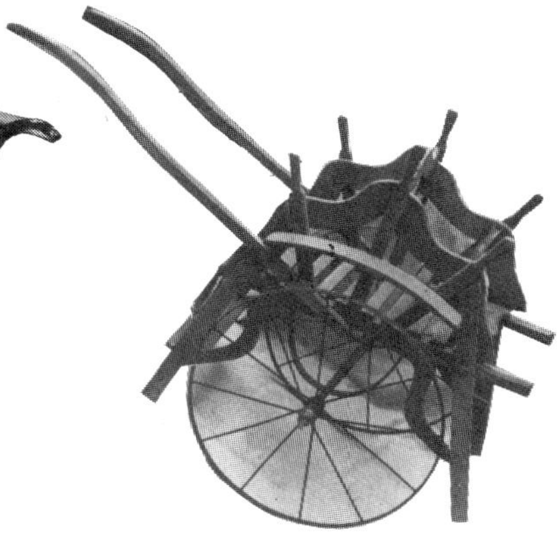

Country style 'mail cart' push-chair with iron wheels. £100

1930's German wickerwork pram with alloy wheel arches and bumpers. £60

Tan-Sad wartime Cot-Kar pram, No. 3214, with wooden body and leatherette hood. £85

A rare T. Trotmans patent 1854 folding pram with carpet back seating and wood and brass wheels. £400

1930's 'Pedigree' pram by A. J. Dale & Son, Warminster. £55

Wooden 'mail cart' pram with carved sides, leather hood and brass trim. £300

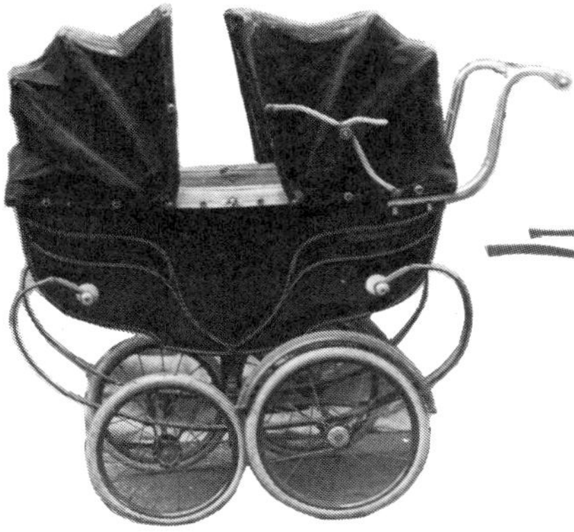

Silver Cross 1930's twin hood doll's pram with metal and wood body and leatherette and fabric hood. £50

Country style oak framed back to back twin pram with brass hubs. £180

PRINTS

One of the attractions of collecting prints is that apart from there being the range to suit all pockets there is always the chance of coming across a real treasure. This is a classic example of where acquiring knowledge could yield a fortune.

On a more moderate level prints by Le Blond, Baxter, Icart and Cruikshank are always worth seeking.

Look for clear impressions, preferably in colour, with good margins and no damage and also keep an eye open for limited editions which will always command a premium.

'The Darktown Yacht Club – On The Winning Tack', published by Currier & Ives, 1885, small folio. (Robt. W. Skinner Inc.) £168

The actor Nakamura Kichie-mon in the role of Mitsuhide, signed and sealed Shunsen. (Christie's) £270

Adonis in Y fronts, by Richard Hamilton, screenprint in colours, 1963, signed and dated in pencil, from the edition of 40, printed by Kelpra Studio, 604 x 815mm. (Christie's) £4,104

'The Celebrated Horse Dexter, 'The King Of The World' Driven By Budd Doble'', published by Currier & Ives, 1867, large folio. (Robt. W. Skinner Inc.) £1,418

Plakat Muim Institut, by Ernst Ludwig Kirchner, woodcut printed in blue and black, 1911, on rose laid paper, 728 x 492mm. (Christie's) £4,860

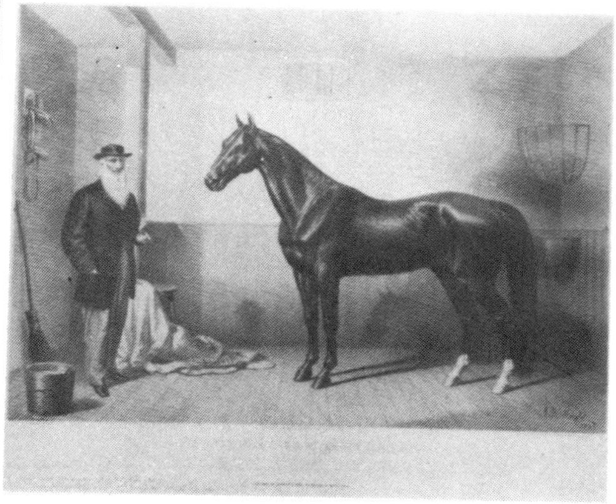

'Rysdyk's Hambletonian', published by Currier & Ives, 1876, large folio. (Robt. W. Skinner Inc.) £1,148

'The Champion in Luck', published by Currier & Ives, 1882, small folio. (Robt. W. Skinner Inc.) £54

Campbell's Soup, by Andy Warhol, screenprints in colours, 1969, on wove paper, 907 x 657mm., and album. (Christie's) £3,780

'The Trotting Mare Goldsmith Maid, Driven By Budd Doble', published by Currier & Ives, 1870, large folio. (Robt. W. Skinner Inc.) £810

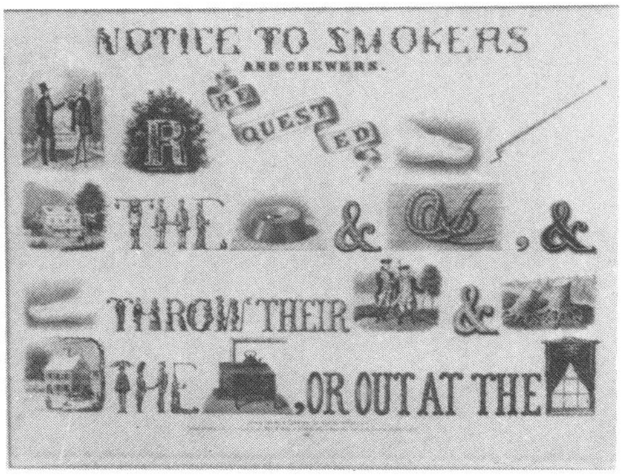

'Notice To Smokers And Chewers', published by N. Currier, 1854, small folio. (Robt. W. Skinner Inc.) £540

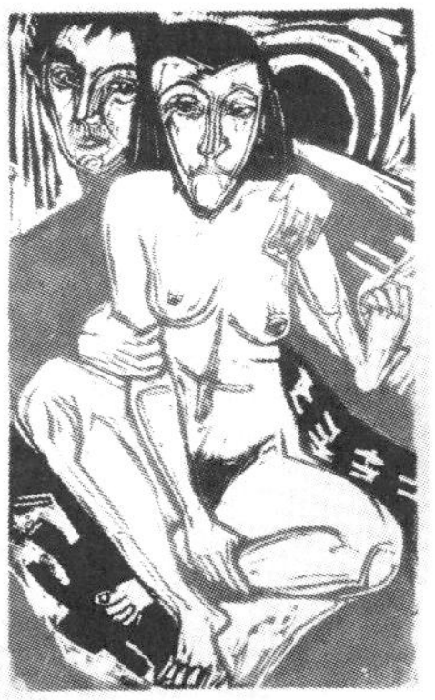

Melancholisches Madchen, by Ernst Ludwig Kirchner, woodcut printed in three colours from one block, 1922, on soft Japan, 752 x 445mm. (Christie's) £43,200

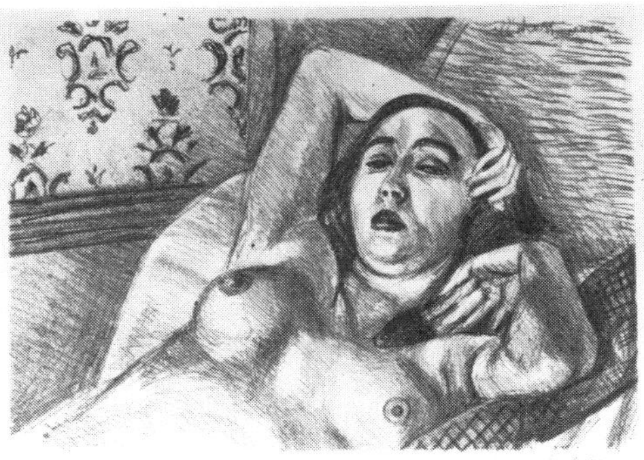

Le Repos du Modele, by Henri Matisse, lithograph, 1922, on Chine volant, signed in pencil, 223 x 304mm. (Christie's) £1,836

'The Great Fire at Boston', published by Currier & Ives, 1872, small folio. (Robt. W. Skinner Inc.) £287

L'Artisan Moderne, by Henri de Toulouse-Lautrec, lithograph printed in colours, 1894, on cream wove paper, 923 x 648mm. (Christie's) £7,020

'The Accommodation Train', published by Currier & Ives, 1876, small folio. (Robt. W. Skinner Inc.) £202

PURSES & HANDBAGS

Apart from any natural deterioration resulting from the passage of time, an attack of moths or storage in a damp place, evening bags and purses are generally found to be in fair condition; used mainly on special occasions they were rarely subjected to the rigors of everyday use.
The body of the pouch was produced in a number of materials including leather, beadwork, tapestry, embroidered silks and a chain mail of gold, silver or steel links. The clasps, and mounts too, were sometimes made of precious metals inset with gem-stones, gilt, silver or silver filigree but more commonly of tortoiseshell.
All types of old handbags are now being appreciated for their 'period' styling and this includes handbags produced up until the 50's and, in cases like the Cartier, to the present day.

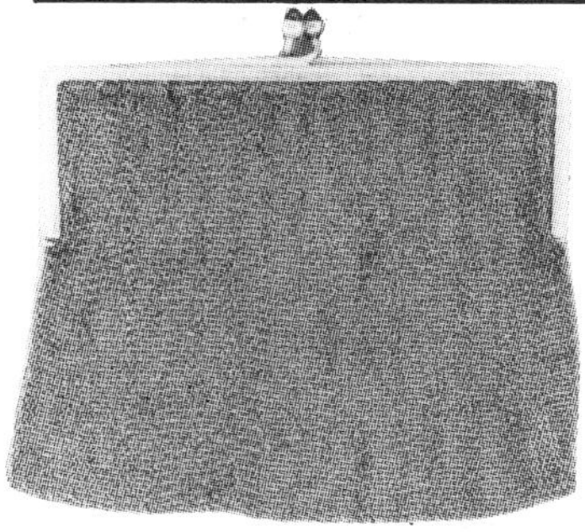

A 20th century French hallmarked 18ct. gold mesh evening bag, 192.8gr. (Robt. W. Skinner Inc.) £1,068

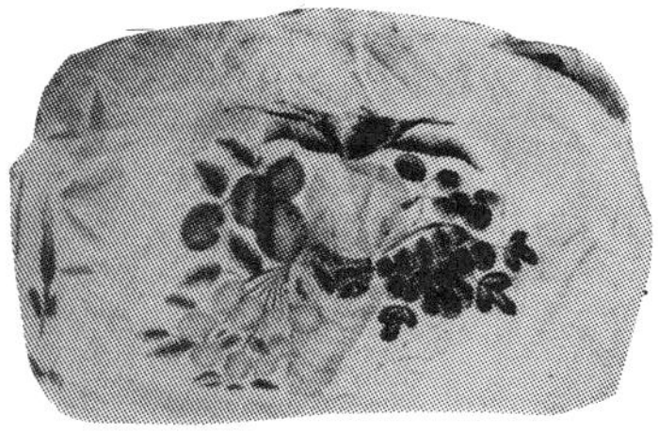

A painted silk purse, inscribed in ink 'Judith N. Peaslee, painted under the care of Miss C. Gage, Bradford Academy, 1812', Mass. (Robt. W. Skinner Inc.) £347

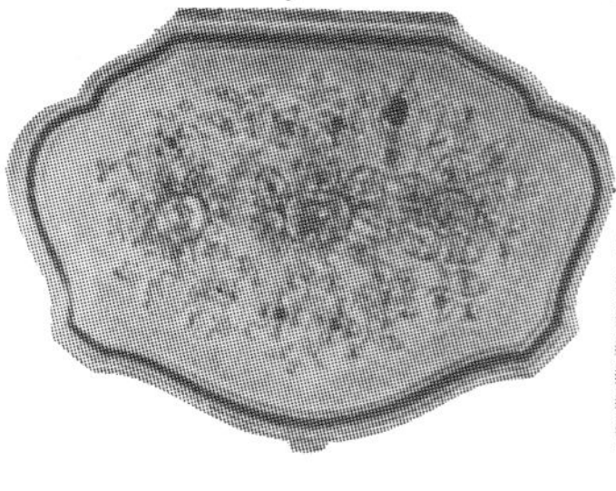

A gold and gem-set cartouche-shaped purse with borders of dark blue enamel, probably Austrian, circa 1870, 7.4cm. £4,204

A Victorian floral beaded bag with sterling top, made in Greece, 10in. long. £33

A fine late 19th century beadwork purse with plated mounts. £22

Early 19th century Palais Royale purse, 6½in. wide. £648

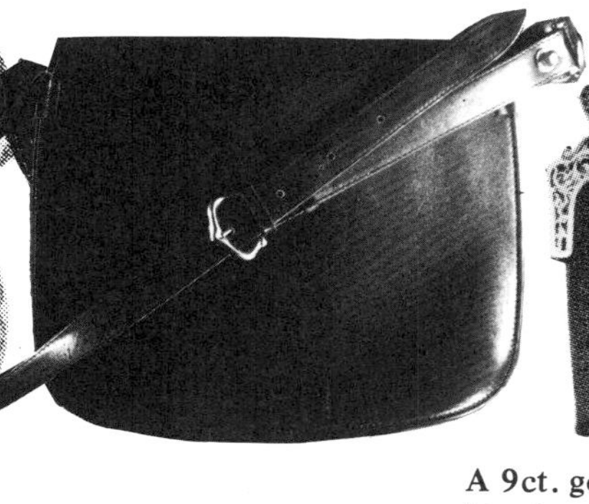

1970's Cartier 'saddle' bag with gold plated fittings. £150

A 9ct. gold mesh evening bag, by S. Blanckensee & Son Ltd., Birmingham 1838. (Lawrence Fine Art) £605

A small soft leather purse decorated with fleurs de lys and with a fake sovereign clasp. £6

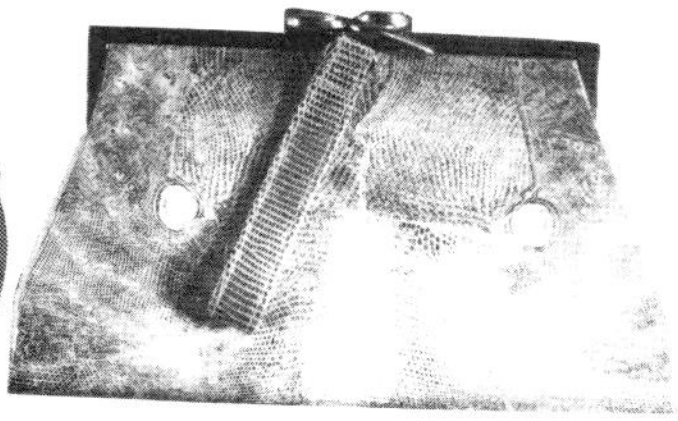

Edwardian snakeskin clutch bag with silver mounts. £100

Mid 18th century Louis XV gold mounted black leather purse from the collection of Madame de Pompadour, 11cm. £1,261

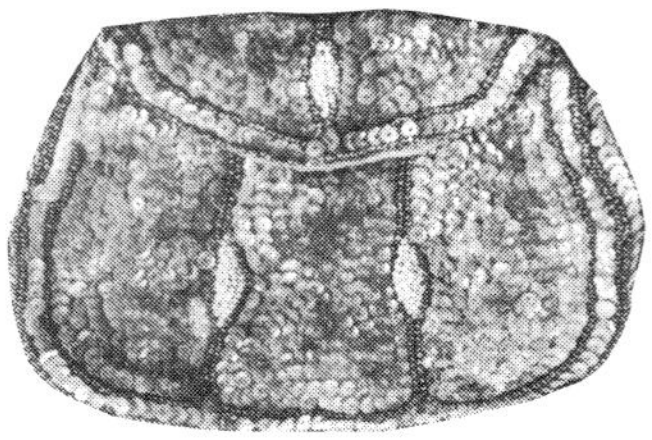

A 19th century beadwork and mother-of-pearl button decorated purse. £7

QUACK MEDICINE BOTTLES

The Victorians swallowed an amazing quantity of quack medicines and the gullibility of the public seems to have known no bounds if the claims on the bottles are to be believed.

The most popular medicines were those which advertised themselves as having been used by royalty and bottles embossed with such claims are now prized by collectors. Some of the rarer and more interesting glass medicine bottles contained materials which cannot be obtained over the counter today like Elixir of Opium or the strangely named Mouse Ear Syrup. There was also Extract of Mistletoe Druid Cure and Seaweed Extract in a green glass bottle. Medicines were produced for babies – Croup Mixture was popular – and for nervous ladies who might have taken Miss Pike's Powders for Fits and Nervous Complaints.

Pre 1850 Ruspinis Styptic in cobalt blue pontilled bottle. £100

Violin shaped clear glass pontilled bottle, 'By the King's Patent Granted to Robt. Turlington – For His Invented Balsam of Life – Jan. 26th 1754. £100

Dr. Wartburg's Fever Tincture, Tonic Medicine, in aqua moulded bottle. £50

Miss Pikes Powders for Fits and Nervous Complaints, in a lead glass bottle, circa 1800. £100

True Daffys Elixir, in a lime green pontilled bottle. £100

'By the King's Patent', True Cephalic Snuff, in a crudely blown pontilled bottle of light green glass. £100

Dr. Solomon's Cordial Balm of Gilead, in moulded aqua glass bottle. £150

Dr. Lobb's Blob Lipped, cylindrical clear glass bottle with an embossed humanoid face on the reverse. £140

Henry's Calcined Magnesia, Manchester, in a lead glass pontilled bottle. £30

Dalby's Carminative, in a cone-shaped aqua bottle. £30

J. Cropper's 'Never Failing Gout Mixture', in aqua coloured glass bottle, circa 1850. £20

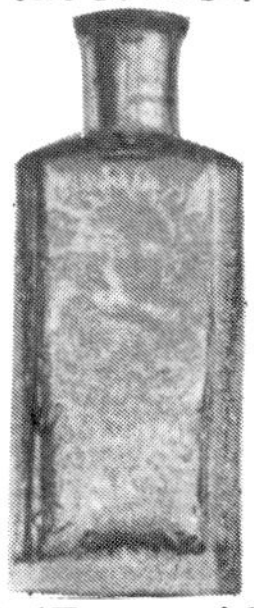

Holden's 'Tommy' bottle, 7½ pence size, Cures Sprains and Sore Throats, aqua glass. £30

QUILTS

Bedcovers and quilts, many of very humble origin indeed, are now most enthusiastically collected in all parts of the Western world.

They are treasured for their intricate designs, colourful patterns and, perhaps more important still, the skill demonstrated in the fine hand stitching. Some examples are considered to be so rare and valuable that they hang, framed and under special glass to prevent fading.

The original concept was a simple one – to make use of odd scraps of fabric in producing a bedcovering with a practical function. As many more women became proficient in the art, traditional patterns developed, but even these formal designs show much individual style.

In setting out the pattern for a quilt, a paper pattern was cut, often from whatever bits and pieces were to hand; letters, household accounts and other documents were used. The paper pieces were sometimes stitched into the backing of the quilt and may provide a clue in dating a piece.

Late 19th century crazy quilt with The Lord's Prayer, America, consisting of velvets, brocades and cottons of varying shapes, 69in. wide. (Robt. W. Skinner Inc.) £256

An appliqued coverlet with pineapple pattern, America, circa 1840, 82 x 98in. (Robt. W. Skinner Inc.) £1,388

A patchwork quilt, Penn., signed and dated in ink on the back, 'Phebeann H. Salem's(?) Presented by her Mother 1848', 8ft.11in. x 9ft. (Robt. W. Skinner Inc.) £1,319

Early 19th century red and blue patchwork Calamanco coverlet, America, 108 x 100in. (Robt. W. Skinner Inc.) £833

A patchwork cover worked with hexagonal pieces of mid/late 19th century printed and plain coloured cotton, 2.50 x 2.34m., lined. (Phillips) £250

A 19th century cotton piecework quilt, American, with a centre star motif, 90 x 91in. (Christie's) £1,259

An appliqued quilt with attached label 'Made by Mrs. J. Walter Marshall of Old Frankport Rd., Lexington, Kentucky', circa 1860. (Robt. W. Skinner Inc.) £1,388

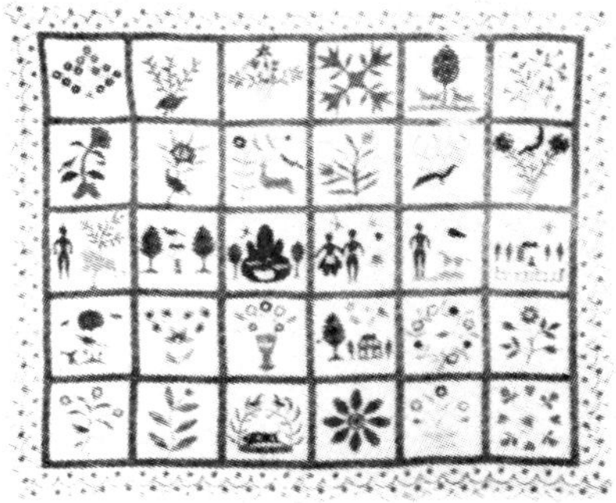

An applique quilt signed and dated 'Sarah Ann Wilson - 1854', consisting of thirty appliqued squares of floral and animal design, 7ft.1in. x 8ft.4in. (Robt. W. Skinner Inc.) £22,222

A 19th century American appliqued quilt, 7ft.1in. x 6ft.2in. (Robt. W. Skinner Inc.) £833

A 19th century patchwork cotton quilt, with unusual tulip border motifs, America, 92 x 92in. (Robt. W. Skinner Inc.) £1,182

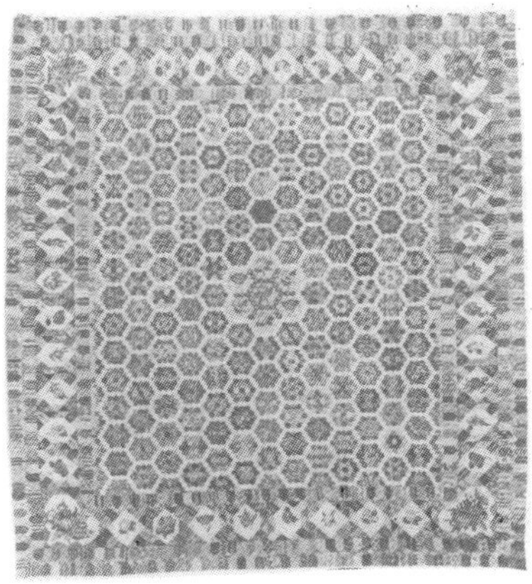

An early 19th century patchwork coverlet in plain and coloured printed glazed cotton, circa 1830, 2.70 x 2.24m. (Christie's) £620

An applique album quilt, New Jersey and Pennsylvania, 1853, 7ft.9in. x 8ft.7in. (Robt. W. Skinner Inc.) £2,325

A pieced and quilted cotton coverlet, lily pattern, American, circa 1900, approx. 84in. long, 80in. wide. (Christie's) £493

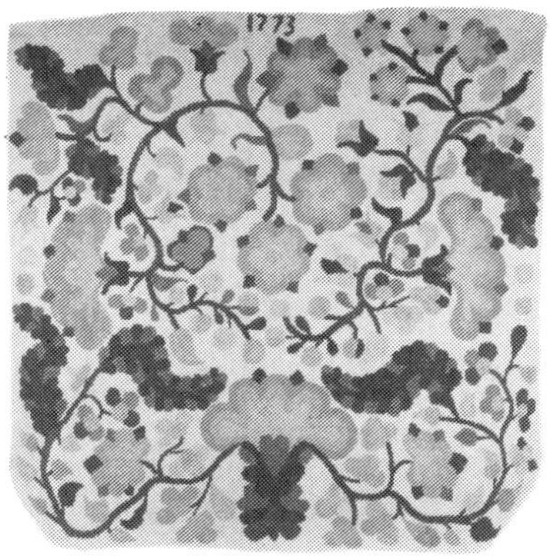

A wool bed rug, worked with a darning stitch in a tree-of-life pattern on a natural wool foundation, dated 1773, 84 x 85in. (Christie's) £7,586

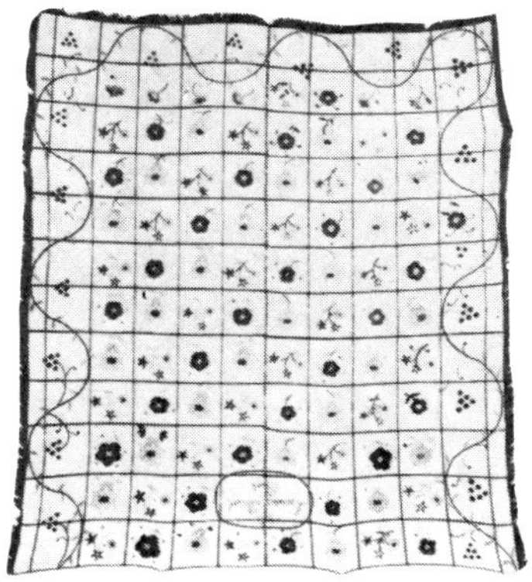

An embroidered blanked, probably New York, 'Lucretia Brush(?) Busti, 1831', large blue and white check, 6ft.4in. x 7ft.4in. (Robt. W. Skinner Inc.) £3,918

RACKETANA

Lawn tennis is the most popular ball game in the world and it has its roots in games played in Persia and Egypt in 500 B.C. From these early games a variety of other racket games evolved ranging from battledore to ping pong and today there is a strong interest in collecting the bats, rackets, balls and shuttlecocks used in those games.

One of the earliest tennis rackets dates back to 1880 but shuttlecocks from as early as 1840 can be found. Early rackets were strung with gut or wire and a few were made of vellum sheets. There were even bats with delicate wooden fretwork faces. Ping pong bats were often also vellum sheeted in the 19th century and the first wooden ones appeared in America in 1900.

Badminton racket made in India, circa 1885. £75

Child's 'toy' racket, only 22¾in. overall, circa 1900. £40

'Lop-sided' lawn tennis racket, maker unknown, circa 1885. £175

Long-headed lawn tennis racket with 'fish-tail' grip by G. G. Bussey & Co., circa 1900. £75

Lawn tennis tacket with steel head and strung with wire, circa 1925. £40

Table tennis battledore with single vellum sheet in bamboo frame, circa 1900, made by J. R. Mally. £40

Pair of wooden 'Ping-Pong' bats by Parker Brothers, U.S.A., circa 1900. £25

De Luxe 'Ping-Pong or Gossima' set in wooden box, by J. Jaques & Son, circa 1900. £200

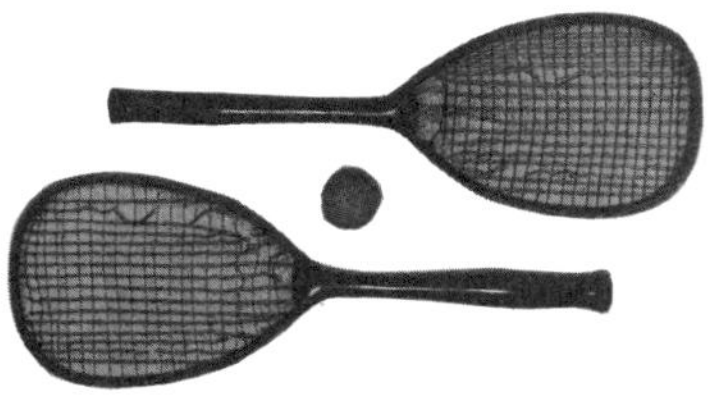

Pair of table tennis rackets, 16½in. overall, by G. G. Bussey & Co., circa 1900. £50

Miniature battledore and shuttlecock set, the battledores faced with vellum and only 8in. overall. £50

Table tennis bat, circa 1900, delicately cut out in fretwork. £40

Very large vellum battledore, 23in. overall, for the game of battledore and shuttlecock, circa 1890. £50

RADIOS

Put an old 78 record on an old wind up gramophone and the atmosphere of a bygone era bursts forth from the elegant horn. It therefore comes as something of a surprise, to find todays 'Six o'clock news' emitting from a 30's bakelite radio, when '2LO calling' might be more appropriate.

Radios have come a long way since Mr. Marconi harnessed the transmission of electro magnetic waves back in 1894 and this is the fascination for collectors.
From Catswhisker and crystal to three valve battery sets in kit form, the plug in coils, grid leaks and flexi valve holders, hold all the magic of a pioneer world in which the reward is a signal from far away places – if assembled in the right order.

'Phillips' Mains AC "Super Inductance" model 830A 1932. £100

Pye 740, 1923, four valve cabinet deluxe wireless set, 14in. high. £750

'Ekco' AC Mains model AC74 bakelite 1939. £50

Marconi, 1923, V2 long range wireless set in a walnut case, 10in. high. £450

1922, Marconiphone, multi valve RB7, 1ft.8in. high, 1ft.7in. wide, a scientific type of set probably used by wealthy amateurs. £1,500

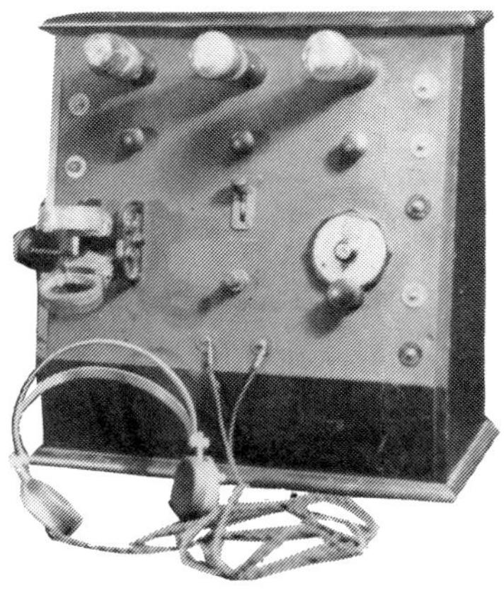

'Fellophone' Super 3 Bright Emitter Battery Set 1922-24. £120

RAILWAYANA

It would seem that the fascination for all aspects of railway transport has been with us since the first locomotive, Trevithicks Tram Engine, hauled a train of trucks at Merthyr Tydfil in 1804.

The first public railway, Stockton & Darlington, opened on 27th September 1825, to be followed by the Liverpool & Manchester on 15th September 1830.
The first broad gauge engine, the 'North Star', was built at Newcastle upon Tyne for overseas railway but was sold to G.W.R. in 1836 – the first broad gauge railway opened on 4th June 1838.

The field is vast, for absolutely everything connected with the railway is collectible, from whole trains to station signs, lamps, clocks, tickets and even the locks of the lavatory doors.

British Rail steel ticket clipper. £10

Cast iron railway sign 'Weight in train'. £20

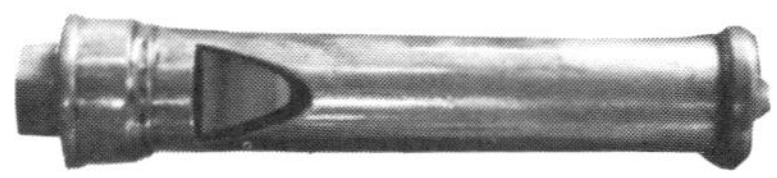

Late 19th century brass train whistle. £45

A fine large British Rail metal lamp with brass fittings. £40

N.E.R. painted metal string tin. £12

British Rail signal indicator. £30

British Rail guard's hat £8

British Rail tin for explosive fog signal. £3

'Andrew Barclay Sons & Co., Kilmarnock, 1942', original cast brass train plate. £85

British Rail tie with insignia 'Forward'. £4

Lancashire & Yorkshire Railway original transfer. £30

RAILWAY TICKETS

Railway tickets have been collected since the earliest days of the railway system. Traditionally collectors have built up their collections by exchange, but in recent years several large collections of tickets have been auctioned and many more offered for sale by collectors. This has enabled a price to be placed on certain of the rarer items. A few examples are shown below. The value placed on any particular ticket is dependant on several factors, such as the age, condition and the station or company of issue.
Platform tickets are also a popular item with many collectors who aim to get one from as many different stations as possible.

Misprinted tickets are also keenly collected as are specialised tickets like those issued to Hop Pickers, Anglers or for a day visit to the Dockyard.
As a rule nationalisation issues (1948) are more available and as such are much cheaper than the earlier tickets issued by individual companies.

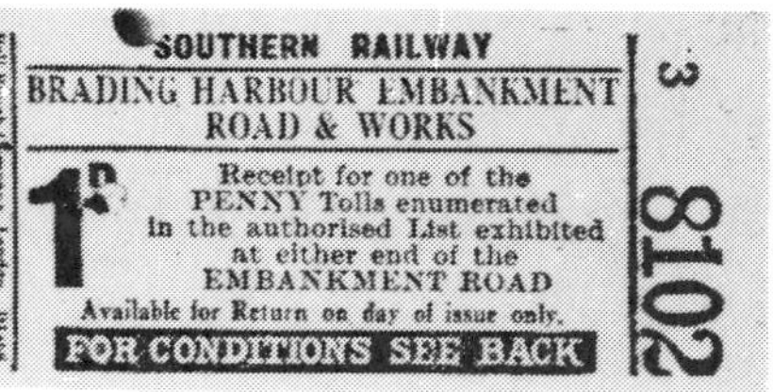

Brading Harbour Embankment Road and Works. £2.50

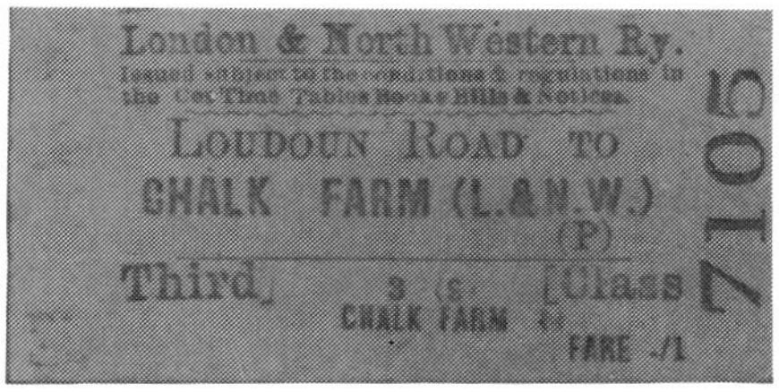

Issued by London & North Western Railway at Loudon Road. £20

Platform Ticket for Ludgate Hill, closed 1929 (record price). £340

Sulgrave Manor, Conducted Tour, British Railways. £2.50

Issued by the Somerset & Dorset Joint Railway in 1899. £20

Chatham, Portsmouth or Plymouth, Navy Week, Southern Railway. £5

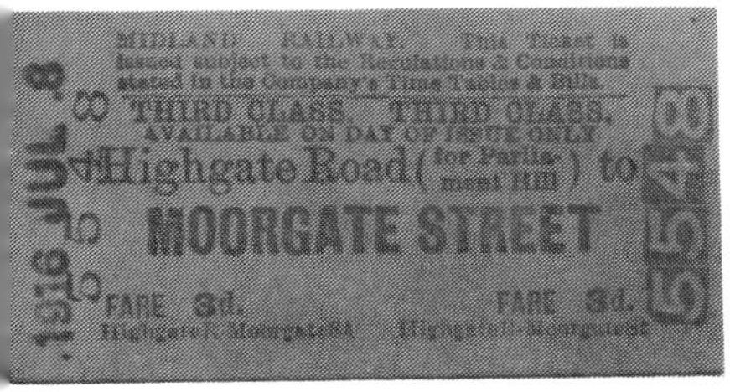

A Midland Railway ticket issued at Highgate Road Station. £20

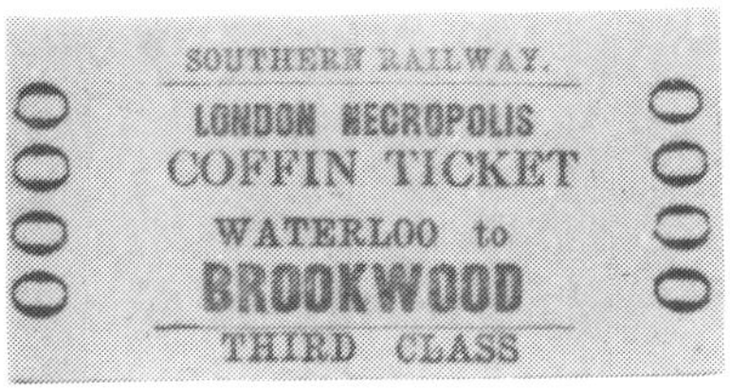

Southern Railway, Coffin Ticket, Waterloo to Brookwood. £25

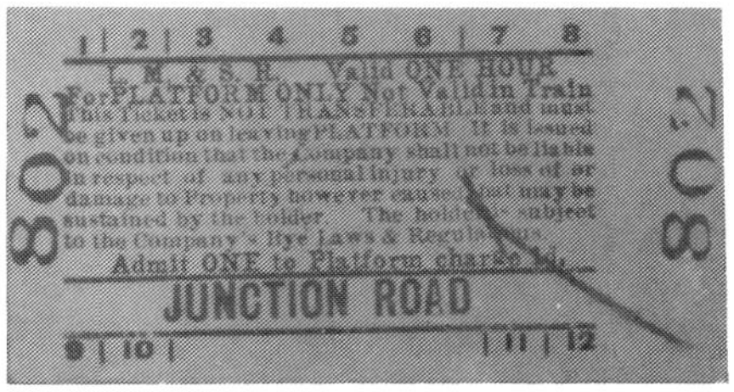

Issued at Junction Road on the Tottenham & Hampstead Joint Line. £100

National Coal Board, Bicycle and Perambulator Ticket. £1.50

Hop Picker Ticket 1938, London Bridge to Tenterden. £2.50

'Rickmansworth' Platform Ticket. £2

RATTLES

Since the beginning of time it has been a tradition to present a young child with a rattle of sorts. Examples exist from the simplest dried gourd with rattling seeds to the most elegant of Georgian rattles crafted by leading silversmiths and decorated with coral. Coral rattles were the most highly prized for the substance was thought to contain medicinal properties beneficial to the child.

As a rule, Georgian rattles are plain and Victorian rattles fussier; having bunnies, elves and other sentimental characters introduced into their design.

One of the most attractive designs was created for the older child. It is known as a poupard and consists of a doll's head and body placed upon an ivory stick incorporating a whistle. When the stick is turned a small musical box within the body of the doll plays a melody.

Rattles of ivory or wood and even the celluloid Art Nouveau type are less expensive and will form the foundation of an interesting collection.

Victorian silver rattle with ivory teether and whistle. £90

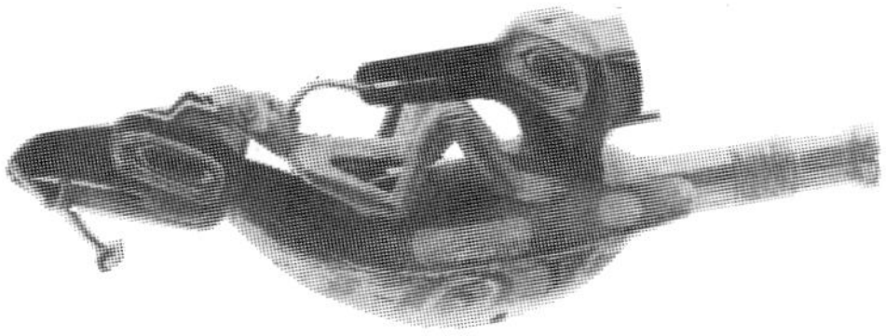

Northwest coast polychromed carved wood raven rattle, carved in two sections, 12¼in. long. (Robt. W. Skinner Inc.) £2,777

A baby's Victorian silver rattle, unmarked, with whistle and carved ivory handle. £150

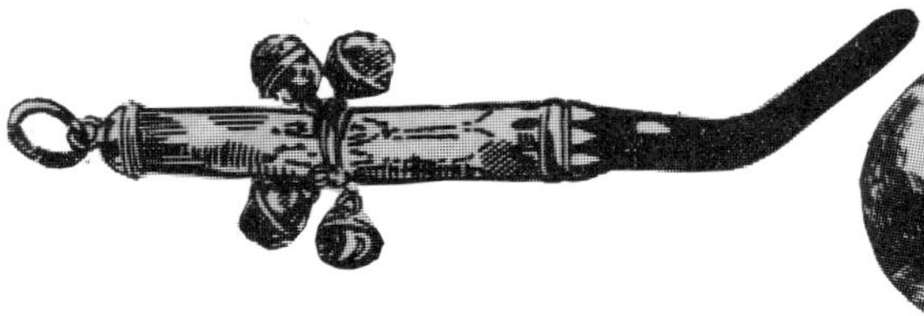

Early 18th century child's silver rattle, 5¼in. long, circa 1700. £360

A Victorian silver rattle dated 1886. £35

18th century child's rattle and whistle by Shem Drowne, Boston, 1749. £220

Georgian silver baby's rattle and comforter, maker's mark GU on whistle mouthpiece, Sheffield, 1818, 5in. long. £125

A 20th century baby's plated rattle. £10

Sterling silver baby rattle with sliding monkey, Birmingham, circa 1905, 6½in. long. £316

17th century child's rattle bearing the Edinburgh date letter for 1681. £1,250

An Edwardian plated baby's rattle. £4

RAZORS

Razor collecting is still a fairly new field and exceptionally fancy specimens can still be bought.
The vast majority of plain black and white handled cut-throat razors are too plain and recent to interest many collectors and these are worth less than one pound each.

Items at a premium are; perfect pearl-handled razors, preferably Sheffield, with carved pearl panels – £15-£20; and Sterling silver handled razors, preferably solid and engraved, though silver on ivory are also desirable at £20-£30.

Good, uncracked 1800 period razors with straight handles are generally more collectible than later items and German razor sets, and imitation ivory sets are always worth less than the equivalent Sheffield made ivory sets.

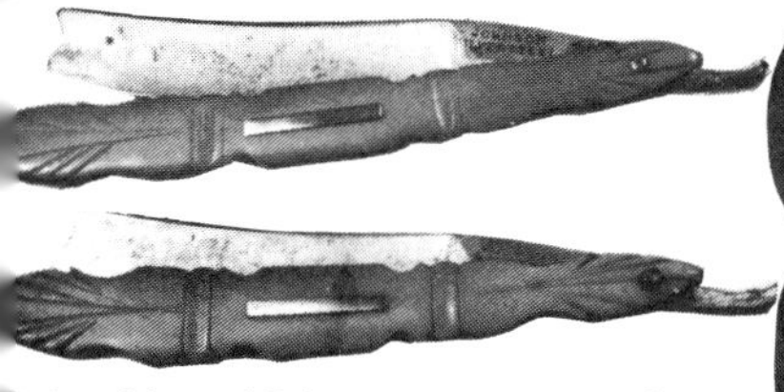

'air of late 18th century razors by ohnson, with pressed horn handles. £20–£30

Pair of mid 19th century razors with embossed silver handles. £100

A rare sailor's twin-bladed razor, with penwork handle, engraved 'Plymouth'. £100

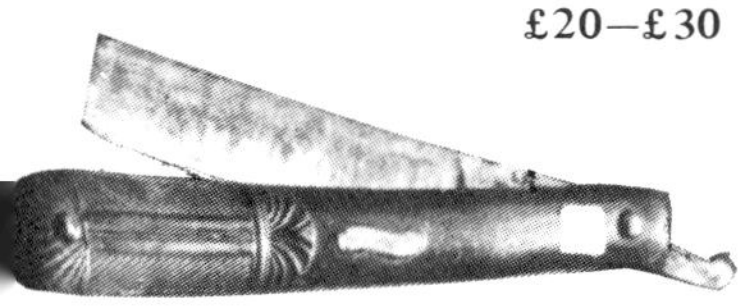

id 19th century razor with pressed ack horn handle. £10–£12

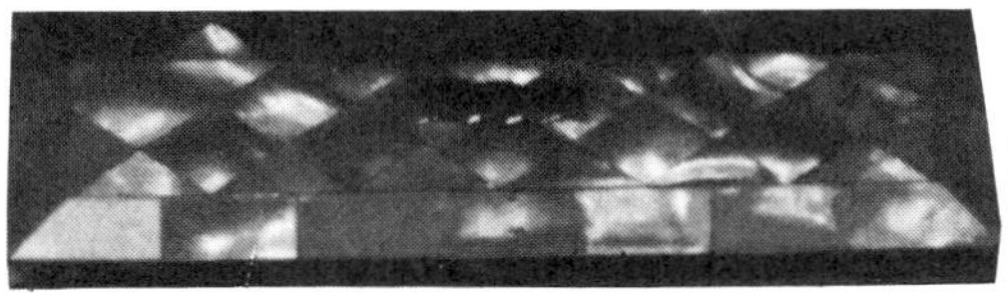

Mid 19th century gambler's travelling razor with dice designs on the handle. £60–£80

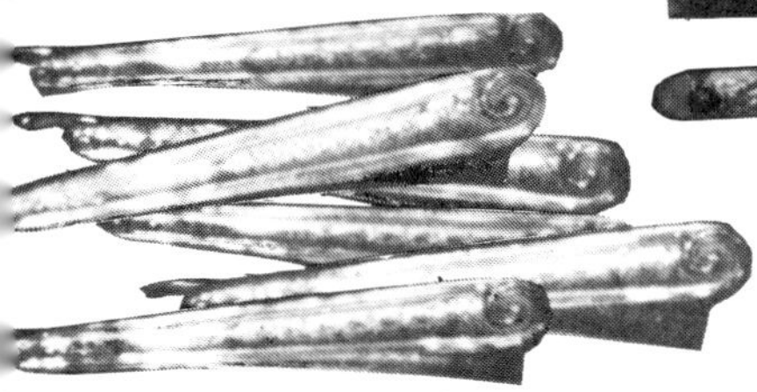

\ possibly unique set of six razors vith silver gilt handles, by Paul torr, with matching strap, 1834. £1,500

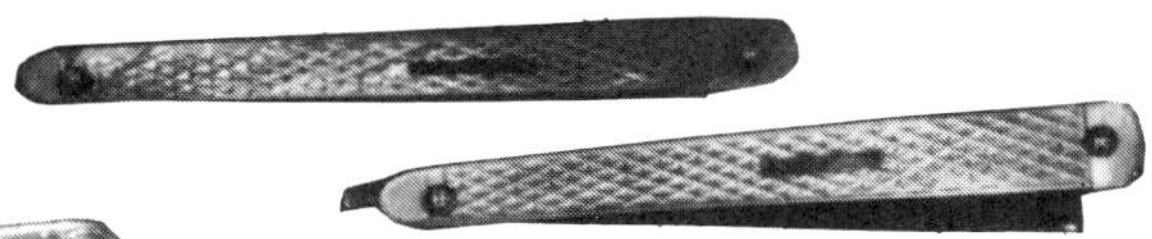

A pair of chequer carved pearl handled razors with solid gold pins, contained in a mother-of-pearl case, by I. H. Farthing, circa 1805. £175

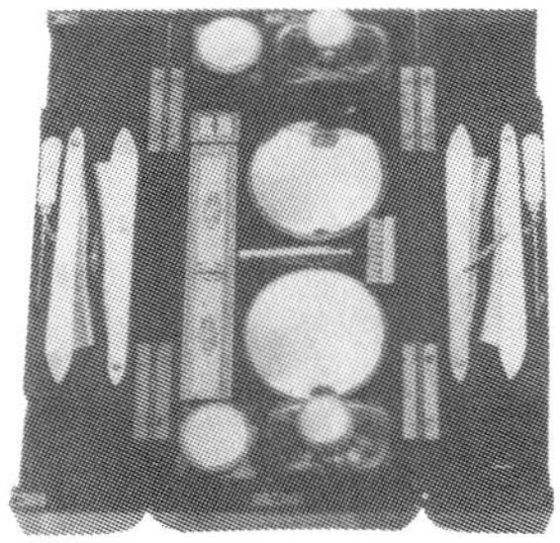

A good late 18th century French, mahogany case necessaire de voyage in silver gilt, including razors. £2,700

Gillette safety razor in metallic box. £2.50

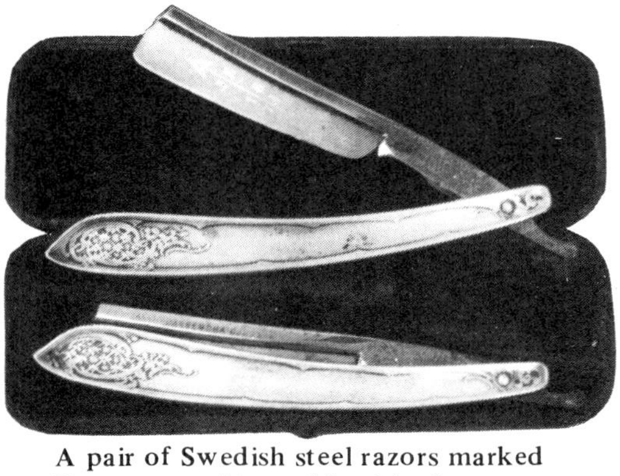

A pair of Swedish steel razors marked Dannemora Gjutstahl, with silver handles, contained in a black leather case, 1874. £85

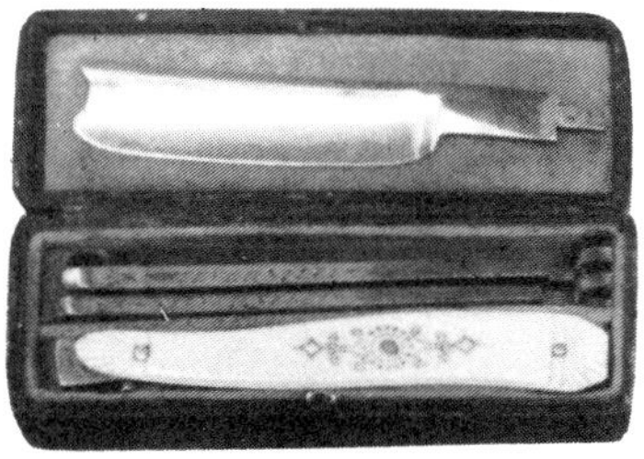

An early 19th century English razor with pinwork ivory handle, contained in a red leather case. £40–£80

RIFLES

The making of weapons, particularly guns, has always been a highly skilled craft. Today there are still master gun makers like Scotland's David McKay Brown whose output is not more than five or six weapons a year but who can demand five figure prices for each of them. These rifles instantly become collectors' items and join the weapons which are eagerly sought after by the world's richest connoisseurs.
The earlist long barrel guns were simply iron or brass tubes fitted to a stock of wood and they first appeared in the late 15th century. A cock was fitted slightly later but the German invention of the wheellock in 1517 gave us the origin of the rifle as we know it today.

Gunsmiths always sought for elegance in their products which went on to include the flint lock, the matchlock which was used by Wellington's armies and the English 'Brown Bess' which first appeared during the reign of William II. By the early 19th century England had become the centre of the gun making industry and pioneered or developed all significant advances including the invention of the double barrelled shotgun which appeared as a novelty in 1784.

Guns to look out for include military firearms produced by gunmaker Robert Murden during the English Civil Wars and 'dragon' carbines from the same period which have long barrels, bellied muzzles and full stocks with flat sided butts on which dragons' heads were carved. From these dragon guns the term 'Dragoon' appeared. Rifles made by London gunsmiths J. Purdey and Sons have been famous for over a century and some collectors specialise in weapons from various campaigns and wars, including those used in the gun battles of America's Wild West.

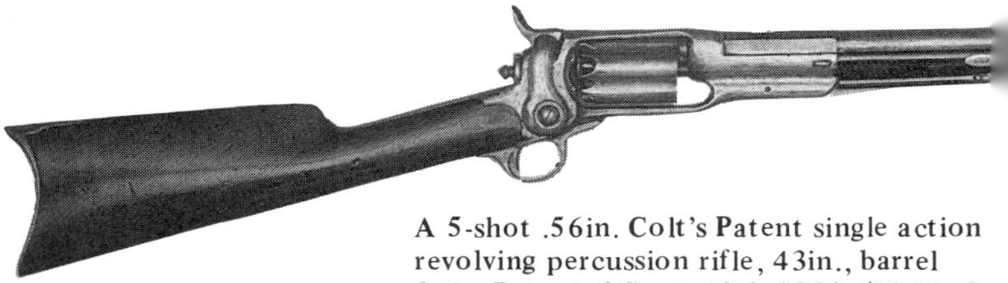

A 5-shot .56in. Colt's Patent single action revolving percussion rifle, 43in., barrel 24in, Patented Sept. 10th 1850. (Wallis & Wallis) £1,700

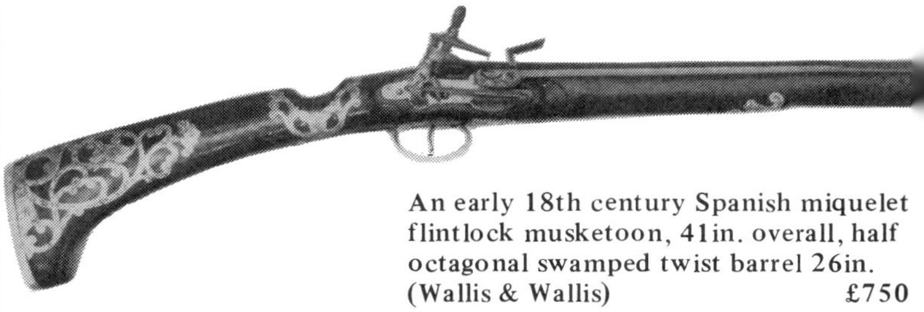

An early 18th century Spanish miquelet flintlock musketoon, 41in. overall, half octagonal swamped twist barrel 26in. (Wallis & Wallis) £750

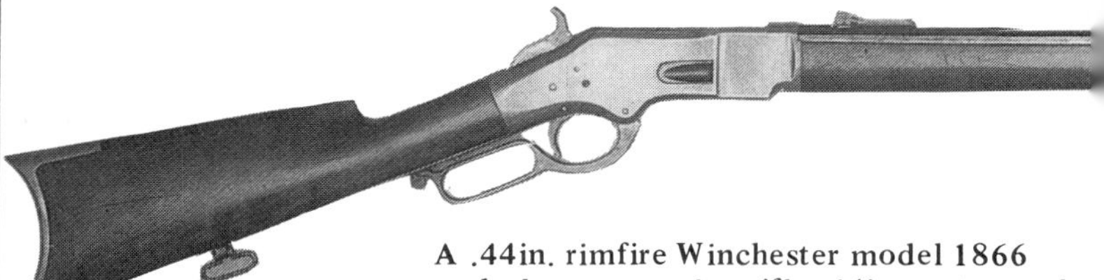

A .44in. rimfire Winchester model 1866 underlever repeating rifle, 44in., octagonal barrel 24in. (Wallis & Wallis) £2,000

A .40in. circa 1800 pump-up reservoir butt tap loading air rifle by Bate, 47½in., octagonal barrel 31½in. to tap. (Wallis & Wallis) £450

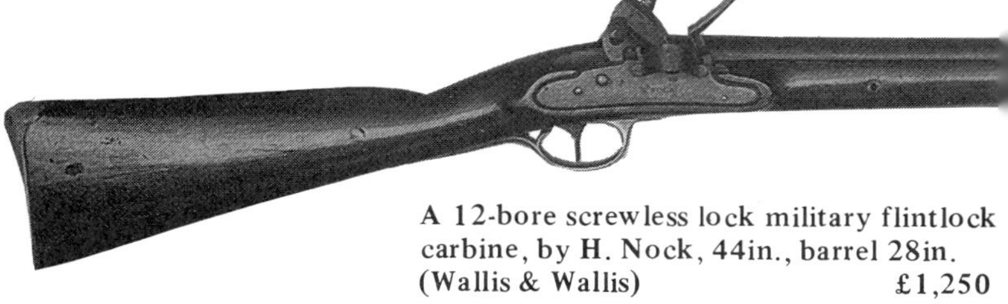

A 12-bore screwless lock military flintlock carbine, by H. Nock, 44in., barrel 28in. (Wallis & Wallis) £1,250

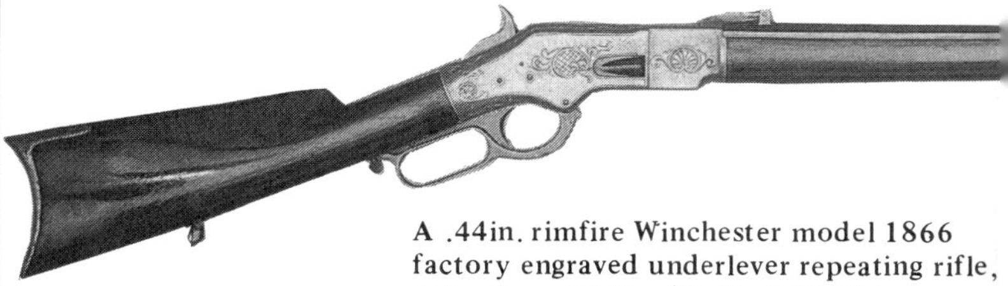

A .44in. rimfire Winchester model 1866 factory engraved underlever repeating rifle, 44in., barrel 24in. (Wallis & Wallis) £4,100

ROBERTSON'S GOLLY BADGES

It was just before the First World War, whilst on a visit to the 'backwoods' of North America, that a son of James Robertson, the founder, noticed a large number of young children playing with little black rag dolls with white eyes made from their mothers' discarded black skirts and white blouses.

The young Mr Robertson was so intrigued by the popularity of the small 'Golly' (the name being the children's interpretation of Dolly) that he thought it would make an appealing mascot and trade mark for the Robertson's range of products.

The first golly badge Robertsons produced was in 1930 commencing with the Golly Golfer. Four years later a series of fruit badges were produced with a Golly head superimposed into the berries. In 1937 came a Union Jack waistcoated Golly with it's arm raised in formal salute and Cricketers with County names printed on them. These early pre war Gollies had pale yellow waistcoats with Golden Shred printed on them.

The scheme was discontinued during the war because of the metal shortage but in 1946 a further series of Gollies were introduced with white waistcoats and the words Golden Shred – sportsmen, scout, standard walking Golly, bagpiper and guitarist.

About 1960 the golly changed, his eyes now looked to the left, hair became wavy and the words Golden Shred removed from his bright yellow waistcoat.

In 1977 came the skateboard and the motorcycle brooches and in the same years a series of 15 woven Golly jeans patches were designed which have become as popular as the brooches.

Post 1960 Gollies with bright yellow waistcoats. 75p—£1

Post War 'Golden Shred' white waistcoated Gollies. £1.50—£2

Pre War 'Golden Shred' pale yellow waistcoated Gollies. £2—£2.50

Fruit badges with Golly heads. £2—£3.50

ROBOTS

Toyland was first invaded by robots in the 1950's and, as you might have guessed, over 90% were made in Japan.
These colourful tinplate mechanical men and other related space toys with their numerous battery operated talents were an immediate success. They were able to perform hitherto undreamed of feats, many combining more than one action i.e., walking, talking, turning, shooting, flashing lights while rotating at a dizzying speed and so on.

Demand was high in the 1960's and the manufacturers entered a 'golden age' of production. In 1970, however, production of the well-loved tinplate models was abandoned in favour of the use of plastics but these were not nearly as pleasing, nor as popular.
As an indication of the current interest in collecting robots of the 50's and 60's, note that Mr Atomic Robot, made in the early 1960's, is now valued at over £400.

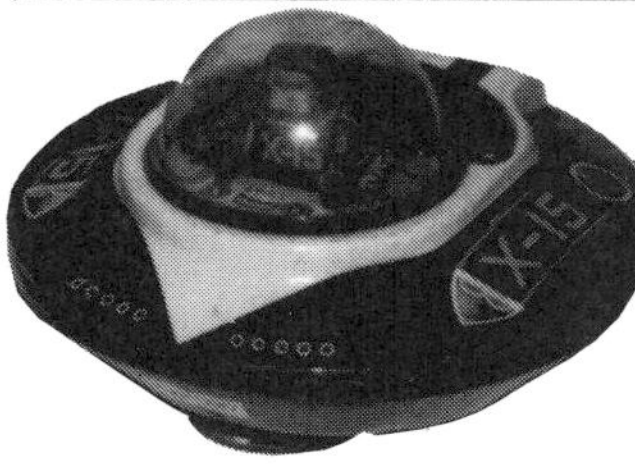

Japanese made 1960's flying saucer, X15, complete with robot operator. £20

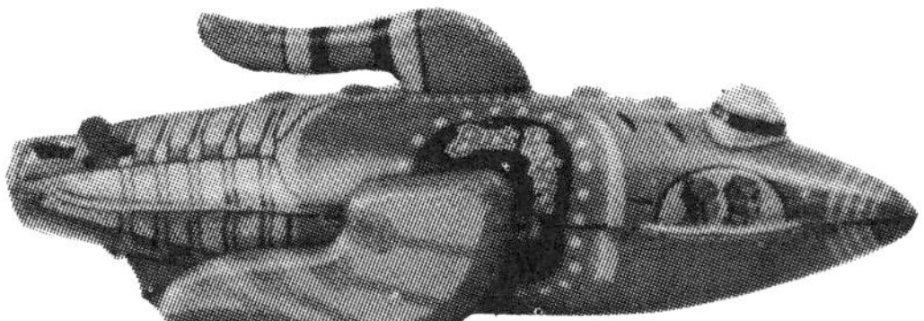

A Marx Buck Rogers spaceship, Pat. 1927, lithographed tin, 12in. long. (Robt. W. Skinner Inc.) £134

1960's Japanese space explorer vehicle with robot operator. £20

'Last in Space Robot', 1970 American, plastic battery operated robot. £80

'Planet Robot', 1960's Japanese plastic. £60

'Dino Robot', 1970, Japanese tin and plastic robot whose head opens to reveal a dinosaur's head. £100

'Astronaut', Japanese 1960, battery operated robot. £60

1960's Japanese flying saucer with robot operator. £20

Marx wind-up 'Buck Rogers' space ship, New York, 1927, 12in. long. (Robt. W. Skinner Inc.) £325

'Space Explorer', Hong Kong plastic battery operated 1960's robot. £25

ROCK 'N ROLL

Anything to do with the early stars, no matter how tenuous the connection, is being collected but it is the items more personally identified with our idols that really fetch money. For example a piano, once the property of Paul McCartney, sold for £9,900. This is perhaps a more obvious treasure but early photographs of John & Paul on stage can fetch upwards of £100 and all promotional material such as Elvis Presley film posters or concert programmes is also readily saleable.

Of particular interest are those items more personally identified with the super group such as an autographed Cavern Club membership book for 1961 which can command as much as £500. Even more sought after would be a signed Royal Variety Performance programme such as one recently sold by Sotheby's for well over £1,000.

But for really amazing money the hand-written lyrics of 'Imagine' by John Lennon, on the reverse of an hotel bill from Majorca dated 20/4/71, will command over £7,000.

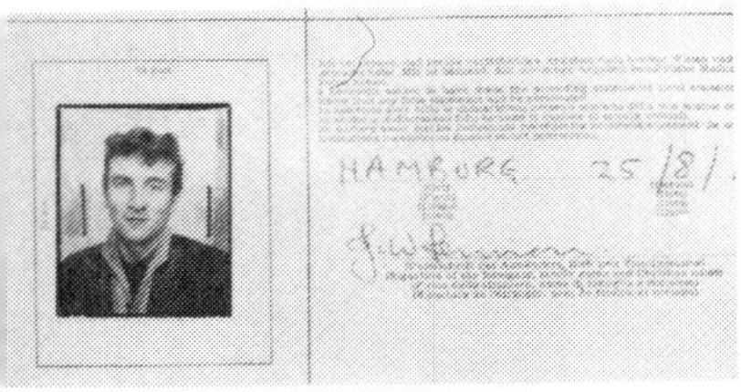

Official documents relating to John Lennon in Hamburg, 1960/63. £1,100

A Raleigh Super 50 Moped once owned by John Lennon, complete with registration book, 69in. long, circa 1965. £2,860

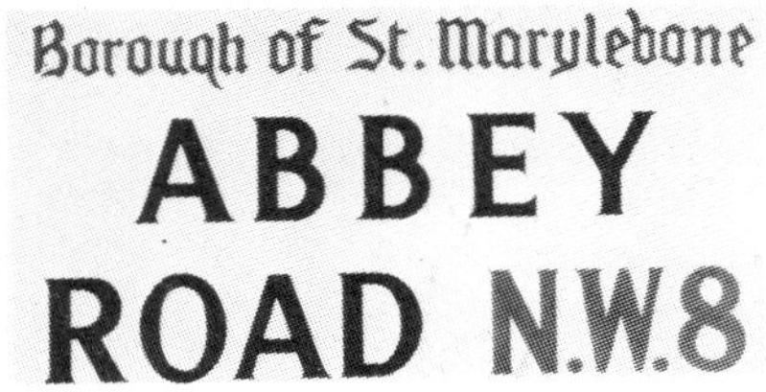

Abbey Road, The Borough of St. Marylebone, enamelled street sign, 30 x 18in. £640

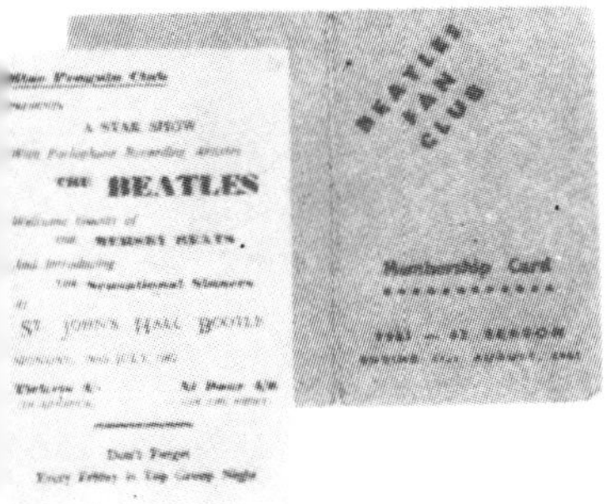

A Beatles 1961-62 fan club card and concert card for a show. £200

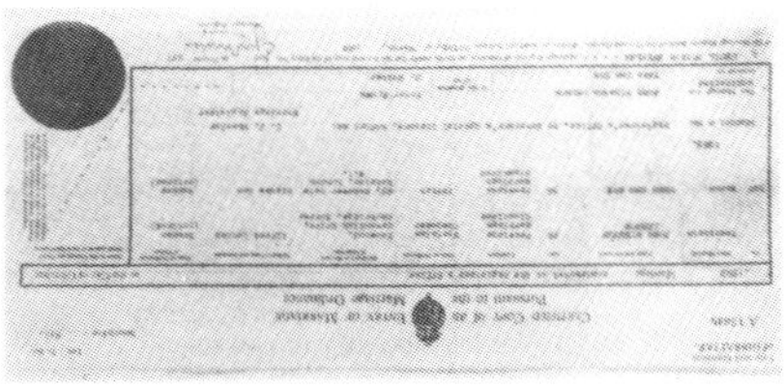

A copy of the Marriage Certificate of John Winston Lennon and Yoko Ono Cox, contracted at the Registrar's Office, in the City and Garrison of Gibraltar, by Governor's Special Licence, on 20th March, 1969. (Christie's) £3,000

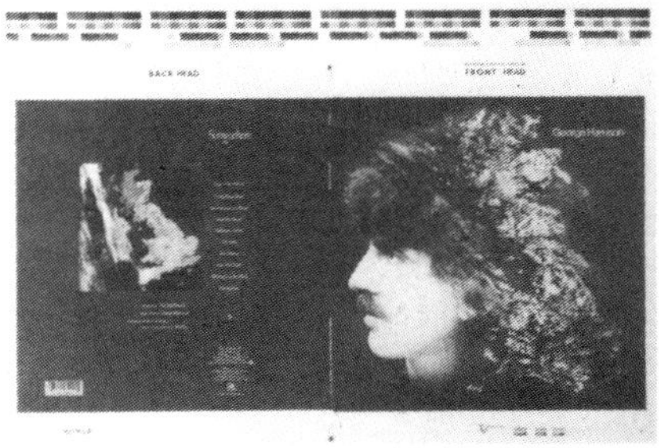

George Harrison, the original artist's proof for an un-issued album cover, 'Somewhere in England', Dark Horse Records, 1981, 18½ x 26in. (Christie's) £650

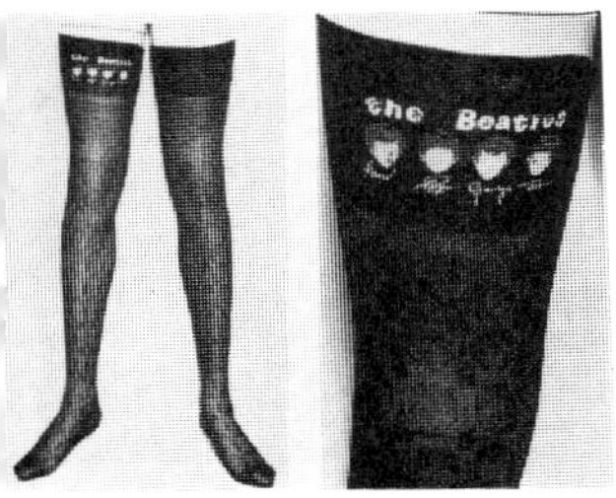

A pair of Beatle woven nylon stockings printed with caricatures of the Beatles, circa 1965. £280

A Beatles gold disc for the LP 'Sgt. Peppers Lonely Hearts Club Band', presented to the Beatles by EMI, dated 1967. £14,300

John Lennon's Broadwood upright piano, with letter of authenticity. £8,800

Astrid Kirchherr, original portrait photograph of John Lennon, George Harrison and Stuart Sutcliffe, 1960. £660

The Beatles LP, VJ 1092, the first LP released in the United States. £44

A Christmas card for 1970 from Apple made from foam rubber. (Worrall's) £120

Eric Clapton platinum disc for 'Backless' presented by RSO Records Inc. for the sale of one million copies, circa 1978. £770

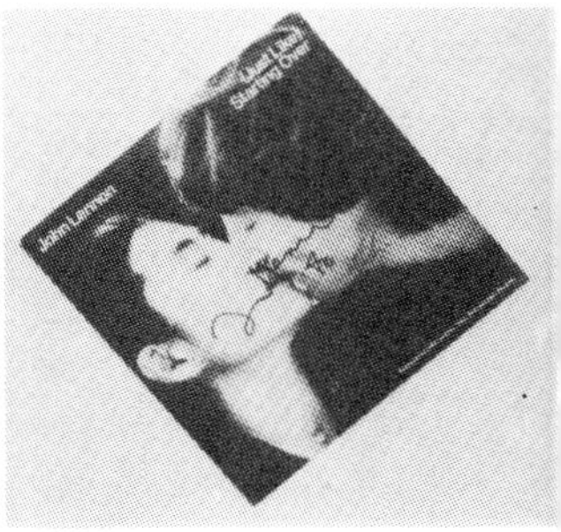

John Lennon 'Starting Over', the paper sleeve to the single bearing signatures of John Lennon and Yoko Ono. £385

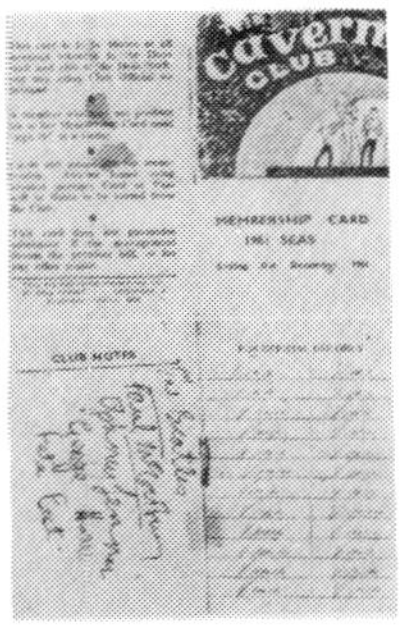

An autographed Cavern Club membership book for 1961, containing the signatures of Pete Best, Johnny Lennon, George Harrison and Paul McCartney, 1961. £462

A radio telephone once the property of Elvis Presley, contained in a leather brief-case with initials E.A.P. beneath carrying handle. £660

An Elvis Presley wristwatch, by M. Tissot, 'Elvis Presley' in raised letters, circa 1970. $2,090

An autographed Beatle concert programme for the 1964 Tour, signed by the four members of the group. £462

Dire Straits, a presentation 'Platinum' disc, 'Brothers In Arms', the album mounted with a 'platinum' cassette above a reduction of the album cover. (Christie's) £400

The Beatles, 'Help', Parlophone 33½ r.p.m., mono, 1965, signed on the cover by each of The Beatles, and inscribed 'All the Best, George Harrison'. (Christie's) £1,200

A quantity of autograph material from Pink Floyd, The Who, Marvin Gaye and 'Auf Wiedersehen Pet'. (Christie's) £200

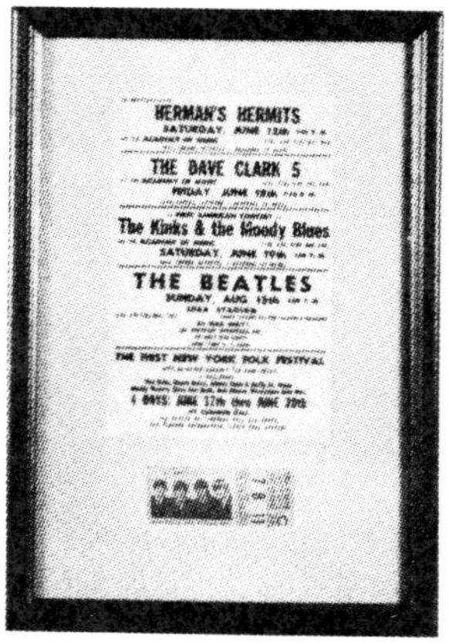

The Beatles in Shea Stadium, hand bill and concert ticket, 1966. £286

The Beatles, a signed menu for the Supper Party following Royal World Premiere "Help!". (Christie's) £420

A 1966-69 Vox Mando 12 String Guitar in sunburst, serial no. 74309. (Christie's) £200

Paul McCartney's Chappell & Co. Ltd. upright piano, 50 x 50 x 24½in., English, circa 1902. £9,900

A 'Presentation' 'Gold' disc of '(I Can't Get No) Satisfaction' by the Rolling Stones. £1,100

A Corgi 'Yellow Submarine' toy, the die cast scale model with two opening hatches revealing figures of The Beatles, circa 1967, 5in. long, in original box. (Christie's) £120

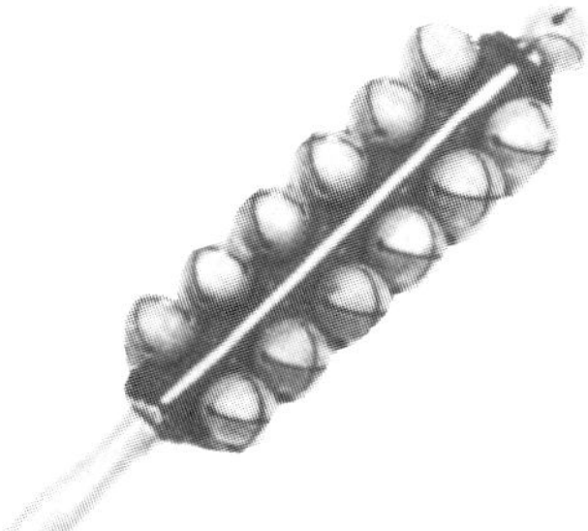

A set of hand 'Reindeer' bells, with red wooden handle used by John Lennon for the recording of 'Happy Christmas (War Is Over)', 1972, 12in. long.(Christie's) £900

Original etching and aquatint of 'The King', by David Oxtoby, signed by the artist, 27 x 21½in. (Christie's) £250

A limited edition resin bronze G.R.P. bust of Jimi Hendrix, circa 1985, by J. Somerville, no. 5 of an edition of 20, 24in. high. (Christie's) £300

Dire Straits, a presentation 'Platinum' disc, 'Brothers In Arms', the album mounted above a reduction of the L.P. cover and a plaque. (Christie's) £320

A Beatle Bubble Gum Machine by Oak Mfg. Co. Inc., American, circa 1965. £418

A rare photograph sold with copyright and negative of the Beatles and NME Poll Winners Trophy, Wembley 1964. £550

A promotional postcard for the release of The Move album, 'Flowers In The Rain', circa 1967. (Christie's) £200

ROYAL DUX

This most distinctive porcelain was produced at the Royal Dux factory established in 1860, in Dux, Bohemia.

The factory quickly gained a reputation for beautifully fashioned portrait busts and ornate vases but the most sought after pieces around today are the scantily clad nymphs of flowing form, more often than not seductively draped around shell-shaped bowls or curved mirror frames.

The most noticeable characteristic of this unglazed porcelain is the colour tones of soft pastel beige, pink and green.

Marks include an embossed pink triangle stamped Royal Dux Bohemia or E (proprietor: E. Eichler) in an oval surrounded by Royal Dux Bohemia.

Dux figures were exported in considerable quantities to America and Australia establishing a lasting international popularity.

Large Royal Dux group with camel and Bedouin seated on its back, 19¾in. high. (Reeds Rains) £580

An Art Nouveau Royal Dux figural vase modelled as a tree trunk with a maiden climbing around the side, 46cm. high. (Phillips) £270

A Royal Dux porcelain group of a peasant man and woman, on leaf decorated base, 22¾in. high. (Dacre, Son & Hartley) £300

A Royal Dux gilt porcelain figure of a girl bather seated on a rock, 19in. high. (Dacre, Son & Hartley) £360

A Royal Dux porcelain group of classical figures, the boy in wolf-skin, and girl wearing a gown, 26in. high. (Dacre, Son & Hartley) £760

A Royal Dux Art Nouveau conch shell group with three water nymphs in relief, 17½in. high. (Reeds Rains) £470

A Royal Dux bust, the young Art Nouveau maiden gazing to the left, raised pink triangle mark, 20in. high. (Christie's) £660

A large Royal Dux figure of a peasant boy leaning on a wooden pitcher, 59cm. high. £375

RUGS

Traditionally, in the east, Oriental carpets have always performed a dual role:

Firstly, as furnishings they have been used not only as floor coverings but also wall hangings, divan covers, and in decoration generally. In Turkey and Iran in particular they satisfy an aesthetic need which, in the west, paintings have fulfilled.

Secondly, in countries where governments and currencies were unstable they performed the function which stocks and shares perform here – a reserve of wealth to fall back upon in bad times.

As an investment in present day Europe and America they similarly should fill both roles – for those who take household furnishings seriously they may combine profit and pleasure.

Remember that, unlike paintings, the value of a rug is more in proportion to its size and type. This is because the intrinsic value of a rug depends upon months or even years of hand knotting.

A Shirvan rug with multiple floral decoration on indigo field, 80 x 51½in. (Reeds Rains) £500

Early 20th century Kazak prayer rug, S.W. Caucasus, a red field with ivory medallion, 4ft.2in. x 6ft.11in. (Robt. W. Skinner Inc.) £1,212

An Isfahan rug, the ivory field with three flower vases and flowering trees, 6ft.11in. x 4ft.10in. (Christie's) £3,024

Late 19th century Eastern Caucasian/Kuba rug, woven in the afshan or 'crab-kuba' design, 3ft.5in. x 4ft.10in. (Robt. W. Skinner Inc.) £378

A Souf silk and metal thread Kashan prayer rug, 6ft.9in. x 4ft.3in. (Christie's) £3,456

Late 19th/early 20th century 'Eagle' Kazak rug, Southwest Caucasus, 5ft. 11in. x 7ft.7in. (Robt. W. Skinner Inc.) £1,448

Late 19th century Bergama Village rug, 3ft. x 3ft.9in. (Robt. W. Skinner Inc.) £568

A Senneh rug, the indigo field divided into panels of flowering plants, wreaths and prayer arches, 6ft.8in. x 4ft. 4in. (Christie's) £3,024

SAMPLERS

Samplers were produced from early in the 18th century right through until after the First World War as a means of showing how adept a young girl could be at the useful art of embroidery, as well as knowing her alphabet.

A variety of coloured silks were worked, most popularly in cross-stitch, on a canvas backing to incorporate the name and age of the exponent, the date, numbers one to ten together with the alphabet, a hymn or a poem and a multitude of designs depending on how clever our young needlewoman was.

An early 19th century American needlework sampler, 19½ x 21in. (Robt. W. Skinner Inc.) £1,909

A George IV needlework sampler, by E.H., 1826, 17 x 12½in. (Graves, Son & Pilcher) £340

A sampler by Julia Matild Paisey, 1845, worked in dark silks, 16 x 12½in. (Christie's) £520

A sampler by Mary-Ann Hayter, aged 8 years, 1823, worked in coloured silks, 15 x 13in. (Christie's) £340

A needlework family register worked by Lucia A. Daniels in 1832, 16 x 18in. (Robt. W. Skinner Inc.) £694

Early 19th century needlework sampler, 'Phebe L. Slessor work aged 11 years', New England, 16 x 16in. Robt. W. Skinner Inc.) £625

A Boston School needlework sampler, made by Sarah Henderson in 1765, aged 12, 21 x 18½in. (Robt. W. Skinner Inc.) £15,384

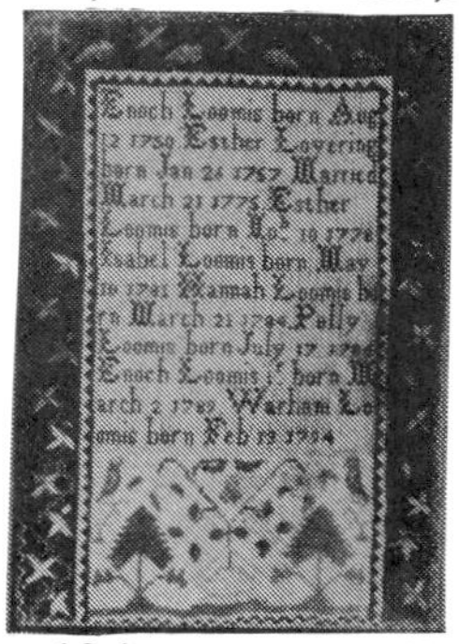

Late 18th century needlework sampler family record, 10½ x 16in. (Robt. W. Skinner Inc.) £2,152

Early 19th century woolwork sampler, worked by Elizabeth Shufflebottoms 1841, 23½ x 23¾in. (Reeds Rains) £300

SARDINE BOXES

Sardine boxes were produced to cater for the sensibilities of the refined middle class in the 19th century who enjoyed eating tinned sardines but did not like the idea of a vulgar tin appearing on their dining tables so they bought pretty boxes of porcelain, cut glass or silver to conceal them. These boxes all had sardines on their lids and though many of them were made by pottery firms in Britain like Spode or Minton, the prettiest seem to have come from Germany or Czechoslavakia. Many of the boxes were set in silver or plate mounts with a fork beside them.

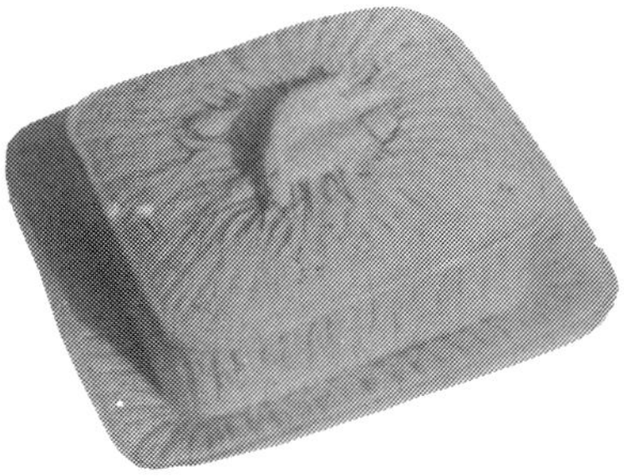

Pottery bamboo design sardine box with woven pattern on lid, made in Alloa, Scotland by Waverley. £70

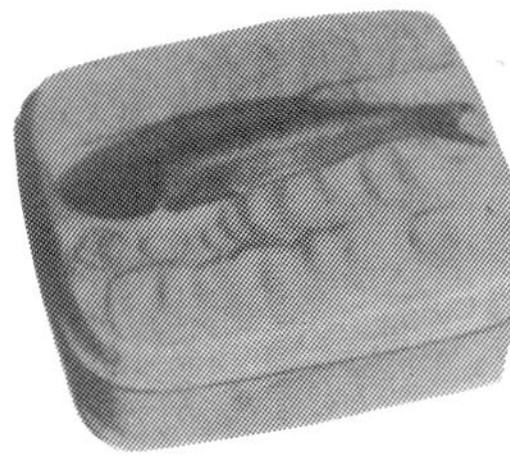

Czechoslovakian porcelain sardine box with a green marbleized effect and a good painted fish. £160

English porcelain sardine box with a finely painted fish with red fins, complete with silver plated stand and fork. £140

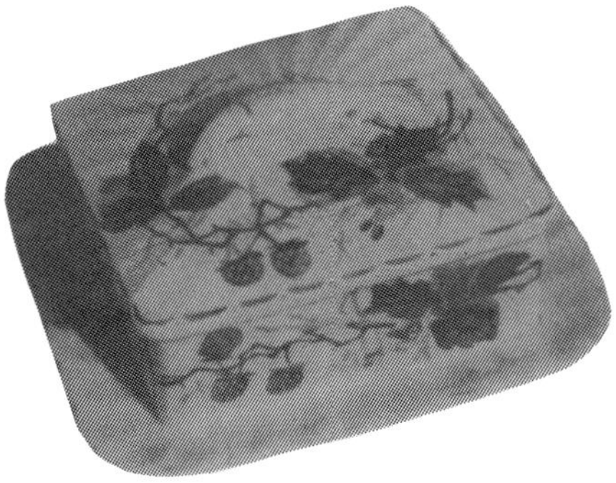

An unusual German porcelain sardine box decorated with gilding and brambles in flower and fruit by Mehlem. £130

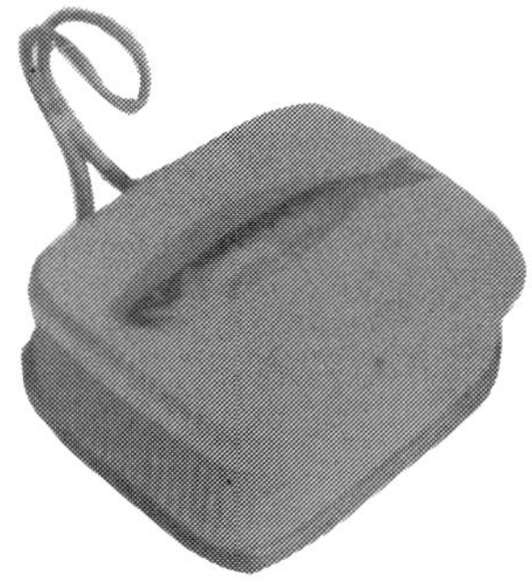

Fluted white porcelain sardine box with a finely painted fish, marked with an eagle, on plated stand. £250

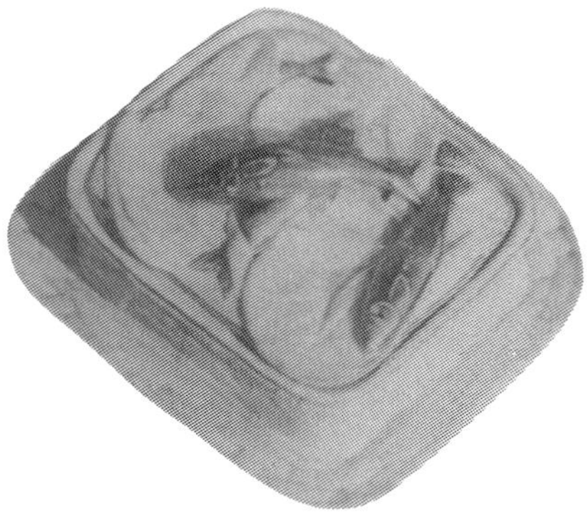

Gilded pottery sardine box with woven sides and decorated lid embellished with water lilies and reeds, unmarked probably English. £70

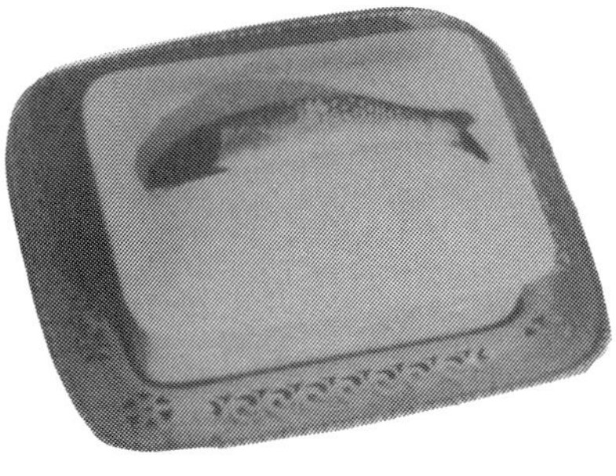

Apricot glaze sardine box marked Flos Maron, with pierced silver plated stand. £140

Cut glass sardine box with silver plated stand and lid, unmarked. £100

China sardine box of plain design with painted roses and a gilded scaled fish, dated 1886, marked MKK. £60

WIW-H

SATSUMA

Satsuma is a type of Japanese pottery which derives its name from Kagoshima, formerly known as Satsuma, the prefecture of Japan in which it was produced. The production of Satsuma ware began in the late 16th century but it was not introduced to the West until it was exhibited at the Universal Exhibition in Paris in 1867. The earliest examples were copies of Korean and Chinese pottery pieces and they were mainly tea ceremony ware in a hard greyish white or parchment coloured faience with a crackle glaze. In the mid 18th century lavishly enamelled and gilded pieces began to be made and these are highly prized by collectors.

A Satsuma pottery cylindrical box, the cover painted and gilded with geishas, 3in. diam. (Reeds Rains) £200

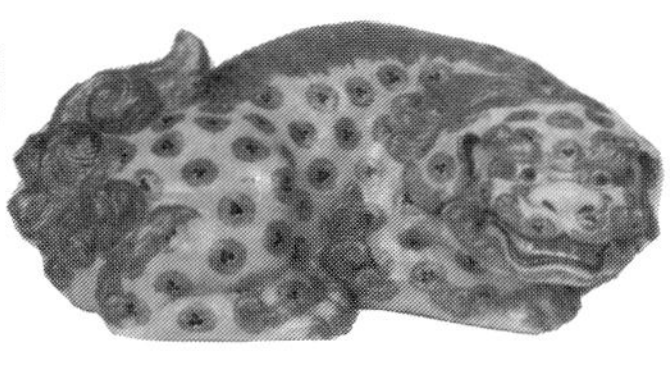

Late 19th century Satsuma model of a recumbent karashishi, 34cm. long. (Christie's) £1,320

A 19th century Satsuma bowl, signed on the base Gyokushu, 15.5cm. diam. (Christie's) £561

Late 19th century Satsuma model of a recumbent caparisoned elephant, signed, 25cm. long. (Christie's) £972

A Satsuma pottery pot pourri bowl on three feet in the form of grotesque heads, 8½in. diam. (Capes, Dunn & Co.) £95

A 19th century Satsuma broad oviform jar and domed cover with knob finial, signed Kintozan, 48cm. high. (Christie's) £486

A Satsuma type bowl of U-shape, signed, 4¼in. diam. (Lawrence Fine Art) £1,100

Late 19th century Satsuma teapot and cover modelled as a stylised bird, 18cm. long. (Christie's) £880

A Satsuma oviform vase enamelled in black, red and green and gilt, 12in. high. (Christie's) £1,500

A Satsuma large lidded jar, gilded figures on black ground, 13in. high. (Barber's Fine Art) £620

Late 19th century Satsuma model of a courtier, signed Dai Nihon, 22.5cm. high. (Christie's) £825

A 19th century large Satsuma oviform vase, signed Satsuma Tansai above an iron-red Shimazu mon, 50.2cm. high. (Christie's) £864

SCENT BOTTLES

Scent bottles can be found made in a number of materials including, silver, gold, enamel and porcelain, but the vast majority are made of glass with a variety of decorations.
Throughout the 18th and 19th centuries, it was customary to carry a container of insoluble crystal salts blended with aromatic essence purchased from a chemist or perfumier.
It was not until the 20th century that perfume was sold in ready filled bottles, and of these, the bottles made by Lalique for Coty and Nina Ricci are particularly sought after.
Examples by Daum, Galle and Webb also fetch good prices but a start can be made with Victorian overlay scent bottles, often double ended, and far more reasonably priced.

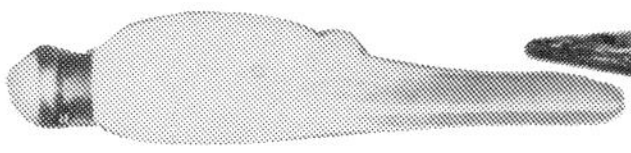

A cameo glass swan's head scent bottle in yellow and white, with silver cap marked Chester, 1884, 22cm. long. £1,210

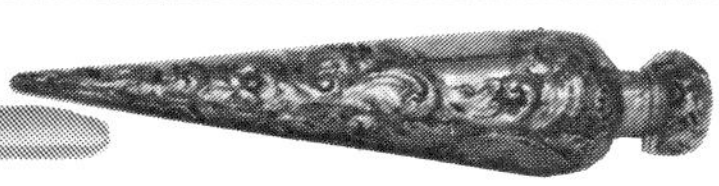

Victorian silver scent phial, Birmingham, 1892, 8in. long, 5oz., in case. (Hobbs & Chambers) £260

19th century cameo glass salts bottle with silver screw top, in case, 4in. long. (Capes, Dunn & Co.) £195

A ruby glass scent bottle of tapering elongated form, with hinged silver cap marked Birmingham, 1880's, 24.5cm. long. £770

An Apsley Pellatt sulphide and cut glass scent bottle and a stopper, 9.5cm. high. (Christie's) £324

One of a pair of Edwardian cut glass cologne bottles, by Wm. Comyns, London, 1905, 5½in. high. (Christie's) £700

A Lalique glass perfume bottle, flattened, square body with central oval depression, 1930's, 12.75cm. high. £300

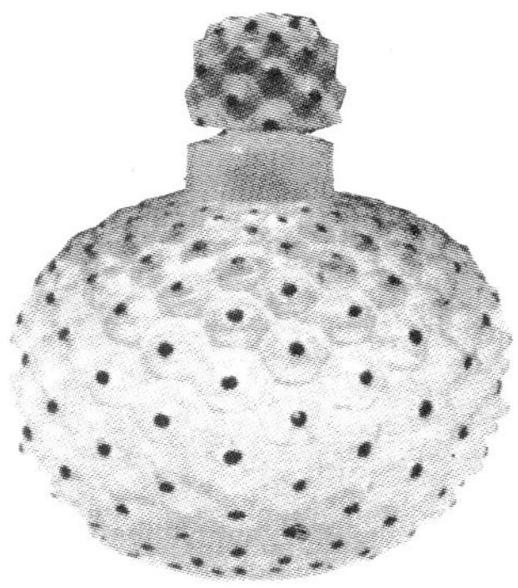

One of a pair of Lalique glass perfume bottles, moulded as sea urchins, 9.5cm. high, 1930's. £150

A Franchini gilt metal mounted scent bottle, the hinged cover with ring and bead chain attachment, 7.5cm. long. (Christie's) £259

'Worth', a Lalique glass scent bottle, with original Worth paper label, 24.5cm. high. (Christie's) £280

A glass scent bottle and stopper, inscribed 'Cigalia, Roger et Gallet, Paris', 13cm. high, in original box. (Phillips) £280

A Baccarat enamelled cut glass scent bottle with gilt metal screw cover, 9.5cm. long. (Christie's) £864

SCOUT BADGES

The collecting of Scout badges has an obvious attraction for those connected with the Scouting movement for it is mainly through attending jamborees and similar gatherings that badges can be acquired, either by purchasing from other scouts or by simply swapping your own county or area badge with those from another.

Most collectors work on a theme of just English counties or Scottish areas while others go worldwide and try to obtain at least one badge from each Scouting country.

Although Northamptonshire takes credit for being the first to have a distinguishing emblem in 1910, Kent claim to be the first to issue a county badge as recognised today on 26th July 1912 depicting a white horse.

Apart from the early metal badges issued by Devon and Dorset and a few printed paper badges issued during the war all county badges have been made of cloth, embroidered at first and woven from the 1930's until the present day.

Most modern badges cost less than 25p. but as in any field of collecting rare items exist which sell for considerably more, such as the aforementioned metal badges or those from counties no longer in existence such as South Warwickshire or Yorkshire West Riding.

Top of the list however are those issued for the World Jamborees in 1937 and 1947. These are worth at least £30 depending on the sub camp, of which there were 10 in 1937, or the French Province, of which there were 15 issued in 1947.

Condition is of importance when assessing value, a mint badge obviously being worth more than a badge which has been on a campfire blanket for a number of years.

France 1947 Jamboree. £30-£40

Somerset. (Printed) £5

South Warwickshire. £20 to £25

Yorkshire West Riding. £20 to £25

Merioneth. £10

Tyrone. (Printed) £5

Dorset. (Felt) £10

County of Edinburgh and Leith. £20 to £25

Midlothian. (Printed) £5

1937 Jamboree, Wereld, Nederland. £30-£40

Peterborough. (Felt) £10

Hunts. (Felt) £10

Gwynedd. 15p

Leeds. £20 to £25

Manchester 15p

Guernsey (Felt) £10

Clydesdale. 25p

Suffolk. (Felt) £10

SCRIMSHAW

Scrimshaw work was a popular pastime for sailors aboard the big whaling ships of the 19th century. The work can best be described as extremely fine engraving on bone or ivory, the incised detail darkened down with black ink or soot.

Usually working on a whale's tooth, though sometimes on whalebone, the sailors most commonly chose a theme relating to life at sea but, just occasionally, one may come across a mildly erotic design.

Scrimshaw work is often mounted for display or used to embellish objects such as gongs, inkstands and a variety of small boxes.

A mid 19th century decorated panbone, 10in. wide. £600

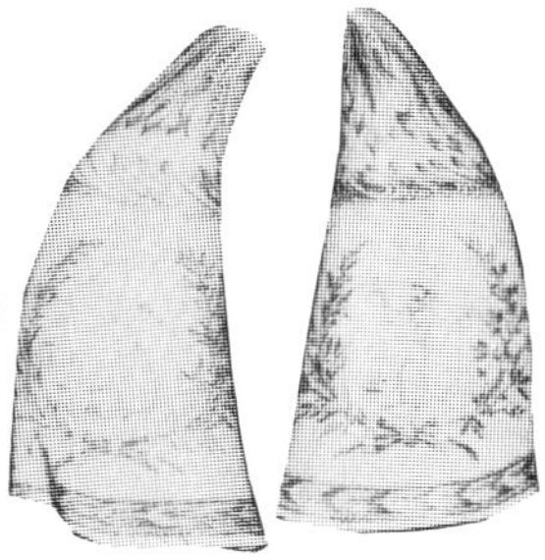

A pair of scrimshawed whale's teeth, well engraved, English, 1830-50, 7in. long. £1,500

The Unicorn Crimper made of scrimshaw. £12,675

Mid 19th century English whale's tooth scrimshaw decorated with a schooner in choppy seas, 6½in. long. £308

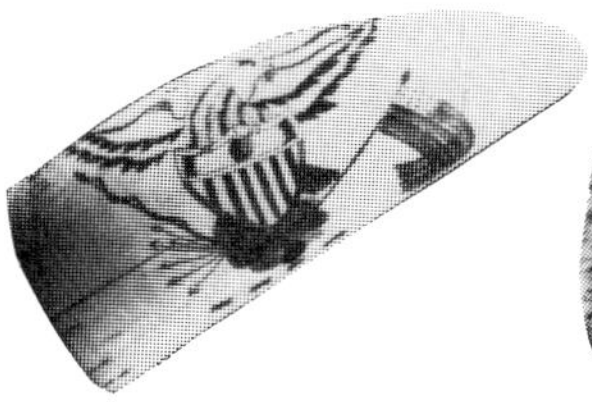

American 19th century engraved scrimshaw whale's tooth, 5¾in. long. (Christie's) £205

Mid 19th century American whale's tooth scrimshaw, decorated as an eagle's head, 5in long. £209

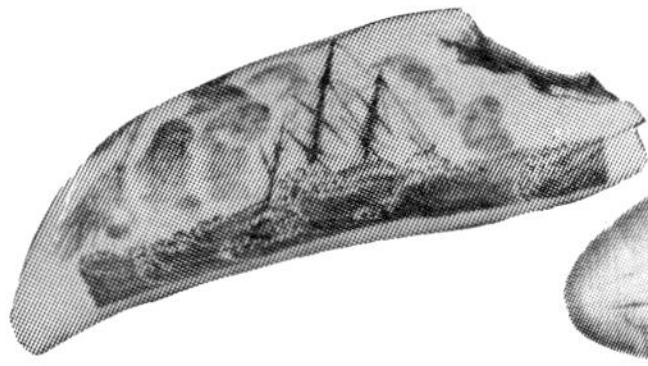

Mid 19th century well-scrimshawed whale's tooth 8½in long. £650

Mid 19th century whale's tooth scrimshaw, 6in long. £440

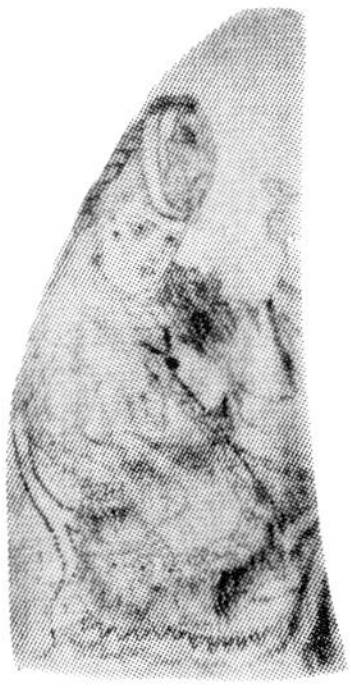

Mid 19th century English whale's tooth scrimshaw, showing a young girl, 6in high. £132

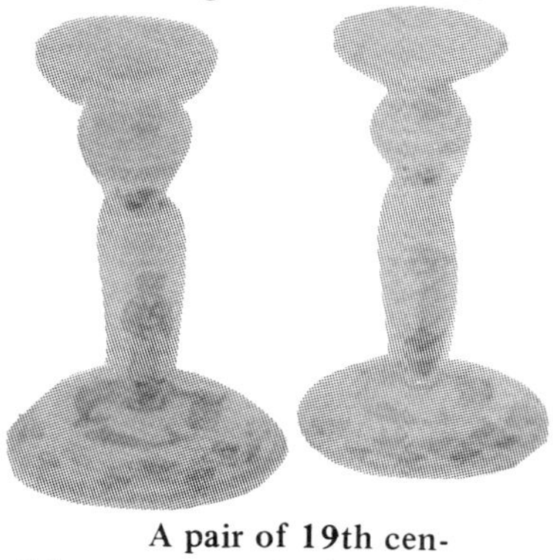

A pair of 19th century scrimshaw candlesticks, America, 4¾in. high. (Robt. W. Skinner Inc.) £608

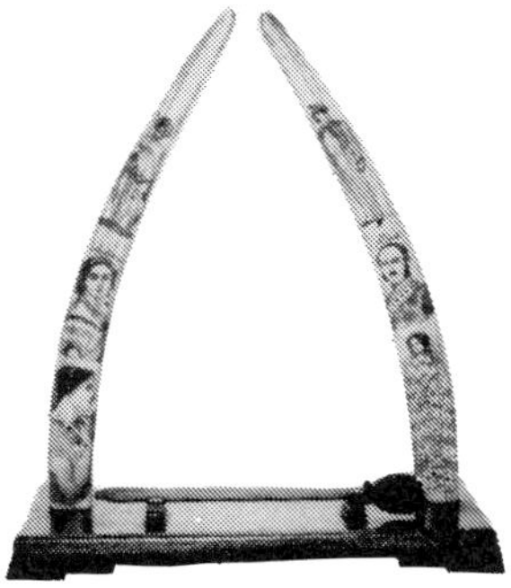

A pair of mid 19th century scrimshawed walrus tusks, English, 48cm. high. £750

An unusual pair of scrimshawed whale's teeth, circa 1840, 8in. high. £700

SERIES WARE

"Adorn yet serve some useful purpose" was the reasoning behind the very successful introduction of Series Ware which was the brain child of Charles J. Noke who joined Doulton's in 1889.
He realised that standard pottery shapes could be decorated with popular images and sold as 'novelty art wares' to the general public who were not able to afford the more expensive creations of individual artists.
Designs, many of them by Noke himself, were transfer printed onto plates, jugs, bowls, mugs and teasets. Refined earthenware or bone china was used and the transfer prints were handcoloured which gave the technique the name of 'print and tint'.
The first series issued was the 'Isthmian Games' in 1889 and it was followed by a new theme almost every year till World War Two.

A Royal Doulton Cecil Aldin Series ware jardiniere, the decoration from the 'Old English Scenes', 18cm. high. £170

Oliver Twist tankard in low relief, designed by C. J. Noke, issued 1949-1960. £60

Sir Roger de Coverley Series teapot, 5in. high, circa 1911, depicting Sir Roger in the garden. £55

Willow Pattern Series jar and cover, 6½in. high, circa 1912. £68

Royal Doulton Series ware coffee pot, 7½in. tall, D5506, 1934. £30

The Gleaners, Series ware sandwich tray. £30

Rural England (Welsh) Series, two-handled vase, 12½in. high, circa 1907, depicting a woman in traditional dress. £58

'Nightwatchman', a Series ware jug by C. J. Noke, 8½in. high, D1198, 1903. £38

SEVRES

King Louis XV established and partly financed the Sevres pottery factory at Vincennes in 1756. They produced a soft paste porcelain as well as hard paste imitation Chinese Ming dynasty eggshell porcelain which was a great success when it was shown at the Great Exhibition in London in 1851.

In 1876 the factory was removed to St Cloud and a great deal of experimentation was done in formulae and pastes which resulted in the discovery of a kaolin based paste which resembled the original Chinese formula and a silicate paste which provided a wide range of colours for decoration of the pieces.
Among the modellers employed by Sevres was the great sculptor Rodin and A. Leonard who made unglazed figures at the turn of the 20th century.

A Sevres ornithological circular sugar bowl and cover, blue interlaced L marks enclosing the date letter U for 1773 and painter's mark of Evans, 11.5cm. high. (Christie's) £540

One of a pair of late 19th century Sevres pattern metal mounted turquoise gound oviform vases, 84cm. high. (Christie's) £5,940

A Sevres biscuit group of The Judgement of Paris, circa 1781, 41cm. high. (Christie's) £1,404

A Sevres-pattern porcelain and ormolu mounted mantel clock, imitation interlaced L and initial marks, circa 1880, 61.5cm. high. (Christie's) £2,592

A Sevres bleu nouveau cylindrical coffee cup and saucer, blue interlaced L marks enclosing the date letters EE for 1782. (Christie's) £540

A pair of Sevres pattern square bottles and stoppers decorated with portraits of Louis XIV and Me. de Lamballe, circa 1880, 15.5cm. high. (Christie's) £1,080

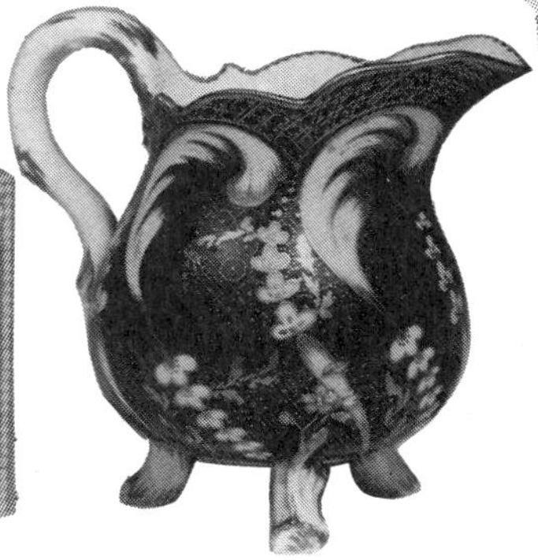

A Sevres bleu nouveau baluster milk jug, blue interlaced L mark enclosing the date letter q for 1769, and painter's mark B, 12cm. high. (Christie's) £432

A pair of large documentary Sevres seaux a bouteille with gilt-edged shell and scroll handles, blue interlaced L marks and with incised marks 7, nu and C 6, 18.5cm. high. (Christie's) £15,120

SEWING MACHINES

The first practical sewing machine was patented in America in 1845 by a machinist named Elias Howe. In the following years up to 1900 rival manufacturers produced many unusually shaped and interesting machines and these are the ones to collect. If the machine looks ordinary, it will be! The Singer Sewing Machine Company produced ten million machines by 1890 and many are still in use. A credit to Victorian technology but not always the most desirable of objects to collectors.

Appearances can be deceptive for some machines of the 1890's copied ideas patented in the 1860's. So be careful and look at machines in collections, read up on as much information as you can find and seek the unusual.

Beware of chipped paint and worn decoration as these cannot be replaced. However, rust is not a problem and neither is oily dirt, as both can be removed.

'The Challenge' lock-stitch machine made by the **Imperial Sewing Machine Co.** of Birmingham. Bears a registration mark of 1871 and a patent of 1874. Elaborately decorated with gilt and with elaborate brass face-plate, circa 1875. £70

Tiny Germany toy chain-stitch machine of pressed metal with elaborate floral decoration. This one pre-1914-18 war but the type made well into the 1920's. £25

'Howe' lock-stitch machine with rubber belt drive and lovely hand-painted floral and gilt decorations. No maker's address nor patent dates, but presumed by Howe Sewing Machine Co. circa 1876. £120

'Advance' lock-stitch machine, made in Germany and imported by **J. Collier & Son,** Clapham Road. Based on the 'Howe' machine and found under several trade names. Gilt transfer decoration, circa 1880. £40

'Prima Donna' lock-stitch machine with brass face-plate and slide-plates. Made by **Whight and Mann** of Ipswich but not so marked. No patent dates, circa 1875. £100

Small chain-stitch machine sold by **James Weir,** Soho Square, as the '55/- Sewing Machine'. Marble base, post 1872 and made in England by Weir but an exact pirated copy of earlier machines supplied to Weir but made in Canada by **Charles Raymond.** £60

SHAVING CREAM POT LIDS

The most common shaving cream pot lids are those produced by Boots the Chemist, as universal in Victorian times as they are today. Shaving cream pots were made by most large pottery companies with Doulton perhaps leading the field and they were sold on to the public by toiletry manufacturers, barbers and chemists. A few were made specially for hotels or men's clubs and some of those can still be found.

Lids with pictorial designs are the most expensive but the majority of them were printed in black and white, green and white or brown and white.

Examples of interesting lids include those sold by the famous West End barber, Trumpers, and the pretty painted ones sold by French toiletry manufacturer Roger and Gallet. Victorian men were particularly fond of shaving cream scented with almonds and one which advertised itself as being used by Prince Albert had a vast sale in the 1850's.

John Gosnell & Co. Ambrosial Shaving Cream, an early lid which changed the reference to Prince Albert after his death in 1861 to 'Patronized by the Nobility'. £50

Henri Freres, Creme D'-Amandes, Ambrosial, a French style lid with an attractive trade mark. £35

Ch. Jaschke's Shaving Cream, Regent St., London, decorated with a gold band. £20

Spratt's Perfect Shaving Cream, a small London lid complete with directions. £20

Carter's Imperial Shaving Cream, an unusual lid with white lettering in a black background. £40

Erasmic Shaving Cream, lid complete with matching pot. £25

Blondeay & Cie, Premier Vinolia Shaving Cream for Sensitive Skins, circa 1920. £25

Roger & Gallet, Creme de Savon, a French lid and pot printed in green. £15

Boots Creme D'Amande for Shaving, probably the most common shaving cream lid. £8

Muire Bouquet Shaving Cream, 'Does not dry on the skin', the French name had sales appeal. £35

Vachon-Bavoux & Cie, 'Creme de Savon', a French lid possibly only sold in France. £35

S. Maw, Son & Thompson, Ambrosial Shaving Cream, Perfumed with Almonds, small size. £25

SHAVING MUGS

The earliest recognisable shaving mugs date back to the 15th century but they were really just small bowls and shaving mugs did not reach the height of their glory until Victorian times. By 1930 they began to disappear because of the advent of the electric razor.
They were made of pottery, porcelain, brass, pewter, copper or silver and some were painted with flowers, fruit, were numbered or even bore the owner's name. Special occasions like Coronations always produced a rash of commemorative shaving mugs and Goss crested shaving mugs are highly sought after.
The rarest type found by collectors are 'four in ones' which held water, soap, a shaving brush and a razor all in separate compartments. 'Three in ones' were slightly less unusual but the most common were the simple mug with a sticking out lip for easy lathering of the brush. French shaving mugs were taller and thinner than those used in Britain and they did not have a handle.

Swan shaped shaving mug with gilt edging, circa 1900. £20–£30

Three in one shaving mug with a place for water, the soap and a brush, circa 1900. £18–£30

Victorian shaving mug with hand-painted floral decoration and gilt edging. £25–£40

Souvenir Coronation shaving mug for for H.M. King George VI and Queen Elizabeth. £15–£25

Large, late 19th century, shaving mug with floral decoration and gilt edging. £15–£25

Souvenir Coronation shaving mug for George V and Queen Mary. £15–£25

Late Victorian shaving mug decorated with floral sprays. £14–£20

Late Victorian pewter shaving mug with embossed floral decoration. £35–£55

Elegantly shaped white shaving mug decorated with pink floral sprays. £12–£20

SHOES

In the past, collectors have followed the history of footwear through collections of highly detailed replica boots and shoes originally designed as containers and made of silver, pewter, brass, porcelain and glass.

Today they are looking for the 'real thing'. Early or unusual examples are being snapped up at auction sales and more antique shops are making space to display footwear from all periods up to the 1940's.

Prices range from a few pounds to a thousand and more, depending on the appeal, rarity and condition of the goods. Late Victorian shoes and little satin low heeled slippers are fairly common and will cost about £25, and Edwardian leather strap shoes about £15.

A pair of lady's shoes of emerald green damask with low heels, mid 18th century. (Christie's) £250

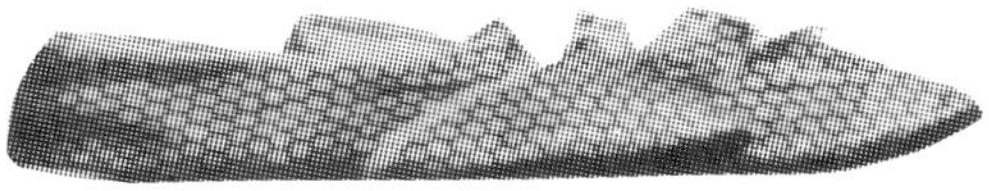

A pair of lady's flat heeled shoes of pink kid stencilled in black with a honeycomb design and bound with ivory satin, circa 1800-10. (Christie's) £320

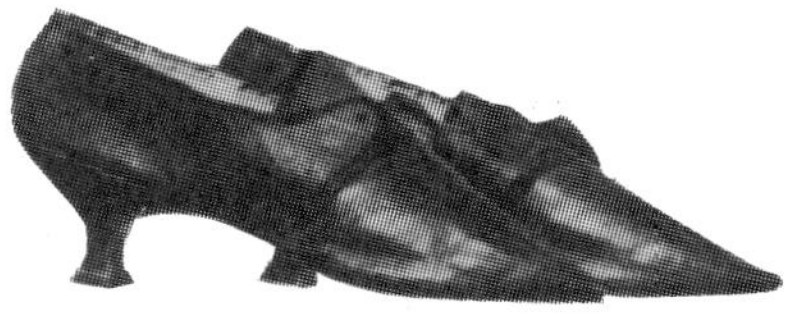

A pair of lady's high heeled shoes of black kid bound with black braid, circa 1785. (Christie's) £190

A pair of lady's shoes of ivory silk brocaded with sprays of pale green and yellow flowers with kid rands and heels, circa 1750. (Christie's) £600

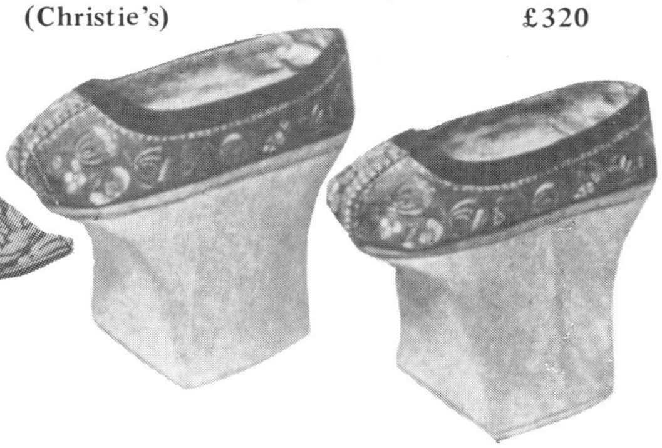

A pair of late 19th century Chinese lady's stilted shoes of red silk with blue silk border. (Phillips) £150

A pair of lady's high heeled shoes of ivory silk embroidered in silver thread, early 18th century. (Christie's) £480

A pair of lady's wedding shoes of ivory satin embroidered with silver thread, belonging to Margaret Gladstone, circa 1784. (Christie's) £450

A pair of lady's high-heeled shoes of royal blue velvet bound with blue braid, English, circa 1640. (Christie's) £8,000

A pair of 19th century tin anniversary skates with adjustable strap at ankle and foot, 9in. long. (Robt. W. Skinner Inc.) £376

SIGNED PHOTOGRAPHS

Collecting signed photographs on a limited budget is still possible and may even prove to be a profitable experience.

A new collector would be well advised to start at the lower end of the market, buying and selling in a comparitively safe area until he has made a few contacts, acquired some knowledge of the subject and learned to identify the mass produced machine signed copies circulating within the market. Many stars of the early cinema, music hall performers, even some of yesterdays' pop idols signed photographs which now change hands at between £1 and £10. This is an interesting area and valuable experience may be gained before moving up into a league where a fine photograph of Tchaikovsky, signed and inscribed by the composer, will fetch over £1,000.

Ronald Reagan, 40th President of the U.S.A., photograph of Reagan when a film star, signed and inscribed 'Good Luck', postcard 5½ x 3½in. £55

'Sincerely Yours, Hetty King, 1/7/07', male impersonator. £30

Field-Marshal Montgomery: photograph with Eisenhower, signed. £55

Piotr Ilyich Tchaikovsky, 1840-93, photograph, signed and inscribed in ink, in Russian, dated 2 May 1885, 159 x 102mm. £1,100

Virginia Woolf, leaf extracted from her passport bearing her photo and signature, both overstamped by the Foreign Office, 18th April, 1933. £170

'To Irene Jones, My best wishes, Ben Lyon, Bebe Daniels'. £12

Sir Winston Churchill, fine photograph of the young Churchill, signed on mount, 9 x 7½in. £250

'Nelson Eddy', signed photograph toether with original envelope. £15

SIGNED PHOTOGRAPHS

Pablo Picasso, full length photograph of Picasso in bathing trunks, signed in ballpoint, 7¼ x 5in. £150

Elvis Presley, photograph of Presley in military uniform in a car, signed in blue ballpoint, with another, 5½ x 3½in. £110

Charles Chaplin, good photograph in black and white signed in black ink. 10 x 8in. £140

Laurel and Hardy, good photograph of them in characteristic pose signed by both, 5 x 7in. £80

'My Best Wishes to you, Gertrude Lawrence'. £8

Johann Strauss, The Younger, carte de visite photograph, signed with an autograph musical quotation of four bars from 'The Blue Danube', framed and glazed. £825

Wilfred Rhodes: photograph of Rhodes in well-worn Yorkshire blazer, signed, 165 x 210mm., n.d. £35

Victoria, the official Diamond Jubilee photograph, signed and dated by the Queen, inscribed on the reverse by her private secretary, Sir Arthur Bigge, to the photographer Downey, 13 x 7½in., April 1897. £620

Robert Browning: Cabinet photograph of Browning, signed and dated 5 May 1886. £450

Mae West, photograph signed, inscribed 'To John Best Wishes Mae West', 10 x 8in. £19

Leo Tolstoy, postcard photograph signed in black ink in English script. £200

'To Miss Rene Jones, Best Wishes from Florie Forde, 1936'. £10

SILVER

Almost every family owns at least one item of silver, tucked away safely and only brought out for special occasions. The status this precious metal occupies is shown by the way it is chosen as the ideal present at times of great significance like births, weddings and 25th wedding anniversaries. The collecting of silver is a vast field because some people concentrate on place of origin – like Scottish provincial silver; on dates; makers like Bateman, Kandler or Ramsay; function of the piece – candlesticks and candelabra are very popular – or the quality of the decoration. Silver was used for as wide a variety of items from walking stick tops or picture frames to embossed wine coolers and vast table centrepieces.

Prices range just as much because a Victorian silver christening mug and spoon may sell for around £100 while presentation pieces like racing cups can soar into six figures. Prices vary according to the weight of the silver used and over the years this has fluctuated considerably as the price of bullion rises and falls. However, a piece of silver by a master craftsman or woman and from an interesting period will always sell for far more than its bullion value.

A George III shaped circular salver, by James Ellis & Co., Sheffield, 1818, 25.8cm. diam., 23.5oz. (Lawrence Fine Art) £308

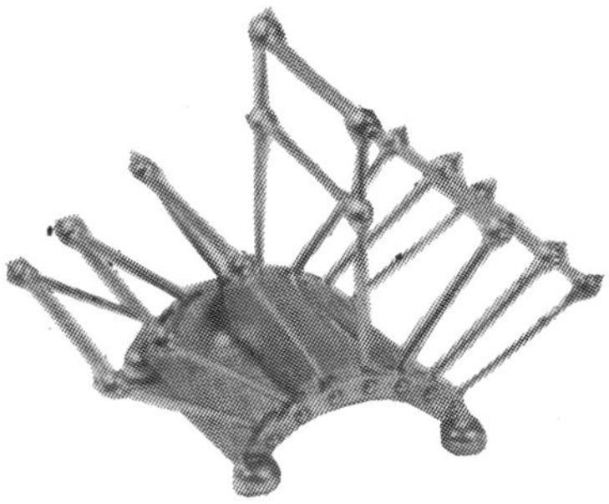

A Hukin & Heath electroplated letter rack designed by Dr. C. Dresser, stamped H & H 2555 and registration lozenge for May 1881, 12.3cm. high. (Christie's) £280

A French Christening set, post 1838 guarantee, with maker's mark of Veyrant, 8.8oz. of weighable silver. (Lawrence Fine Art) £352

A George III plain circular tea kettle, stand and burner, the kettle by H. Bateman, 1783, the stand and burner by Chas. S. Harris, 1881, 63oz. (Christie's) £1,080

A late 19th century English silvered bronze group of a jockey on horseback, signed and dated J. Willis Good, 1875, 27cm. high.(Christie's) £2,500

An Art Nouveau silver photograph frame, stamped maker's marks W.N. and Chester hallmarks for 1903, 22.3cm. high. (Christie's) £300

George III chamber candlestick, by John Crouch and Thos. Hannam, London, 9oz. (Bermondsey) £400

A George III sugar basket, by Abraham Peterson, 1795, 17cm. across. (Lawrence Fine Art) £352

A pair of George III silver circular salts, maker possibly S. C. Young & Co., Sheffield, 1813, 3½in. diam., and a pair of salt spoons. (Edgar Horn) £310

A silver sugar box and scoop of scuttle form, maker's mark S.D.L.D., London, 1911, 17½oz. (Parsons, Welch & Cowell) £390

Three pieces from a dressing table set, die stamped with foliage in the Art Nouveau style, Chester 1903/04/05, by W. Neale. (Lawrence Fine Art) £77

George III silver mustard pot, by Edward Capper, London, 1797, 3¾in. high. (Bermondsey) £225

A 19th century Indian silver deep bowl, 8½in. diam., 33 troy oz. approx. (Robt. W. Skinner Inc.) £291

A George III oval epergne, 1802, maker's mark IP, probably for Joseph Preedy, with cut glass bowl, 10in. high, 38oz. (Christie's) £1,512

A George II plain baluster mug, London, 1733, 13cm. high, 11oz. (Christie's) £275

A tazza designed by Georg Jensen, stamped 1921, G J 830 S 263, 18.8cm. high, 16oz.5dwt. (Christie's) £972

A George III pear-shaped coffee pot, by Francis Butty and Nicholas Dumee, London, 1765, 11½in. high, 31.75oz. gross. (Christie's) £800

A pair of crocus-shaped embossed silver vases with leaf decoration, 6¼in. high. (Dacre, Son & Hartley) £100

An early Victorian silver bellied body teapot, by W. R. Smily, London, 1852, 6½in. high. (Edgar Horn) £170

A Liberty & Co. silver biscuit box with Birmingham hallmarks for 1902, 20oz.14dwt., 14cm. high. (Christie's) £432

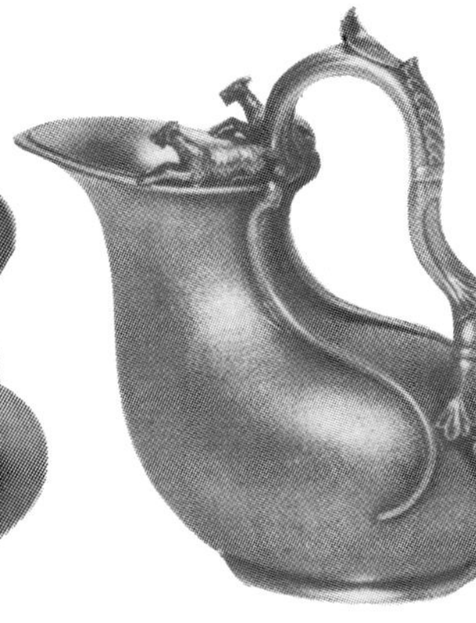

A Victorian 'ascos' jug, by Hunt & Roskell, 1844, 33.25oz. (Phillips) £1,350

A George IV claret jug, maker's mark probably that of Joseph Angell, 1829, 29cm. high, 31oz. (Lawrence Fine Art) £1,650

An Indian circular sugar bowl and cover on four fluted lion's paw supports, by Davd. Hare, Calcutta, circa 1820, 6½in. high, 21oz. (Christie's) £2,592

A pair of George III circular decanter stands, by Thomas Robinson I, London, 1809. (Christie's) £940

A George IV kitchen nutmeg grater with tongue and dart borders, by Charles Rawlings, 1824. (Phillips) £420

Pair of George III table candlesticks, London marks of 1776 overstriking the original Sheffield marks, 27.9cm. high. (Lawrence Fine Art) £528

A Regency egg cruet with six matching egg cups, London, 1820, together with six George IV eggspoons, by Eley & Fearn, London, 1824, 32oz. (Woolley & Wallis) £820

An Arts & Crafts Movement chalice in medieval style, by Omar Ramsden & Alwin Carr, London, 1912, 5.2in. high, 10oz. all in. (Christie's) £760

A George III oval tea caddy, by Thos. Phipps and Edward Robinson II, 1784, 12.4cm. high, 12.4oz. (Lawrence Fine Art) £990

An Elizabeth I plain wine cup, engraved 'The Towne of Wollterton, 1568', by Peter Peterson, Norwich, 5¼in. high, 6oz. (Christie's) £3,456

A George III plain, inverted, pear shaped cream jug, London, 1774, 11cm. high. (Christie's) £75

A two-handled shaped oval soup tureen and cover, by Elkington & Co., Birmingham, 1909, 126oz. (Christie's) £3,240

One of a pair of mid 18th century style three-branch candelabra, with scrolling branches, 10¾in. high, 75oz. (Christie's) £900

One of a pair of pounce pots, by John McKay, Edinburgh, 1798, 3oz. (Worsfolds) £230

A German silver gilt beaker, by J. P. Hofler, Nuremberg, circa 1690, 3¾in. high, 4oz. 17dwt. (Christie's) £864

An Indian tapering cylindrical tankard, by Robert Hamilton, Calcutta, circa 1812, 6in. high, 19oz.8dwt. (Christie's) £2,376

One of a pair of wine coolers, stamped Georg Jensen GI 925S 289, 9.8cm. high, 29oz. 9dwt. (Christie's) £3,780

A plain cylindrical sugar caster with domed cover, by Goldsmiths & Silversmiths Co., London, 1911, 7¼in. high, 11.50oz. (Christie's) £150

A Victorian electroplated tea urn with domed cover, 58cm. high. (Lawrence Fine Art) £704

A William IV silver gilt vine leaf fruit dish. by John Watson, Sheffield 1834, 12in. wide, 29oz. (Christie's) £2,160

A Queen Anne plain tapering cylindrical chocolate pot, by Nathaniel Lock, 1708, 8¾in. high, 18oz.18dwt. gross. (Christie's) £2,916

A vase shaped ewer, by B. C. Frobisher, circa 1816-25, 11.1/8in. high, 25oz. (Christie's) £658

SNUFF BOTTLES

Chinese snuff bottles usually resemble small vases about 6cm. (2½in.) high, and are made of a variety of materials including porcelain, ivory, jade, cloisonne, horn, agate, glass and bronze. Most sought after, and therefore most expensive are those made of porcelain from the late 17th and early 18th century, closely followed by carved hardstone such as agate, quartz and amethyst. A guide to quality, although it is not infallible, is the size of the hole in the neck (the smaller the better) and the degree of hollowing out – those with a large interior being the best. This also applies to glass bottles which were generally carved out of a solid piece as opposed to being blown.

An inside painted glass rounded square snuff bottle with jade stopper. (Christie's) £378

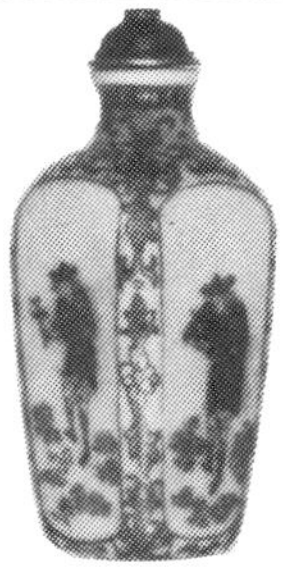

A porcelain tapering square snuff bottle with green glass stopper. (Christie's) £432

An agate rounded rectangular bottle with acorn finial. (Christie's) £345

A five-colour overlay glass disc snuff bottle with glass stopper. (Christie's) £378

A jasper rounded square snuff bottle with matching stopper.(Christie's) £1,080

An agate rounded square snuff bottle with turquoise stopper. (Christie's) £702

Chinese 19th century white jade snuff bottle, 2¾in. high. (Robt. W. Skinner Inc.) £100

An inside painted rock crystal rounded rectangular snuff bottle, dated 1919, with blue glass stopper. (Christie's) £194

A white jade disc-shaped globular bottle with coral glass stopper. (Christie's) £3,780

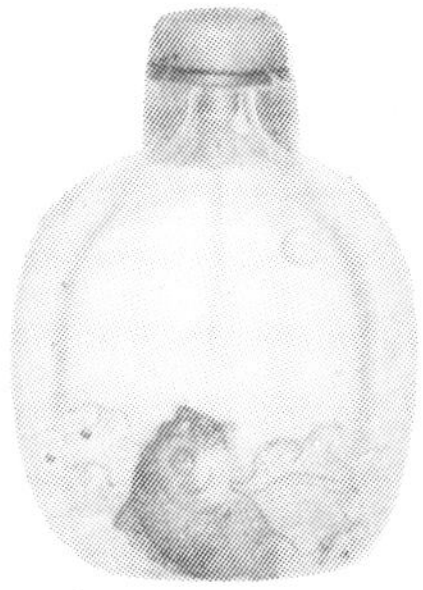

A rock crystal rounded rectangular flattened snuff bottle with mottled green jade stopper. (Christie's) £2,808

A Suzhou style chalcedony snuff bottle carved with a monkey, 1750/1850, tourmaline stopper. £286

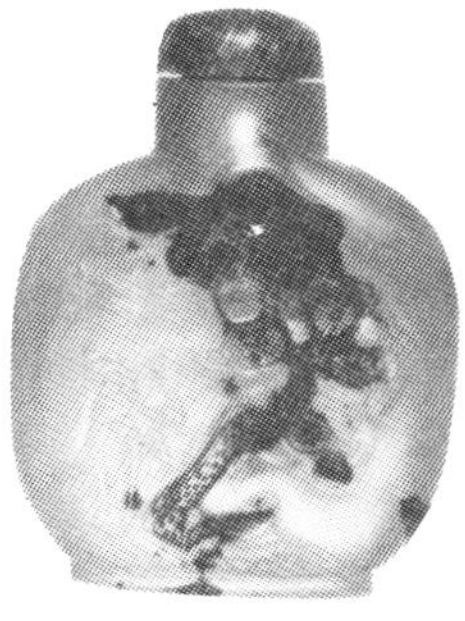

An agate rounded square snuff bottle with lapis lazuli stopper.(Christie's) £486

SNUFF BOXES

They come in all shapes and sizes and made from many materials including gold, silver, tortoiseshell, papier mache, and enamel ware. Like the vinaigrette, many have gilt interiors. Generally the lids are decorated and here the variety is infinite. They may be painted, inset with semi-precious stones or inlaid with contrasting materials. Those ornamented with representations of the famous castles, 'castle-tops', are particularly desirable boxes, notably that of Windsor Castle by Nathaniel Mills.
Unusual examples have two compartments so that snuff can be separated into grades and a most uncommon box may have a watch inset in one section.

An early Victorian castle top snuff box, by N. Mills, Birmingham, 1838, 7.2cm. long. (Lawrence Fine Art) £396

A silver gilt cartouche-shaped snuff box, probably German, circa 1760. £500

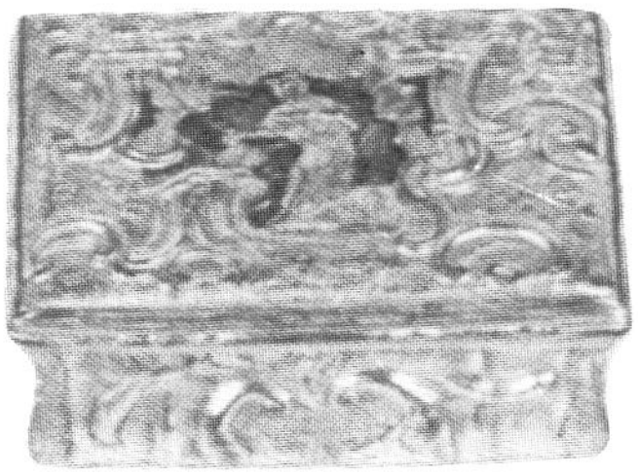

An English gilt metal and aventurine snuff box, probably Birmingham, mid 18th century, 2½in. wide. £198

19th century circular snuff box set in the cover with a micro mosaic of Pliny's doves of Venus, 2.7/8in. diam.(Christie's) £702

A George IV tortoiseshell snuff box in the form of a tortoise, by T. Wallis & J. Hayne, London, 1820, 3¼in. long. £2,310

An English oval pressed horn snuff box, by John Obrisset, 1712, the lid decorated with the arms of Sir Francis Drake, oval 4in. £286

An Italian rectangular silver gilt mounted hardstone snuff box, by Giacomo Sirletti, Rome, 1811-36, 3½in. long. (Christie's) £3,132

An early 18th century oval mounted tortoiseshell snuff box, impressed with a portrait of Queen Anne and signed 'OB' for Obrisset, circa 1710. (Phillips) £200

A late 18th century Italian silver gilt circular snuff box, Venice, circa 1770, 5.6cm. diam. (Phillips) £250

A shallow tortoiseshell snuff box, circa 1740, possibly French, 3.1/8in. wide. (Christie's) £702

A George II silver gilt fox mask snuff box, by T. Phipps & E. Robinson, 1807, 3¼in., 3oz. 10dwt. (Christie's) £2,160

An oval baluster form snuff box, by Charles Murray, Perth, circa 1830, 2¼in. high. £825

SOUVENIRS

Although people travelled to a limited degree it was not until about 1880, when trains and paddlesteamers made the journey easier, that people started flocking to the seaside.

Wages and working conditions had improved greatly during the previous decade, and with sea bathing being made respectable, nay beneficial by Victoria, the resorts were packed throughout the summer. Added to this were the daytrippers, all seeking some little momento to take home for their friends, which meant a massive growth in the souvenir business.

Although they had been made on a commercial scale since the opening of the Thames Tunnel in 1843, and given a boost by the Great Exhibition of 1851, it was W. H. Goss, with his little porcelain urns and vases bearing Coats-of-Arms, who really took advantage of the market.

An unusual six-sided brass seal depicting views of London, circa 1845, ¾in. sq. £25

Souvenir shaving mug by W. H. Goss, 4in. tall. £36

Souvenir ashtray by W. H. Goss. £10

Shakespeare's cottage by W. H. Goss. £70

Souvenir Pixie jug from 'St. Columb Minor'. £1

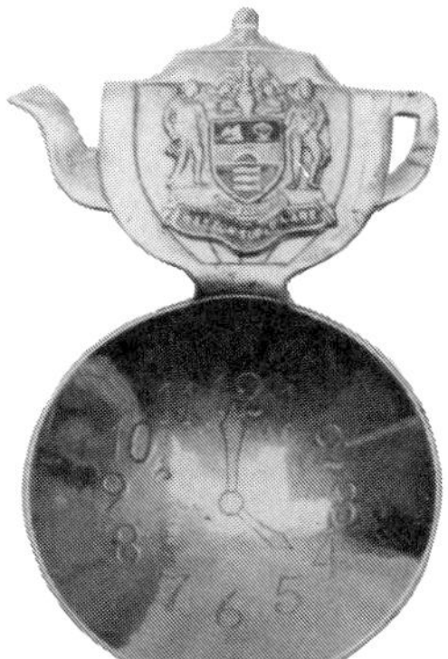

Weston-super-Mare brass caddy spoon. £1

Souvenir plate from Lerwick with a pierced edge. £8

A Lowestoft 'trifle' mug with scrolling handle, 3½in. high, circa 1795. £935

Souvenir toby jug 'A Present from Ludlow', 6in. high. £2

1950's Oriental souvenir cushion cover. £2

Souvenir match holder from Brentford. £7

Leather souvenir jewellery box, 'Anstey's Cove Torquay'. £4

STAFFORDSHIRE

If you stand in the car park in the centre of Stoke and turn full circle, you will be confronted by numerous chimneys emblazoned with the household names of the most famous potteries. Drive a few miles and the road signs tell of Fenton, Longton, Hanley, Burslem, Tunstall and Burmantofts, all familiar names to collectors of Staffordshire pottery. At one time there were over four hundred factories going full blast to meet the insatiable demand of the Victorians to have a pottery figure covering every available surface.

Most are press moulded and decorated in underglaze blue and black with touches of colour in overglaze enamel and gilding. Early examples have closed bases or sport a small hole in the base, while 20th century pieces are usually slip cast in Plaster of Paris moulds and are open ended.

Vast quantities of these earthenware figures were produced from around 1850 right up until the First World War. They are referred to as Staffordshire figures although many were produced at factories in the north of England and in Scotland.

A Staffordshire Toby jug of conventional type, seated holding a frothing jug of ale, circa 1780, 24.5cm. high. (Christie's) £432

A Staffordshire part tea service printed in grey monochrome with bust and other portraits of Wellington. (Christie's) £280

A group of Napoleon III and Empress Eugenie, the oval base named in gilt moulded capitals, circa 1854, 12in. high. (Christie's) £160

A money box modelled as a chapel, inscribed Salley Harper Hougate March 16th 1845, 6¾in. high. (Christie's) £450

A figure of a huntsman, holding a hunting horn in his right hand, circa 1795, 9¼in. high. (Christie's) £170

A Staffordshire jug depicting Wellington at Salamanca, 5½in. high. (Christie's) £90

An Obadiah Sherratt group of Polito's menagerie, circa 1830, 29.5cm. high. (Christie's) £16,200

STANDS

If you are one of those happy souls whose habit it is to arrive home late on rainy evenings with muddy boots, library book in one hand, a walking stick in the other, rubber plant and fruitcake clutched to your chest and umbrella held aloft in a vain attempt to keep your new hat dry; and if, when you do arrive home so encumbered, you find that the power workers have called a lightning blackout and you have to grope your way about in candle-light – just relax. All you need is a collection of appropriate stands and your problems are over.

There are candlestands, plant stands, reading and music stands, cake stands, kettle stands, umbrella stands, hat stands, boot stands, shaving stands, even wig stands. Such was the ingenuity of past craftsmen and designers that there is a purpose built stand for just about everything from whips to cricket bats.

An 18th century mahogany adjustable knee rest, 13¼in. £242

A 19th century mahogany whip and boot rack, 39½in. £110

A Regency rosewood duet music stand, the pierced top filled with lyres. (Christie's) £702

A Chippendale mahogany birdcage candlestand with a dished and moulded circular tilt top, 1760-90, 23½in. diam. (Christie's) £3,208

A Swiss carved pine umbrella stand in the form of a standing bear, 4ft.9in. high, circa 1900. £462

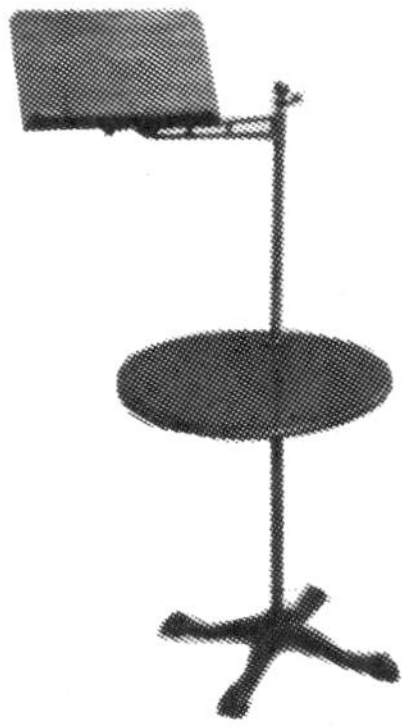

Victorian oak and cast-iron reading bracket and circular table. (Butler & Hatch Waterman) £95

Unusual Victorian music stand with papier-mache top inlaid with mother-of-pearl, circa 1850. £660

Gustav Stickley oak plant stand, circa 1903, 28in. high. (Robt. W. Skinner Inc.) £500

STEVENGRAPHS

When the government of 1860 removed the ban on imported silk goods, it had a disastrous effect on the weavers of Coventry, forcing many of them out of business. It did, however, spur on a certain Thomas Stevens to try out some of his new ideas. By adapting his looms to weave small, multi-coloured pictures and bookmarks instead of the traditional ribbons, he found instant, overwhelming success. He also produced Christmas, birthday and Valentine cards, plus calendars, sashes and badges, all of which were offered to a totally new market, since they were sold through booksellers and fancy goods shops.

Stevens travelled to trade fairs all over Britain, Europe and America taking along with him portable looms so that visitors could watch the production at first hand and buy whatever took their fancy. The response in America was so favourable that he went on to export great quantities of pictures which explains why there are so many excellent collections in that country today.

Although a variety of woven silk pictures can be found, those by Stevens usually bear the inscription 'woven in pure silk by Thomas Stevens, Coventry' printed on the front of the mount.

Thomas Stevens died in 1888, leaving the business to his two sons. Their products continued to be popular until the outbreak of the First World War but, although they continued to turn out a few portraits after that time, main production became geared to the manufacture of hatbands and the like. The firm survived until 1940, when the factory was completely demolished in the blitz.

'H.R.H. Prince of Wales', facing left with flags below. £45

'Charles Stewart Parnell M.P.', with yellow harp and clover leaves below portrait. £35

'Rt. Hon. W. E. Gladstone MP', looking ahead with sprays of thistles and roses. £20

'For Life or Death', Heroism on Land, a horse drawn fire engine. £45

'R.M.S. Orcoma', postcard in fair condition. £20

'The Finish', the same scene as **'The Struggle'** renamed after 1879. £35

'S.S. Columbia' Hands across the Sea, postcard. £10

'International Exhibition', Glasgow 1888, original mount. £60

STONEWARE

The production of saltglazed stoneware had been carried on at Lambeth for centuries when John Doulton first went into the pottery business there in 1815.
At first his firm continued the prevalent output of cheap mass produced items like bottles, jugs and barrels and it was not until John's son Henry joined the business that more complex modelling and detail began to be introduced.
It was Henry who diversified into architectural stoneware and who started to turn his Lambeth Pottery into a centre for the production of decorative stoneware.
In 1866 he took into the company a group of students from the Lambeth School of Art and in the Paris Exhibition of 1867 their work was highly acclaimed.
The people who produced decorative stoneware at this time included the three famous Barlows, Frank Butler, George Tinworth and many others including women like Eliza Simmance.

A biscuit barrel with plate cover and mounts, the sides painted in pate-sur-pate with four cockatoos, r.m., 1886, 5½in. high. £130

A jug with incised green and yellow plants with blue flowers, c.m., 1878, 7¼in. high. £110

A cream jug and sugar bowl with an incised frieze of rabbits above green and blue leaves, c.m., 1880, 1886, 4½in. high. £380

A cylindrical jug with a dark brown glaze and applied flower heads, blue triangles and white beads, c.m., 1878, 6¾in. high. £85

A water filter with incised, carved and applied decoration on a buff bround, DSL, 14½in. high. £120

A large pair of vases, each with an incised frieze of wolves and their cubs amongst foliage, r.m., 1885, 16½in. high. £520

A golfing jug, sprigged in white, with the panels of the 'Last Ball', 'Putting' and 'Driving', impressed Lambeth mark, circa 1880, 20cm. high. £280

A monkey group inscribed 'A United Family', sitting on a bench and sheltering under an ochre umbrella, r.m. & e., circa 1892, 5in. high. £850

SWEET CIGARETTE PACKETS

The special packages produced in the early part of the 20th century and designed to contain chocolate cigarettes are probably the most sought after by collectors. Names to look for in these pre war issues are Fry's with 'Campaign', Lyons, Maynards and Clarnico.

Following World War II the popular sugary sweet cigarettes were sold loose and it was not until the mid 1950's that we see any great variety in packet designs. Subsequent to the 'Coronation' series of 1953 and the 'Olympics' issue of 1956 there were new and colourful designs appearing every week.

Eager to promote sales the manufacturers took their themes from popular children's television programmes, depicting action packed scenes from current favourites such as Wagon Train, The Lone Ranger, Wyatt Earp and Hawkeye. Science Fiction was also well represented with Star Trek, Thunderbirds and Fireball XL5. Barratt & Co. issued a series of Walt Disney characters featuring the much loved Mickey Mouse and Snow White and these always command a high price.

The quantity of the packet contents varied with 5, 6, 7, 10, 20 and 25's being generally available and – joy of joy's – a presentation pack of 50 appearing around Christmas.

Probably because the packet was designed to imitate the 'real' tobacco version, new E.E.C. regulations stipulate that this confection should now bear the name 'Candy Stick' leaving us with little or no trace of the old favourite 'Sweet Cigarette'.

Buccaneer, Cadet Sweets, 1957. £5

The World of Ships (ships printed on reverse), Sweetule Products, set of 24. £50 set

Snow White, Barratt & Co., 1930's. £15

Wyatt Earp, Como Confectionery Co., 1962. £5

Star Trek, Primrose Confectionery, 1971. £3

Olympic Achievement, Comet Sweets 1956, set of 22. £25 set

SWORDS

From earlist times, a man's sword stood for a great deal, not only was it used for protection but it signified his status and his pride. It is significant that the most popular item of booty has always been a sword and handing it over was symbolic of defeat. Mementoes of campaigns far back in history can still be found hanging in the homes of the victors. Collectors today can buy Japanese swords taken during the 1939-45 war which have blades many hundreds of years old and prized by the owners' family so highly that they were passed down through the generations. These blades were often signed by the craftsmen who forged them.

There are swords in collections from Turkish campaigns, from the Crimea, from the Napoleonic Wars and the U.S. Civil War – in fact from almost any war since recorded history began. Warriors were buried with their swords and the engraving on a sword blade and the elaboration of its hilt gave a clue to the importance of the man who carried it. Recently the finely carved ivory lion's head hilt of a Shamsir sword ensured that it sold for £3,200 at auction.

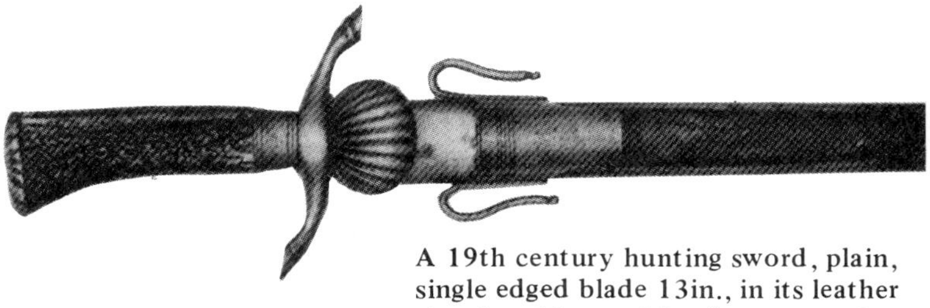

A 19th century hunting sword, plain, single edged blade 13in., in its leather sheath, with provision for companion knife. (Wallis & Wallis) £60

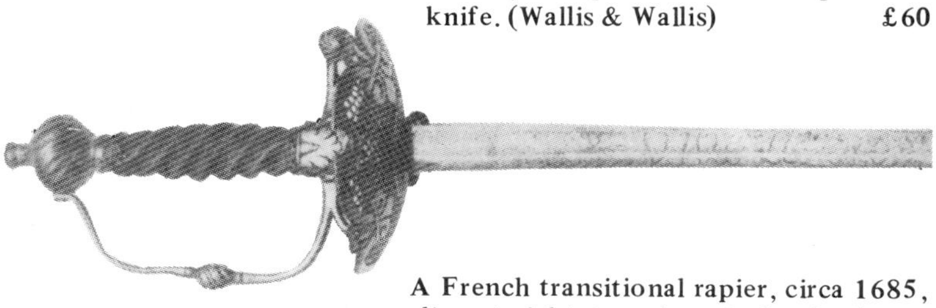

A French transitional rapier, circa 1685, slim, straight, tapering, single edged blade 37in. (Wallis & Wallis) £400

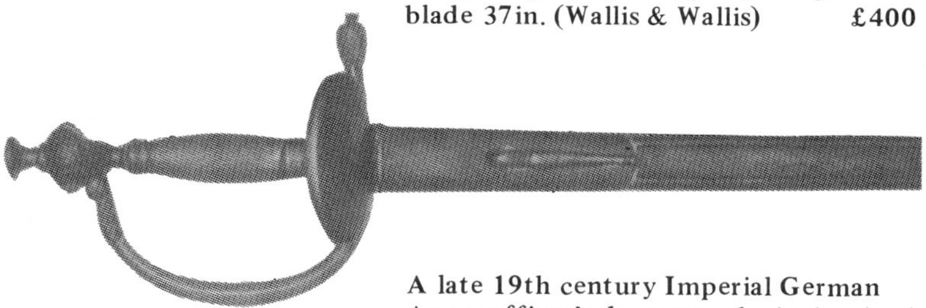

A late 19th century Imperial German Army officer's dress sword, single edged blade 32in., by E. & H. Peekhaus. (Wallis & Wallis) £115

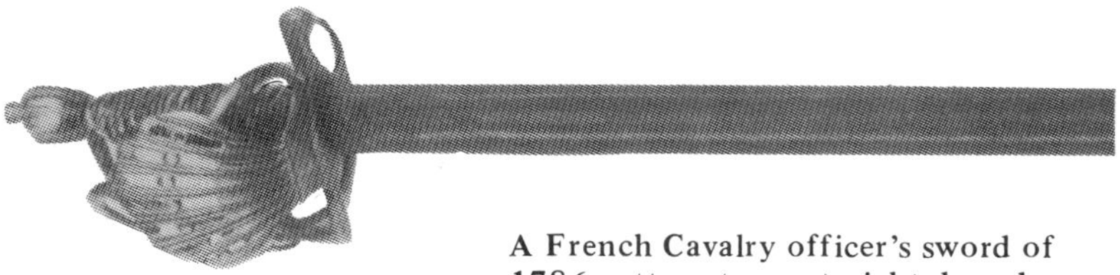

A French Cavalry officer's sword of 1786 pattern type, straight, broad single fullered, single edged blade 38in., with false edge. (Wallis & Wallis) £190

A wakizashi, the red lacquered scabbard simulating cherry bark, fitted with a gilt kogai and shakudo-nanakoji kozuka, 16th century, 34.2cm. (Christie's) £4,104

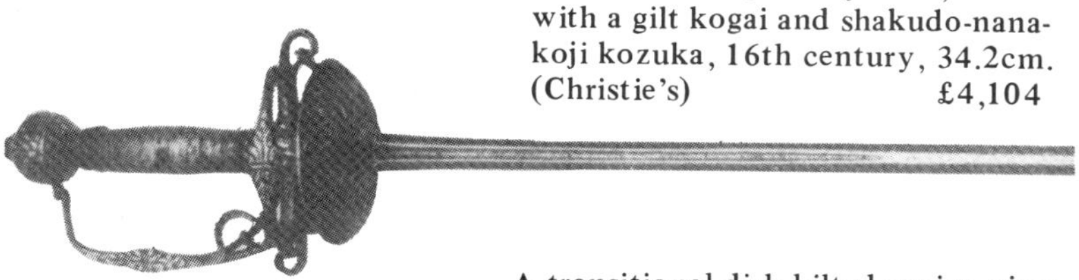

A transitional dish hilted rapier, circa 1630, slender blade 41½in., stamped Sebastian Hernantis in the fullers. (Wallis & Wallis) £330

TAXIDERMY

Taxidermy was not perfected technically until the beginning of the 19th century. The interest in collecting and preserving birds and animals increased as the century progressed, coinciding with a general awakening of interest in natural history until, by the 1880's, almost every town and village in the country had its own taxidermist. The interest began to wane shortly before the Great War, and did not return until the 1960's, since which time cased taxidermy has become steadily more collectible.

The quality of the work produced during the heyday of taxidermy (1860-1914) varied enormously, but it is only the top quality work which has any real value today, and this represents perhaps less than 5% of all that was actually produced.

Although it is not essential, it is a good idea to look for the taxidermist's label which is usually placed inside or on the back of the case. Variations include Peter Spicer of Leamington who, for example, incorporated a signed pebble into the groundwork of his cases. Condition is of prime importance: taxidermy specimens are notoriously susceptible to attacks from moths and beetles.

The quality of the taxidermy and case setting is equally important: the bird or mammal must be mounted in a lifelike manner and be set in an artistic but appropriate simulation of its natural habitat. Within these limits, each taxidermist evolved his own particular and distinctive style, and the very best cases are today recognised as works of art.

The photographs chosen are mostly items from the top end of the market, and the prices, which are considered to be the current market values for each case, reflect this.

Pair of albino pheasants by G. White of Salisbury, circa 1900. £100

Domestic pigeon in dome, 1922. £50

Fox mask on shield by Peter Spicer & Sons, circa 1920. £50

Pair of grey squirrels by Rowland Ward of London, circa 1900. £100

Pair of Arctic hares by J. Hutchings of Aberystwyth, circa 1905. £125

Golden eagle by Macpherson of Inverness, circa 1900. £300

TEAPOTS

Teapots dating from early in the 18th century will always command high prices for at first the famous leaf was an incredibly expensive luxury supped only by the very wealthy. Teapots of this period are accordingly very rare and of a high quality.

The duty on tea was reduced dramatically midway through the 18th century, considerably increasing its popularity which continued, unabated, throughout the 19th century.

Teapots have therefore been made in every conceivable shape, style and material for a very long time and as a result any would-be collector will need to be pretty discriminating, sticking strictly to a chosen type – be it Staffordshire barge teapots at under £100 to early saltglaze examples costing over £1,000.

A stoneware teapot and cover by Lucie Rie, covered in a matt manganese glaze, circa 1958, 15cm. high. (Christie's) £324

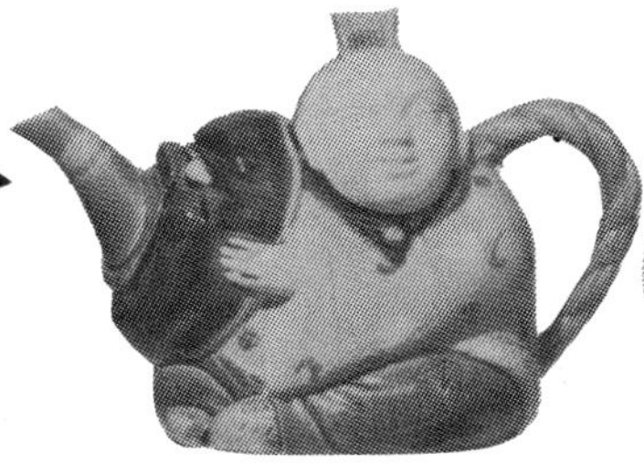

A Minton teapot modelled as a Chinaman holding a mask from which the spout projects, circa 1875, 14.4cm. high. (Christie's) £540

A Royal Worcester aesthetic teapot and cover, modelled as the upper part of a body, 15.5cm. high. (Christie's) £756

A Wedgwood creamware globular teapot and cover, painted in the manner of David Rhodes, circa 1768, 15cm. high. (Christie's) £2,052

An 18th/19th century Kakiemon type mokkogata teapot with shallow domed cover and arch-shaped handle, 19cm. long. (Christie's) £918

A Satsuma miniature teapot, signed on base, 4in. high. (Reeds Rains) £320

A Meissen teapot and cover, decorated in cisele gold, 12cm. high, red lustre workman's cross mark, 1725. (Lawrence Fine Art) £6,050

A Linthorpe teapot, the design attributed to Dr. C. Dresser, 21.3cm. high. (Christie's) £118

TEDDY BEARS

President Reagan has one, so has Princess Anne, together with Enoch Powell and Pope John Paul, although his stays in the Vatican. Mrs Thatcher's is called Humphrey and he often raises money for charity and Lord Bath's friend called Clarence wears spectables. Arctophily is the name of the game – they all have bears.

Margaret Steiff, a crippled dressmaker, is credited with making the first bear about 1900, but it wasn't until Teddy Roosevelt refused to shoot a bear on an organised hunt (it was, after all, tied to a stake by someone eager to please) that the Teddy Bear really took off in popularity.

Early bears have a hump on the back, jointed arms, head and legs and are generally stuffed with straw. The best have glass or button eyes and come complete with a growl.

Most early bears are often described as 'well loved' which is why those in good condition will always command a premium.

A long plush-covered teddy bear with black button eyes, with Steiff button in the ear, 25in. high. (Christie's) £1,300

A golden plush-covered musical teddy bear, playing Sonny Boy by Al Jolson, 20in. high, circa 1930. (Christie's) £550

A golden plush covered teddy bear, the front unhooking to reveal a metal hot water bottle, by Steiff, 17in. high.(Christie's) £1,100

A Steiff blonde plush teddy bear, with metal disc in left ear, 17in. high. (Lawrence Fine Art) £990

A teddy bear of grey plush with brown button eyes, embroidered nose, hump back and long paws, 13in. high. (Christie's) £320

A Steiff pale plush teddy bear with black thread stitched nose and straw stuffed body, with button in left ear, 33cm. high. (Phillips) £500

German teddy bear by Steiff of pale plush colour, renewed pads, snout and nose, circa 1909. (Phillips) £1,100

A plush-covered teddy bear with round ears, button eyes, pronounced hump and long paws, probably by Steiff, 21in. high. (Christie's) £300

THIMBLES

Thimbles date back to Roman times; and since then have been made of gold, silver, bronze, brass, pewter, iron, porcelain, enamel, ivory, bone, wood and leather.

Very early thimbles are rare and valuable and few on the market today date from earlier than the turn of the 18th/19th century. Up to the late 19th century silver thimbles were not always hall marked but, it may be useful for identification purposes to note that, before the middle of the seventeenth century, thimbles were hand punched and show irregularity in the indentations.

The growing interest in thimbles has led to an escalation of current values but, condition is all important if a high price is to be fetched. If the tops are perished to any extent this will detract from the value.

Goss china thimble 'Heckington'. £15

Chelsea thimble in hinged silver filagree case, circa 1700. £1,200

Near East, silver thimble, circa 1910. £18

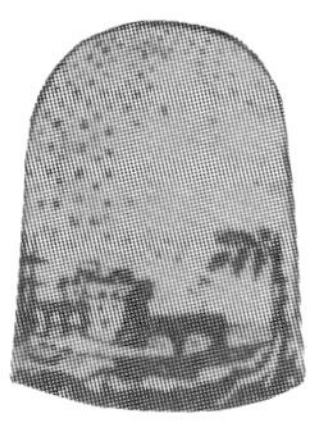

Meissen thimble decorated in Schwarzlot and gold by I. Preissler. £4,250

Silver 'stone top' thimble, circa 1890. £33

A fine filagree silver thimble, circa 1800. £250

Filagree silver thimble, circa 1800. £250

Dorcas silver thimble, size 5, circa 1890. £12

Silver thimble containing a bottle, circa 1800. £300

Elizabeth II coronation thimble. £78

Pewter thimble depicting the 'House of Commons' and 'Big Ben £5

Great Exhibition 1862 thimble. £168

Mrs. Thatcher re-election thimble. £20

Patent guard silver thimble. £45

Coral and silver thimble, circa 1880. £48

TOBACCO TINS

Cigarette and tobacco tin collecting has become very popular not only in Britain but also abroad, with collectors in America, Australia, and New Zealand. As a result, the varied and beautifully designed early tins, in good condition, are becoming increasingly scarce and consequently rising in price.

1880-1930 was probably the golden age for pictorial tins, as this period saw many tobacco companies, large and small, competing with one another in the tobacconist's window, trying to catch the eye of the smoker with their colourful tins; a pretty girl, a man about town image or more popularly a naval theme.

Sadly most of these early tobacco companies have gone, never the less, the tins can still be found and what a thrill for the collector to spot a tin bearing the name of Taddy, Lusby or Kriegsfeld.

Gallaher's **'Rich Dark Honeydew'**, circa 1900-20. £20

Hignett's **'Cavalier Bright Flake'**, circa 1900-20. £15

Hignetts **'Pilot Flake'**, circa 1900-20. £20

'Sweet Leaf' smoking mixture, circa 1900. £20

Lambert & Butler **'Log Cabin'**, circa 1900-20. £10

Cohen, Weener & Co. Ltd. **'Afrikander Smoking Mixture'**, tin, 3 x 4in. £2

The 'Greys' Silk Cut Virginia tobacco tin. £2

Carroll's **'Mick McQuaid'** cut plug, circa 1900-10. £20

Player's **'No Name'** tobacco tin. £2

TOOLS

Medical, nautical and draughtsman's instruments have always been recognised as precision made tools worthy of the attention of collectors.
Now the old tools of all professions, vocations and crafts are appreciated for their beautiful workmanship and charm.
Those particularly sought after are, the carpenter's mortice gauges and brace and bits made of ebony and brass, also butcher's cleavers and bone saws. Woodworking chisels will form a splendid collection on their own as will the infinite variety of different sized woodworking planes.
Certain items, of course, have been moving upwards in price for some time and this applies in particular to the wood plane. There are over fifty different types of plane, ranging from the 3in. plane used by violin makers to the 17in. jack plane, and nowadays, some of the early 'named' examples can fetch hundreds rather than tens of pounds.

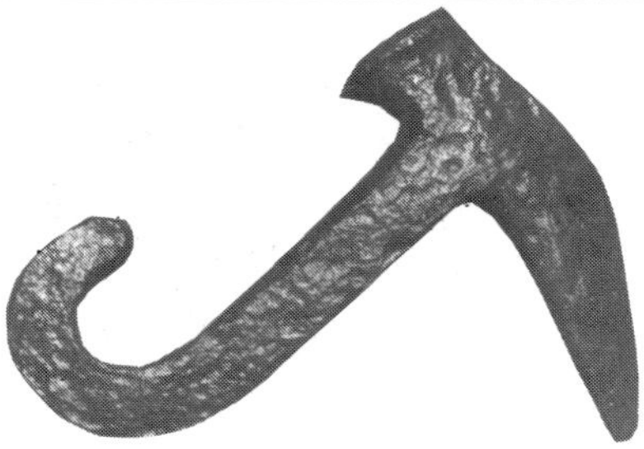

Iron wood jack for rope attachment after hammering into wood. £6

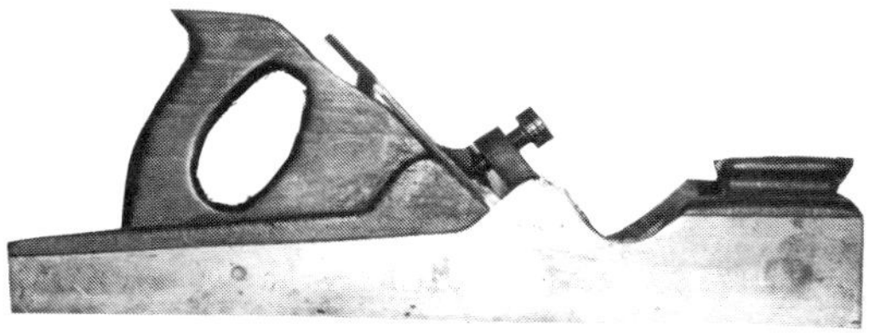

A large good quality plane by Robert Sorby, Sheffield. £154

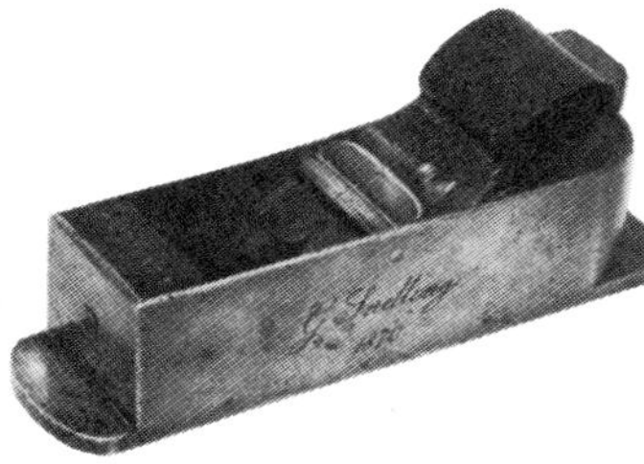

Mid 19th century mitre plane with brass box-shaped body, stamped G. Snelling and C. Keate, 7.1/8in. long. £176

An unusual late 19th century wood and brass billiard cue sharpener, 6in. long. £20

An 18th century beechwood router or 'Old Woman's Tooth', 9½in. long. £770

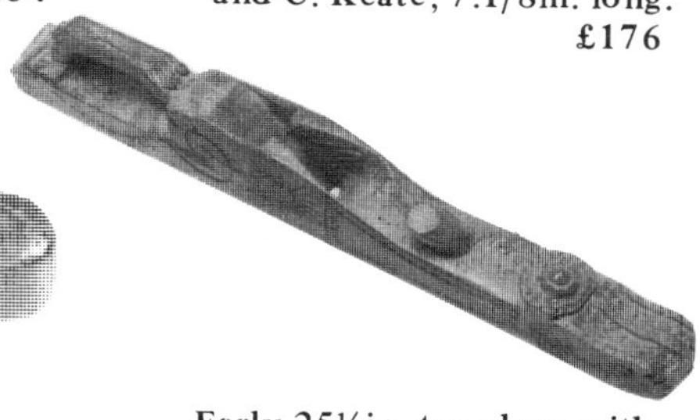

Early 25½in. try plane with flat iron handle. (David Stanley Auctions) £360

An early all metal side valve lifter. £14

Nicely shaped brick hammer, 14in. long. £12

A 19C two-handled French floor plane. (David Stanley Auctions) £100

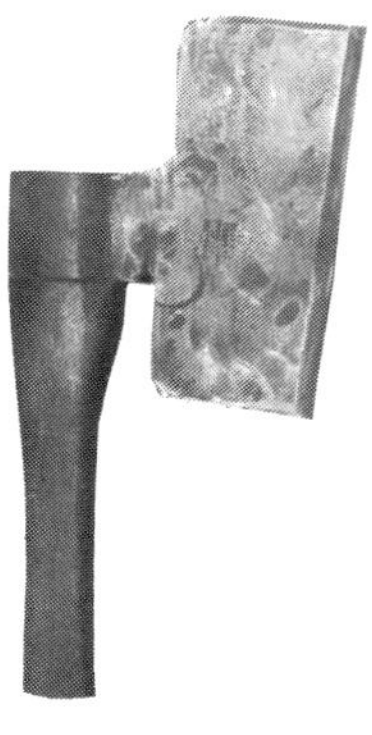

A cooper's (barrel makers) hatchet with short handle. £40

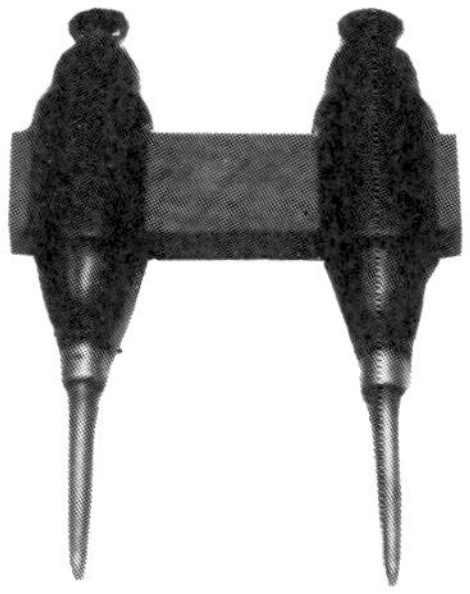

Pair of mahogany steel tipped trammels with knurled brass tightening screws, 9in. overall. (David Stanley Auctions) £115

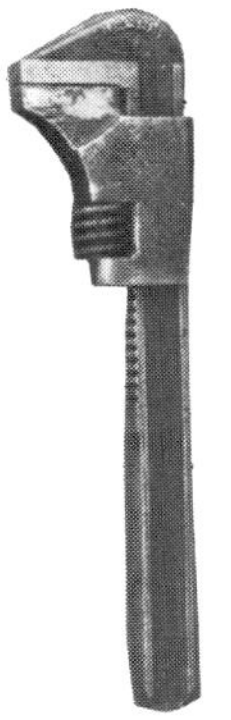

Large all metal wrench by Shelley. £8

A mid 18th century Dutch beechwood plane dated 1766, blade stamped Robt. Moor, 8in. long. £825

A screwstem plough with boxwood stems and nuts, by J. Miller, Clayton St. (David Stanley Auctions) £70

A beech plough by Gabriel, with brass thumb screw at the end of the stems. (David Stanley Auctions) £700

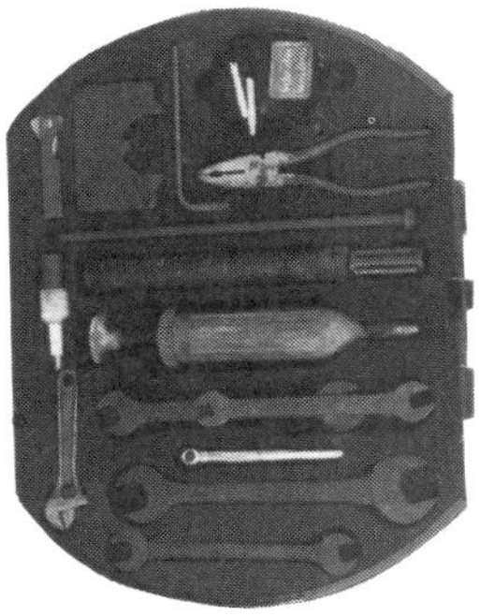

A Jaguar tool kit in a fitted case. £50

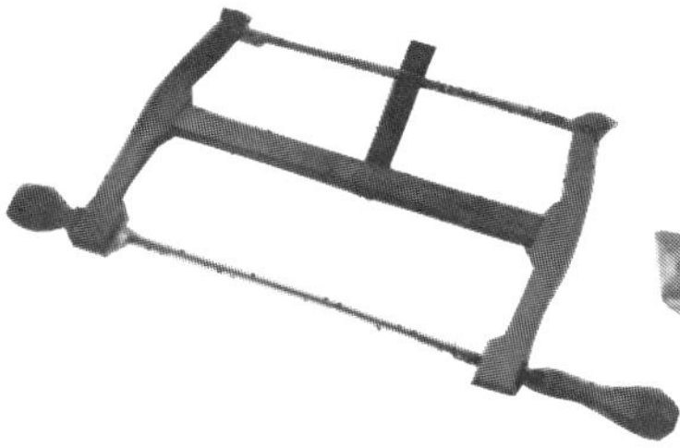

Late 19th century wooden framed fret saw. £15

A mahogany sash fillester with boxwood fence and stem wedges. £115

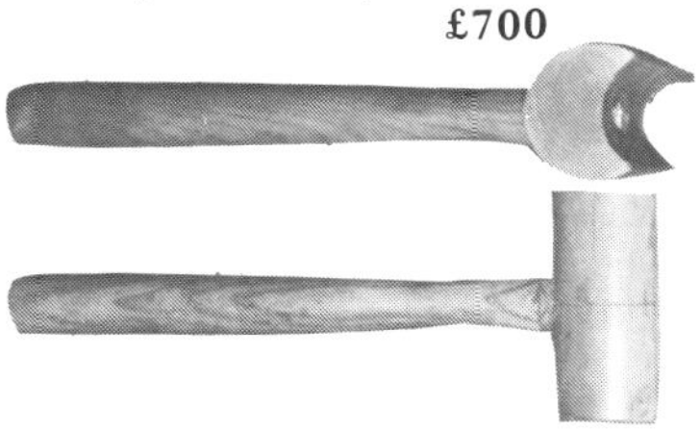

A Naval serving mallet of boxwood for serving shipped ropes. £15

Stanley plane No. 45 with wooden handles and original box. £70

An early 18th century lignum vitae and steel upholsterer's hammer, inscribed J. Sarney and 1716, 9½in. long. £605

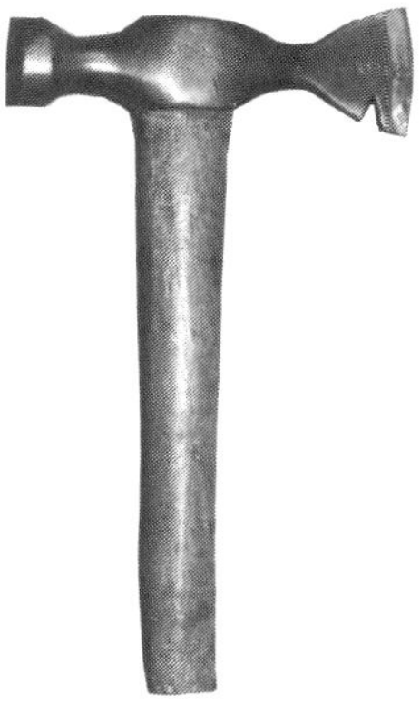

Victorian scaffolder's hammer for tightening lashings in pinewood pole scaffolding. £20

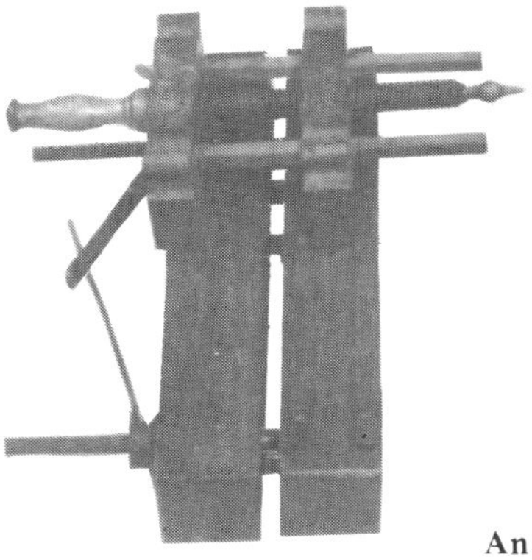

A bookbinders plough complete with cutting press. (David Stanley Auctions) £80

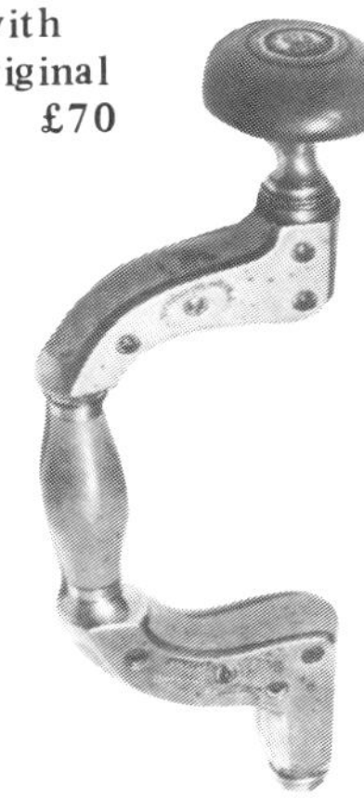

An ultimatum brace by Wm. Marples with boxwood infill, handle and head with ebony ring. (David Stanley Auctions) £1,550

A rosewood box plane with cast brass sole plate and steel blade by Hearnshaw Bros., 7½in. long. (Dacre, Son & Hartley) £65

WIW-I

TOYS

If every child treated his toys with the utmost care, didn't bang them into the skirting board, and carefully packed them away in their original boxes after use, it would have left a legacy of toys for future generations, but we would not be seeing some of the astronomical prices certain toys sell for at auction now.

A tin plate car by Carette sold for £6,700, a doll by A. Marque £24,000, a 1953 Vulcan Bomber by Dinky over £1,000 and a set of lead soldiers for £10,000.

It is all to do with supply and demand for suddenly old toys are big business, well out of the reach of the children they were designed for.

Age is not the criteria, for even the Japanese plastic space toys of the 50's and 60's are now eagerly sought after and are starting to make good money.

'Mac 700', a printed tinplate motorbike with rider, by Arnold, W. Germany, circa 1955, 7½in. long. (Christie's) £220

A Bing hand-enamelled early two-seater Benz racing car, with steerable front wheels, German, circa 1904, 11¼in. long. (Christie's) £9,200

A hand enamelled 'New Orleans Paddle Wheeler', probably by Dent, U.S.A., circa 1903, 10½in. long. (Christie's) £400

A painted wood dapple grey 'pony size' rocking horse, with horse hair mane and tail, 56in. long, British. (Christie's) £350

A printed and painted tinplate model of a four-door limousine with clockwork mechanism, by Tipp & Co., circa 1928, 8¼in. long. (Christie's) £480

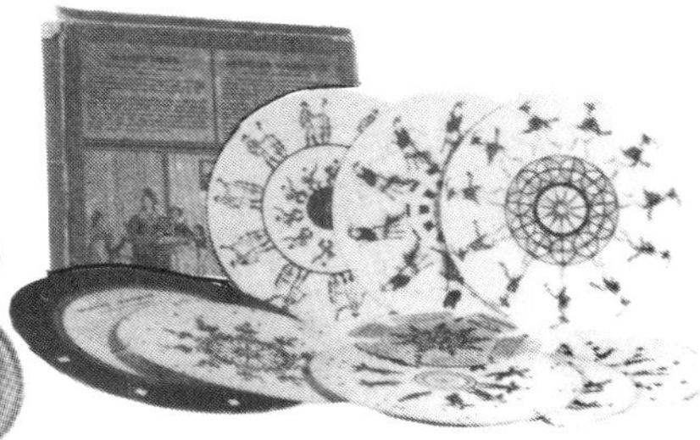

A Magic Disc phenakisticope optical toy with 8 discs, each 7in. diam., a viewing disc, 9in. diam., and a Fantascope disc, 5in. diam. (Christie's) £480

A Triang Minic pre-war taxi (M), boxed, with key. (Phillips) £350

A Dinky model Guy van with upright radiator grill, unboxed. (Hobbs & Chambers) £42

A Triang Minic pre-war 59 ME Searchlight lorry, boxed (M). (Phillips) £180

A Jep painted tinplate 'Panhard Levassor', finished in tan with red lining, French, circa 1925, 30½in. long. (Christie's) £650

A tinplate model of a fairground traction engine, with a four-wheeled car containing a carousel, by Bing, circa 1906. (Christie's) £480

An early painted metal gunboat with clockwork mechanism, by Bing, circa 1904, 10½in. long. (Christie's) £220

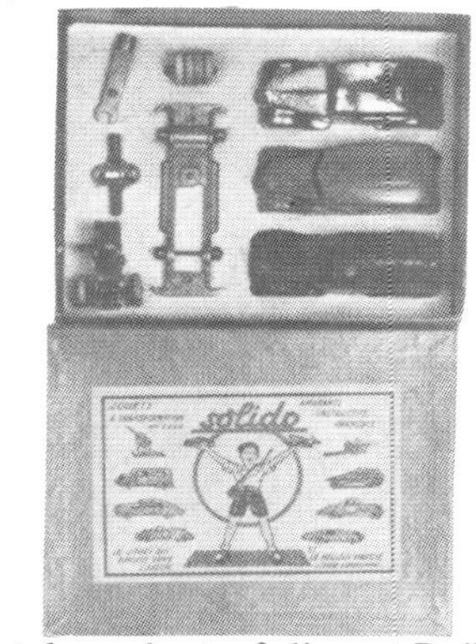

A boxed set of diecast Build-Yourself vehicles, by Solido. (Phillips) £45

Various model road signs, nine Dinky petrol pumps, three street lamps and seven figures, unboxed. (Hobbs & Chambers) £30

A Triang Minic pre-war Rolls Tourer, boxed, with key. (Phillips) £220

A clockwork automaton toy of a bisque headed doll pulling a wooden two-wheeled cart with driver, 13in. long. (Christie's) £1,300

'Bulky Mule, The Stubborn Donkey', EPL No. 425, by Lehmann, circa 1910, 7½in. long.(Christie's) £150

A gauge 1 signals gantry, with four signals, oil fired lamps and ladders on both sides, by Bing, circa 1910, 21in. high. (Christie's) £440

Meccano, No. 2 Constructor Car constructed as a tourer, boxed. (Phillips) £1,200

A Carette lithograph limousine, with clockwork mechanism, German, circa 1911, 8½in. long. (Christie's) £720

A Triang Minic pre-war Learner's car, boxed, with key (M). (Phillips) £300

Dinky 28M green delivery van advertising "Atco Motor Mowers'. (Christie's) £280

Part of a collection of five tinplate toys, comprising two prancing horses, a steam engine, a circular saw bench and another item. (Lawrence Fine Art) £10

A carved and painted rocking horse with hair mane and tail, America, circa 1880, 52in. long. (Robt. W. Skinner Inc.) £810

A Crown illuminated Panorama optical toy theatre, illuminated by a candle mounted behind, 9½in. wide. (Christie's) £180

A painted metal model of an Austin J40 Roadster pedal car, 64in. long, British, circa 1950. (Christie's) £750

A Hess printed and painted tinplate toy of Dreadnought, with clockwork mechanism, circa 1911, 8½in. long. (Christie's) £60

A tinplate toy gramophone, printed 'Made in Germany', 1930's, 8¼in. long. (Lawrence Fine Art) £60

An early Lines Bros. pedal car, the wooden body painted suede grey with sprung chassis, 39in. long. (Lawrence Fine Art) £550

An early painted tinplate fish, with clockwork mechanism causing the fish to flap its fin, 8¼in. long, by Bing, circa 1910. (Christie's) £220

A painted tinplate cat, 'Nina', EPL No. 790, by Lehmann, circa 1907, 11in. long. (Christie's) £1,000

An early printed and painted tinplate automobile, 'Tut Tut', EPL No. 490, by Lehmann, circa 1910, 6¾in. long. (Christie's) £900

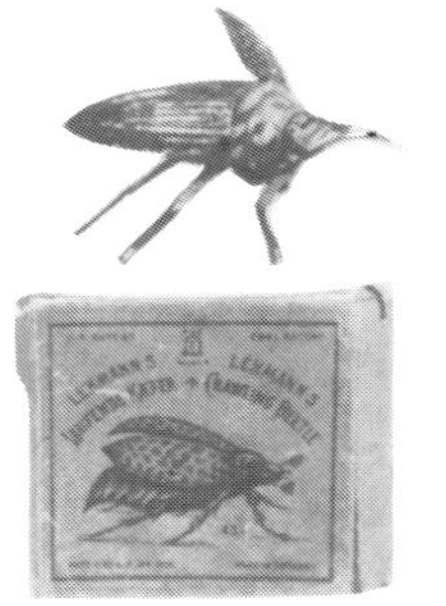

A printed and painted tinplate beetle, EPL No. 431, by Lehmann, circa 1906, 3¾in. long. (Christie's) £100

'Baker and Sweep', E.P.L. No. 450, by Lehmann, circa 1905, in original box. (Christie's) £1,600

A painted tinplate model of a P2 Alfa Romeo racing car, with clockwork mechanism, by C.I. G., France, circa 1926, 21½in. long. (Christie's) £800

Dinky 917, Guy van advertising 'Spratts'. (Christie's) £100

A Gunthermann painted and lithographed four-door limousine with clockwork mechanism, German, circa 1910, 11½in. long. (Christie's) £800

'Popeye the Sailor', No. 268, a printed and painted tinplate toy of the cartoon sailor in a rowing boat, 14in. long, by the Hoge Mfg. Co., Inc., U.S.A., circa 1935. (Christie's) £1,300

'New Century Cycle', EPL 345, with clockwork mechanism, by Lehmann, circa 1910, 5in. long. (Christie's) £850

Gunthermann, Gordon Bennett clockwork racing car, finished in yellow with gold detail, 28cm. long. (Phillips) £4,000

A Britains' farmer's gig, No. F28 with horse, together with Fordson tractor, unboxed. (Hobbs & Chambers) £30

An early Carette carpet toy tinplate sailboat, with flywheel mechanism, German, circa 1905, 11¾in. long. (Christie's) £180

'Mickey Mouse Organ Grinder', tinplate toy with clockwork and musical mechanisms, by Distler, circa 1930, 6in. long. (Christie's) £650

A Dinky Series 28 first pattern delivery van, painted in black and red with gilt decals, 'The Manchester Guardian', circa 1935. (Lawrence Fine Art) £240

A painted tinplate toy of a monkey on a four-wheel musical carriage, German, circa 1903, 7½in. long. (Christie's) £280

TRENCH ART

Trench Art is a term embracing all those curious oddities made by our fighting troops from spent bullet and shell cases when they were not winging off mortars towards the enemy lines.

Most take the form of ashtrays or cigarette lighters, often sporting cryptic messages with names and dates, which give an added interest, while other pieces are quite ambitious and take the form of aeroplanes, tanks and field guns.

Polished brass shell cases can make a useful addition to the hearth for housing spills and fireirons as can souvenir shells complete with the business end, when buffed and polished. Beware though, for it has been known for a First World War trophy to sit quite contentedly for decades by a roaring fire in a live condition – never assume they are harmless.

Brass trench art aeroplane made from bullet cases. £22

Combined lighter and ashtray dated 1944. £7

Second World War metal matchbox holder decorated with 'peace' symbols. £7

Cigarette lighter made from a brass bullet case. £5

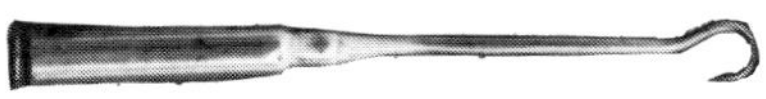

Brass bullet case button hook. £4

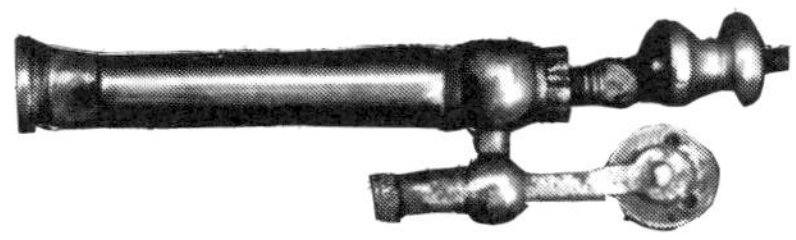

First World War lighter made from a bullet case. £3

Leather riding crop with two 303 brass bullet cases forming the handle. £4

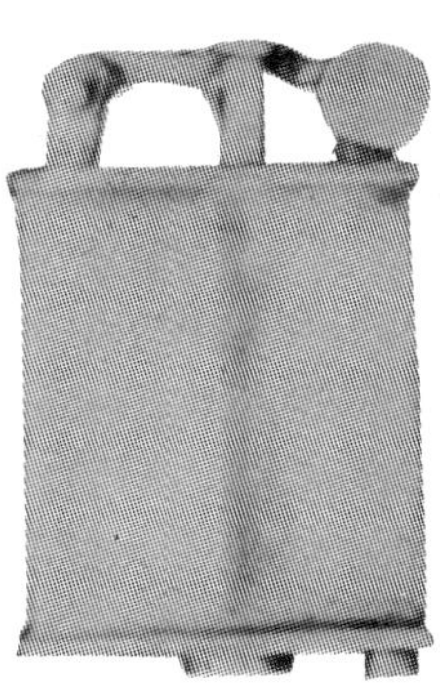

Handmade World War I brass petrol lighter. £6

A large brass and aluminium table lighter. £12

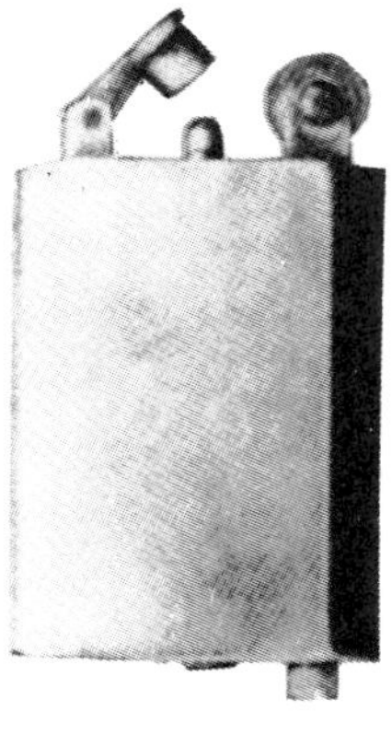

World War I initialled petrol lighter made by Frank Stanley. £7

Polished brass shell case, 12in. high. £8

TREEN

Treen is one of those collective terms which embrace a disjointed array of articles with the common factor being that they are all made of wood, and all have been produced on a lathe either in part or whole.
The majority are functional household articles, many originating in the kitchen, made from finely grained hardwoods such as yew, lignum vitae, sycamore and olivewood, which acquire a fine warm patina over the years.
Largely ignored little more than a decade ago, prices for good quality treen can now be measured in hundreds of pounds rather than tens.
Early 18th century American treen is particularly desirable and it is not unknown for a single bowl to fetch over £1,000.
The variety of objects embraced by the term is endless and includes bowls, spoons, goblets, coasters, moulds, napkin rings, egg-cups, mortars, boxes and boot trees.

An early 19th century mahogany cheese board, 10in. diam. £264

A treen bucket on ebonised turned stem with brass swing handle, 14½in. high. (Lawrence Fine Art) £484

A 19th century mahogany egg cup stand, 7½in. high. £418

A lignum vitae mortar and boxwood pestle, mortar 6½in., pestle 9½in. £93

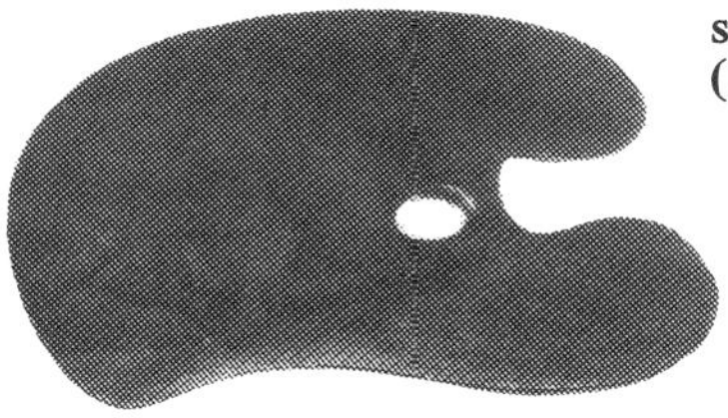

A late 18th/early 19th century mahogany artist's palette, 18in. long. £38

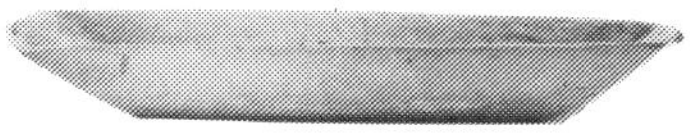

Early 19th century American elongated wooden bowl with small carved handles, 29½in. long. £225

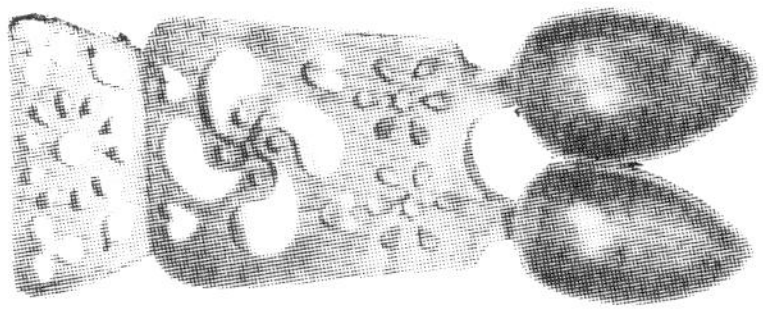

An 18th century yewwood double love spoon, 9in. long. £396

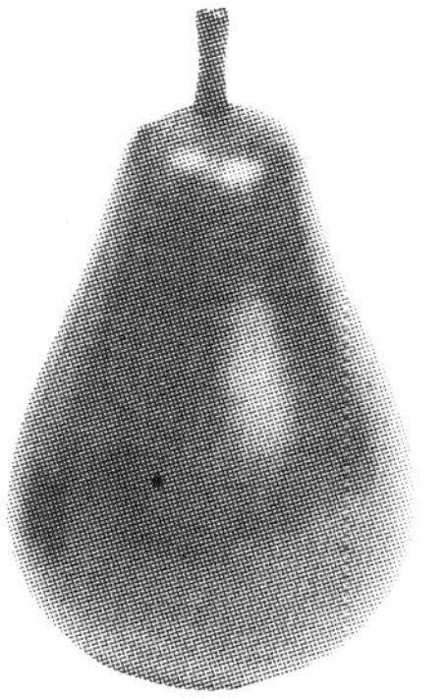

A 19th century lignum vitae paperweight in the form of a pear, 5¼in. £264

A George III mahogany cistern, the vase shaped body with lead lining, 17in. diam. (Christie's) £2,052

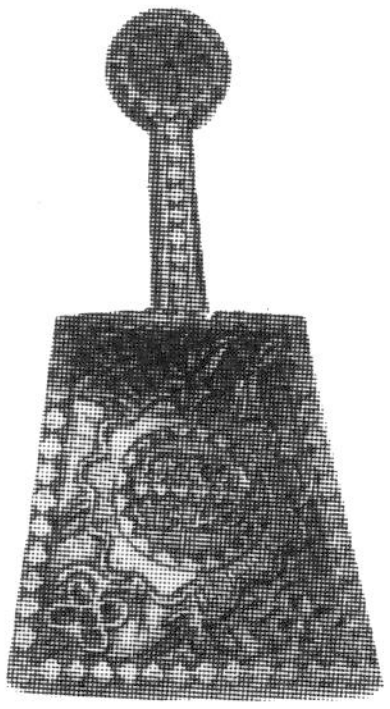

A Scandinavian beechwood washing bat, dated 1842, 15in. long. £253

A Biedermeier walnut cradle, the oval body with detachable tin liner, 52in. wide. (Christie's) £4,104

TSUBAS

Tsubas (hand protectors from a Japanese sword) are usually about 2in. across, are made of iron, brass or copper – occasionally with gold or silver decoration – and have a wedge-shaped hole in the centre for the blade (tang). There are usually other openings for the sword knife (kogatawa) and skewer (kogai).

Some are simply patterned while others bear decoration, either inlaid or applied, depicting a variety of subjects including landscapes, animals, historical events and folklore. Later examples were sometimes decorated with cloisonne or Champleve enamel.

At first they were made by the swordsmith but as they became more important armourers took over their production until finally specialist craftsmen emerged who made nothing but tsubas.

A Japanese iron Nara School tsuba, 5.8cm. of irregular form. (Wallis & Wallis) £50

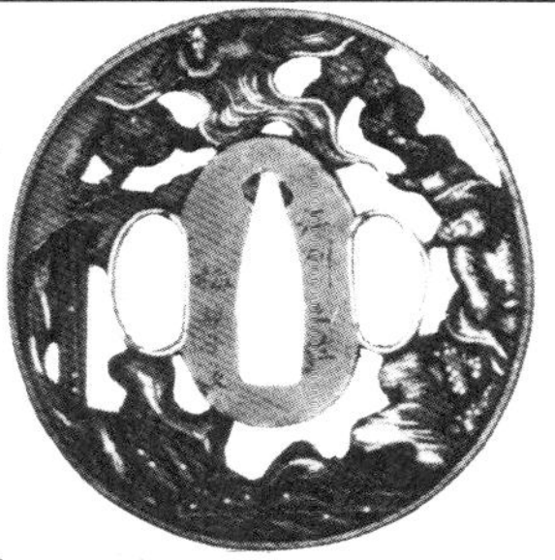

A circular iron Soten tsuba, 7.3cm., signed Goshu ju Soheishi sei, details in gold nunome. (Wallis & Wallis) £105

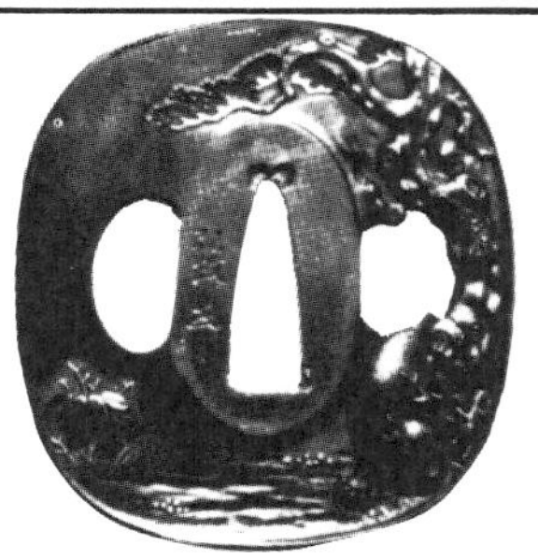

A dark Shibuichi rounded-square tsuba, signed Hiromasa, mid 19th century, 6.7cm. (Christie's) £453

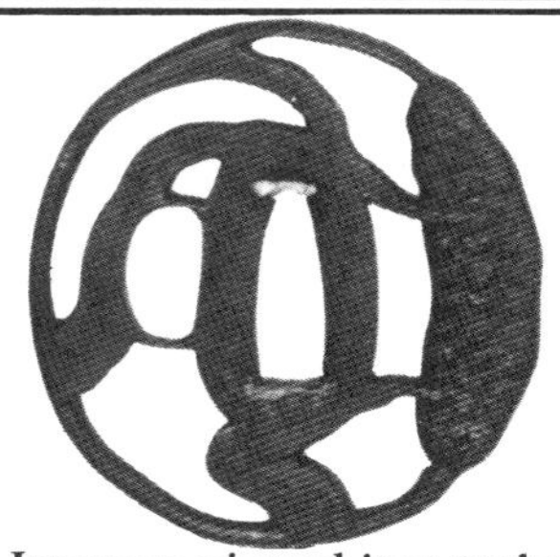

A Japanese pierced iron tsuba, 7.4cm., of irregular form, chiselled as an ear of corn in low relief with leaves. (Wallis & Wallis) £32

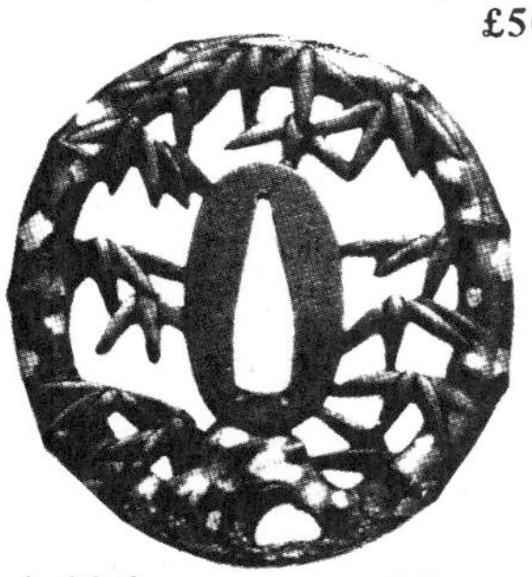

A 19th century oval iron tsuba, signed Choshu ju Toyonobu saku (Okamoto School), 7.9cm.(Christie's) £300

A Mokkogata iron tsuba, signed Yamashiro Kuniju Umetada Mitsuyoshi, 8.4cm. (Christie's) £270

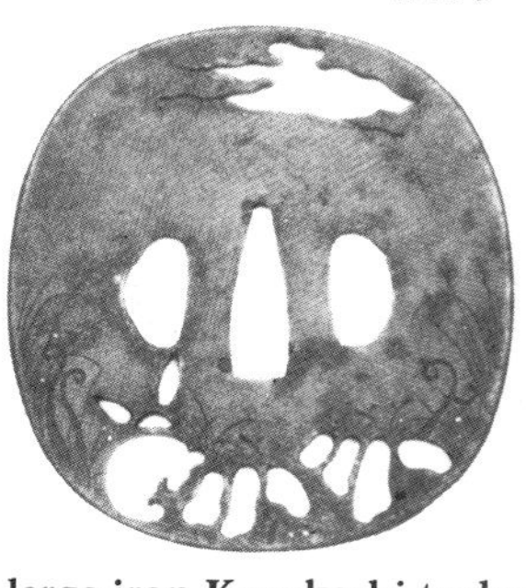

A large iron Kosukashi tsuba of square form, 8.7cm., finely pierced in negative silhouette. (Wallis & Wallis) £170

A 19th century copper and sentoku hari-ishime hariawase tsuba, Mito Kinko School, 8.4cm. with fitted box. (Christie's) £1,836

An 18th century circular iron tsuba with black patina, signed Echizen ju Kinai saku, 8.6cm. (Christie's) £756

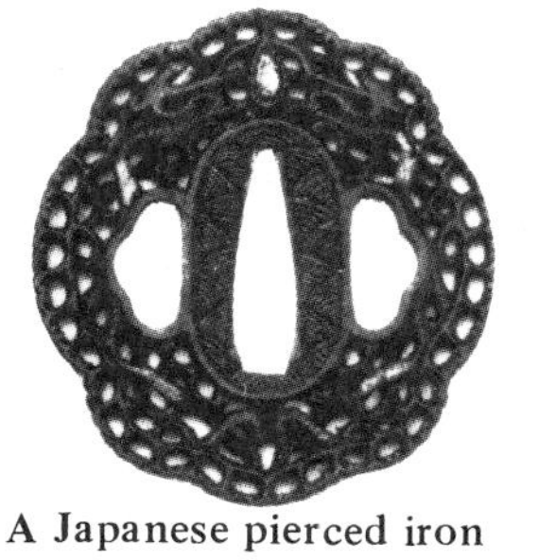

A Japanese pierced iron Nambam tsuba, 6.2cm., with gold nunome details. (Wallis & Wallis) £50

A fine Jakushu School iron tsuba of squared form, 6cm. (Wallis & Wallis) £145

A large oval iron tsuba, 7.9cm. inlaid with brass key pattern overall. (Wallis & Wallis) £38

TUNBRIDGEWARE

In the 17th century, visitors flocked to take the waters at the spa town of Tunbridge Wells in Kent. Local craftsmen, eager to meet the demands of a growing souvenir trade, developed a method of producing thin sheets of patterned veneer known as Tunbridgeware or 'English mosaic'. Thin strips of different woods in a variety of colours, were set in an arranged pattern then stuck together to form a block from which thin sheets could be cut. This way the pattern could be repeated over and over again. The decorative veneer was applied to a great variety of objects and in particular to boxes.

The earliest pattern was made up of cube shapes and later veneers show a great number of intricate designs including flowers, birds and landscapes.

The popularity of Tunbridgeware continued throughout the 18th and 19th centuries and it is from this period that most examples originate; the last firm in production was Boyce, Brown and Kemp 1837-1927.

A rosewood book tray, the whole outlined with mosaic borders, 1ft.3in. wide. £300

A domed top rosewood ground box, depicting a ruined castle, 10½in. wide. (Geering & Colyer) £135

A rosewood visiting card tray of rectangular shape, 10¾in. wide. £200

A rosewood writing slope, the interior fitted with compartments and ink-wells, 12¼in. wide. £220

A mahogany and rosewood watch stand on inverted bun feet, 6½in. high. £100

A rosewood and Tunbridgeware tea caddy of waisted form, the domed top depicting Battle Abbey, 9in. wide. (Parsons, Welch & Cowell) £350

A rosewood single division tea caddy, 5½in. wide. £150

A thermometer stand by H. Hollanby, 4½in. high. £100

A rosewood jewellery box with mosaic borders, with velvet lined interior, 7in. wide. £100

A miniature chamber candlestick with mahogany base inlaid with an end grain mosaic panel, 1¾in. high. £90

An English burr-walnut nautical writing box, 13½in. wide. £297

A rosewood games box, the top and cavetto sides banded with 'Berlin woolwork' borders, 10½in. wide. £200

TYPEWRITERS

Many 19th century typewriters had a double keyboard with one key for each capital together with one for each of the small letters and the major disadvantage of most was that it was impossible to read the typed sheet until after the work had been completed.

The breakthrough came with a machine, based on a design by Sholes, incorporating the shift key mechanism – very much on the same principal as modern manual machines.

In the first ten years of manufacture 50,000 were sold by Remington, Oliver, Smith, Underwood and Yost; names still well to the fore in typewriter manufacture today.

Interest in these early machines has increased considerably and the trends of the last few years, points to a worthwhile investment.

A Hall typewriter with rubber type sheet (defective), in walnut case with instructions in lid. (Christie's) £190

A Lambert typewriter No. 2908, by The Lambert Typewriter Co., New York. (Christie's) £180

An Edelmann typewriter on shaped cast iron base, German, circa 1897, 10½in. wide. £240

Rare Corona special folding typewriter in red lacquer body, circa 1910, 12¼in. wide. £220

A Hammond No. 1 typewriter, American, with piano type ebony keys, circa 1884. £600

Williams No. 2 typewriter with grasshopper action type bars, length of platen 8¼in., circa 1893. £350

A Mignon Model 2 typewriter. £1,300

American Colombia typewriter No. 2, with circular letter index, 9¾in. wide, circa 1890. £440

A Hall typewriter, No. 2498, in a mahogany case, American, circa 1885, 15¼in. wide. £200

VALENTINE CARDS

On St. Valentine's Eve, it was a custom for young people to meet and draw by lot, one of a number of names of persons of the opposite sex. Once two names were paired, the gentleman was then bound to the service of his Valentine for the period of one year. This practice was adapted to form the custom we observe today; that of sending an anonymous greeting to a sweetheart. Valentine cards from about the 1850's were romantic with lashings of frills, lace, ribbons and flowers. Many survive, but not so many survive in perfect condition.

The Valentine postcard came into use around 1900 and, for twenty years or so, enjoyed a period of great popularity. The better examples in this category are good artist drawn, chromo litho cards by publishers such as Ettinger, Tuck, Hildesheimer, Wildt & Kray, Schwerdtfeger etc. Unfortunately, although many well known artists illustrated these cards, very few were ever signed.

To My Valentine, Raphael Tuck & Sons, 1930's. £2.25

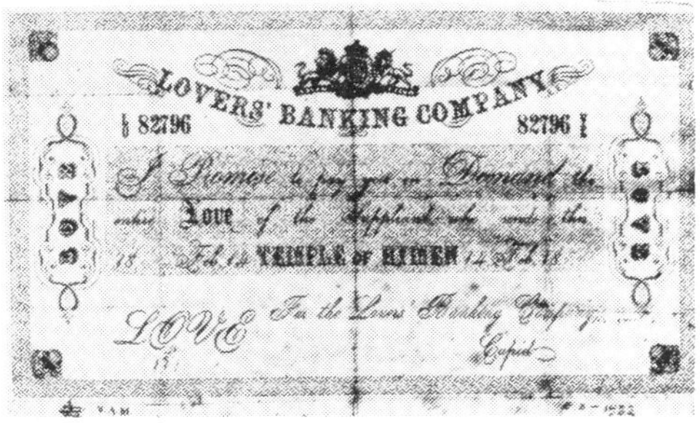

Early Victorian Valentine in the form of a banknote. £12.50

Forget Me Not For I'll Remember Thee. £5

Max Ettinger Royal Series No. V104, embossed chromo hearts and flowers 'With Love's Greeting'. £3.50

A Valentine For Someone Often In My Thoughts. £2

Max Ettinger Royal Series No. V96, chromo embossed envelope 'My Valentine', 'Think of Me'. £4.50

Comic Valentine card 'To Arms, to Arms, ye British brave'. £10

'Faith, Hope and Charity', four in set, sometimes three in set. G. B. & Co. Series, embossed chromo litho with gold leaf applique. £2 each

'Maiden thy little heart to let.' £9

VINAIGRETTES

There were many thousands of small useful boxes and among the most precious – and the smallest – are those known by the unlikely name of 'vinaigrettes'.

Descendants of the pomander and, before that, the pomme d'ambre, vinaigrettes began to appear towards the end of the 18th century. Their function was to contain, under a pierced grille, a small piece of sponge or wadding soaked in aromatic oils and 'vinegars' whose vapours were thought to ward off disease and could be sniffed to counteract the less pleasant effluvia not uncommonly encountered in the days before efficient municipal refuse collection.

These little boxes were carried either in a pocket, muff or purse or, were worn suspended from a chain on a chatelaine or pocket watch and some have little fixing rings attached. The inside was almost invariably gilded to avoid corrosion.

Occasionally made of gold but more commonly of silver, pinchbeck, glass or porcelain and sometimes inset with precious stones, vinaigrettes have the advantage over many collectible items in that they are usually particularly beautifully made and, being so often constructed of precious metals, they are fairly certain to resist those fluctuations of fashion which can so easily undermine the investment potential of less stable items.

Prices and values naturally vary according to the maker, quality, material, age and condition of the pieces. Vinaigrettes by Nathaniel Mills are particularly desirable, especially those with embossed scenic views on the lid.

An early Victorian castle top vinaigrette, the cover case with a view of Windsor Castle, by John Tongue, Birmingham, 1845, 4cm. long. (Lawrence Fine Art) £418

A George IV rectangular vinaigrette, by Thos. Newbold, Birmingham, 1821, 3.2cm. long. (Lawrence Fine Art) £154

A George IV vinaigrette in the form of a purse, by Lawrence & Co., Birmingham, 1821, 3cm. long. (Lawrence Fine Art) £198

A 19th century Chinese Export oblong vinaigrette with engine-turned base, by Khecheong of Canton, circa 1850. (Phillips) £120

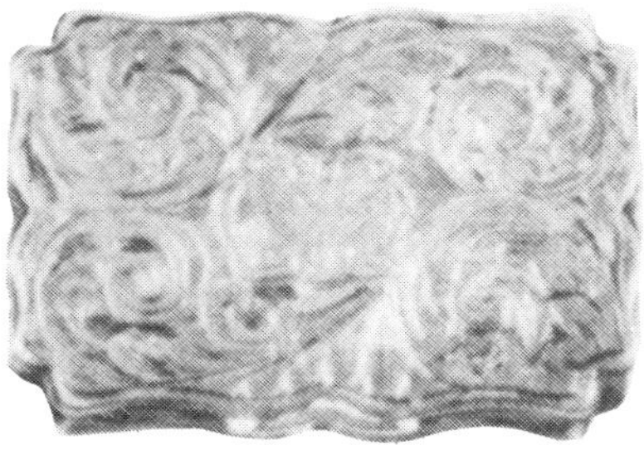

A Victorian gilt lined, bright cut, shaped oblong vinaigrette with vacant scroll cartouche, by F. Clarke, Birmingham, 1846. (Christie's) £75

A George IV engine-turned and gilded vinaigrette, L. & Co., Birmingham, 1822. (Christie's) £140

An oblong silver 'Castletop' vinaigrette chased on the cover with a view of Westminster Abbey, by N. Mills, Birmingham 1842, 1¾in. long. (Christie's) £648

A William IV silver gilt engine-turned vinaigrette with reeded sides, by Thos. Shaw, Birmingham, 1830. (Christie's) £90

WALKING STICKS

Walking sticks have been collected for a very long time and a survey of the current market shows no decline in their popularity as collector's items.
Relevant factors to consider when starting any collection must be availability, variety and of course, space available to display the chosen objects. The walking stick seems to fulfil all of these requirements with ease.

A good collection will include examples on an international scale which in turn leads to a healthy exchange of information and objects in a field where everyone involved can indulge their own individual taste while selecting from the great variety of items available.

Some collectors will prefer walking sticks with handles of carved ivory, silver, hardstone or gold while others favour the simpler animal handles or the more humble and very individual 'country stick' which is usually made from a piece of wood selected from a hedgerow or special tree and carved according to the skill of the craftsman.

Walking sticks are often designed to serve a dual purpose, the shaft cleverly concealing the mechanism for a variety of functions. Since sticks were 'worn' as part of the 17th/18th century gentleman's dress the inclusion of such accessories as a watch, telescope or drinking flask seemed a very sensible idea. A typical example is the sword stick with a slender steel blade attached to the cane handle and concealed within the shaft of the stick.

This category has always had great appeal for collectors but anyone can join in and the chance of finding a unique interior fitting is always a possibility.

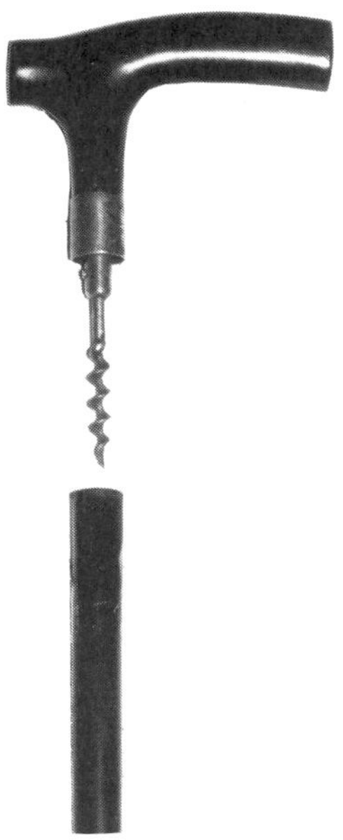

Victorian corkscrew cane with black horn handle and silver collar, bayonet fitting, 34in. long, circa 1880. £250

Rare percussion muzzle loading umbrella gun with Birmingham proof stamps, the brolly being ornamental, 35in. long, circa 1840. £600

Rosewood cane with carved wood walrus head handle with ivory tusks and gilt metal collar, circa 1880, 35in. long. £130

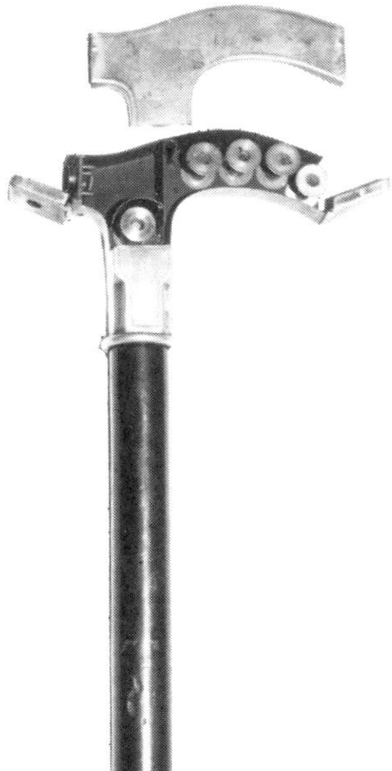

The 'Ben Akiba' camera cane invented by E. Kronke, Berlin 1903, and manufactured by A. Leh, with 24 exposures and ten spare rolls of film carried in the shaft, 35in. long. £4,000

An early Victorian telescope walking stick the horn screw-off handle fitted with a compass and presentation silver band, 34in. long, circa 1850. £600

German stick with Malacca shaft and finely carved ivory handle featuring a seated lion, circa 1840. £400

WATCHES

Although watches with single hands were made in the 17th century it wasn't until the 18th century that the need for an accurate timepiece was required specifically as an aid to navigation aboard ship.
This prompted a number of significant developments such as, the lever and cylinder escapement and established a wealth of watchmakers whose work is most sought after today. Among them are Mudge, Tompion, Graham, Quare, Frodsham, Breguet, Leroux, Barraud and Ellicott.
Watches were originally carried in the 'fob pocket' in the waistband of the trousers only moving up to the waistcoat pocket in the 19th century. Wrist watches are basically a product of the 20th century.
Recent manufacturers to look for are Rolex, Movado, Piquet and Cartier.

A gold World Time wristwatch, signed Patek Philippe & Co., Geneva, no. 929572, the leather strap with 18ct. gold buckle. (Christie's) £13,333

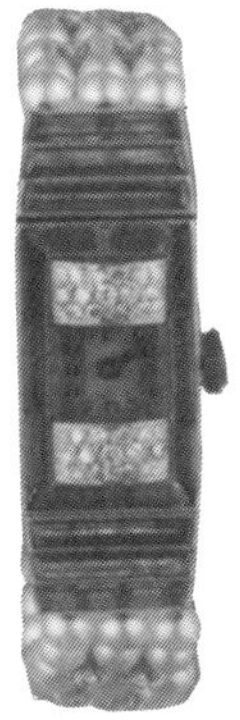

A Concorde Watch Co. lady's watch, yellow metal set with peridots, topaz, diamonds and pearls. (Christie's) £2,160

A gold wristwatch, signed P. Philippe & Co., Geneve, nickel eighteen-jewel cal. 23-300PM movement. (Christie's) £1,062

A gold wristwatch within an 18ct. gold case, signed Audemars Piguet, with 14ct. mesh bracelet. (Christie's) £696

A Swiss gold and enamel musical automaton verge watch, circa 1820, 60mm. diam. (Christie's) £12,960

A verge watch, the movement signed Daniel Delander, London, 334, 55mm. diam. (Christie's) £648

A chased and enamelled platinum openface watch, signed P. Philippe & Co., no. 200063, 43mm. diam. (Christie's) £910

A gold duplex watch, the movement signed Radford, Leeds, No. 2588, 53mm. diam. (Christie's) £972

A multi-colour gold filled hunter cased pocket watch, signed Illinois Watch Co., fifteen jewel movement, 53mm. diam. (Christie's) £189

A French gold and enamel cylinder watch, the movement signed Breguet A Paris, 51mm. diam. (Christie's) £1,620

A small gold openface five-minute repeating watch, signed Fayette S. Giles, 36mm. diam. (Christie's) £1,138

A gold openface quarter repeating watch with automaton, 18ct. gold case, 56mm. diam. (Christie's) £1,821

An 18ct. gold wristwatch, signed P. Philippe & Co., Geneve, nickel eighteen-jewel cal. 9'''-90 movement. (Christie's) £2,125

A lady's platinum wristwatch, signed P. Philippe & Co., Geneve. (Christie's) £476

A gold wristwatch, signed Patek Philippe & Co., Geneva, no. 794766, with 18-jewel cal. 23-300 movement. (Christie's) £1,320

An 18ct. gold wristwatch with fifteen jewel movement, signed Le Coultre Co., dated 1934. (Christie's) £1,062

A Swiss gold openface skeletonised quarter repeating verge watch with erotic automaton, circa 1820, 56mm. diam. (Christie's) £4,554

A silver pair cased verge watch with automaton, signed Sylvester, London, no. 6788, 55mm. diam. (Christie's) £607

A Dutch enamel and silver pair cased verge watch with false pendulum, signed Martineau, London, 52mm. diam. (Christie's) £1,024

An 18th century verge pocket watch with silver dial and case, by J. Hocker, Reading. (Capes, Dunn & Co.) £190

WEATHERVANES

If there was any doubt that collecting weathervanes is a subject for serious investment, it was dispelled recently in America when an entire auction was devoted to the sale of just one weathervane with historical connections to the patriot Paul Revere.

Weathervanes have also been disappearing mysteriously from atop some of the highest churches in New York State as the result of daring helicopter raids at dawn, no less. A sure indication of their worth.

American weathervanes tend to be more adventurous in their design than their British counterpart and feature running horses, Red Indians, stagecoaches, sailing ships and butterflies as well as the universal cockerel.

Late 19th century American copper weathervane depicting a cow, 14½in. high, 24in. long. (Christie's) £303

Mid 19th century American copper horse and groom weathervane, 20½in. high. (Robt. W. Skinner Inc.) £451

Late 19th century American copper weathervane in the form of a pig, 35in. long. (Christie's) £7,586

A cast metal and copper rooster weathervane figure, American, circa 1890, 27in. high. (Robt. W. Skinner Inc.) £1,319

'Flying Horse' weathervane, A. L. Jewell & Co., Waltham, Mass., circa 1870, 35½in. long. (Robt. W. Skinner Inc.) £4,895

An iron prospector's weathervane, Penn., circa 1900, 27½in. high. (Robt. W. Skinner Inc.) £520

A gilded centaur weathervane, probably A. L. Jewell & Co., Waltham, Mass., circa 1860, 40in. long. (Robt. W. Skinner Inc.) £81,250

A moulded copper 'North Wind' weathervane, in the form of a cherub's head blowing stylised air, 23in. high, 56½in. long. (Christie's) £11,472

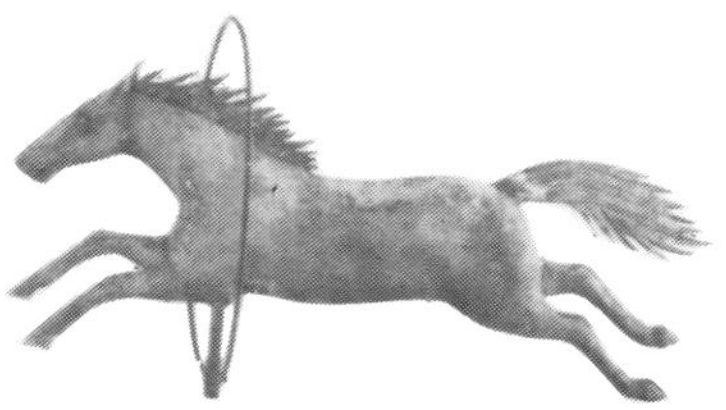

A 19th century running horse and hoop weathervane, America, 30in. long. (Robt. W. Skinner Inc.) £2,635

A sulkie and rider with horse weathervane figure, attributed to T. W. Fiske, America, circa 1880, 36in. long. (Robt. W. Skinner Inc.) £1,689

A locomotive and tender copper weathervane, America, circa 1882, 61in. long. (Robt. W. Skinner Inc.) £115,625

A late 19th century American carved wooden weathervane in the form of Gabriel blowing his horn, 47in. long. (Christie's) £1,204

A 19th century sheet iron silhouette weathervane, a prancing horse with military rider, 27in. long. (Robt. W. Skinner Inc.) £1,351

Mid 19th century American copper cow weathervane, possibly from the Howard Co., 15½in. high. (Robt. W. Skinner Inc.) £555

A cast metal and moulded copper horse weathervane figure, attributed to J. Howard, circa 1880, 21in. high, 29in. long. (Robt. W. Skinner Inc.) £2,291

Early 19th century gold leaf dove figure, America, 13in. high, 23in. wide. (Robt. W. Skinner Inc.) £866

A moulded copper stag weathervane, attributed to J. Harris & Co., Boston, circa 1879, 30½in. high. (Robt. W. Skinner Inc.) £19,444

Late 19th/early 20th century American gilt copper weathervane depicting a peacock, 29in. long overall. (Christie's) £2,427

Ethan Allen running horse weathervane figure, America, circa 1880, 26½in. long. (Robt. W. Skinner Inc.) £405

Late 19th century running horse with jockey weathervane figure, possibly J. L. Mott & Co., circa 1880, America, 16in. long. (Robt. W. Skinner Inc.) £1,351

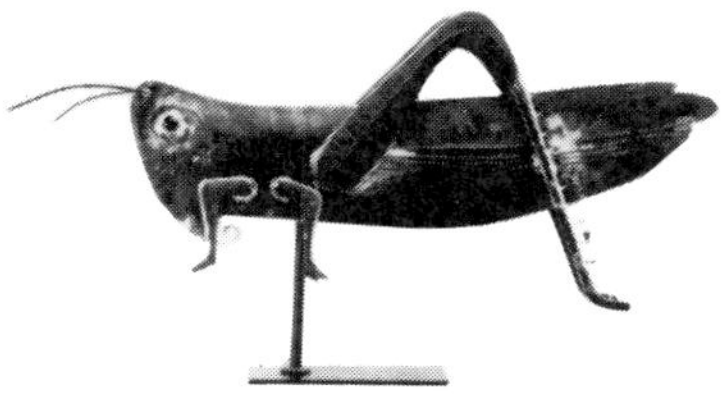

A 20th century grasshopper weathervane figure, the moulded copper figure with verdigris, 19in. high, America. (Robt. W. Skinner Inc.) £625

WEDGWOOD

Josiah Wedgwood established his first pottery at Burslem in 1759. In 1769 his Etruria factory was opened but the original Burslem factory closed in 1774. In 1940 the factory moved to Barlaston.

The Wedgwood pottery was renowned for its green glazed wares, its cream coloured wares, black basalt, jasper and cane ware. Parian busts, marketed as Carrara busts, appeared in 1848 and bone porcelain was produced on a sizeable scale from 1878 onwards.

The company experimented in lithography which gave an imitation of oil painting on pottery and they also produced high quality relief decoration. At the end of the 19th century, Wedgwood transfer printed tiles were very popular as were their basalt vases, majolica ware and pottery decorated with printed landscapes which was exported to America in large numbers.

Among the best known Wedgwood artists were A. and L. Powell who experimented in freehand designs, and K. Murray whose work was decorated with grooves and fluting.

A Wedgwood & Bentley black basalt hare's head stirrup cup, circa 1775, 16cm. high. (Christie's) £9,180

A Wedgwood blue and white jasper bulb pot and cover, impressed mark and V, circa 1785, 24cm. high.(Christie's) £1,296

A pair of Wedgwood bronzed black basalt triton candlesticks of conventional type, impressed marks, circa 1880, 27cm. high. (Christie's) £702

A Wedgwood blue and white jasper portrait medallion of William Pitt The Younger, circa 1790, 9.5cm. high. (Christie's) £432

A Wedgwood vase designed by Keith Murray, 16.5cm. high. (Christie's) £86

A Wedgwood pot pourri vase and pierced cover, the central area painted by H. Beardmore, signed, 34.5cm. high. (Phillips) £300

A Wedgwood charger, the cobalt blue ground with raised polychrome decoration, 38.5cm. diam. (Christie's) £864

A 19th century Wedgwood blue and white jasper vase, 12in. high. (Christie's) £500

WHISTLES

New collectors tend to gather these little whistles without much system or discrimination then, realising that there are so many different types and styles, they quickly start to specialise.
Dog whistles and those in the form of a dog are particularly attractive, especially those made of porcelain by the Derby factory.

Others collect just military or police whistles including the bosun's call which is often made of silver and has a special fascination all of its own.

There are whistles for train guards and whistles for referees but most interesting of all are those disguised within the form of another object, such as, a penknife, spoon, peeper, pencil, or tape measure.
Materials will include silver, gold, jet, agate, brass, porcelain, wood and ivory.

Japanese Special plated brass whistle. £1

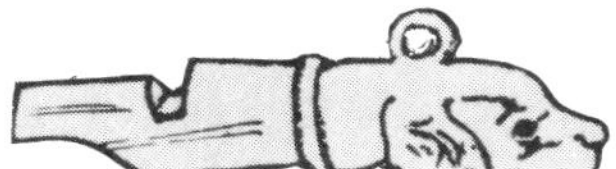

Silver dog whistle, dated 1898, Birmingham. £50

Victorian silver whistle with niello decoration. £100

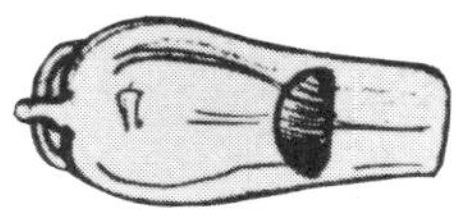

Victorian silver whistle of bulbous form. £35

The Acme Thunderer with plated chain, circa 1950. £2.50

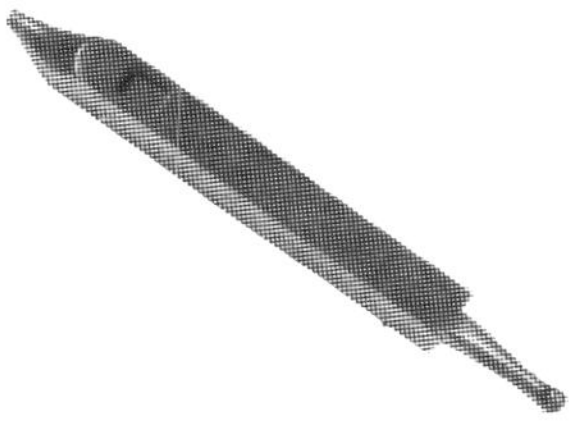

An 18th/19th century mahogany choir master's pitch pipe, 12½in. long. £143

A small 'Acme' plated whistle. £4

A goldwashed silver and coral rattle whistle, hallmarked Birmingham, 1862, 6in. long. (Robt. W. Skinner Inc.) £235

A plated Metropolitan Police whistle. £3

A 19th century sheep's horn sheepdog whistle, 5in. long. £20

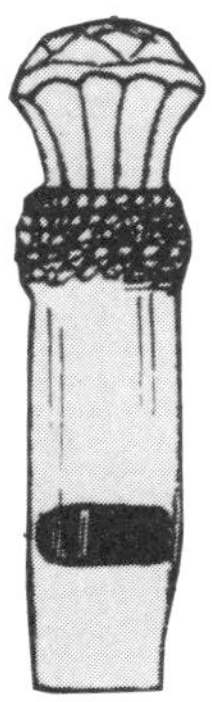

Scottish silver thistle whistle, dated 1906. £65

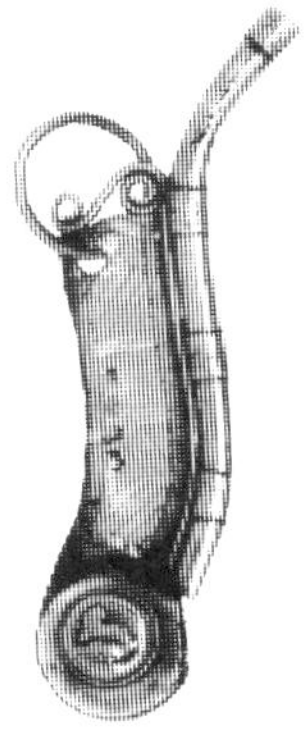

Rare George II bosun's whistle, London, 1740, 4¼in. long. £1,870

1970's plastic whistle, made in Japan. 30p

WINE GLASSES

Wine glasses began to replace metal goblets on rich men's tables from the 17th century onwards and since then glass workers have vied to produce more elegant and unusual designs.
Venetian glasses were always marked by the elaboration of the design; the Bohemians first discovered how to cut glass so that it looked like a jewel and their heavy, ruby coloured goblets are now very valuable. Wine glasses were also used to pass messages and the supporters of the Jacobite cause after the 1715 and 1745 rebellions drank their toasts out of glasses engraved with roses which symbolised their Stuart sympathies. These glasses now change hands at prices around £300 each. Some of the most elegant old glasses have air twist stems and others are decorated with gilt or are intricately engraved by skilled artists. Jacob Sang of Amsterdam was an 18th century engraver whose work is among the most beautiful in the world.

A composite stemmed wine glass of drawn trumpet shape, circa 1750, 18cm. high. (Christie's) £129

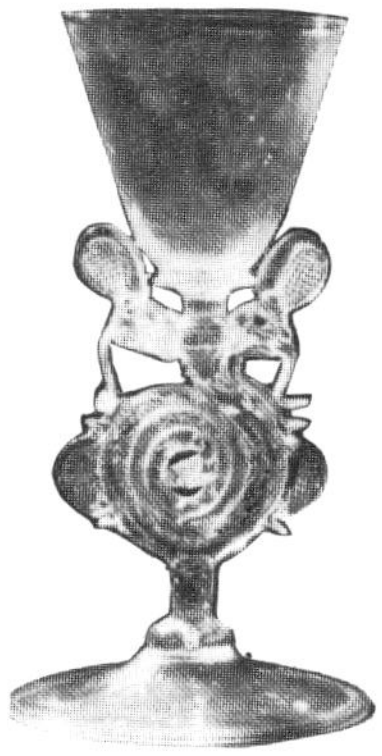

An 18th century serpent-stemmed glass, the funnel bowl supported on a merese, 18cm. high. (Christie's) £194

A baluster wine glass, the bell bowl with a small tear to the solid lower part, circa 1715, 14cm. high. (Christie's) £280

An unrecorded signed Royal armorial goblet by Wm. Beilby, circa 1762, 25cm. high. (Christie's) £56,160

A wine glass by David Wolff, the stem cut with diamond facets, 1790-95, 15cm. high. (Christie's) £3,780

A colour twist wine glass with waisted bucket bowl, circa 1760, 17cm. high. (Christie's) £1,944

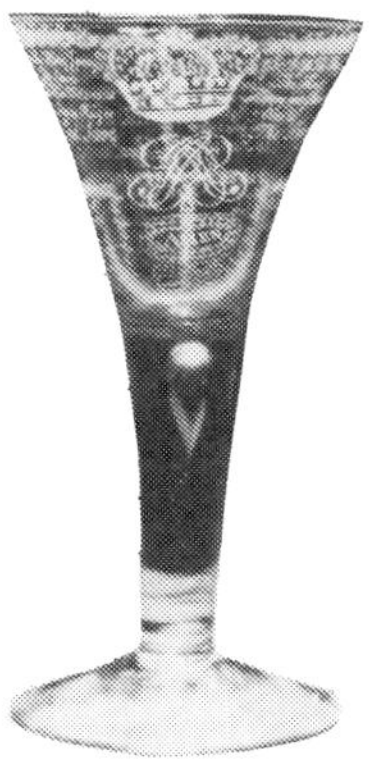

The 'Beves' 'Amen' glass engraved with the Jacobite version of God Save the King, circa 1750, 18cm. high. £13,750

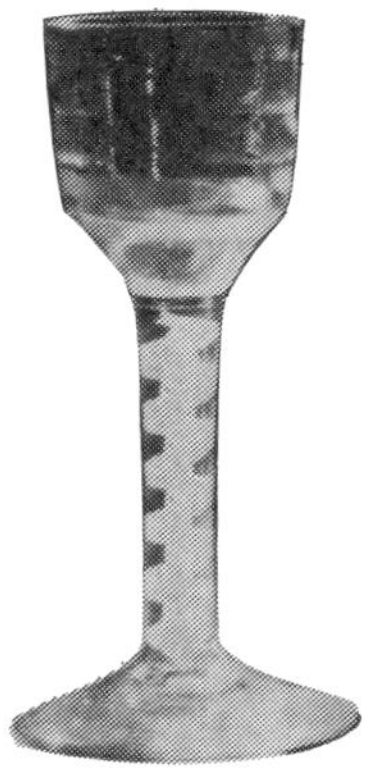

A 'Lynn' opaque twist wine glass with horizontally ribbed ogee bowl, circa 1775, 14cm. high. (Christie's) £345

WOOD

Prior to the 18th century, the average piece of English pottery was a pretty crude affair but, with the discovery of a hard white stoneware suitable for more delicate modelling, a new era dawned.

Part of the glazing process involved throwing common salt on the pottery while it was still in the kiln, the heat causing it to combine with the surface of the object to form a vitreous coating – hence the term "saltglaze". Figures glazed in this way were extensively made in Staffordshire, notably by Wedgwood and Astbury, and later by the Wood family throughout the 18th and early 19th century.

Ralph Wood, Senior (1715–72) and his brother Aaron (1717–85), sons of a Chedleton miller, developed a unique style for their productions, perpetuated by their respective sons, Ralph Jr. (1748–95) and Enoch (1759–1840). Their products were particularly noted for their delicate colouring and fine design but Aaron's son, Enoch, was later tempted by the prospect of increased production, as a result of the industrial revolution, and a good deal of the quality associated with the family was lost in the process.

All of their wares are clearly marked. The rarest of these takes the form of an impressed 'R. Wood', which although taken to be the work of Ralph Wood Senior has been recorded as late as 1794; 22 years after his death.

Enoch Wood started his own factory in 1784 and later, in 1790, went into a partnership with James Caldwell which continued trading successfully until 1818. During this time they shipped vast quantities of their tableware to America marked 'Wood & Caldwell' impressed around an American eagle.

A Ralph Wood Bacchus mask jug, circa 1775, 23.5cm. high. (Christie's) £410

An Enoch Wood model of a stag, circa 1800, 29cm. high. (Christie's) £1,836

A Ralph Wood bust of Milton, on a shaped rectangular socle, circa 1790, 22cm. high. (Christie's) £432

A Ralph Wood oval plaque of Patricia, circa 1775, 29cm. high. (Christie's) £1,512

Ralph Wood jug, modelled by Jean Voysey, circa 1788, 25cm. high. £425

A Ralph Wood group of the Vicar and Moses of conventional type, circa 1770, 21.5cm. high. (Christie's) £453

A Ralph Wood Toby jug of conventional type, circa 1770, 25cm. high. (Christie's) £626

A Ralph Wood oval plaque portrait of a woman, perhaps Charlotte Corday, circa 1780, 20cm. high. (Christie's) £594

A Ralph Wood triple spill vase modelled as two entwined dolphins, circa 1775, 20cm. high. (Christie's) £1,188

WORCESTER

Robert Chamberlain and Co. began in 1783 at Worcester and continued in operation till 1850. In 1852, the company took the name of Kerr and Binns. By 1862, this company was renamed the Worcester Royal Porcelain Company.
Dessert ware and comports in glazed porcelain supported by parian figures are among the best known Worcester pieces and their Limoges ware was exhibited in the Paris International Exhibition of 1855. The firm is best known, however, for the heavily jewelled decoration of its table services. The effect was achieved by building up the decoration by many firings. In the 20th century the company was noted for high quality painting and lavish gilding. They also produced figures in ivory paste or white porcelain with bright glazes and enamelled decorations. The birds modelled by D. Goughty are especially famous.

A Royal Worcester reticulated globular vase in the manner of George Owen, inscribed January 4th 1895, 11cm. high. (Christie's) £453

A pair of Royal Worcester figures modelled as a lady and gentleman, 14in. high, circa 1887. (Christie's) £1,000

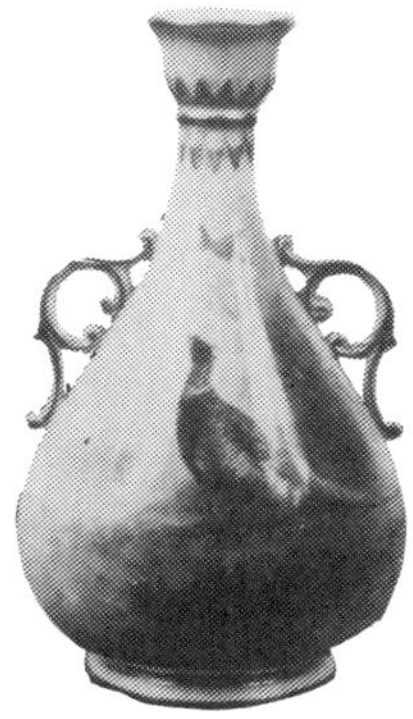

One of a pair of Royal Worcester vases painted by Stinton, signed, 6in. high. (Reeds Rains) £340

A Royal Worcester figure of Karan Singh, the trinket maker, 13cm. high, from the Indian Craftsman Series, shape 1204, 1884. (Lawrence Fine Art) £374

A Worcester plate painted in the atelier of James Giles, circa 1770, 22.5cm. diam. (Christie's) £594

A Worcester flared wine funnel painted in a famille verte palette with an Oriental holding a fan, circa 1755, 13.5cm. high. (Christie's) £12,960

A First Period Worcester apple-green teacup and saucer, crossed swords mark and 9 in underglaze blue. (Lawrence Fine Art) £396

A Worcester, Flight & Barr, canary-yellow ground flared flower pot with fixed gilt ring handles, circa 1805, 16cm. high. (Christie's) £1,404

INDEX

INDEX